The Foundations of Management Knowledge

What really counts as the knowledge of management? How is this best conveyed and how does it relate to the needs of contemporary managers? These are crucial questions for contemporary management knowledge – questions that are currently being hotly debated in Government, Industry, and Professional Bodies. However, in a contemporary context of radical restructuring in complex organisations and managerial work, alongside extensive changes in management ideas and the modes of management learning, authoritative responses to these key questions are hard to find.

This volume brings together distinguished contributors from the US and Europe to this broad debate about the current status and directions for development of the knowledge of management. The book critically examines established understandings of the foundations of management knowledge in the light of contemporary challenges from the worlds of both theory and practice. Its distinctiveness is that the contributions are orientated to the investigation of fundamental relationships between management ideas, management learning and management practice. The book's relationship to the foundations of management knowledge is quizzical, pursuing awkward questions about fundamental relationships that have become exposed (and unavoidable) through contemporary debate.

The book comprises three main sections, each of which focuses on key issues or challenges:

- Management knowledge and the challenge of professionalisation
- Management knowledge and the challenge of learning
- Re-situating management knowledge

Over the course of this discussion, management knowledge becomes understood as a complex field that is concerned with practices of bounding and ordering (i.e. organising) and their thresholds and limits of transition (i.e. managing), both operationally and conceptually. In this light, the book argues that management offers a distinctive and versatile field of knowledge well able to contribute to the interdisciplinary and interoperational challenges of the twenty-first century.

Paul Jeffcutt is Professor of Management Knowledge in the School of Management and Economics of Queen's University Belfast.

Routledge Advances in Management and Business Studies

The Foundations of Management Knowledge

Edited by Paul Jeffcutt

 Routledge
Taylor & Francis Group

LONDON AND NEW YORK

First published 2004
by Routledge
2 Park Square, Milton Park, Abingdon, Oxon, OX14 4RN

Simultaneously published in the USA and Canada
by Routledge
270 Madison Ave, New York NY 10016

Routledge is an imprint of the Taylor & Francis Group

Transferred to Digital Printing 2007

Typeset in Baskerville by Taylor & Francis Ltd

British Library Cataloguing in Publication Data
A catalogue record for this book is available from the British Library

Library of Congress Cataloging in Publication Data (to follow)

A catlog record for this book has been requested

ISBN10: 0–415–20778–9 (hbk)
ISBN10: 0–415–43984–1 (pbk)

ISBN13: 978–0–415–20778–2 (hbk)
ISBN13: 978–0–415–43984–8 (pbk)

Publisher's Note
The publisher has gone to great lengths to ensure the quality of this reprint but points out that some imperfections in the original may be apparent

Dedicated to
Raymond Alec Jeffcutt (1918-2000)

Contents

**PART III
Re-situating management knowledge 167**

Notes on Contributors

Robert Chia is Professor of Strategy and Organisation, School of Business and Economics, University of Exeter, UK. He is the author of several books and journal articles on Organisation Theory and Management and has presented conference papers in North America, Europe and the Asia Pacific. His research interests revolve around the issue of world-views and their implications for managerial decision-making.

Stanley Deetz is Professor of Communication at the University of Colorado at Boulder, USA. He specialises in the study of communication, power and decision-making from a critical/cultural/philosophic perspective. His publications include *Leading Organizations through Transitions* (Sage, 2000), *Doing Critical Management Research* (Sage, 2000), *Transforming Communication, Transforming Business* (Hampton, 1995) and *Democracy in an Age of Corporate Colonization* (SUNY, 1992).

Stephen Fox is Senior Lecturer in Management Learning and head of the Department of Management Learning at Lancaster University. His research interests centre upon a critical appreciation of learning as a practical social and material achievement informed by a range of social theories and perspectives on learning, knowledge and inquiry.

Silvia Gherardi is Associate Professor of Sociology of Work at the Faculty of Sociology of the University of Trento, Italy. She has a degree in sociology and has been trained in sociology of organisation at the University of Exeter (UK). She has also conducted research studies and training programmes for the development of women's competencies and participation in organisations. Gender and organisational cultures was the theme of her last book, *Gender, Symbolism and Organizational Cultures* (Sage, 1995).

Christopher Grey is Senior Lecturer at the University of Cambridge, UK, and Fellow of Wolfson College. He previously held posts at Leeds University and UMIST and is Visiting Fellow at Stockholm University. He is editor-in-chief of *Management Learning*. His research is in the area of Critical Management Studies, including professional socialisation, management education and the sociology of management and organisations.

Tanni Haas is Assistant Professor in the Department of Speech Communication Arts & Sciences at Brooklyn College, USA. His research on the theory and practice of public journalism, journalism codes of ethics, organisational communication ethics and qualitative research methods has appeared in more than a dozen scholarly journals and books. He currently serves on the editorial board of *Journalism & Mass Communication Educator* and *Newspaper Research Journal*

Paul Jeffcutt is Professor of Management Knowledge and Director of the Centre for Creative Industry, Queen's University Belfast, UK. His research interests concern the interdisciplinary field and changing practices of management knowledge, particularly knowledge dynamics in the organisation and management of creativity and innovation. He has published extensively in these areas and has held guest editorships with a range of international academic journals.

Ewart Keep is Deputy Director, Economic and Social Research Council (ESRC) Centre on Skills, Knowledge and Organisational Performance, Warwick Business School, University of Warwick, UK. He has published extensively on the learning organisation, the skills strategies of UK organisations, aspects of 14–19 education and training, and on the link between skills and competitive performance. He has acted as an advisor to the Department for Education and Skills (DfES), Department of Trade and Industry (DTI), Cabinet Office, the Chartered Institute of Personnel and Development (CIPD), the Nuffield Foundation and the Scottish Parliament.

Willem Koot is Professor of Organisational Anthropology at the Vrije Universiteit, Amsterdam, the Netherlands. His main research interests are ethnicity, identity formation and the dynamics of organisational culture; he is also interested in the emergence of local management models in the context of globalisation and localisation processes. His publications include *Contradictions in Context* (VU-University Press, 1996) and *Beyond Complexity: Paradoxes and Coping Strategies in Managerial Life* (Rozenberg Publishers, 2002).

Robert R. Locke is Emeritus Professor of History, University of Hawaii at Manoa. He was Visiting Professor at Reading University (1988–2001) and at Queens University Belfast (1999–2002). He is the author of numerous works on comparative management and educational history in Europe, Japan and America, and is currently working on the Americanisation of management education in France, Germany and the Czech Republic in the information age.

David Sims is Professor of Management at the Cass Business School, City University, UK. He is the author or co-author of some 80 books and journal articles about management thinking and learning, about narrative approaches to studying management, about the storied nature of managerial and other lives, and about the consequences of such a narrative understanding.

Roy Stager Jacques is the owner of Ravenheart of Sedona Coffee, Sedona, Arizona, USA. To date, the theme of his research has been the discursive construction of organisational realities and power relations. This has been pursued through gender studies in some of his work and through historical discursive analysis elsewhere (e.g. *Manufacturing the Employee*, Sage, 1996). His present interest is to better understand the significance of such research in the world of applied business practice.

Alan B. Thomas is Senior Lecturer at Manchester Business School, University of Manchester. His research interests include organisational leadership, inter-corporate relations and the sociology of management education. He is the author of *Controversies in Management: Issues, Debates, Answers* (Routledge, 2003). His latest book is *Research Skills for Management Studies* (Routledge, 2003).

Hugh Willmott is Diageo Professor of Management Studies in the Judge Institute of Management at the University of Cambridge, UK. He is currently working on a number of projects whose common theme is the changing organisation and management of work. His books include *Critical Management Studies* (Sage, 1992, co-editor), *Making Sense of Management: A Critical Introduction* (Sage, 1996, co-author) and *Management Lives* (Sage, 1999, co-author).

Foreword

As the number of business schools and management researchers grows by leaps and bounds throughout the developed and developing worlds, there has been an explosion in management education and learning. This growth in management knowledge has encompassed a number of issues, from the ethical to the technological, to the conflicts in dominant modes of management thought.

The world of work is changing dramatically, with jobs less secure and organisational structures more 'flexible', with downsizing, outsourcing and the short-term contract culture firmly in place. In response, management theory and research is seeking to better understand the dynamics of managers, management, organisational structures and organisational change in a global economy.

This volume on the foundations of management knowledge, therefore, is a welcome addition to the literature in raising the key issues in 'management knowledge' and in the management of knowledge. The various authors highlight the central dilemmas, conflicts and challenges for the future. This should be essential reading for all scholars and practitioners in the field of management.

Professor Cary L. Cooper, CBE
Manchester School of Management, UMIST
President of the British Academy of Management

1 Contemporary management knowledge

The parameters of debate

Paul Jeffcutt

The field of management knowledge

As befits a relatively young field, historical studies of the development of management are a fairly recent phenomenon.[1] Over the past decade or so, studies have been completed of the management traditions of the US, the UK, France, Germany, the Netherlands, Scandinavia and Japan (e.g. Locke 1989; Engwall 1992; Alvarez 1998). From this work it is clear to see that the field developed distinctively in different countries and continents, with the US tradition having had a significant, some would argue hegemonic, influence (e.g. Alvesson and Willmott 1996; Locke 1996).

This exploration of the similarities and differences between the management traditions of different nation-states has contributed to the development of a broader framework for the investigation of management as an area of knowledge. The consideration of management as an area of knowledge has been shaped by the investigation of three main themes:

- *Concepts*: the mix of ideas, academic fields and disciplines that comprise the 'subject' of management (e.g. Clegg and Palmer 1996; Tranfield and Starkey 1998).
- *Carriers*: the means by which management knowledge is conveyed, covering a broad spectrum from more *formal* media – such as award-bearing management education programmes (i.e. master's in business administration – (MBA) etc.), management journals and books (e.g. French and Grey 1996; Furusten 1999); to more *informal* media – such as in-service training, popular publications, TV and video, management consultants (e.g. Clarke and Fincham 2001; Jackson 2001).
- *Practices*: the action, behaviour and technique of management professions and managerial work in complex organisations (e.g. Watson 1994, 2001; Watson and Harris 1999).

Given that each of these thematic areas is substantial and complex, their interrelationship produces an awkward territory with multiple interfaces, stakeholders and flows of influence. This territory, necessary for the understanding of management as a field of knowledge, provides the domain in which this book is located.

As the book shows, the relationships between these three main themes have always been in tension, but over the past decade in particular the territory of management knowledge has become increasingly turbulent. In the context of radical restructuring in complex organisations and managerial work, alongside extensive changes in management ideas and the modes of management learning, relationships within and across the three themes have become difficult and more contested. The contemporary territory of management has thus become actively criss-crossed by its many stakeholders making powerful contributions to what can be appreciated as a vigorous (and sometimes acrimonious) debate about the current status and directions for development of the knowledge of management.

The scale of this 'debate' has become extensive,[2] involving government departments (e.g. Education and Employment, Trade and Industry), scientific bodies (e.g. National Science Foundation, Office of Science and Technology, Economic and Social Research Council – (ERSC)), industry bodies (e.g. US Chamber of Commerce, Confederation of British Industry), professional bodies (e.g. American Academy of Management, British Academy of Management) and international journals (e.g. *Academy of Management Review, Organisation, British Journal of Management*).

The 'debate' has largely taken place through a series of investigations, reports and special publications (e.g. from ESRC 1994 to BJM 2001) involving the above stakeholders (separately and in diverse combinations). This 'debate' (although, it has not necessarily been conducted in these terms) has essentially been questioning the nature and effectiveness of the established relationships between concepts, carriers and practice in management knowledge at a time of increasing disorder in each of the three main arenas that constitute the field. Briefly (for this chapter, amongst others, will go on to consider this matter in more detail), this disorder appears to have fundamentally challenged established understandings of complex organisation (e.g. virtual firms), management practice (e.g. distributed knowledge work), the reliability of management research (e.g. post-positivist paradigm shifts) and the robustness of management ideas (e.g. rapid turnover of fads and gurus).

The present volume brings together distinguished contributors to this broad debate about the current status and directions for development of the knowledge of management. Its distinctiveness is that their contributions are oriented to the investigation of fundamental relationships (i.e. between concepts, carriers and practice) that constitute management knowledge. The purpose of the book is to critically examine established understandings of the foundations of management knowledge in the light of contemporary challenges from the territories of both theory and practice. Hence the book's relationship to the foundations of management knowledge is quizzical, pursuing awkward questions about the constitution of these foundations that have become exposed (and unavoidable) through contemporary debate. As this chapter will go on to observe, this is an approach that connects management with other fields of knowledge that have been seeking to address the complexity of tensions between the spheres of science and society (e.g. Gibbons *et al.* 1994; Nowotny *et al.* 2001).

The book unfolds across three main parts, each of which focuses on key issues or challenges:

I   Management knowledge and the challenge of professionalisation
II Management knowledge and the challenge of learning
III Re-situating management knowledge

This opening chapter draws together and elaborates themes from across these three parts of the book, drawing attention to the in-depth contributions to the overall debate that are being made by the various contributors. It will also seek to synthesise and draw conclusions around the key issues and challenges that are being considered across the book as a whole.

The modern foundations of management knowledge

In Part I of the book, the interrelationships between modern management knowledge and processes of managerial professionalisation (both formal and informal) are explored. Working back from the contemporary 'crisis', Alan B. Thomas (in Chapter 2) describes a series of paradigms of 'management formation' that became overlaid on each other during the 20th century. His baseline is an 'old paradigm' that became established in the 19th century, in which management knowledge was an art or craft that was primarily developed in context. As a consequence, management education in the 'old paradigm' was largely positional and two-tier: as a liberal art for a social elite – providing 'rounding' for persons who had been born to assume leadership; and as in-service technical and commercial training for supervisory staff (undertaken either on the job or part-time).

The third quarter of the 20th century, particularly within Western Europe and North America, was crucial for the establishment of the 'new paradigm' of management knowledge (see Locke 1989; Engwall and Zamagni 1998). During this period, management began to achieve the status of a science – becoming established in higher education (departments of engineering or economics being influential hosts) and developing a formalised mainstream of theory (based around the applied behavioural sciences, such as psychology and sociology). During this phase of development, management was becoming positioned as an 'applied science', seeking to emulate established professional fields such as law or medicine that were structured around the effective flow of basic knowledge downstream from academia to practice. Formative in this process, Locke argues, was the allied experience of the Second World War, where huge logistical and operational problems on a global scale had been surmounted through the application of organisational systems and management principles to the industrial-military war effort.

In the 'new paradigm', Locke observes , 'management became the focus of science and science the focus of management as never before' (1989: 26). The novelty of the 'new paradigm' was a virtuous circle of relevance, where management became both truthful and useful – in other words, structured around a series of universal principles of management knowledge that were ubiquitous in their application to a diversity of organisational practice. This transition was achieved through the synthesis of earlier established disciplines (predominantly economics, engineering, sociology and psychology, converging around decision/general systems theory) in the formation of a body of knowledge that was authoritative, ubiquitous and readily translatable (downstream) to the professionalising practice of managing in a diversity of circumstances and contexts. In the UK, the key carriers of this management knowledge were, first, centres for post-experience management development, following the establishment of Henley in 1945 and the British Institute of Management in 1947; and, second, specialist business schools providing MBA education (university based, founded on the US model), initiated in 1965 in London and Manchester.

In retrospect, the significance of the 'new paradigm' was twofold: on the one hand, it constructed a quasi-scientific frame for the integration of the social and technical sciences concerned with the systematisation of the behaviour of both people and technologies; on the other hand, it represented organised life as composed of discrete, coherent and manipulable components which were interacting in a complex, changing but ultimately manageable world (see Cooper 1986, 1989; Clegg 1990).

These foundations provided the underpinnings for substantial growth; however, as Christopher Grey illustrates (in Chapter 3), they included significant flaws: on the one hand, management sought to be a positivistic science but was 'demonstrably unscientific'; on the other, its technical practice was increasingly divergent from actual managerial experience. This latter point is strongly reiterated in Robert Locke's analysis (in Chapter 4) of the successful development of the information and communications technology (ICT) sector in the USA being attributable to a contingent set of socio-political and economic factors. Indeed, this new entrepreneurial sector grew strongly in California despite the prevailing management knowledge of US business schools, which was more concerned with the separation of tacit and formal knowledge and the maintenance of a technical curriculum that had limited applicability in the economy.

Management, as Grey observes (in Chapter 3), has thus far failed to professionalise (in terms of the medical model), and instead of achieving authoritative closure around the licensing of its knowledge (via the MBA, for example) it remains fragmented and ad hoc (see also Whitley 1995, 1999). However, in spite of these 'flaws', the 'new paradigm' for management knowledge has sustained the considerable expansion and proliferation of management knowledge. As Ewart Keep shows (in Chapter 5), the rapid expansion of management education in the UK (since the mid-1980s) has been unable to match the burgeoning increase in demand. Indeed, Bosworth (1999) calculates that, at current rates, it would take UK business schools over 500 years to educate all current managers in the UK to MBA standard. Whatever the timescale, Keep then sets out a persuasive array of obstacles and challenges to the effective development of a management education and training system for the UK.

In this light, the contemporary context of management knowledge can be appreciated as unstable and disordered – a situation characterised by paradoxical forces: on the one hand, expansion and implosion; on the other, complacency and critique. The past decade or so (in particular) has witnessed what appears to be increasing disorder in both the theoretical and empirical foundations of the field of management – very considerable changes in the behavioural sciences have been paralleled by very considerable changes in complex organisations and management practice. Furthermore, the pace, scale and complexity of these changes is continuing to intensify.

As I shall outline below, these developments have raised significant tensions which have problematised both the usefulness and the truth of management knowledge – in other words, challenging the foundations of the 'new paradigm':

1 *Whilst the usefulness of management knowledge has been more problematised, management practice has become expanded and reasserted.* As contemporary socio-economic transition has become ever more intensive, unstable and uncertain, managerial 'solutions' to the organisational problems of states (such as Russia), sectors (such as healthcare) and institutions (such as the British Broadcasting Corporation – (BBC)) have also proliferated. However, as complex organisations have downsized and delayered through corporate re-engineering, managerial functions have also become shifted and dispersed as work has been intensified and displaced within organisational networks (e.g. Lash and Urry 1994; Pettigrew and Fenton 2000). In parallel, there has been a substantial expansion of provision in management education and training (taking place at all levels from post-experience to the secondary school), as well as a global explosion in management consulting activity. Hence, management has rapidly become the largest undergraduate and postgraduate subject in the UK (in 2000/2001 registering over 13 per cent of all students), whilst corporate 'universities' have proliferated in both scope and scale (Huff 2000). However, alongside this expansion the relevance of management education to organised life has increasingly been challenged (by governments, industry, professional bodies, academics and practitioners; see French and Grey 1996; Starkey and Madan 2001), leading to a series of national investigations and reports. Indeed, as the contemporary modern crisis in organised life has intensified, the managerial 'solutions' proposed appear to have become all the more evangelical, reactionary and desperate – as the commodities of the new genre of 'popular management' exemplify (see Micklethwait and Wooldridge 1997; Jackson 2001).

2 *Whilst the truthfulness of management knowledge has been more problematised, the field of management as a modern science has become expanded and reasserted.* In its 'new paradigm', management was established as a synthetic, multidisciplinary field – the dominant process by which the field has repaired and developed

its theoretical mainstream has been through the continuing assimilation and reworking of material from more marginal academic territories (see Jeffcutt 1994; Jeffcutt *et al.* 2000). However, over the past decade or so this often colonial process has intensified, both in terms of the variety and scope of novel ideas as well as in terms of the rapidity of their turnover. Indeed, as the disciplines of the social and behavioural (or human) sciences were redefining and reorienting themselves through post-structural paradigm shifts (Geertz 1983; Gibbons *et al.* 1994), management was experiencing a cacophony of gurus and a bewildering array of fads, alongside the proliferation of novel and adversarial academic areas of analysis (Abrahamson 1996; Jackson 2001). Significantly, these narratives are both parallel and sympathetic – each articulating reliable routes to better understood and better organised futures (through both theory and practice). In this context, the number of university management schools in the UK has expanded sevenfold (from 14 to 101) over the past decade, with management academics coming to represent one in four of all active social science researchers (ABS 2000). Most recently, the UK research councils for the social sciences and engineering sciences have collaborated to establish a major Management Research Initiative with substantial public funds which will found a National Institute for Advanced Research in Management. Thus, as the coherence of the social and behavioural sciences as bastions of truth and expertise has become increasingly destabilised and undermined, the field of management knowledge (the ubiquitous science of managing organised life) has become more performative, seeking to remodel itself as the authentic voice of the 'leading edge' of progress, however disorganised and apparently unmanageable.

So, to summarise, two interrelated processes of contemporary change can be observed in the empirical and intellectual foundations of management knowledge. On the one hand, there is a continuing process of unbounding and pluralisation of the (macro and micro) socio-economic order in a globalised society, exemplified by the instabilities of transition in Eastern Europe and East Asia as well as in the everyday world of complex organisations and managerial work (e.g. Burton-Jones 1999; Castells 2000). Across both these macro and micro arenas, established structures have become increasingly compromised through processes of 'delayering', 'downsizing' and 'outsourcing', with knowledge work in organisational networks (multi-stakeholder, project based and virtual) as the flourishing operational form (e.g. Baumard 1999; Prichard *et al.* 2000). On the other hand, there is the further unbounding and pluralisation of the human sciences (see Geertz 1983; Gibbons *et al.* 1994), exemplified by paradigm shifts and emerging interdisciplinary arenas (e.g. the post-structural redefinition of 'subjects', territories and practices of knowledge), with intellectual networks (multi-stakeholder, project based and virtual) as the flourishing operational form (see Caswill and Shove 2001; Nowotny *et al.* 2001). Configured by competing understandings of the thresholds and boundaries of knowledge and of transition in organised life, the everyday world of organisational analysis has thus become increasingly compromised and hyperactive (see also Hassard and Parker 1993; Burrell 1997).

Through these interrelated processes of unbounding and reshaping in both the theoretical and empirical foundations of the field, the mainstream of management knowledge has become both more pluralised and more performative. As I have suggested, the peculiar juxtaposition of expansion and implosion symptomises a field that seems to have become increasingly destabilised. Indeed, the contemporary problematisation of both the truth and usefulness of management knowledge underpins (although not explicitly in these terms) an extensive debate that has been taking place on the future of the field, involving a wide range of constituencies and stakeholders. A key term in the critiques that have been made is 'relevance', and there appear to be two broad interpretations of this term, which together encapsulate key problems for contemporary management knowledge:

- first, that contemporary management knowledge is intellectually limited because it remains based around a narrow mainstream of knowledge (e.g. positivist and functionalist behavioural science) that is out of touch with intellectual developments across the human sciences and not flexible or versatile enough to engage in fruitful opportunities for theory building (e.g. Alvesson and Willmott 1996; Clark 2000);
- second, that contemporary management knowledge is operationally limited because it remains based around outmoded understandings of practice (i.e. organisational and occupational stability) that are out of touch with the complexity and ambiguity of contemporary organised life and not flexible or versatile enough to inform practitioners who are learning to work with the unmanageable (e.g. Watson 1994, 2001; Watson and Harris 1999).

These critiques were neatly joined in the report of the UK Commission on Management Research which described a 'double challenge of relevance' for management knowledge and acknowledged the substance and significance of these hurdles for the majority of the mainstream (ESRC 1994; Pettigrew 1997). In this light, the evidence examined over the course of this chapter presents a key question: has management knowledge so shifted over the last half century that it has become *neither* truthful *nor* useful? In other words, has management gone from a virtuous to a vicious circle of relevance – becoming dominant but with really nothing to say?

This is a serious question which requires a considered response – to achieve this necessitates coming to a judgement on the processes by which the contemporary problems of management knowledge have arisen. The choices appear clear cut – essentially, one needs to judge whether contemporary pressures and tensions can be understood primarily as root causes of change in the field, or whether they should be understood primarily as catalysts of change in the field. The first option suggests that the foundations of management knowledge are *secure* but contemporary conditions have posed serious challenges that the field needs to adapt more effectively to. The second option suggests that the foundations of management knowledge are *insecure* and contemporary conditions have served to amplify and intensify fundamental problems that are inherent to the nature and form of modern management knowledge.

Whichever understanding is reached, it needs to be based upon a considered exploration of the foundations of modern management knowledge (the purpose of the book as a whole and this chapter in particular).

Revisiting the foundations

Earlier in this chapter I suggested that the constitution of management knowledge in its 'new paradigm' rested on a complex double synthesis between 'theory' and 'practice', in which significant tensions between (and within) behavioural science disciplines and organised contexts were able to be rationalised and reconciled. Drawing on themes that are being developed across the book, it is thus appropriate now to unpack and examine some of these constitutive tensions of management knowledge in a little more detail. This will be done by examining a series of propositions about the constitution of management knowledge, as follows:

- *Management knowledge is a field that is inevitably multidisciplinary.* This conceptual field concerned with the analysis of organisation and management, which has become increasingly established over the past century, was formed from theoretical foundations that were largely dominated by behavioural science disciplines (e.g. economics, psychology, sociology) which developed earlier in the 19th century. The behavioural science core of this field, which became synthesised and formalised in the establishment of the 'new paradigm', has since become extended to both the humanities (e.g. drawing on history and philosophy in the study of business ethics) and the natural sciences (e.g. drawing on mathematics and physics in the study of complexity).
- *Management knowledge is a field that is inevitably multi-contextual.* This operational field concerns a variety of forms of managerial work (diverse arenas of skill and professional activity) in a variety of organised settings (bounded in terms of place, size, sector, scale, scope, etc.) that are joined together by practices of ordering. Over the past century, a territory of management practice has become increasingly established that has sought to manage such difference in the pursuit of progress, both across and within the diverse settings of organised activity. As numerous studies have shown (see Chapters 3 and 13), these practices of managing and organising were again formed on foundations of practice which emerged earlier in the regulation of modern society (e.g. developed in armies and prisons). From a longstanding concentration on the domain of private industry, the mainstream practices of management have more recently been explicitly extended to domains such as public services, cultural activities and sport.

- *Management knowledge is a field that is inevitably plural, being both 'multidisciplinary' and 'multi-contextual' (not just either/or).* The plurality of management knowledge has come to reflect the functional areas of organisation and enterprise, such as the specialisms of marketing, personnel, production and accounting, whose competing concerns there have been attempts to integrate through the more ubiquitous practice of management. Equally, this is a plurality which has reflected the behavioural sciences, where the field of management knowledge has developed over the past century as a hybrid arena of contestation and collaboration between already established disciplines which sought to pursue broader questions of order/disorder and modern transition through complex organisation.

- *Management knowledge is a field that is both a practical science of management and a theoretical science of manageability (not just either/or).* This tension, often experienced as ambiguity or ambivalence, is fundamental to management knowledge – its presence can be seen in the early development of the field, as the following illustration shows. A century ago, as the modernisation of efficiency systems and the extension of bureaucracy into organised life was being facilitated (e.g. through the management practices of Taylorism), the coercion, provisionality and alienation that accompanied this particular search to extend progress through the management of complex organisations were being recognised and articulated (e.g. through the more broadly focused sociological work of Weber and Durkheim). Such patterns of divergence and selective focusing have been significant in shaping the development of management knowledge throughout the twentieth century. Whether bifurcated around theory/practice or order/disorder, these means of managing this fundamental tension appear to have become structural for management knowledge.

From the foregoing, management knowledge can be recognised as a field that is both concerned with and constituted by complex boundaries and tensions. Or, put another way, the territory of management knowledge addresses practices of bounding and ordering (i.e. organising) and their thresholds and limits of transition (i.e. managing), both operationally and conceptually. From this basis, management knowledge is inevitably heterogeneous and hybrid – since it is constituted by complex knowledge flows that link together raggedly bounded arenas, which we have been exploring as concepts, carriers and practices.

Yet the mainstream development of the field has been characterised by the glossing and oversimplification of these complex interconnections in a search to manage their tension and ambivalence. As Cooper (1986, 1989) observed, this process has produced a selective focusing on 'order' in the understanding of organisation and management that has been consistently linked to the corresponding censorship of 'disorder'. These patterns of attention have shaped the development of a 'mainstream' in which order became interiorised within relatively stable boundaries in both complex organisations and the field of management theory (see also Hodgkinson and Herriot 2001).

According to Wagner (1994), the 20th-century project of the human sciences has been the 'large scale conventionalisation' of modern transition, based upon principles of securing and extending the 'intelligibility and shapeability' of the modern world. In this light, management knowledge (particularly in its 'new paradigm') needs to be understood as an important contributor to this project. Wagner (1994) goes on to argue that a widespread *fin-de-siècle* disorder, evident across modern science and modern society, signifies a major transitional process – the 'second crisis of modernity', the effective novelty of the 'second' modern crisis being that the intensity, scope and scale of its symptoms (e.g. unbounding and pluralisation) have made the problematic principles of modern ordering both more explicit and more bereft. For management knowledge, the 'second' modern crisis has exposed an important paradox – since this field (most closely associated with the organisation and management of progress in the modern world) would appear to be proliferating as its fundamental limitations have become increasingly exposed.

In this light, it is probably also clear that my response to the key question posed at the end of the previous section is that the foundations of management knowledge (consolidated through its 'new paradigm') are insecure, with contemporary conditions having served to amplify and intensify fundamental problems that are inherent in the nature and form of modern management knowledge. This understanding does not mean that the future for management knowledge becomes impossible – but that the nature of fruitful ways forward, through a complex landscape of pitfall and possibility, are particularly challenging. It is with these problems and opportunities that Parts II and III of the book are concerned.

Contextualising the foundations

The second major section of the book concerns management knowledge and the challenge of learning (i.e. the relationship between management knowledge and the theory and practice of management learning). As Steve Fox shows (in Chapter 6), the formal management education and training system is but the tip of a learning iceberg, with the overwhelming majority of management learning (both structured and unstructured) taking place informally. Earlier it was argued that the 'new paradigm' of management knowledge emphasised the separations between the formal and informal spheres of knowledge and also prioritised their relationship, management knowledge becoming constructed as free standing and ubiquitous, being produced by a scientific community and disseminated downstream to practitioners, where it was readily applicable to a diversity of contexts.

The crucial concern shaping these relationships is the role of context in the production and consumption of management knowledge. In the 'new paradigm' management knowledge is decontextualised (i.e. shorn of managerial context) through its process of production and then banked within an abstract system of knowledge from whence it becomes packaged for consumption (i.e. recontextualisation) through a formal educational process of dissemination/acquisition. From this perspective, context-sensitive management knowledge, developed through everyday experience and informal learning, is merely anecdotal (i.e. unscientific, even contaminated).

Steve Fox (in Chapter 6) builds a persuasive argument for socially situated management knowledge, arguing (following Lave and Wenger 1991) that the production of knowledge is indissociable from its consumption. All knowledge is thus practised, whether in the academy or on the shop floor, and this crucial contextualising process is interactive and emergent. The significant juxtaposition is that management knowledge in its new paradigm contrives to hide the skilled craftwork of privileged knowledge producers (the contextualisations of the scientific community) whilst actively denying the correspondingly skilful knowledge work of practitioners.

Hugh Willmott (in Chapter 7) is concerned with the critical possibilities of the everyday knowledge work of practising managers. He focuses on action learning, a well-established management development process whereby managers learn in self-managed groups by discussing, acting and reflecting on 'live' organisational problems. His concern is the scope and depth of this process and in particular the limitations that the social and institutional context provides for the critical possibilities for learning. He examines one case in detail, arguing that in conventional action learning managers are not empowered to question the coherence and ethics of procedures from which they derive both authority and security (see also Jackall 1988; Thomas and Al-Maskati 1997) – as a consequence, their development agendas are often narrow (i.e. task and technique oriented). He concludes by arguing for critical action learning, a learning process which explicitly engages with these framing issues of identity and power in management development.

David Sims (in Chapter 8) is concerned with how the informal contexts of management learning operate, investigating the value and potency of managers' informal knowledge through the key process of storytelling. He argues that storytelling enables managers to manage their information-rich environments – this process of exchange helping to build a responsive organisational knowledge framework of the tacit, provisional and hybrid (in other words, a cultural capability that is living and lived). Echoing earlier behavioural analyses of managerial work (e.g. Jackall 1988; Watson 1994), Sims observes that storytelling is a major function of the everyday work of managers – stories are skilfully authored, interpreted, adapted and critiqued, being traded as a valuable currency that circulates managerial tacit knowledge around organisational environments.

Context is thus crucial to the production and consumption of management knowledge. The 'new paradigm' sought to manage context through a series of practices that organised relationships for the construction of knowledge between producers and consumers – on the one hand, these practices effaced and discounted context in the process of production and, on the other, these practices dispensed context (pre-packaged) for consumers to operationalise.

From this perspective, the 'relevance' debate in management knowledge can be seen as a recent articulation of the poverty of key knowledge relationships between producers and consumers. Earlier in this chapter it was recognised that the volume and scope of this contemporary dissatisfaction are significant. Yet, as Alan B. Thomas (in Chapter 2) reminds us, degrees of consumer dissatisfaction have, to some extent, always been evident, although, in line with the terms of the 'new paradigm' knowledge contract, these have typically been discounted by producers. However, when the dissatisfaction involves both producers and consumers, and when its scope is not confined to the formal management learning system (i.e. the tip of the iceberg) but is played out across an expanding framework of influential carriers of informal management learning, these matters become more influential.

As Starkey and Madan (2001) show, the volume and significance of informal management learning continue to grow rapidly, evidenced by the proliferation of popular management publications, corporate universities, video and internet-based in-service training, and management consulting (amongst other things). However, as I suggested earlier, what appears to be happening is that the whole management learning 'iceberg' is growing as the privileged relationship of the formal 'tip' to the informal bulk continues to be undermined. This process reflects the limitations of the structure and content of the formal management learning system as well as the desires of an increasing number of consumers to structure knowledge relationships and to engage with the complexities of context in their own way. Indeed, as everyday managerial life becomes increasingly unmanageable, so the informal carriers that provide 'useful' managerial knowledge both proliferate and compete, with products that range from the authentic and engaged to the trivial and exploitative.

These important and ongoing revisions to the knowledge relationships between the producers and consumers of management knowledge need to be understood in terms of broader changes that have been observed in the contemporary knowledge economy. An influential analysis of these matters has been provided by Gibbons *et al.* (1994), who argue that intensifying over the late 20th century has been a fundamental shift in knowledge relationships. Based on an investigation of the development of the humanities and of the natural and social sciences, they argue that a new mode of knowledge production (Mode 2) has come to be overlaid upon a dominant mode of knowledge production (Mode 1) that was established earlier in modern society.

They characterise Mode 1 as the conventional scientific model, which privileges the production of basic ('pure') knowledge within unified and concentrated subject areas (i.e. mono-disciplinary) for dissemination downstream to a separate category of knowledge consumers – 'users'. As has already been shown, this is precisely the mode that management knowledge in its 'new paradigm' has sought to emulate.

They characterise Mode 2 as more interactive, distributed and dynamic – arguing that in contemporary society the key repositories of knowledge and capability are distributed across conventional disciplinary and organisational boundaries (i.e. those established under Mode 1). Furthermore, the effective networking of these resources would appear to enable more effective engagement with the complex problems of contemporary society, which have not tended to present themselves conveniently sectioned up in terms of the subject specialisms laid down in the modern university. Mode 2 is thus:

- transdiciplinary (working beyond the boundaries of any one discipline);
- networked (socially distributed knowledge-production sites that interconnect stakeholders, who exchange perspectives and ideas);
- interactive (knowledge is produced in the context of application through relationships between theory and practice).

These characterisations of Modes 1 and 2 and their interrelationship have generated widespread debate across the sciences and social sciences – here there is only opportunity to consider that part of the debate concerning management knowledge. In this context, a key role has been played by the British Academy of Management (BAM) and its scholarly publication, the *British Journal of Management* (BJM). Building from a substantial discussion within the British Academy of Management on the nature and focus of management research, Tranfield and Starkey (1998) argued that management knowledge is in practice not a Mode 1 field – being both 'soft' (having no unifying paradigm) and 'divergent' (researchers being loosely knit within a broad intellectual space). They concluded by proposing policies for sustaining the development of management as an explicitly Mode 2 field. This argument was taken up in subsequent annual conferences of the British and American Academies of Management and the debate was consolidated in a recent special issue of the *British Journal of Management* (BJM 2001).

Perhaps unsurprisingly, the debate within management on Gibbons *et al.* (1994) has been similar in character to that taking place more broadly (i.e. in other scientific communities; see Caswill and Shove 2001). For many commentators the debate has tended to be either/or in character, with argument (explicitly or implicitly) for the development of the status quo (i.e. Mode 1) by those who feel that Mode 2 represents a dilution of academic rigour (e.g. Grey 2001; Kilduff and Kelemen 2001) countered by argument for a development of the Mode 2 agenda by those who feel that this offers a strategic way forward for a field that has lost direction (e.g. Starkey and Madan 2001; Hatchuel 2001).

In an either/or type of debate there is little space for the recognition that the argument itself extends beyond polar opposites and cannot thus be resolved by dichotomous choice. For example, Gibbons *et al.* (1994) argue that Mode 1 has been overlaid upon Mode 2 and that this produces a complex interface of transition. Indeed, within management knowledge we have seen this interface to be particularly confusing, with diverse stakeholders arguing for more insightful and responsive solutions to 'fuzzy' problems whilst individual and institutional reward structures (e.g. Research Assessment Exercise in the UK) are emphasising more conventional knowledge-production activities (Anderson *et al.* 2001). In the BJM special issue a limited number of papers explicitly address the complex dynamics of knowledge relationships in management knowledge – arguing for multifaceted approaches to the exchanges between modes of knowledge production/consumption (Pettigrew 2001; Weick 2001; Hodgkinson *et al.* 2001; Huff and Huff 2001).

Earlier in this chapter I argued that management is a field of knowledge that is inevitably hybrid – comprising plural knowledge(s) with multiple application(s), what Whitley (1995, 1999) describes as 'fragmented adhocracies'. Pursuing this direction of argument, the crucial concern becomes whether these characteristics describe failings or advantages. However, these are questions that have been actively pursued for at least a decade (although not necessarily in these terms), as my earlier examination of the intensive 'relevance' debate in management knowledge showed. The content and positioning of the BJM special issue thus emphasises a number of the conclusions drawn in the present chapter: first, the enduring strength of this debate and its predominantly adversarial parameters; second, the irresolvability of the debate in the terms in which it has largely been pursued. In this light, the concluding section of the present chapter (and book as a whole) will be concerned with approaches which seek fruitful ways of taking these questions further forward.

Re-situating management knowledge

In the previous section I concentrated on the nature of context in management knowledge, arguing that, however represented, context is always present in knowledge relationships (i.e. explicitly or implicitly, whether these activities are concerned with production or with consumption). In these respects, it is significant to note that the follow-up book to Gibbons *et al.* (1994) emerged from the authors' concern with the oversimplification of their arguments about Modes 1 and 2, and concentrates on addressing the problem of context in knowledge relationships (Nowotny *et al.* 2001). In short, the authors argue that all knowledge is contextualised (both Mode 1 and Mode 2), arguing that the key difference is between how strongly and weakly this contextualisation is effected – extending the debate beyond the confines of reliability and validity (i.e. limited dialogue between knowledge stakeholders) towards robustness (i.e. extensive dialogue between knowledge stakeholders).

This reframing of the knowledge debate from its form of production (Mode 1 and 2) to its process of contextualisation (robustness, stakeholder voice) leads to the foregrounding of three key issues:

*   the framing of problems and solutions;
*   the nature and distribution of expertise;
*   the epistemological core.

As readers will recognise, these are concerns that have already been shaping the argument of this chapter and the contents of this collection. The final section of the book engages explicitly with these concerns, arguing for the further development of management as a strongly contextualised field of 21st-century knowledge.

Robert Chia (in Chapter 9) examines management knowledge as a fundamental process of ordering that is reality-constituting and world-making – an activity that is intrinsic to human behaviour and not just about techniques that are applicable to the economy. His chapter considers major transitions in the history of civilisation as formative of the modern mindset with its fundamental taxonomic urge to clarify, attribute and predict. In doing so, his overarching purpose is to give voice to the tacit and unrepresentable forms of knowledge that modern knowledge glosses over – engaging with forms of knowing appropriate for a postmodern world.

From this foregrounding, subsequent chapters concentrate on the problems and opportunities for different aspects of plurality in management knowledge and contemporary organisational life.

Willem Koot (in Chapter 10) is concerned with paradoxical processes of identity formation in contemporary organisations. He examines how organisations deal with cultural and ethnic complexity – global/local processes that lead to severe tensions between forces of homogenisation and standardisation, on the one hand, and with forces of differentiation and fragmentation on the other. His chapter underlines the paradoxical nature of the identities that are constructed in contemporary hybrid organisations – emphasising trust and commitment as well as insecurity and fear of failure.

In the next chapter (Chapter 11), Stanley Deetz and Tanni Haas undertake a radical analysis of information flows across organisational boundaries between 'internal' and 'external' stakeholders. They argue that a unified incorporation of these multiple flows and perspectives is not possible; hence corporate entities (as conventionally understood) need to be disassembled and reconstructed to enable an ethical dialogue between stakeholders fruitfully to take place. Their approach has radical implications for both the governance of corporations and the scope of managerial work.

Silvia Gherardi (in Chapter 12) uses the metaphor of citizenship to extend our understandings of gender in organisations. Her approach to citizenship brings together the fields of law, political science and sociology in an analysis of social processes in organisations that construct identities and memberships around gendered differences. Her purpose is to move beyond discussions of gender in terms of dichotomy and hierarchy, in order to understand gender in organisations as a plural process that is both symbolic and cultural.

The final chapter in the collection (Chapter 13) draws together several themes and concludes with an imperative for action. Roy Stager Jacques critically contrasts management knowledge at the end of the 19th and the start of the 21st centuries – two important historical points in the industrial and the post-industrial eras. He examines the foundational assumptions, relationships and knowledge-development practices that have informed and sustained management knowledge at both of these points. He finds contemporary management knowledge to be wearing blinkers that were formed in the 19th century – largely reinterpreting contemporary phenomena in terms of long-established conventions and thus unable to see clearly the provenance of emerging systems for producing and distributing knowledge. He argues that management knowledge now needs to be focused on that which it has overlooked – how will new social spaces in the post-industrial knowledge economy be occupied, what new social actors will be constructed and what will this mean for formerly privileged stakeholders (e.g. the industrial business school)?

From such a perspective, the failings that have made management an inadequate science in the traditional mode (i.e. its intellectual and operational heterogeneity, its diversity of carriers and stakeholders) are advantages that make it a versatile science in the contemporary mode. Hence the 'new paradigm' of management knowledge can be considered as not only based upon a mode of knowledge production and contextualisation that was inappropriate to the foundations of the field of management, but also based on a paradigm that was itself outmoded. So, having been obstinately wedded to a doubly inappropriate 'identity' for a substantial time, the contemporary problems of management knowledge become more complex, more difficult and more urgent.

In the UK context, as a relatively 'new' field of knowledge, management has striven for acceptance by its stakeholder communities – both academic and operational. Thus far, the outcome has largely been bifurcation and oversimplification around a theory/practice divide (as the 'relevance' debate exemplified), with no great achievement in terms of acceptability with either major stakeholder community. For example, in terms of the contemporary research university, management knowledge is still too messy and contaminated to be academically mainstream (as the Oxford University debate over the siting of the Said Business School illustrated, management is clearly on the 'wrong side of the tracks'), whilst, in terms of the contemporary knowledge-intensive enterprise, management knowledge is still too remote and narrowly contextualised to be translatable into understandings that can guide operational improvements (as the recent national review by the Council for Management and Leadership found, CEML 2002).

In these respects, the Advanced Institute for Management (AIM) in the UK presents both a timely and a unique opportunity to intervene in support of the healthy development of the field. The AIM has the potential to become a pluralist agora for complex and dynamic debate between the diverse constituencies of management knowledge to help shape the further development of management as a strongly contextualised and fruitful science of the 21st century (Nowotny *et al.* 2001). Equally, the AIM also has the potential to become a bunker for restricted discussions between the existing elites within management knowledge, a development that is most likely to consolidate the position of management as a weakly contextualised and feeble science of the 20th century.

In conclusion, it needs to be reiterated that the recent trajectory of the development of management knowledge (i.e. unbounding and pluralisation) has intensified the existing problems of the field in a contemporary context of more widespread change in processes of knowledge production and consumption. As has been suggested, these problematics have become exacerbated because the inherent hybridity and heterogeneity of management knowledge form a complex landscape of interconnection without the possibility of a unified authoritative centre. This means that the transdisciplinarity and transcontextuality of the 'field' become articulated through subtle and fragile exchanges between 'communities of practice' that cannot be conveniently reduced and separated into discrete (theoretical or practical) arenas. Furthermore, in the absence of any feasible centre we have to be fully concerned with the nature and form of the exchanges which both cross and reform boundaries of knowledge in the field (i.e. the complex interrelationships between concepts, carriers and practices). For contemporary management knowledge, this means the building of a syncretic dialogue (see Stewart and Shaw 1994) – a dialogue which recognises both mutuality and difference; a dialogue that is both diverse and hybrid as well as creative and critical.

This has to be seen as a difficult path that needs to be pursued in awareness of the colonial practices by which management knowledge has traditionally and consistently sought transcendence and renewal (Knights and Willmott 1997). Indeed, as the form and content of the 'new paradigm' have become increasingly exhausted and bereft, so the character of transition in the mainstream has become more turbulent, fragmentary and reactionary. Indeed, we all need to beware of such competitive fundamentalism (whether academic or operational) – since it is positioned on a slippery slope above a 'balkanised' fight to the death between specialisms to decide which is the one 'true' centre for the field of management knowledge.

In contrast, it also needs to be appreciated that the creative and contested nature of management knowledge makes it a territory of endeavour well suited to fruitfully engage with such ambiguity and complexity. Given its inherent hybridity and heterogeneity, management knowledge is intimately concerned with effective dialogue (translation and mediation) in complex exchanges between concepts, carriers and practices. Indeed, in my view this very 'contact zone' is what makes management knowledge such a distinctive, versatile (and exciting) arena of contemporary work.

Over the course of this chapter I have presented management knowledge as a field that addresses practices of bounding and ordering (i.e. organising) and their thresholds and limits of transition (i.e. managing), both operationally and conceptually. Re-situating management knowledge in such terms describes a distinctive and versatile science well able to contribute to the interdisciplinary and interoperational challenges of the 21st century. Despite the inadequacies of its mainstream (the 'new paradigm') over the majority of the 20th century, the ugly duckling of management knowledge may ultimately be really learning to fly. Thus, we have reached a picture of possibility for management knowledge in the 21st century that links versatility with capability and fruitfulness with dynamism.

Notes

1   A pronounced historical perspective within management studies is a relatively recent and welcome development. There has, of course, been a strong historical perspective evident within fields of social science, such as economic history, that have concerns

which overlap with those of the field of management. Whilst this work has been valuable (particularly in the absence of relevant historical studies in management), it does need to be recognised that such analyses have tended to foreground micro and macro issues (e.g. Pollard 1965), with organisational and managerial concerns (meso-level issues) being given relatively limited attention (see Anthony 1986).

2   As recent historical studies of management traditions show, the shape and direction of the development of this field have to some extent always been contested. The key point here is the increasing intensity and scale of this debate over the past decade. This particular emphasis does not overlook the contribution of earlier work to these matters (see Chapter 2), including several important reports from the 1980s (e.g. Handy *et al.* 1987; Constable and McCormick 1987; Porter and McKibbin 1988).

3   I should like to acknowledge the helpful comments of Robert R. Locke and Gerard P. Hodgkinson on an earlier draft of this chapter.

References

Abrahamson, E. (1996) 'Management fashion', *Academy of Management Review* 21: 254–85.

ABS (2002) *Pillars of the Economy: Developing World Class Management Performance*, London: Association of Business Schools.

Alvarez, J.L. (ed.) (1998) *The Diffusion and Consumption of Business Knowledge*, New York: St Martin's Press, Inc.

Alvesson, M. and Willmott, H. (1996) *Making Sense of Management*, London: Sage.

Anderson, N., Herriot, P. and Hodgkinson, G.P. (2001) 'The practitioner–researcher divide in industrial, work and organizational (IWO) psychology: where are we now and where do we go from here?', *Journal of Occupational and Organizational Psychology* 72: 391–411.

Anthony, P.D. (1986) *The Foundation of Management*, London: Tavistock Publications.

Baumard, P. (1999) *Tacit Knowledge in Organizations*, London: Sage.

BJM (2001) *British Journal of Management* 12, Special Issue: S1–S2.

Bosworth, D. (1999) 'Empirical Evidence on Management Skills in the UK', paper prepared for the DfEE workshop on Management Skills, 5 July, Manchester, UMIST (mimeo).

Burrell, G. (1997) *Pandemonium: Towards a Retro-Organization Theory*, London: Sage.

Burton-Jones, A. (1999) *Knowledge Capitalism: Business, Work, and Learning in the New Economy*, Oxford: Oxford University Press.

Castells, M. (2000) *The Rise of the Network Society*, Oxford: Blackwell.

Caswill, C. and Shove, E. (eds) (2001) *Science and Public Policy: Special Issue on Interactive Social Science* 27(3).

CEML (2002) *Managers and Leaders: Raising our Game*, London. Council for Excellence in Management and Leadership.

Clark, P. (2000) *Organisations in Action: Competition between Contexts*, London: Routledge.

Clarke, T. and Fincham, R. (eds) (2001) *Critical Consulting: New Perspectives on the Management Advice Industry*, Oxford: Blackwell.

Clegg, S.R. (1990) *Modern Organizations: Organization Studies in the Post-modern World*, London: Sage.

Clegg, S. and Palmer, G. (eds) (1996) *Constituting Management*, Berlin: De Gruyter.

Constable, J. and McCormick, R. (1987) *The Making of British Managers*, London: British Institute of Management.

Cooper, R. (1986) 'Organisation/disorganisation', *Social Science Information* 25(2): 299–335.

——— (1989) 'Modernism, postmodernism and organizational analysis 3', *Organization Studies* 10(4): 479–502.

Engwall, L. (1992) *Mercury Meets Minerva*, London: Pergamon.

Engwall, L. and Zamagni, V. (1998) *Management Education in Historical Perspective*, Manchester: Manchester University Press.

ESRC (1994) *Report of the Commission on Management Research*, London: HMSO.

French, R. and Grey, C. (eds) (1996) *Rethinking Management Education*, London: Sage.

Furusten, S. (1999) *Popular Management Books*, London: Routledge.

Geertz, C. (1983) *Local Knowledge*, New York: Basic Books.

Gibbons, M., Limoges, C., Nowotny, H., Schwartzman, S., Scott, P. and Trow, M. (1994) *The New Production of Knowledge: The Dynamics of Science and Research in Contemporary Societies*, London: Sage.

Grey, C. (2001) 'Re-imagining relevance: a response to Starkey and Madan', *British Journal of Management* 12, Special Issue: 27–33.

Handy, C., Gordon, C., Gow, I., Moloney, M. and Randlesome, C. (1987) *The Making of Managers*, London: National Economic Development Office.

Hassard, J. and Parker, M. (1993) *Postmodernism and Organisations*, London: Sage.

Hatchuel, A. (2001) 'The two pillars of new management research', *British Journal of Management* 12, Special Issue: 33–41.

Hodgkinson, G.P. and Herriot, P. (2001) 'The role of psychologists in enhancing organizational effectiveness', in I. Robertson, M. Callinan and D. Bartram (eds) *Organizational Effectiveness: The Role of Psychology*, Chichester: Wiley.

Hodgkinson, G.P., Herriot, P. and Anderson, N. (2001) 'Re-aligning the stakeholders in management research: lessons from industrial, work and organizational psychology', *British Journal of Management* 12, Special Issue: 41–9.

Huff, A. (2000) 'Presidential address: changes in organizational knowledge production', *Academy of Management Review* 25: 288–93.

Huff, A.S. and Huff, J.O. (2001) 'Re-focusing the business school agenda', *British Journal of Management* 12, Special Issue: 49–55.

Jackall, R. (1988) *Moral Mazes: The World of Corporate Managers*, Oxford: Oxford University Press.

Jackson, B. (2001) *Management Gurus and Management Fashions: A Dramatistic Inquiry*, London: Routledge.

Jeffcutt, P. (1994) 'The interpretation of organisation: a contemporary analysis and critique', *Journal of Management Studies* 31(2), March: 225–50.

Jeffcutt, P., Pick, J. and Protherough, R. (2000) 'Management and the creative industries', *Studies in Cultures, Organizations and Societies* 6(2):123–7.

Kilduff, M. and Kelemen, M. (2001) 'The consolations of organization theory', *British Journal of Management* 12, Special Issue: 55–61.

Knights, D. and Willmott, H. (1997) 'The hype and hope of interdisciplinary management studies', *British Journal of Management* 8(1): 9–22.

Lash, S. and Urry, J. (1994) *Economies of Signs and Space*, London: Sage.

Lave, J. and Wenger, E. (1991) *Situated Learning: Legitimate Peripheral Participation*, Cambridge: Cambridge University Press.

Locke, R. (1989) *Management and Higher Education since 1940*, Cambridge: Cambridge University Press.

——— (1996) *The Collapse of the American Management Mystique*, Oxford: Oxford University Press.

Micklethwait, J. and Wooldridge, A. (1997) *The Witch Doctors*, London: Mandarin.

Nowotny, H., Scott, P. and Gibbons, M. (2001) *Rethinking Science, Knowledge and the Public in an Age of Uncertainty*, Cambridge: Polity.

Pettigrew, A.M. (1997) 'The double hurdles for management research', in T. Clarke (ed.) *Advancement in Organizational Behaviour: Essays in Honour of D.S. Pugh*, London: Dartmouth Press.

—— (2001) 'Management research after modernism', *British Journal of Management* 12, Special Issue: S61–70.

Pettigrew, A.M. and Fenton, E.M. (2000) 'Complexities and dualities in innovative forms of organizing', in A.M. Pettigrew and E.M. Fenton *The Innovating Organization*, London: Sage.

Pollard, S. (1965) *The Genesis of Modern Management*, London: Edward Arnold.

Porter, L.W. and McKibbin, L.E. (1988) *Management Education and Development: Drift or Thrust into the 21ˢᵗ Century*, New York: McGraw-Hill.

Prichard, C., Hull, R., Chumer, M. and Willmott, H. (eds) (2000) *Managing Knowledge: Critical Investigations of Work and Learning*, London: Macmillan Press Ltd.

Starkey, K. and Madan, P. (2001) 'Bridging the relevance gap: aligning stakeholders in the future of management research', *British Journal of Management* 12, Special Issue: 3–27.

Stewart, C. and Shaw, R. (1994) *Syncretism/Anti-Syncretism*, London: Routledge.

Thomas, A.B. and Al-Maskati, H. (1997) 'Contextual influences on thinking in organizations: learner and tutor orientations to organizational learning', *Journal of Management Studies* 34(6): 851–70.

Tranfield, D. and Starkey, K. (1998) 'The nature, social organisation and promotion of management research', *British Journal of Management* 9(4): 341–54.

Wagner, P. (1994) *A Sociology of Modernity*, London: Routledge.

Watson, T. (1994) *Understanding Management*, London: Routledge.

—— (2001) 'The emergent manager and processes of management pre-learning', *Management Learning* 32(2): 221–35.

Watson, T. and Harris, P. (1999) *The Emergent Manager*, London: Sage.

Weick, K.E. (2001) 'Gapping the relevance bridge: fashions meet fundamentals in management research', *British Journal of Management* 12, Special Issue: 71–7

Whitley, R. (1995) 'Academic knowledge and work jurisdiction in management', *Organization Studies* 16(1): 81–105.

—— (1999) *The Intellectual and Social Organization of the Sciences*, 2nd edition, Oxford: Oxford University Press.

Part I

Management knowledge and the challenge of professionalisation

2 The coming crisis of Western management education

Alan B. Thomas[1]

Introduction

The aim of this chapter is to explore the contention that Western management education has entered a period of 'crisis' and to examine the implications of such a development. Drawing on historical studies of management education in America and Europe, four modes of management 'formation' are identified, each of which has been dominant in a particular period. From its pre-paradigmatic beginnings, management education has been successively transformed under an 'old' and latterly a 'new' paradigm. Current changes in and critiques of the 'new' paradigm imply that Western management education is entering a post-paradigmatic mode. The implications of this post-paradigmatic turn are considered in relation to management practice, management knowledge and management 'formation'.

In *The Coming Crisis of Western Sociology*, the late Alvin Gouldner argued that sociologists in the 1960s were living 'in a fluid, transitional era' (1971: 7) in which the dominant sociological theories of the day were losing their grip on practitioners. Experiencing a growing divergence between their personal and professional realities, some sociologists at least were engaged in a fundamental questioning of the established canon of sociological beliefs and were actively constructing alternatives. To the extent that such developments implied a radical reconstruction of the sociological project, sociology was entering a period of crisis.

In this chapter we are concerned not with Western sociology in the 1960s but with Western management education[2] today. Yet there seem to be some telling similarities between the state of sociology then and of management education now, for management education seems at present to be in a state of fluidity and transition. In the face of considerable turbulence in both the 'fields of action' and the 'fields of knowledge' (Lupton 1984), management education in both Britain and America has become the object of substantial criticism (see, e.g., French and Grey 1996).

The significance of today's critical mood is, however, unclear. Given that management education, like education itself, has seldom been entirely free from questioning, current expressions of dissatisfaction and doubt might well be regarded as little more than background noise. On the other hand, it seems possible that there might be something distinctive about the current situation, and that Western management education is entering, or perhaps has already entered, a period of 'crisis' with profound implications for its future.

The purpose of this chapter is to explore this contention, or hypothesis, and to consider its implications. In the next section we define some key terms, and then examine some prima facie indications of crisis. We then present a historical account of the development of management education in order to situate current tendencies. Finally we outline some aspects of the challenge to the dominant assumptions of the field and speculate on their implications for the future.

Some key terms

The key terms in this discussion are 'crisis', 'Western' and 'management education'. Since the meanings of these terms are not self-evident, we briefly describe the ways in which they are understood here.

'Crisis' has perhaps become an overused word, and it would be easy to level the charge of hyperbole in applying it to the current state of management education, as if one were holding up the spectre of dissolution, collapse or 'death'. However, as Gouldner points out:

> The central implication of a crisis is *not*, of course, that the 'patient will die'. Rather the implication is that a system in crisis may, relatively soon, become something quite different than it has been. A system undergoing crisis will change in significant ways from its present condition. While some of these changes may be only temporary and may soon restore the system to its previous condition, this is not the distinctive implication of a system crisis. A crisis, rather, points to the possibility of change that may be more permanent, producing a basic metamorphosis in the total character. When a system undergoes crisis, it is possible that it will soon no longer be the thing it was; it may change radically or may even fail to survive in some sense.
>
> (Gouldner 1971: 341)

We are interested, then, in the possibility that management education is undergoing changes that imply a 'basic metamorphosis' such that 'it will no longer be what it was' rather than in its likely disappearance or demise. Moreover, it is important to point out that a crisis need not be thought of in negative terms. It is just as possible to celebrate the onset of a crisis as it is to bemoan it. A crisis may thus be seen as liberating rather than disabling, although individuals' reactions are likely to differ according to how they perceive their relation to the status quo.

By 'Western' management education I mean to refer to a conception of management education which originated in the United States but which came to inform its practice elsewhere, especially in Britain and, to a lesser extent, in continental Europe. As Locke has pointed out, the American business school 'propagated, if it did not invent, the idea of management itself' (1989: 163) and, more especially, the idea of management as a profession. In turn it invented the business school and what later became known as the 'professional' or 'traditional' model of management education.

Although most clearly expressed in the major American business schools, this model, or something like it, was exported to Europe, and especially to Britain, in the immediate post-war period when Europe was particularly open to the influence of American culture. Its reception there was not, however, uniform. Britain, having no prior tradition of management education, was particularly open to American influence, British management's attitudes and practices having tended to remain closer to America than to continental Europe (Dufour 1994; Haire *et al.* 1966). Germany, however, was largely resistant to it, France rather less so. Even so, management education in Europe initially drew much of its inspiration from American practice (Dufour 1994).

The influence of America on British practice was especially clear at the time of the establishment of the two 'British Harvards' at London and Manchester in the 1960s. As Turner (1969) pointed out, business schools are about as British as drum majorettes. Although these British schools were keen to establish their own identities, they nonetheless drew heavily, if tacitly, on American assumptions about management education (Whitley *et al.* 1981).

Western management education is thus taken here to refer not to the sum total of provision in America and Europe but to a set of assumptions about its purpose and practice which originated in America and which came to inform management education elsewhere and most especially in Britain. If there is a crisis it is thus likely to be experienced most visibly in those countries.

Finally we turn to the concept of 'management education'. One of the problems which bedevils educational debate is the vagueness and overlapping meaning of many key terms such as 'training', 'education', 'development', 'general', 'technical', 'vocational', 'liberal', and so on (see, e.g., Thomas and Anthony 1996). Although it is impossible to avoid such words, it has seemed preferable whenever possible to refer to management 'formation', a French term intended here to designate all those processes associated with the transmission and acquisition of knowledge, attitudes and skills. Formal management education, institutionalised in the education system, can thus be seen as one specific mode of management formation but not as the only one.

Prima facie indications of crisis

What preliminary indications are there to suggest that Western management education is in a state of crisis? We turn first to the United States and then to Britain.

It has been noteworthy that in America in recent years there has been a growing tendency not to celebrate the achievements of its business schools but to blame them for the country's declining competitiveness and faltering economic performance. An early note was sounded by Hayes and Abernathy (1980) in their paper 'Managing our way to economic decline', where they argued that the business school curriculum was a shallow concept which encouraged analytical detachment and which failed to develop the hands-on skills of management. More recently the Porter and McKibbin (1988) report concluded that management education and development activities in the United States are in danger of casually drifting into the 21st century. In 1992 the *Harvard Business Review* published a debate on the MBA, asking 'is the traditional model doomed?', in which Mintzberg stated that 'business school education as it currently stands is undermining U.S. business'. He went on to say that he was 'increasingly convinced that the more Harvard and similar business schools succeed, the more U.S. business fails', and he referred to 'the damaging effects of conventional MBA education' (Mintzberg 1992: 129). Similarly, Aaronson, commenting on her survey of graduate business schools between 1945 and 1960, has wondered 'whether America might have been better off without such reliance upon business education for executive suite preparation' (1992: 173).

Criticisms of management education in America have been summarised by Cheit (1985). On the basis of an analysis of 200 articles he identified four groups of criticisms: business schools emphasised the wrong model of management education; ignored important work such as that on behavioural skills; failed to meet society's needs; and fostered undesirable attitudes of arrogance, short-termism and careerism. In short, the legitimacy of management education in America appears to be under severe questioning.

In Britain, Willmott has claimed that 'established understandings of management practice and education are currently being unsettled by a number of developments' and that some management academics share 'a deep scepticism about the value, relevance and practical efficacy of established management theory and the way that this is imparted to potential or practising managers' (1994: 105–6). Miller has asked whether the MBA is 'in crisis' (1993: 32), French and Grey (1996) have called for a fundamental rethinking of management education, and, in a European context, Dufour has asked whether 'we really want to continue our MBA programmes as such' (1994: 15). Finally, Anthony has suggested that 'as things stand, it seems that it might be a matter of no great consequence if management education as we know it simply came to an end' (Thomas and Anthony 1996: 33).

Although it would be wrong to suggest that there is, as yet, a general consensus on the current condition of Western management education, there seem to be sufficient indications of discontent to support the view that Western management education is indeed in a critical state.

Some reactions to the crisis hypothesis

If there seems little doubt that management education is currently the object of considerable criticism and questioning, this need not lead one to conclude that this is a sign of crisis. We briefly consider three possible reactions below.

Business as usual

One reaction might be to argue that management education has always operated in a state of incipient crisis, especially in Britain. In part this is because of the difficulty, inherent to the task, of demonstrating its efficacy in a compelling manner. Since management education is sustained to a large degree by faith, and since faith is fragile, management education has always been open to criticism. Current expressions of discontent represent simply the latest instalment of a long-running show and are of no particular interest.

Crisis? What crisis?

Alternatively, it could be suggested that although management education experienced a birth crisis, most obviously in Britain, it successfully overcame this and has long been a securely established institution. America has more than a century of tradition in management education; Britain offers MBA courses in over a hundred establishments; students continue to enrol in management courses in large numbers. Thus management education is fundamentally healthy and talk of a 'crisis' is no more than hyperbole, used by a traditional range of critics – narrow-minded practitioners, elitist academics, utilitarian governments and leftist scholars – to 'talk up' an artificial crisis as a way of advancing their pernicious agendas.

The crisis is real

Finally, it could be proposed that although management education has achieved a substantial degree of legitimacy in the eyes of academia, government and management practitioners, and although it has always faced criticisms of its aims, content and methods, current questioning is so fundamental and so widespread as to herald the onset of a genuine crisis. On this view, management education is on the brink of a genuinely transformational moment in its history.

Whilst I do not want to deny or underestimate the significance of the first two of these views nor to overestimate the plausibility of the third, it is the latter which will chiefly be addressed in the rest of this chapter. Is Western management education in crisis?

The development of Western management education

To understand the current state of Western management education it is important to set recent developments in their historical context, for, as Oxenham has observed, 'Knowing how things have got the way they are is a precondition for judging whether the institutions we have represent a rational response to the challenges for which they were designed, or whether we have problems' (1984: 26).

To do so we employ the historian's device of periodisation together with the notion of 'paradigms', where a paradigm is to be understood in Locke's (1989: 1) sense as the set of assumptions upon which people base their practice of (in this case) management education.[3] As depicted in Figure 2.1, each paradigm defines a mode of management 'formation', a set of assumptions concerning the nature of management knowledge, the possibilities for the transmission of that knowledge, the forms of application of that knowledge to management practice, and the relations between these elements (see, in a different context, Jamous and Peloille 1970).

As the dates in Figure 2.1 imply, each paradigm takes up a central position of dominance which it occupies over a given period. The arrows indicate that paradigms 'drift' into a dominant position and are then displaced by alternatives which emerge during the prior period. Each transition period is marked by focal concerns which seek to reject the old paradigm in favour of the new and which engage adherents of established and emerging paradigms in struggles for dominance. The outcomes of such struggles are conditioned by a complex array of social, cultural, political and organisational factors, so that there is no straightforward way of predicting outcomes. For example, potential new paradigms may emerge but fail to achieve dominance in the short run or at all; thus in Britain advocates of formal management education had to wait many years before there was any significant positive response from the education system (Thomas 1980).

Each period can thus be distinguished in terms of the dominant assumptions held about managerial knowledge, managerial learning and managerial practice which serve to inform modes of management formation. It is misleading, however, to treat these modes as if they succeeded each other by replacing and obliterating their predecessors. Rather, successive modes are better seen as over

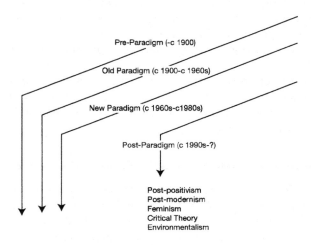

Figure 2.1 Succession of modes of management 'formation'

laying, rather than replacing, earlier ones, so that formerly dominant modes may persist 'in the background' alongside their dominant successors, sometimes located in different institutions and sometimes even within the same institution. Most obviously, what I have called the pre-paradigm mode, in which management formation is located exclusively in the workplace, has continued to flourish alongside alternative conceptions which give pride of place to formal management education within the education system.

Before turning to discuss these modes in more detail, a few general points need to be made about the different histories of Britain and America. In the United States, management education was well established before the 1960s under the old paradigm. But most of this was undergraduate education, with the graduate school at Harvard (established in 1908) being a prominent exception. The major expansion of graduate management education came only after 1945, so that by 1959 there were as many business schools in America as there are MBA courses in Britain today (Aaronson 1992). In Britain, with the exception of a few commercial and management courses and the ill-fated National Scheme of Management Studies, there was no graduate management education until the 1960s. As Locke (1989: 185) has pointed out, in America management education tended to begin at the undergraduate level and then move to the MBA, whereas in Britain the reverse has been the case. Most importantly for the purposes of this discussion, management education in Britain effectively began under the sway of the new paradigm.

The pre-paradigm mode (–c.1900)

In the pre-paradigm mode of management formation, the generation, transmission and application of management knowledge was based on the assumption that these processes could only, or could best, be carried out in the workplace itself as part of the everyday process of managing organisations. Management knowledge was thus conceived of in essentially local terms, consisting of the rules of thumb, guidelines, everyday recipes and practices which management practitioners discovered or invented for themselves, or which they received as established wisdom based on custom and habit. This knowledge was derived largely from experience and was not, and perhaps could not, be codified or formalised as a body of knowledge, although occasionally management practitioners set out their ideas in textual form (e.g. Freedley 1853). Learning about management was assumed to be possible only through direct experience of managing – that is, by 'natural learning' (Burgoyne and Hodgson 1983) in the course of day-to-day working life. Management knowledge, management learning and the practice of management were thus seen to be intimately related and essentially workplace based. Specialised education in management via the education system was barely conceivable,[4] as was the notion of a science of management.

The old paradigm mode (c.1900–c.1960s)

What Locke (1989) has called the 'old paradigm', or what Cheit (1991) refers to as the 'old consensus', emerged as management education began to be established in the education system. In America, basic provisions for commercial education in private business colleges and trade schools developed in the early 19th century, but these were largely concerned with training clerks in such tasks as bookkeeping rather than with management and administration (Hugstad 1983). As such they lacked the prestige to be considered as appropriate for the education of managers, much as the technical colleges were later to do in Britain. However, the founding of the Wharton School at the University of Pennsylvania in 1881 is generally seen as marking the beginnings of management education in the American higher education system.

At this time the management knowledge that was to be conveyed by education was not conceived of in vocationally specialised, technical or scientific terms. Management education was seen as an exercise in liberal, general education intended to equip gentlemen with the moral and intellectual capacities befitting their future status as leaders. Thus the Wharton School, for example, was deliberately located in the liberal arts college at the University of Pennsylvania rather than in the economics department in order to create a liberally educated class of leaders for American society (Sass 1982). The designation of such education as management education might be thought, then, to be tangential in the sense that whilst being education *for* managers its content was general rather than vocational.

In the early 20th century management education in America moved away from its liberal arts roots towards a more practical, functional orientation. Thus, according to Cheit:

> During the first half of the 20th century, the concept of management, as well as the curriculum in business schools, represented a consensus of the views of both practitioners and professors. Practice played an important role in instruction, most of which was at the undergraduate level, and was frequently offered by instructors from the world of business. Because the entry-level employment needs of business firms were most influential in shaping the concept of the manager and of management education, the emphasis in the curriculum was on how to perform the functions of business. And there was agreement among practitioners and professors about the importance of the principles of management, a body of thought that later became known as the classical theory.
>
> (Cheit 1991: 196–7)

The old paradigm therefore maintained a close association between management knowledge, defined in functional terms, management learning, the acquisition of functional competence through formal instruction, and management practice as a source of management knowledge, of teachers and as the aim of management education.[5] It differed from pre-paradigm assumptions in that it assumed that management knowledge could be codified and taught by means of formal instruction. What it lacked, however, was the assumption that management knowledge could be scientific or that management could, like medicine, be a science-based profession.

The new paradigm mode (c.1960s–c.1980s)

The post-war years saw the emergence of a new paradigm for management education that assumed that it was both possible and necessary to create a science, or a series of sciences, of management and to teach them to managers as a basis for their practice (Locke 1989). This paradigm arose from a complex set of interrelated developments, including transitions in various fields of knowledge – in economics, mathematics, statistics, organisation theory – the emergence of operations research and systems theory, encouraged by the exigencies of the Second World War and the subsequent Cold War, and various institutional changes such as the growth of large firms. Thus by the 1960s 'management had become the focus of science and science the focus of management as never before' (Locke 1989: 26), and management was to be conceived of as a 'profession'.

In the United States, these developments were crystallised for management education by the publication of the Gordon and Howell (1959) and Pierson (1959) reports. These reports were highly critical of American management education, which was seen to be 'too vocational' and insufficiently concerned with rigorous, scientific, disciplinary knowledge. The business schools responded by increasing the disciplinary orientation of their curricula and by recruiting growing numbers of disciplinary specialists. This 'trend to appoint new faculty from the social sciences, combined with the increasing popularity of business faculty trained in technical specialities within mathematics and engineering schools, led to a noticeable decline in demand for business faculty grounded primarily in business practices' (Hugstad 1983: 21). The adoption of the new paradigm thus went hand in hand with a 'transference of influence and power from the business community to the academy' (Hugstad 1983: 21) and fitted neatly with business school academics' interest in raising the prestige of their vocation (Kephart *et al.* 1963).

In 1960s America a growing gap was perceived to be developing between business schools and business practitioners, so that 'by the end of the decade the concerns regarding overemphasis on vocational concerns had been replaced by criticism that business programs were becoming too esoteric and theoretical' (Hugstad 1983: 41). Thus Koontz (1961) spoke of a 'management theory jungle' populated by burgeoning 'schools' of management thought which were becoming unintelligible to practitioners and too far removed from their practical concerns. Returning to the matter in 1980 (Koontz 1980), he noted that the six schools he had identified 20 years earlier had grown to 11 and that only one, in his view, was concerned with the actual process of managing.

This growing remoteness of management education from management practice is exemplified in the business schools' curricula. Cheit (1991) examined the MBA curricula of 12 leading American business schools for 1987–88 and found that management amounted to only 2 per cent of the required part of the programs. He commented that 'most institutions have no course with this name...the curriculum is increasingly specialised and academic and not primarily about managing' (Cheit 1991: 206, 209).

As we have said, in Britain management education in the universities was from the start based on the assumptions of the new paradigm. In his report on British business schools, Franks (1963) declared that the curriculum would be based partly on 'framework' subjects, such as economics, sociology and psychology. He went on:

> The second main kind of useful knowledge consists in certain skills or techniques of management which have mostly been elaborated in and since the last war.... Operational research, linear programming, resource allocation and strategic planning, decision theory and its applications, the use and application of computer techniques [represented] a far-reaching extension of the principles of scientific method and quantitative analysis into new fields, and as such they are coming to constitute an important element in the contemporary climate of ideas.
>
> (Franks 1963: 9)

In Britain the major expansion of management education thus came at a time when the new paradigm was already being instituted in America, and in an era of optimism about technology and social science. British management education thus never experienced the 'old consensus' between practitioners and professors identified by Cheit (1991) for America. As the founding of the business schools at London and Manchester showed, any consensus in Britain was shallow and fragile for they rapidly came under attack (Thomas 1980). What consensus there was was a consensus within the education system – that establishing business schools and MBA courses was a profitable venture. Even then it is not at all clear that there has ever been an agreed model of management education among management educators themselves. Thus, for example, the recent 'back to basics' movement expressed in the Management Charter Initiative has proved to be controversial (see Chapter 5).

The post-paradigm mode (c.1990s–?)

The developments outlined above can be summarised in terms of the nature and extent of consensus on the dominant modes of management formation. Thus under the pre-paradigm mode there was a consensus among academics and practitioners concerning management formation, albeit a negative one: both parties tacitly agreed that management formation was to take place in the workplace. Under the old paradigm the consensus took the form of an understanding that management formation could, at least in part, be effectively undergone in the higher education system. Under the new paradigm, whilst the academic consensus persists there is substantial dissent on the part of practitioners. Finally, under post-paradigm conditions practitioner dissent is joined by dissent from within – management educators themselves are now not only critics but perhaps the leading critics of their own practice.

Moreover, it is the character of much of that critique from within that is noteworthy. For whilst sometimes the concern is largely with alternative forms of pedagogy (McLaughlin and Thorpe 1993) or with curriculum design (Watson 1993), there is also a strong strand of radical criticism stemming from postmodernism (Boje 1996), feminism (Mills and Tancred 1992), critical theory (Alvesson and Willmott 1992; Willmott 1994), environmentalism (Berry 1995) and elsewhere (Anthony 1986; Thomas and Anthony 1996). These latter orientations raise fundamental issues concerning not only management education but the conduct of management itself (Grey and French 1996).

It seems that there might be more here than simply the worries of academics about the respectability of their work or of management practitioners about the relevance of MBA education to business. Although one can hardly refer to a chorus of criticism, a substantial number of critical voices are being raised today which speak from a wide variety of viewpoints and which address issues basic to the whole project of management education. This seems to support the contention that contemporary management education is indeed potentially open to crisis.

The coming crisis: challenges to the new paradigm

Since management formation is concerned with processes of generating, transmitting and applying managerial knowledge (in the broadest sense), it might be expected that all three facets of this process have become the focus of deep questioning, as indeed I believe they have. But largely for reasons of space, and also because it seems most fundamental, I will concentrate on the issue of knowledge.

Management knowledge as science: the post-positivist challenge

As we have already seen, under the new paradigm managerial knowledge became heavily associated with science, and especially with positivist conceptions of science. Mitroff and Churchman comment that whilst 'there has never been any coherent or sound philosophy of management or of knowledge itself...positivism is still the dominant ideology of academia' and that ' business schools have jumped on the positivist bandwagon in the desire to attain academic respectability' (1992: 134). Yet positivism has been widely critiqued by philosophers of social science and abandoned as the dominant epistemology of the human studies. So, for example, Polkinghorne (1983) has spoken of the current 'post-positivist' era and of the 'post-positivist challenge', a theme reflected in today's postmodern drift.

Dissent from established assumptions about managerial knowledge and their implications for management education has perhaps been most convincingly expressed by Schon (1983), who argues that the technical programme of positivism is of marginal relevance to management practice in today's rapidly changing world. Whereas the new paradigm assumes that effective management practice is based on the application of the sciences of management, Schon argues that this is misleading. Such a view requires the application of general, abstract, reductionist schemes to unique, concrete, complex cases; does not indicate how to cope with alternative frameworks for interpreting problems; and does not deal with value issues. He thus advocates the reflective practicum as the appropriate mode of formation, in which learning by doing is central rather than peripheral and in which traditional conceptions of teaching are replaced in favour of coaching. By such means an 'epistemology of practice' might be constructed.

Management education has, until now, been largely insulated from these foundational challenges, a consequence in part of the institutional isolation of business schools from the wider academic community. Yet there are signs that at least some of the basic management disciplines are beginning to feel the influence of these epistemological stirrings: in economics (Ormerod 1994), in marketing (Brown 1995; Morgan 1992), in accounting (Power and Laughlin 1992), in operational research (OR) (Mingers 1992), in human resource management (Legge 1995; Steffy and Grimes 1992), in organisational behaviour (Boje and Dennehy 1994; Sims *et al.* 1993; Tsoukas 1994) and in strategic management (Knights 1992). Whether these critical currents will lead to a basic transformation of these fields remains to be seen, but the current situation does at least seem very different to that which prevailed in the relatively recent past.

In principle the 'post-positivist challenge' opens up management education to alternative forms of knowledge and of formation, to non-positivist social science, to postmodernism and to the long-lost humanities (Johnston 1986). But adherents of such disciplines are faced with a crucial problem, that of 'relevance'. In effect, management education is caught in a trap: positivism holds out the promise of techniques for controlling the world; managers want and expect to be provided with technical knowledge; therefore to dethrone positivism seems like a suicidal act, at least as management education is currently conceived. But positivism does not work; to put it in an (obviously oversimplified) nutshell, positivistic management knowledge seems subject to the inverse utility law: the more it adheres to positivistic conceptions of rigour, the less useful it is – other than for purely rhetorical purposes.

Of course, these observations are highly contentious. Some, such as Donaldson (1985) and Kay (1994), seem to believe that positivism can be rescued. But I am more inclined to agree with Butler who, noting that the 'treasured dream' of a management science has failed to materialise, concludes that 'a science of managing seems to be as elusive as a science of living' (1986: 147). At the very least it seems that deep questioning of the nature of managerial knowledge and its relation to management practice is likely to continue under post-paradigm conditions. Thus Locke, for example, has noted the growing concern in the 1980s among some American management experts with the 'crumbling epistemological foundation' of the dominant American model of management, with the result that 'the epistemological and psychological assumptions upon which American managerialism built its house collapsed' (1996: 175, 191).

Management as a discipline: the unfulfilled promise

If there has been a failure to establish a convincing managerial science, there has also been a failure to establish management as a discipline or field, whether scientific or otherwise. Although the seeds for such a development were sown by the classicists of old and nurtured, with some difficulty, by their neo-classical successors, it seems subsequently to have been siphoned off into the nearest available receptacle, organisational behaviour, where it has languished ever since. This marginalisation of management within the new paradigm seems, like the problem of managerial knowledge, to be symptomatic of the current crisis of management education.

When we consider the ways in which knowledge is produced in society we might well focus on its codification, the establishment of disciplines and the creation of formal institutions in which such knowledge is subsequently developed and transmitted to learners. But alongside this we must place the less visible forms of everyday knowledge developed, for example, within occupational communities and maintained and passed on as an oral tradition. In the case of management, it is evident that it is the latter form of knowledge that provided the initial basis for the codified forms which could be taught in the education system. Fayol, for example, saw just this process of codifying the everyday knowledge of experienced management practitioners as the indispensable basis for management education (see Thomas 1993).

The insertion of management into the education system under the assumptions of the new paradigm has, however, proved problematic. Far from establishing management as a discipline, closely focused on the tasks of management practice, management has been successively redefined according to the orientations of academics to the point that it ceases to be recognisable to managers or disappears entirely from the curriculum. We have already noted Koontz's (1961, 1980) surveys of the state of management knowledge in which he depicted a growing fragmentation and remoteness from the practitioner's world. Today, perhaps not surprisingly, the teaching of management appears to have been all but eliminated from current business school curricula. Cheit (1991) reports that in America MBA programmes generally fail to teach management, and although we lack up-to-date information on the management education curriculum in Britain it seems doubtful that the situation there is much different.[6]

It could be, of course, that the classicists were wrong and that there is no distinct practice that can be labelled 'management'. It could also be that there is such a practice but that it is difficult or impossible to capture and codify it within a disciplinary framework. Stewart notes that 'management is not yet a well-defined discipline' (1984: 323) and that 'what is missing is any integrating conception of the nature of management' (*ibid.*: 324). She goes on to suggest that 'the desire for academic prestige and perhaps also the background and education of management teachers, have made us over-rate the extent to which management is a knowing, as distinct from a doing, occupation' (*ibid.*: 325). If management is indeed primarily a 'doing' occupation, then we have to consider 'the possibly very limited contribution of academics' (*ibid.*: 325) to learning how to do it. Universities have traditionally been concerned with the advancement of knowledge by teaching and research rather than with developing skilled practice, with the possible exception of training in medicine. It may be, then, that institutional constraints are such that management, as a discipline focused on practice, cannot readily secure a strong presence in the universities.

In the early days of management education in Britain, Revans saw these constraints very clearly. Referring caustically to the business professors who were busily constructing the business school curricula at London and Manchester, he wrote:

> Knowing little of business reality, incurious as to what might form an effective experimental syllabus, and fearful of the responsibilities of whatever real world action might have helped them to discover it, they simply carried on doing what they had always done, and even what their own teachers had done before them. When they filled up the timetable with lectures upon economics, sociology and mathematical bric-a-brac, it was not because these subjects had been proved essential to the prosecution of better management; they offered them because, like the mountebank in front of the shrine, it was all they had to offer. There was simply nothing else they could do.
>
> (Revans 1980: 194–5)

At a time of burgeoning MBA programmes, the failure to establish management as a discipline produces a very curious result – a management education which barely concerns itself with teaching its recipients how to manage.

The post-paradigm prospect

Is there a crisis in Western management education? Insofar as the tight coupling of formal education and management practice under the old paradigm has become progressively weakened, and insofar as this is now seen to be rooted in the very forms of knowledge (positivist technicism) and modes of instruction (formal teaching) institutionalised under the new paradigm, it does not seem far-fetched to suggest that there is. What, then, of the prospects for the future?

If the Western model of management education as it has become established in the post-war period is clearly undergoing substantial reassessment from a variety of quarters, the outcome of this scrutiny remains, of course, uncertain. As Figure 2.1 suggests, management formation under post-paradigm conditions is likely to become increasingly diverse, with no one mode holding an unchallenged place. Most management formation seems likely, as ever, to take place in the pre-paradigm mode. Learning about managing will continue, for better or worse, in organisational workplaces, with or without the contribution of formal management education. The old paradigm also seems likely to persist in some parts of the education system and within those organisations large enough to make their own provisions. Formation in the new paradigm mode hardly seems likely to disappear, if only because, whatever the criticisms, the market will probably continue to support it as it has done in the past. And, of course, there are likely to be a variety of hybrids combining elements from each mode. The crisis may thus be 'resolved' in several different ways. Below, we briefly examine three possibilities.

From management education to management studies

One possibility, discussed by Grey and French (1996), is that of divorcing the study of management entirely from a concern with management practice. On this view, to conceive of management education as a form of 'professional' preparation focused on the development of vocational techniques and skills is mistaken both practically and morally, the former because there is no genuine applied science of management to teach and the latter because the desirability of enhancing managerial effectiveness is questionable. Management should therefore be approached as a liberal study, much as political studies or religious studies are, taught primarily to enhance the learners' understanding and without any presumption of vocational commitment.

In essence, this view posits a withdrawal of the higher education system from participation in management formation and so points to a return to the pre-paradigm mode. Since current investments in the new paradigm are substantial, there seems little likelihood of this view achieving a position of dominance as the basis for a new consensus.

From management studies to 'real' management education

A second possibility, discussed by Thomas and Anthony (1996), envisages a division of labour akin to that implied by Grey and French but with an important difference. On the one hand, the 'external' study of management, which is open to any and all intellectual perspectives and disciplines, might be explicitly formulated under the rubric of management studies, perhaps in academic schools. Alongside this, however, the 'internal' study of *managing*, based closely on the realities of management practice, might be institutionalised separately but still within the education system. Such a division is seen to be advantageous since it avoids maintaining the pretence that academic interest in proliferating 'perspectives' on management is conterminous with preparing managers for their practice, and it facilitates the emergence of a clear focus within the academy on the processes of managing (perhaps revitalising the management discipline project).

This view can be seen to advocate a combination of the old and new paradigms, separately institutionalised in academic and professional schools. The prospects for its achieving dominance would appear, however, to require a revolution in the knowledge base of management practice as well as a radical recasting of current institutional commitments.

From management education to action learning

An interesting convergence has emerged in some quarters on the part of critical theorists (e.g. Willmott 1994) and 'liberal' theorists (e.g. Schon 1983) on the central importance of action learning in management education. From a critical point of view, action learning is seen to be significant chiefly as a means of advancing the emancipatory project, whereas for liberal theorists it is seen chiefly as a means of enhancing managerial effectiveness (though it should not be thought that the two are necessarily mutually exclusive). For both parties, action learning is nonetheless seen to be an important and emerging alternative to traditional forms of management education (see also McLaughlin and Thorpe 1993).

It is difficult to see how action learning can achieve much more than a minor position as one element within the post-paradigm mode. Being labour intensive in character at a time when major pressures are being exerted on higher education institutions to economise on academic labour, the emergence of action learning as a dominant mode of management formation would require a major institutional transition.

From this all too brief discussion of three currently canvassed possibilities for avenues of development for management education, it seems clear that none is likely to achieve a dominant position as a mode of management formation. Rather, we might expect them to form elements in an increasingly diverse and polycentric post-paradigmatic array.

Any truly radical break with prevailing practice seems likely, however, to take place outside the established institutional structure of management education, in what Grant and Riesman (1978) have called 'telic' institutions – that is, institutions 'charged with a sense of mission and distinctiveness' (Klein 1990: 36). Klein points out that such institutions, which emerged, for example, in the 1960s to advance interdisciplinary forms of education, approached the status of social movements or generic protests against contemporary life. They pointed towards a different conception of the ends of undergraduate education, ends that could not be met simply by reforming existing curricula or inventing new instructional technology. New programs and, in some cases, entirely new institutions were required.

(Klein 1990: 36)

In the case of management education in Britain, in its early stages the London and Manchester business schools could be seen to be examples of just such telic institutions. At Manchester Business School (MBS) (which I obviously know best) the sense of mission and distinctiveness and the claim to 'a high degree of autonomy and freedom to act with respect to the mother disciplines and the bureaucracy of the university' (Van Baalen 1995: 36), characteristic of telic institutions, was very clear in its early years (see J.F. Wilson 1992). Yet, as Van Baalen (1995) notes, the tendency has been for telic institutions located in the universities to 'regress' to the disciplinary structures which are privileged by their environments. In the case of MBS, for example, recent pressures have induced a noticeable reversion to traditional modes and forms.

In the light of the pressures currently being exerted on British universities (T. Wilson 1991; Willmott 1995) the prospects for the emergence of new telic institutions in management education seem doubtful. At the very least this would require the creation of a new consensus, or perhaps a series of them, on alternative conceptions of management education, together with the capacity to secure the resources necessary to institute them. In an era of financial stringency, fragmentation and post-paradigmatic chaos it may be that only small-scale, local agreements can be reached. Yet, as chaos theory suggests (Hall 1992), such small-scale local disturbances may turn out to be 'strange attractors' which divert the system in new directions.

As was noted earlier, the implication of a system crisis is not that 'the patient will die' but that the system may be radically transformed so that 'it will no longer be the thing it was'. It seems clear that some of the conditions necessary to such a transformation in Western management education have begun to emerge, reflecting growing diversity, complexity and turbulence in the fields of both knowledge and action (Lupton 1984). The post-paradigmatic array of modes of management education thus seems likely to become increasingly heterogeneous in terms of forms of knowledge, methods of transmission, possibilities of application and their institutionalisation.

Insofar as the crisis promises to open management education to continuing critical examination and revision, it may be considered virtuous rather than vicious.[7] Whether such questioning is a cause for celebration or a matter for regret is, of course, open to argument. But we should, perhaps, follow Winter, who, reflecting on the contemporary transformation of the university and academic work, proposes that this ought not to signify the doleful ending of a sacred tradition; rather it should constitute the current challenge to our understanding of our role in an historical process which it would be futile to ignore, and which (like earlier phases of the process) offers not only threats but also opportunities.

(Winter 1995: 141)

Notes

1 An earlier version of this paper was presented to the Annual Conference of the British Academy of Management, Aston University, Birmingham, 16–18 September 1996.
2 In a number of the cited sources the term 'business education' is used rather than 'management education'. Since the current debate has been conducted largely in terms of 'management education', this generic term has been adopted here.
3 Locke refers to the set of assumptions 'upon which people base their study of management' (1989: 1).
4 As Freedley put it: 'A collegiate education cannot be recommended, and if attainable is not desirable. A counting-house is the business man's college' (1853: 20).
5 Hugstad comments that between 1900 and 1918 'the business schools moved towards the [management] profession to such a degree that it was difficult to distinguish whether faculty were teachers or businessmen' (1983: 3).
6 A minor indication of the status of management within British business schools is given by the comment of one business school dean who recently stated that the title of professor of management was only given to someone when nobody really knew what they did!
7 The statement elaborating the theme of the 1996 British Academy of Management conference, 'What Have We Really Learned in Management Theory?', exemplified this mood of unrestrained questioning. The issues raised in this brief statement included 'how useful and scholarly the subject really is…are management theorists really in a position to offer sound and effective advice to practitioners in all sectors of the economy…what should business schools be teaching…is management theory itself merely a fabrication of predominantly structuralist researchers with little to say and even smaller room for intellectual development?'

References

Aaronson, S.A. (1992) 'Serving America's business? Graduate business schools and American business, 1945–60', *Business History* 34(1): 160–82.
Alvesson, M. and Willmott, H. (eds) (1992) *Critical Management Studies*, London: Sage.
Anthony, P.D. (1986) *The Foundation of Management*, London and New York: Tavistock.
Berry, A.J. (1995) 'Approaching the millennium, transforming the MBA curriculum: education for the stewardship of the planet's resources', paper presented at a conference on New Perspectives on Management Education, University of Leeds, January.
Boje, D.M. (1996) 'Management education as a panoptic cage', in R. French and C. Grey (eds) *Rethinking Management Education*, London: Sage.
Boje, D.M. and Dennehy, R.F. (1994) *America's Revolution Against Exploitation: The Story of Postmodern Management*, Dubuque, IA: Kendall Hunt.
Brown, S. (1995) *Postmodern Marketing*, London and New York: Routledge.
Burgoyne, J.G. and Hodgson, V.E. (1983) 'Natural learning and managerial action: a phenomenological study in the field setting', *Journal of Management Studies* 20: 387–99.

Butler, D.W. (1986) 'The humanities and the MBA', in J.S. Johnston (ed.) *Educating Managers: Executive Effectiveness Through Liberal Learning*, San Francisco: Jossey-Bass.

Cheit, E.F. (1985) 'Business schools and their critics', *California Management Review* 27(3): 43–62.

—— (1991) 'The shaping of business management thought', in D. Easton and C.S. Schelling (eds) *Divided Knowledge: Across Disciplines, Across Cultures*, Newbury Park, CA: Sage.

Donaldson, L. (1985) *In Defence of Organization Theory*, Cambridge: Cambridge University Press.

Dufour, B. (1994) 'Dealing with diversity: management education in Europe', *Selections*, winter: 7–15.

Franks, Rt Hon. Lord (1963) *British Business Schools*, London: British Institute of Management.

Freedley, E.T. (1853) *A Practical Treatise on Business*, London: Thomas Bosworth.

French, R. and Grey, C. (1996) *Rethinking Management Education*, London: Sage.

Gordon, R.A. and Howell, J. (1959) *Higher Education for Business*, New York: Columbia University Press.

Gouldner, A.W. (1971) *The Coming Crisis of Western Sociology*, London: Heinemann.

Grant, G. and Riesman, D. (1978) *The Perpetual Dream: Reform and Experiment in the American College*, Chicago: University of Chicago Press.

Grey, C. and French, R. (1996) 'Rethinking management education: an introduction', in R. French and C. Grey (eds) *Rethinking Management Education*, London: Sage.

Haire, M., Ghiselli, E.E. and Porter, C.W. (1966) *Managerial Thinking: An International Study*, New York: Wiley.

Hall, N. (ed.) (1992) *The New Scientist Guide to Chaos*, London: Penguin.

Hayes, R. and Abernathy, W. (1980) 'Managing our way to economic decline', *Harvard Business Review* 58(4): 67–77.

Hugstad, P.S. (1983) *The Business School in the 1980s*, New York: Praeger.

Jamous, H. and Peloille, B. (1970) 'Changes in the French university-hospital system', in J.A. Jackson (ed.) *Professions and Professionalization*, London: Cambridge University Press.

Johnston, J.S. (ed) (1986) *Educating Managers: Executive Effectiveness Through Liberal Learning*, San Francisco: Jossey-Bass.

Kay, J. (1994) Plenary address to the Annual Conference of the British Academy of Management, University of Lancaster, September.

Kephart, W., McNulty, J. and McGrath, E. (1963) *Liberal Education and Business*, New York: Institute of Higher Education, Columbia University.

Klein, J.T. (1990) *Interdisciplinarity: History, Theory and Practice*, Detroit: Wayne State University Press.

Knights, D. (1992) 'Changing spaces: the disruptive impact of a new epistemological location for the study of management', *Academy of Management Review* 17(3): 514–36.

Koontz, H. (1961) 'The management theory jungle', *Journal of the Academy of Management* 4: 174–88.

—— (1980) 'The management theory jungle revisited', *Academy of Management Review* 5: 175–87.

Legge, K. (1995) *Human Resource Management: Rhetorics and Realities*, Basingstoke: Macmillan.

Locke, R. (1989) *Management and Higher Education since 1940*, Cambridge: Cambridge University Press.

—— (1996) *The Collapse of the American Management Mystique*, Oxford: Oxford University Press.

Lupton, T. (1984) 'The functions and organisation of university business schools', in A. Kakabadse and S. Mukhi (eds) *The Future of Management Education*, Aldershot: Gower.

McLaughlin, H. and Thorpe, R. (1993) 'Action learning – a paradigm in emergence: the problems facing a challenge to traditional management education and development', *British Journal of Management* 4: 19–27.

Miller, P. (1993) 'Teaching the world to manage in perfect harmony', *Personnel Management* 25(8): 32–5.

Mills, A. and Tancred, P. (eds) (1992) *Gendering Organizational Analysis*, London: Sage.

Mingers, J. (1992) 'Technical, practical and critical OR – past, present and future?', in M. Alvesson and H. Willmott (eds) *Critical Management Studies*, London: Sage.

Mintzberg, H. (1992) 'Debate', *Harvard Business Review*, November/December: 129.

Mitroff, I.I. and Churchman, C.W. (1992) 'Debate', *Harvard Business Review*, November/December: 134.

Morgan, G. (1992) 'Marketing discourse and practice: towards a critical analysis', in M. Alvesson and H. Willmott (eds) *Critical Management Studies*, London: Sage.

Ormerod, P. (1994) *The Death of Economics*, London: Paper.

Oxenham, J. (1984) *Education versus Qualifications? A Study of Relationships Between Education, Selection for Employment and the Productivity of Labour*, London: George Allen & Unwin.

Pierson, F. (1959) *The Education of American Businessmen*, New York: McGraw-Hill.

Polkinghorne, D. (1983) *Methodology for the Human Sciences: Systems of Inquiry*, Albany, NY: State University of New York Press.

Porter, L. and McKibbin, T. (1988) *Management Education and Development: Drift or Thrust into the 21st Century?*, New York: McGraw-Hill.

Power, M. and Laughlin, R. (1992) 'Critical theory and accounting', in M. Alvesson and H. Willmott (eds) *Critical Management Studies*, London: Sage.

Revans, R.W. (1980) *Action Learning: New Techniques for Management*, London: Blond & Briggs.

Sass, S.A. (1982) *The Pragmatic Imagination: A History of the Wharton School 1881–1981*, Philadelphia: University of Pennsylvania.

Schon, D. (1983) *The Reflective Practitioner*, London: Temple Smith.

Sims, D., Fineman, S. and Gabriel, Y. (1993) *Organizing and Organizations: An Introduction*, London: Sage.

Steffy, B.D. and Grimes, A.J. (1992) 'Personnel/organization psychology: a critique of the discipline', in M. Alvesson and H. Willmott (eds) *Critical Management Studies*, London: Sage.

Stewart, R. (1984) 'The nature of management? A problem for management education', *Journal of Management Studies* 21(3): 323–30.

Thomas, A.B. (1980) 'Management and education: rationalisation and reproduction in British business', *International Studies of Management and Organization* 10: 71–109.

—— (1993) *Controversies in Management*, London and New York: Routledge.

Thomas, A.B. and Anthony, P.D. (1996) 'Can management education be educational?', in R. French and C. Grey (eds) *Rethinking Management Education*, London: Sage.

Tsoukas, H. (1994) *New Thinking in Organizational Behaviour*, Oxford: Butterworth-Heinemann.

Turner, G. (1969) *Business in Britain*, London: Eyre & Spotiswoode.

van Baalen, P.J. (1995) 'Disciplinarisation and inter-disciplinarisation in Dutch management sciences', *NOBO*, November: 31–40.

Watson, S.R. (1993) 'The place for universities in management education', *Journal of General Management* 19(2): 14–42.

Whitley, R.D., Thomas, A.B. and Marceau, J. (1981) *Masters of Business*, London: Tavistock.

Willmott, H. (1994) 'Management education: provocations to a debate', *Management Learning* 25(1): 105–36.

—— (1995) 'Managing the academics: commodification and control in the development of university education in the U.K.', *Human Relations* 48(9): 993–1, 027.

Wilson, J.F. (1992) *The Manchester Experiment: A History of the Manchester Business School 1965–1990*, London: Paul Chapman.

Wilson, T. (1991) 'The proletarianisation of academic labour', *Industrial Relations Journal* 22: 250–62.

Winter, R. (1995) 'The University of Life plc: the "industrialization" of higher education?', in J. Smyth (ed.) *Academic Work: The Changing Labour Process in Higher Education*, Buckingham Society for Research into Higher Education (SRHE)/Open University Press.

3 Management as a technical practice

Professionalisation or responsibilisation?[1]

Christopher Grey

Introduction

There is a long-running tension, or even a paradox, which lies at the heart of management – both as a social practice and as an academic discipline.[2] Briefly stated, that paradox is that, on the one hand, management has been seen as being capable of representing itself as a technical practice (Reed 1989) which dominates ever more, and more diverse, areas of social activity (Deetz 1992) whilst, on the other, it has been seen as being incapable of sustaining a project of professionalisation (Abbott 1988; Whitley 1995). This is a paradox because if management is held to be a technical practice, then why is it not possible for managers to achieve closure around a body of technical knowledge and, consequently, to license and control managerial work? If, on the other hand, management is incapable of professionalisation, what is the source of its ability to enter and dominate ever more areas of social activity?

The nature of this paradox can initially be apprehended in terms of what has been perhaps the most influential modern work on the professions, namely Andrew Abbott's *The System of the Professions* (1988). According to this analysis, the 'system of professions' (1988: 86) is a continual battle for jurisdiction over particular territories of expertise, territories which are contested between groupings in a zero-sum game. There are limits to the extent to which the territory of other professions can be raided, however, since 'no profession can stretch its jurisdictions infinitely' (1988: 88). On this understanding of the nature of a profession, management does not qualify, since, 'despite numerous efforts, the area of business management has never been made an exclusive jurisdiction' (1988: 103).

The reason for this failure is held to be deficiencies in the nature of knowledge in the field of management.[3] Management is simply incapable of generating the type of systematic knowledge which would allow closure around managerial activities by a professional grouping of managers. Still less is it possible to generate the abstractions and generalisations which would facilitate the expansion of management into the territories of other professional groups. The supposed deficiencies of the knowledge base which might underpin managerial professionalisation lead directly to the nature and status of management education. The premier management education qualification, the MBA, covers extremely diverse forms of training and knowledge, and an equally diverse body of abstractions about how the work ought to be done. Psychology, sociology, administration, economics, law, banking, accounting, and other professions all claim some jurisdiction in business management.

(Abbott 1988: 103)

Via a different type of analysis, Richard Whitley (1984a, 1984b, 1995) has, through a series of publications, come to similar conclusions to Abbott about the relationship between the knowledge base of management and the weakness of managerial professionalisation. Management studies is a 'fragmented adhocracy' (Whitley 1984a) characterised by low levels of mutual dependence between researchers and high levels of task uncertainty in research. Hence:

The professionalization of managerial skills on the basis of academic knowledge is, then, unlikely to develop very strongly, even in Anglo-Saxon societies where 'professionalism' represents an important occupational ideal.

(Whitley 1995: 103)

Yet, despite the apparent failure of management to professionalise, the most cursory knowledge of contemporary organisational life reveals management in the ascendant. This is a statement not about industrial relations, to which it may nevertheless be linked, but rather about the ability of management to do precisely what Abbott's analysis suggests it should be unable to do: to extend its jurisdiction at the expense of other forms of expertise. The managerialisation of the public sector is a particularly high-profile example because of its political sensitivity. The repeated complaint made by professionals in the UK National Health Service, for example, is that their judgement, values, expertise and autonomy are being circumscribed by those of management and managers.

As well as extending the locus of its operation, management seems to be consolidating its grip on its more traditional sphere of operations (i.e. the industrial corporation). A bewildering variety of jargon and techniques has been spawned – from MBO (management by objectives) to TQM (total quality management) to BPR (business process re-engineering) – acquaintance with which is part of the currency of career success (Watson 1994, 1995) and requires considerable effort to acquire. Thus management training and education, whether in the form of the MBA or as part of the development of the 'learning organisation' (Senge 1990), are becoming increasingly unavoidable.

The power of management within the industrial corporation, and its dispersal outside this setting, has been identified as no less than a colonisation of the life-world (Deetz 1992) and as a new ideology supplanting both capitalism and communism (Enteman 1993), whilst for Ritzer (1993) it is part of the 'McDonaldization of society'. Such analyses are recent exemplars of well-established (albeit diverse) critical traditions which point to the nature and consequences of encroaching administration, managerialisation, bureaucratisation and rationalisation in modern societies (Weber 1968, vol. 2; Weil 1988;

Rizzi 1939; Burnham 1945; Whyte 1956; Marcuse 1964; Jacoby 1973; Foucault 1979; Habermas 1987).[4]

From such critical perspectives, the story which we might expect to be telling about the linkages between management as a technical practice, management as a profession and management education would be as follows (in schematic fashion): management is represented as a technical practice in order to legitimate and extend its social power (in relation to the elite interests of managers; or in relation to class domination; or as part of a process of rationalisation; or...). Professionalisation represents the most developed form of legitimation, resting as it does upon ideologies of integrity, independence, service and expertise. Management education acts as an institutional means through which management as a technical practice is represented and entry to the profession of management is controlled.

The problem such a story runs into (apart from anything else) is the failure of management to professionalise. Yet it remains true that management is represented as a technical practice, and plainly there are issues of legitimation at stake here. Furthermore, if management education[5] is not the link between technical practice and professionalisation, how else is it to be conceptualised? There is a longstanding tradition in the theorisation of education which stresses its role in the reproduction of social domination (Bowles and Gintis 1976). More recently, Foucauldian work has provided analysis of the discursive 'construction of governable persons' in a number of different contexts, including managerial and organisational ones (e.g. Rose 1989; Townley 1994), and enumerated some of the social technologies through which this is effected. Such analysis lays stress upon the notion of 'responsibilisation' – in other words, the regulation of subjectivity in ways which inculcate habits of self-control, self-management, planning, etc. In this chapter, it will be suggested that management education may be read in this light and that it constitutes one type of response to the 'trust' problem in organisations through the responsibilisation of managers.

In summary, then, this chapter attempts to explore the nexus of management as technical practice, as profession, and management education by offering some perspectives on each element. Inevitably, because of the breadth of the concerns and the complexity of some of the literatures involved it has been necessary to skate over some difficult issues in order to present a brief and (hopefully) coherent argument.[6] The intention in the first two sections of the chapter is to set out some basic groundwork for what is to follow in the third section.

In the first section management as a technical practice is discussed, with particular reference to the invocation of science and what this means for the constitution of management. In the second section management as a profession is considered. Rather than discuss this in terms of the knowledge base of management, the sociological conditions for professionalisation are discussed. In the third section an understanding of management education is offered which stresses its role, not in the professionalisation of management, but in the 'responsibilisation' of managers just alluded to. Moreover, management education in a broad sense is held to be implicated in the development of a 'management-speak' industry, and it is this as much as anything which accounts for the way in which managerial discourse is able to insinuate itself into ever more diverse areas of social life.

Management as a technical practice

Management has often – even usually – been represented as a technical practice. On this view, there exists a body of scientifically validated knowledge which is applied by managers in different settings. A weaker version of such a view would be that even if such a body of knowledge does not yet exist it is in the process of emerging and is retarded, not by any barriers of principle, but only by those of time, resources and intellect.[7]

In a comprehensive overview of the sociology of management, Michael Reed states:

> The technical perspective offers a conception of management as a rationally designed and operationalised tool for the realisation of predominantly instrumental values concerned with the systematic co-ordination of social action on a massive scale.... Management...constitutes the neutral social technology necessary to attain collective goals that are unrealisable without it.
>
> (Reed 1989: 2–3)

Whilst rival perspectives on management certainly exist, it is not unreasonable to claim that these have largely been subordinate to an understanding of management as a technical practice founded upon a body of established scientific knowledge. Such an understanding should certainly be seen as an *accomplishment* – that is to say, as a social construction reflecting certain exercises of power.[8] Thus, to take just one episode in the history of management, according to Child (1969) management developed in the context of a movement for industrial democracy in the late 19th and early 20th centuries. Management could act as a way of defusing growing trade unionism, whilst offering a more legitimate ethical basis for industrial authority than that of ownership. Yet this purpose shifted in the period following the First World War:

> management based upon expertise would...be in the legitimate and most effective position to define just what the industrial situation required. It is therefore not surprising to find that eventually most management writers joined in the reaction against the idea of joint manager–worker decision-making. This rejection was...excused in terms of the technical prerequisites for efficient industrial performance.
>
> (Child 1969: 54)

What this should suggest is that management was not initially and necessarily understood as a technical practice and, indeed, that such an understanding was an 'excuse'. In other words, management was constituted as a technical practice for reasons of legitimation.[9] For such legitimation to be effective, it was necessary that a body of technical knowledge be articulated. To put this at the most general level:

> Managerial authority, in its typical, Weberian, rational-legal form, rests on the claim that its knowledge base is scientific and, as such, is characteristic of thinking in an epoch which has been labelled modernist.
>
> (Jackson and Carter 1995: 198)

That is not to say that such knowledge was 'cynically' – or, for that matter, deliberately – brought into existence for legitimatory purposes – given the scientistic and taxonomic preoccupations of the Modern era (Foucault 1970), it must have seemed an obvious way to proceed. But, having emerged, such knowledge had effects in terms of legitimating management. Or, to put it another way, it is hard to see how in the absence of the development of a body of technical knowledge management could have sustained and developed its social power.

The most obvious manifestation of the constitution of managerial technical expertise is scientific management, as publicised and popularised by F.W. Taylor. But it is well known that Taylor was but one, and perhaps not even the most original, of those engaged in similar endeavours. Fayol, Urwick, Brech and Ure are often cited in this regard (see Wren 1994), and there are a host of less well-known figures. For example, in the United States, Daniel McCallum was a mid-19th century railway engineer who proposed a system of division of labour, reporting procedure, surveillance and quality control of an essentially Taylorist type (Chandler 1965). In Britain, writers like Herbert Casson popularised and synthesised emerging writing on management:

> I propose to prove that Business is now being developed into a Science.
>
> (Casson 1915: 9)

Casson goes on to enumerate 16 'axioms' of business which are seen to be the foundations of the new science of business management. These are a strange mixture of the self-evident and the dubious, interspersed with analogies from physics, geometry and biology. This very juxtaposition of management (or business) with more established sciences is plainly a key to its appeal, however. It is a tendency which remains at the heart of much contemporary management studies, where 'positivism is still the dominant ideology' (Mitroff and Churchman 1992: 134).

The positivism of management studies is a broad and problematic issue which cannot be addressed in detail here. Positivism in this context, following Giddens (1974: 1–4), has three broad characteristics:

1   The concepts and methods of the natural sciences (e.g. in terms of experimentation and the generation of general laws) are the most (or only) appropriate means for studying human activity.

2　Knowledge arises from direct perceptions of the world, and nothing is real which is not knowable in this way.

3　Value judgements are not knowable in this way and are inappropriate to scientific enquiry.

Such a position has become increasingly suspect, if not discredited, in much social science (Bernstein 1976), perhaps especially in sociology (Game 1990). To a much more limited extent, it has been questioned in management studies (e.g. Alvesson and Willmott 1992; Knights 1992).

But the positivistic commitments of management are rather different to those of social science. In social science the debate about positivism has had, to give an exceedingly concise review, two key elements. First, is social science like natural science? The answer, at least since Winch (1958), has increasingly been negative. Second, does natural science conform to the received model of social scientists? Again the answer, at least since Kuhn (1962), has tended to be negative. In management these debates are marginal, partly because they miss the point. Positivism is not the philosophy of management but the ideology. That is to say, the language of science has been invoked to bestow legitimacy.[10] One could of course argue that the same is true for social science, but the emergence of the social sciences from the Enlightenment was always a more philosophically engaged project than in management, so that, whereas social science may have looked to a received version of natural science for legitimation, management has looked to a received version of social science, and thus its philosophical engagements are more attenuated and marginal.

What is striking about the emergence of a technical body of knowledge in management, then, is the way 'scientific management' deployed a truncated and probably philosophically indefensible conception of science. In other words, whilst the positivism of social science has become increasingly problematic because of shifts in the philosophy of science and social science, the positivism of management would *never* have stood up to much scrutiny, even at the time when positivism was in vogue in the social sciences. Instead, the key feature of the positivism of management was its stress on systematisation, which might be a part of scientific method but scarcely exhausts such method. Systematisation has the rhetorical effect of seeming to capture the scientific 'mood', without the need for the kind of methodological reflection which has always characterised the history of both natural and social science. As Nyland (1988: 56) notes, the pioneers of scientific management were 'systematisers', and they left an enduring engineering ideology in managerial discourses (Willmott 1984).

Although the issues of the scientific status of management have been dealt with only briefly here, the importance, for present purposes, is this: it is largely irrelevant that much of what constitutes the scientific knowledge of management is demonstrably *unscientific* according to most understandings of science (Jackson and Carter 1995). For example, the Hawthorne experiments have been widely criticised (e.g. Carey 1967) in terms of the extraordinary laxity of their methodology. Yet this hardly diminishes the significance of the attempts to put management on a scientific footing, for, once again, the issue is the legitimation of management as a body of knowledge and, hence, the claims of managers, uniquely, to be able to operationalise such knowledge. No matter how flawed they may have been, the Hawthorne experiments, like Taylor's scientific management experiments and the whole parade of organisation science studies, continue to be reproduced as bedrocks of management thought and are correspondingly influential in defining management as a technical practice.

The deployment of scientific rhetoric in the constitution of management as a technical practice has two linked elements which are of crucial significance. The first is the development of a corpus of knowledge to which managers have privileged access, exemplified by Taylorism, but no less by, say, total quality management. The second element is the development of the notion of the neutrality of management (MacIntyre 1981). The existence of a body of technical management knowledge is bound up with a distinctive form of rationality which has been widely discussed. It is the rationality of means, referred to by Weber (1968) as formal rationality and by others (Habermas 1971) as technical or instrumental rationality. The focus of such rationality is the use of rational means towards the achievement of a given end. Thus, according to Weber, bureaucratic organisations are characterised by high degrees of formal rationality, in that they utilise the most technically efficient means towards their ends.

Again, it is beyond the scope of this analysis to discuss issues of rationality in detail, but the point for present purposes is that the domination of formal or instrumental rationality rapidly slides into a 'technocratic consciousness' (Alvesson 1987) wherein management techniques are merely means to some other end. That is to say, they are represented as normatively neutral because they can be put into the service of a range of ends (which may themselves not be neutral). Management is a technique, on this view, and whether it is used to run concentration camps or hospitals is not something which inheres in that technique, but a contingent attribute of its deployment.[11]

The linkage between the neutrality of management and the appeal to science is not coincidental. The received version of positivism found in management draws a strict separation between fact and value, and thus the supposed facticity of scientific management and its value-neutrality go hand in hand. Moreover, the importance of developing a set of generalised 'laws', such as Casson's axioms or Taylor's principles, must be recognised. If management were situation specific it would not be possible to sustain the idea that managers had particular access to expertise. Rather, expertise would be a feature of habituation in a particular location. The importance of management as a technical practice is that it establishes principles or techniques whose application is universal – from concentration camp to hospital – and this again requires the assumption of neutrality, in that separating management from its context also thereby separates it from its moral and political implications.

The twin features of an appeal to science and the claim of neutrality might be seen as providing a strong basis for professionalisation. And management has long had aspirations to be regarded as a profession, certainly since the early part of the last century (e.g. Brandeis 1914). In the following section, the failure of management to professionalise is considered.

Management as a profession

There are some occupations which have the status of classical professions. They include medicine, law and – albeit more problematically – accountancy. They are classical professions because they are able to exercise high levels of closure around particular skills, and these are skills which are economically and socially valued. So, at least, goes one kind of fairly conventional account in the sociology of professions literature (Wilensky 1964). Of course it might equally well be argued that the ability to be persuasive of an entitlement to be regarded as 'classical' is in fact one aspect of the power of particular occupational groups to achieve these high levels of closure.

The Abbott (1988) view, referred to earlier, of professions not just closing around particular occupational territories but also seeking to extend those territories tends to mean in practice that contestations occur at boundaries. For example, at the boundary of medicine there are contestations between psychiatric and psychological treatments of mental conditions, and between conventional and complementary medicine. Similarly, there are contestations over newly emerging fields of potential professionalisation such as management consultancy, where, amongst other players, both accountants and bankers lay claim to expertise.

So classical professions turn out to be those which have managed to (at least) hold on to their territory over a fairly long time period. It is not that some kinds of occupations are *inherently* professional,[12] and it is important not to fall into the rather facile error of giving professions an analytical value, which ignores, or takes as unproblematic, the fact that that value is part of the very process of professionalisation. This is a significant point in the context of the present discussion, since it means that the failure of management to professionalise should not be seen as an outcome of it being 'the wrong kind of knowledge'. This seems to be Abbott's (1988) view of management, and, moreover, he argues that where the 'right kind' of management knowledge exists – such as cost accounting – it was rapidly assimilated into the accounting profession. Yet if we consider accounting it is plain that its knowledge base can readily be shown to be a social construct (Hines 1988) and its power an outcome of a series of ideological posturings and state intervention (Sikka and Willmott 1995). So accounting, like management, represents itself as a technical practice. Accounting is no more inherently a technical practice than management, but it has been much more persuasive both in its claims to be so and in its project to professionalise. Thus, rather than consider management as a professional practice in terms of its knowledge base it is necessary to look at the sociological conditions of professionalisation.

The ability of a profession to exert monopolistic or near-monopolistic control over a particular occupation is a complex matter. One of the key characteristics is that of licensing. In other words, there is a requirement of qualification and accreditation as a precondition of professional practice. Here universities often play a key role in controlling the disbursement of the relevant qualifications (Larson 1977: 36). Typically, however, universities are but one of the parties involved, with professional associations or other training institutions (e.g. hospitals or inns of court) having a role. In some cases, such as accountancy, the role of universities can be relatively slight, with accounting degrees offering, at most, some limited exemption from the examinations of professional bodies. Moreover, as Abbott points out, there is variation not just between professions but between different nation-states as to the precise role played by universities in the licensing of professional knowledge and the provision of professional training (1988: 195–211). Nevertheless, even where universities have little formal role in profession formation they can act as a first precondition of professional practice, where such practice requires graduate status, and can act as institutions of professional socialisation in a rather diffuse sense (Larson 1977: 153).

But the licensing of practice is not the only element in the professionalisation of particular occupations. Professions also act to regulate their members. Self-regulation is a hallmark of professional knowledge because, precisely by virtue of the closure around that knowledge, it is held that outsiders will lack the comprehension necessary to undertake regulation. Part of that regulation includes the development of codes of ethics, and this links directly to the appeal which professions typically make to the notion of the 'public interest' – which they purport to serve (Kimball 1992). Moreover, successfully professionalised occupations have the capacity to define and redefine the tasks they perform, so that professions do not simply occupy a particular organisational territory but also orchestrate the topography of that territory.

So what about management? As shown earlier, Abbott, amongst others, is very clear that management is not a profession, and this is to be explained by certain characteristics of management knowledge, in particular its failure to generate appropriate abstractions. But that type of explanation has already been rejected, since it relies on the assumption that some types of knowledge are inherently professionalisable. What matters is not having the 'right kind' of knowledge, but the ability to represent a certain body of knowledge in the 'right way'.

A more comprehensive account of the failure of management to professionalise is offered by Reed (1989: 161–4). He identifies three central reasons for this failure. First, following Child *et al.* (1983), Reed sees management as being internally fragmented, and also as having historically lacked state support for professionalisation. Second, the location of management within formally rationalised bureaucracies means that managers are organisationally dependent and less able to develop the autonomy associated with professions. Third, and relatedly, managers, or at least middle managers, are increasingly subject to surveillance and monitoring as their work becomes routinised, as is argued by Clegg *et al.* (1986). Given all of these circumstances, there are limited possibilities for management to effect closure around a skill base, to define tasks and standards, and to self-regulate. In all these dimensions, then, management differs from the characteristics of the 'classic' professions.

Still, there are some difficulties with this explanation of the failure of management to professionalise, or at least some further nuances which require discussion. First, fragmentation is not in itself a barrier to professionalisation: in the medical profession, for example, there is considerable fragmentation, even hostility, between specialisms. There seems to be no reason to think that the distinction between, say, personnel and marketing managers is any greater than that between surgeons and physicians. In the latter case, each specialism has its own association but that does not detract from the overarching professional formation of medicine. In the case of management, specialist groups have sought to construct professional bodies and identities, but with limited success and without the construction of an overarching professional formation of management. Of groups associated with management, accountants have been the most successful, along perhaps with information and computing specialists. But in these cases part of the process of professional definition has been a distancing from 'general management'. It is also the case that the state has not been entirely neglectful of management (Locke 1984, 1989). At least spasmodically, there has been a concern with the development of management education. Thus the inception of business schools in the UK, for example, grew directly out of the Franks Report, commissioned by the National Economic Development Council (Whitley *et al.* 1981: 44–6).

The issue of the location of managers in bureaucratic organisations is also less than straightforward.[13] Shifting organisational structures mean that the overweening rationalisation which might have been held to have undercut the possibility of autonomous professional organisation appears less attenuated than hitherto. On the other hand, given that one of the key effects of 'post-bureaucracy' (Heckscher and Donnellon 1994) has been to fragment managerial careers and disrupt the relationship between individual managers and corporations, it follows that the organisational specificity of managing too may be on the wane. Larson distinguishes professions and bureaucracies by suggesting that bureaucratic authority is collective and structural, residing in managers by virtue of their role, whereas professional power, whilst asserted collectively, bestows freedom and trust upon individual professionals (1977: 206). One might argue that this analysis overstates the depersonalised character of bureaucracy. But, in any case, the changes just alluded to make it an unrecognisable picture of contemporary organisations.

In more recent work, Reed and Anthony have suggested that

> a 'professional model' of management education and occupational formation may be more feasible than the critics imply.
>
> (Reed and Anthony 1992: 598–9)

This possibility exists in part because of the shifting patterns of managerial work just alluded to. Thus we can expect

> the emergence of new groups of managers who will apply their expertise in such a way that cognitive diversity and collective learning will be enhanced.

The reintegration of conception and execution within the 'mega corporation', made possible by information technology and its organizational
consequences, will produce new foundations for managerial authority.

(Reed and Anthony 1992: 602)

This view receives support from Heckscher (1995), who analyses changing
patterns of managerial employment to conclude that there is a need for a professional model for managers divorced from specific organisational settings. Such a
development, as Reed and Anthony recognise, poses a challenge to conventional
management education. In particular, they point to the need to move away from
firm-specific needs and skills and narrow vocationalism (Reed and Anthony
1992: 601). This is a challenge which, arguably, has still to be met (French and
Grey 1996; Grey 1996a) but suggests at least in principle that one of the barriers
to the professionalisation of management may be broken. On the other hand, it
could be argued that this basis for managerial professionalisation is but new
words to an old tune. The MBA degree has long been predicated on the assumption that there is, or the desire that there should be, some set of knowledge which
transcends the firm-specific know-how of managers. Yet, as indicated earlier, the
MBA has failed to identify such a knowledge base.

Reed and Anthony develop their argument in part through an engagement
with Abbott (indeed they quote the same passage), and they invoke Abbott's
(1988: 325) notion of organisational professionalism as the basis for the claim of
the potential for management to professionalise (Reed and Anthony 1992: 599).
Yet the implication of Abbott's discussion at this point is that professionalising
projects in general are likely to be rendered ineffective by organisation. Thus the
prospects for management seem dimmer, not brighter, if Abbott's argument is
accepted.

Finally, the third of Reed's (1989) barriers to managerial professionalisation,
the proletarianisation of managerial work, will be considered. There is certainly
plenty of evidence that this has occurred, not least as a result of the technological changes which Reed and Anthony (1992) mention. The routinisation of
more junior managerial tasks has been responsible for generating unprecedented
levels of job insecurity amongst managers. For example, the development of
credit-rating systems in the banking sector has been responsible for the deskilling
and 'de-professionalisation' of bank managers. Yet, again, it is not plain that this
constitutes an insuperable barrier to professionalisation, any more than the
routinisation of lower-level legal work destroys the legal profession. Routinisation
is likely to shift the lines of demarcation between professionals and others, and
perhaps to reduce the size of professional associations, rather than to destroy
professions as such.

Management education, technical expertise and professionalisation

So far, two themes have been sketched. One suggests that the dominant representation of management is as a technical practice. The other suggests that, for a variety of rather complex reasons, management has not achieved professional status. In both of these aspects, management education plays a pivotal role, which has only been alluded to tangentially so far. Management education in this context denotes a broad set of concerns which are not reducible to the simple transmission of knowledge. Equally important are the production of knowledge and the production of credentials.

The notion of management as a technical practice is, to some considerable extent, an artefact of management education. It is of course true that many of the so-called pioneers of management thought (such as Taylor or Fayol) derived their techniques, rules and systems explicitly from experience. Yet throughout the 20th century, from Mayo to McGregor to Michael Porter, the university has produced and legitimated new theories and techniques of management, as well as incorporating and reproducing the work of industrial 'pioneers'.[14] Similarly, the university has been centrally implicated in the project of professionalisation, which, for all that it may have failed in relation to 'classical' conceptions of professions, has had a significant impact upon the managerial labour market, especially in the USA, where a significant number of managers have the MBA qualification. If we add to this the much greater number of people who take management as all or part of an undergraduate degree the influence of the university is still greater. And if we add the number of people exposed to business school theories through in-house training courses, consultants' interventions, guru seminars and self-help literature (Garsten and Grey 1997) it becomes clear that the role of management education in the dissemination of managerial discourse is profound.

Is such managerial discourse necessarily articulating an understanding of management as a technical practice? Elsewhere (Grey and Mitev 1995; Grey 1996a), I have claimed that this is so as regards the mainstream of representations of management in 'textbook knowledge'. Others have made similar claims. Jackson and Carter (1995) argue that management education routinely reproduces notions of management as science, even though, paradoxically, this means that

> facts which are, *prima facie*, incorrect are being taught to generation after generation of students destined to be the managers of the future.
>
> (Jackson and Carter 1995: 200)

Similarly:

> The business school speaks the artificially clarified and semantically impoverished language of hypothesis testing alone.
>
> (Jacques 1996: xi)

Plainly this links directly to the notion that positivism is the dominant 'ideology' of management thought, referred to earlier, and this observation is by no means detracted from by the existence of the panoply of 'new age', 'postmodern' and 'post-bureaucratic' writings on management. Such writings lay claim to alternative 'human' or 'phenomenological' understandings of management, yet they remain wedded to a faith in wielding techniques of control. Guidelines for the manipulation of organisational symbols are no less a manifestation of management as a technical practice than the algorithms of operational research (a point much misunderstood by some avowedly critical management academics).

To accord management education a central role in the elaboration of management as a technical practice is to present a sharp contrast to one of the dominant understandings of the history of management education. As long ago as 1776, Adam Smith, in *The Wealth of Nations*, bemoaned the fact that universities showed no interest in emerging issues of business and technology (see Bendix 1956: 22–34 for context and discussion). Casson, referred to earlier as a would-be architect of business science, commences with a scathing attack on universities conducted in terms which are still often heard today:

> Naturally the Universities could not give us a Science of Business. Professors have never been in touch with the business world. They have never properly appreciated and respected Business. They have had the snobbish hallucination that Business was not a proper subject for professors to investigate…. Consequently, there is no Chair of Business Science in any great British University. Not even in the United States, where Business has a higher social status, are there more than five or six Universities that have officially recognized Business as a fit subject of investigation…. If there is ever to be a Science of Business, it will have to be developed by business men themselves. It must not be the work of theorists.
>
> (Casson 1915: 13–14)

That universities did indeed hold such views seems to be confirmed by the contemporary writings of the American Thorstein Veblen:

> A college of commerce is…peculiarly incompatible with the cultural purpose of the university. It belongs in the corporation of learning no more than a department of athletics.
>
> (Veblen 1918: 209–10)

Again, this is a view which finds many contemporary echoes. But before concluding that management theory (or business science, or commerce, or however we choose to denote the representation of management as a technical practice) was developed in the face of the opposition of the university, it is worth remembering that Veblen was *bemoaning what had already happened*. He saw the American university as having already been corrupted (not simply by the existence of commerce departments, but by the business orientations of university administrators). And, according to Bledstein, Veblen in fact massively underestimated the extent to which American universities had already become enmeshed in a middle-class 'culture of professionalism' (as against disinterested scholarship) from at least 1870 onwards (1976: 287–8).

In fact, admittedly mainly outside universities, various forms of technical and 'management' education can be found in abundance throughout England (and especially Scotland) from the mid-18th century onwards (Pollard 1968: 127–47 provides massive and detailed historical evidence for this). It is important to avoid anachronistic understandings both of university education and of management, both of which were substantially made or remade in the course of the 19th century. But if we count as management education schools teaching commercial subjects,[15] then the evidence is that it flourished in Britain from the Industrial Revolution onwards.

The opposition to universities as a place to educate managers came as much from outside as from within (Pollard 1968: 132). Even though Casson (1915) bemoans the snobbish lack of interest of 'professors', he also makes it clear that they are so unworldly and theoretical that it would be unlikely that they would have much to contribute. Engwall (1992) discusses the meeting between Mercury (the Roman god of merchants) and Minerva (wisdom) in a detailed history of management education. This study confirms that there was severe resistance from both sides to the development of university-level management education. But it also shows that, despite this resistance, such education was developing very rapidly – albeit under heterogeneous labels – from the last quarter of the 19th century. In the United States, in particular, business schools developed rapidly from the 1880s, and by the 1950s, partly as a result of state intervention, were conceptualised as sites for the development of organisational and management science (Barley and Kunda 1992; Engwall 1992; Locke 1984, 1989). It is a conceptualisation which, whilst by no means unchallenged, appears still to be dominant.

The contention, then, is that the representation of management as a technical practice emerges from, or at least is authorised by, the university. More than this, it can be argued that it developed not just in the face of opposition from, but actually in opposition to, managers. Kanter (1977) suggests that one of the key problems faced in the 19th-century expansion and bureaucratisation of the family firm was that of recruiting trustworthy managers (see also Littler 1982; Rueschemeyer 1986). And the 'trust problem' is by no means of solely historical interest – indeed trust has emerged as one of the most significant topics in contemporary organisational theory (Kramer and Tyler 1996). In the 19th century this problem was resolved by employing managers who were known personally to owners, or who seemed to share similar social characteristics with owners. This tended to lead to a homogeneity and homosociality amongst managers, attributes which continued with the development of large-scale bureaucracies in the 20th century. Whilst this poses issues about the elitism and exclusivity of the managerial classes, the present point is a different one. The scope for appointing trustworthy managers from the ranks of one's social peers clearly has limits – the limits of personal acquaintance and, of course, the fact that such acquaintances are not necessarily trustworthy anyway. No doubt patronage continues in many forms within and between organisations, but one of the key features of bureaucratic rationality was the stress it placed on recruitment and promotion on the basis of qualifications, experience and competence. Whilst managerial experience might lie outside the purview of the university, it was the university which was able to license qualifications and competence, and, increasingly, did so. At around the time that the trust problem loomed in family firms, so business schools emerged, with the foundation of the Wharton School in 1881.

Somehow, the claims of expertise underwritten by such institutions were able to stand proxy for a certain claim of 'moral' respectability. This might seem a puzzling claim to make if one adhered to more conventional accounts of management and management education. These accounts might suggest that the need for qualified managers arose because of the increasing levels of size, complexity and functional specialisation in organisations. However, this view assumes that the skills acquired through management education contribute to enhanced individual and organisational performance and in this sense that management education has a functional justification. Yet such a contribution has never been conclusively demonstrated, and a number of influential commentators, such as Henry Mintzberg, have suggested that management education may actually be damaging to effective managerial practice.

If the attraction to organisations of business school graduates is not their technical competence *per se*, an alternative explanation might be that the most significant thing about management education is its capacity to 'responsibilise' managers, to render them trustworthy and predictable by virtue of their beliefs and behaviours. A close analogy would be the role which accounting degrees play in the accountancy profession. It is commonplace for graduates with such degrees to be recruited by accounting firms, even though it is well known within such firms that the qualification is of very limited relevance to their work and, even, that graduates with this background find training more difficult than 'non-relevant' graduates. Yet the attraction of accounting graduates is that they are seen to have indicated their commitment to the 'idea' of accountancy and, in short, have shown themselves to be the 'right kind of person', an attribute of considerable value in the successful development of an accountancy career (Grey 1994).

Returning to management education, the role of MBA programmes in reproducing certain kinds of norms has been commented upon from several perspectives. Leavitt (1991), noting the importance of socialisation processes in producing MBAs, argues for the need to try to direct and enhance this socialisation in ever more controlled ways. Whitley *et al.* (1981) show the relationship between the MBA and wider structures of social inequality and elite reproduction. More recently, Sinclair (1995) shows the male and masculinist bias built into the MBA experience. Thus there is considerable support for the view that MBA programmes embody and transmit *values*.

To put matters plainly, the point about having an MBA is not the technical utility of the content but the fact that it denotes a certain orientation which renders graduates receptive to 'corporate needs'. One aspect of this is that the MBA offers a means of acquiring cultural capital and social prestige (Whitley *et al.* 1981; Collin 1996). But this is part of a Faustian pact in which the student accepts that s/he must learn and give respect to (and even accept) the 'scientific truths' of management propounded in the business school. This is why it is possible for business schools to get away with teaching to generation after generation facts which are incorrect, as Jackson and Carter (1995, quoted above) demonstrate. It also explains why studies of managerial work (Carlson 1951; Stewart 1967; Mintzberg 1973; Kotter 1982; Watson 1994) consistently find a divergence between this work and rationalistic, technicist management theory accounts of what that work is supposed to consist of. Finally, it explains why, at the level of pedagogy, it is reported (Thompson and McGivern 1996) to be so difficult to persuade students of the truth of the textbook abstractions of management education, or, alternatively, why students will collaborate in accepting these 'truths' through a 'contract of cynicism' (Watson 1996) in order to gain credentials.

The capacity of business schools to responsibilise their graduates should be seen as a specific aspect of the types of social control entailed in the reproduction of subjects as 'docile' – a notion much favoured by Foucauldian scholars, amongst others. Whilst this should not be taken to imply that resistance to managerial responsibilisation is absent, it does suggest that managers are as much a target for organisational control as 'workers'. The existence of 'maverick' managers who betray the trust placed in them indicates that managerial responsibility is an accomplishment which is underwritten by specific social arrangements. As soon as we move away from envisaging power and control as being imposed by one powerful group (e.g. managers) upon another less powerful group (e.g. workers), we are obliged to consider the ways in which social order is reproduced through the co-production of both the notionally powerful and the powerless. In this regard, managers cannot simply be understood as agents of domination, but must also be seen as themselves being constituted through exercises of power. The responsibilisation of managers through their initiation into the 'technical expertise' of management is one such exercise of power.

Conclusion

On the argument which has been advanced here, the constitution of management as a technical practice is not something which should be seen simply as part of a (largely failed) project to professionalise management or solely as an ideological project to legitimate managerial authority, but also as a way of responsibilising managers. It could, however, be argued that it is part of a professionalising process within the developing 'management-speak' industry of academics, trainers, consultants and 'portfolio careerists'. For these, access to the recondite languages and arcane techniques of each and every business fad is the key to their continued employment. Particularly for management consultants, claims to expertise via the deployment of specialist language might be a key part of the process of presentation to clients (Clarke 1995). Similarly, for many management academics the promotion of management as a technical practice is an extremely useful technique of classroom control in the face of insecurity about their legitimacy (Grey and Mitev 1995: 81), enabling pedagogy in 'expert' mode (Grey *et al.* 1996: 98–100). As exponents of technical truths couched in specialist language authenticated by science, no less, such academics (who also grade the exams, of course) are able to persuade or coerce managers into acceptance of models which bear scant resemblance to reality.

None of this implies that managers do not gain considerable legitimacy and attendant rewards by virtue of the representation of management as a technical practice. Nor should one overstate the power of management academics to define the reality of management, which is certainly circumscribed by many factors. But the significance of the 'management-speak' industry, of which management education is a key part, should not be underestimated. Furusten (1995) shows through detailed example how popular management knowledge, with all its attendant ideological baggage, has been able to become widely diffused. What is at issue is not simply the spread of an irritating vocabulary, but the attendant shifts in practices which management discourse legitimates.

Elsewhere (Grey and Mitev 1995; Grey 1996a; Grey and French 1996) it has been argued that management education should not be seen as something which serves the functional needs of managers, but should expose managerial practices to critical scrutiny. The implications of the present chapter are slightly different. If management education has developed 'against' rather than 'for' managers, it means that those management educators who conceive of their task as assisting individual managers are, even within the terms of their own aspirations, mistaken. It makes the task of reconstructing management education along critical lines all the more urgent. But it also reveals the ambiguities of such a project. For the argument in this chapter is that the utility and truth of the content of management education have never been its most important purpose: rather, what has mattered is to find ways both of mystifying students and of encouraging them to accept prevailing social and managerial orthodoxies.

It is important, then, that 'critical' management education does not merely become some new set of mystifications to be learned by management students. Some current developments in 'critical management education', such as those inspired by postmodernism (Boje and Dennehy 1993; Chia and Morgan 1996) which seek a reconstruction based upon notions of empowerment, difference, flexibility and communication, might be seen to fall into just such a trap. A similar criticism might be made of less theoretically sophisticated conceptions of a 'new paradigm' for management education (Raelin and Schermerhorn 1994). Insofar as these merely constitute ways to responsibilise and socialise students into changing understandings of 'organisational needs' they are inadequate. Only when management education becomes infused with social critique will it cease to be a way of controlling managers.

Moreover, if this chapter has been persuasive in its analysis of the paradox set out at the beginning, then this conclusion will no longer seem paradoxical: it may only be possible for management to professionalise if it articulates an independent and critical view of the supposedly technical character of its practice, and thereby distances itself from those whose interests are served by the responsibilisation of managers. If responsibilisation is understood as an exercise of power to reproduce managers who behave in 'appropriate' ways, the route to their own 'empowerment' must surely lie in a refusal of those social technologies which are conducive to their conformity to managerial and organisational orthodoxies, and the task of management educators is to provide the resources for such resistance.

Notes

1 This chapter is based upon research work undertaken as Visiting Fellow, Stockholm Centre for Organisational Research (SCORE), University of Stockholm, Sweden. An early draft of the paper was presented at the SCORE staff seminar and at the Department of Business Administration, Gothenburg University, Sweden. A later draft was presented at the Institute for Organisational Analysis, University of Hull, and at the Management School, Bath University. Many thanks to all who made comments at those seminars and to Paul Jeffcutt and an anonymous reviewer for their comments.

2 Throughout this chapter, the term 'management' is used in this sense: management as social practice and as academic discipline. It might be more accurate, but clearly more cumbersome, to use the term 'the discursive and non-discursive practices of management'. Where what is being discussed is management simply as an academic subject in universities, the term 'management studies' is used; where what is being discussed is management simply as social practice, the term 'managerial practice' is used. 'Management' is not used in the industrial relations sense of 'the management'.

3 Subsequently I will argue that this is not an adequate account of the failure of management to professionalise.

4 The diversity of the references given and the relationships between the authors and the different concepts invoked in this paragraph beg questions of such scope and complexity as to be inappropriate for the present occasion. My intention is simply to flag up the connection between the contemporary debates about management and much more longstanding arguments about the nature of *society*.

5 Here, I mean, of course, management education as currently managerially conceived. The *raison d'être* of management education on this view is its utility to managers, organisations and the economy. On this view, management education must have some functional relation to managerial practice. See Grey and Mitev (1995) for a different view.

6 For detailed introductions to the debates with which the chapter engages, see Reed (1989), Reed and Anthony (1992) and Abbott (1988).

7 This vision of the prospects for management studies is extremely pervasive, and has been so throughout the history of the subject, most recently in Kay (1994). It reflects an 'evolutionary' view of scientific knowledge and a positivistic understanding of management as a branch of that scientific knowledge. That management studies is always 'becoming' but never 'becomes' might give pause for thought, but of course the real function of such rhetoric is legitimatory. See Jacques (1996) for a fascinating discussion of positivism and evolutionary thinking in management. For an explicit statement of the evolutionary view, see Wren (1994).

8 Of particular interest are the ways in which the understanding of management as a disreputable practice (Pollard 1968; Mant 1977) disappeared in the course of the 19th century.

9 It should not be assumed that the use of technical/scientific expertise is, or was, the only strategy available for the legitimation of managerial authority. Perhaps the classic study in this field (Bendix 1956) indicates that a range of 'ideologies of management' can be detected, including those which relate to the entrepreneurship as much as the technical expertise. Such sources of legitimation have in recent years again become more important under the influence of discourses of the enterprising self within the work organisation and in management theory (Du Gay 1995). Nonetheless, the making of management as a technical practice would seem to have been a more general trend, although the *content* of managerial technical practice can be seen to be subject to periodic transformations (Barley and Kunda 1992).

10 There is an argument that positivistic science is itself ideological (Habermas 1971) and if this is so the distinctions drawn between natural science, social science and management may appear redundant. But the concern is to point to the specific ideological issues in relation to management.

11 See Grey (1996b) for a fuller discussion of management, rationality, science and neutrality.

12 Indeed, it is important to note the cultural specificity of the very concept of a 'profession' (Sarfatti Larson 1984).

13 Perhaps more significant than organisational structure in the restriction of managerial autonomy is the structure of ownership. Whilst the view of managers as being simply and solely agents of capital has been rightly criticised, the existence and demands of shareholders place limits upon the autonomy of individual managers and also erode the potential capacity for a putative management profession to self-regulate. After all, managers are also employees (Jacques 1996).

14 One probably hears more of Taylor, and certainly of Fayol, in the business school than on the shop floor or in the boardroom!

15 Languages, bookkeeping, shorthand, commercial law (of various countries), political economy, navigation (Pollard 1968: 131).

References

Abbott, A. (1988) *The System of the Professions: An Essay on the Division of Expert Labour*, Chicago: University of Chicago Press.

Alvesson, M. (1987) *Organization Theory and Technocratic Consciousness: Rationality, Ideology and the Quality of Work*, Berlin: de Gruyter.

Alvesson, M. and Willmott, H. (eds) (1992) *Critical Management Studies*, London: Sage.

Barley, S. and Kunda, G. (1992) 'Design and devotion: surges of rational and normative ideologies of control in managerial discourse', *Administrative Science Quarterly* 37: 363–99.

Bendix, R. (1956) *Work and Authority in Industry: Ideologies of Management in the Course of Industrialization*, New York: John Wiley.

Bernstein, R. (1976) *The Restructuring of Social and Political Theory*, Oxford: Blackwell.

Bledstein, B. (1976) *The Culture of Professionalism: The Middle Class and the Development of Higher Education in America*, New York: Norton.

Boje, D. and Dennehy, R. (1993) *Managing in the Postmodern World: America's Revolution Against Exploitation*, Dubuque, IA: Kendall Hunt.

Bowles, S. and Gintis, H. (1976) *Schooling in Capitalist America*, London: Routledge & Kegan Paul.

Brandeis, L.D. (1914) *Business: A Profession*, Boston, MA: Small, Maynard & Co.

Burnham, J. (1945) *The Managerial Revolution*, London: Penguin.

Carey A. (1967) 'The Hawthorne studies: a radical criticism', *American Sociological Review* 32: 403–16.

Carlson, S. (1951) *Executive Behaviour*, Stockholm: Almqvist & Wiksell International (reprinted 1991).

Casson, H. (1915) *The Axioms of Business*, London: The Efficiency Exchange.

Chandler, A. (1965) *The Railroads: The Nation's First Big Business, Sources and Readings*, New York: Harcourt Brace.

Chia, R. and Morgan, S. (1996) 'Educating the philosopher-manager: de-signing the times', *Management Learning* 27: 37–64.

Child, J. (1969) *British Management Thought: A Critical Analysis*, London: Allen & Unwin.

Child, J., Fores, M., Glover, I. and Lawrence, P. (1983) 'A price to pay? Professionalism and work organization in Britain and West Germany', *Sociology* 17: 63–78.

Clarke, T. (1995) *Managing Consultants: Consultancy as the Management of Impressions*, Milton Keynes: Open University Press.

Clegg, S., Boreham, P. and Dow, G. (1986) *Class, Politics and the Economy*, London: Routledge & Kegan Paul.

Collin, A. (1996) 'The MBA: the potential for students to find their voice in Babel', in R. French and C. Grey (eds) *Rethinking Management Education*, London: Sage.

Deetz, S. (1992) *Democracy in an Age of Corporate Colonization*, New York: SUNY Press.

du Gay P. (1995) *Consumption and Identity at Work*, London: Sage.

Engwall, L. (1992) *Mercury Meets Minerva. Business Administration in Academia: The Swedish Case*, Oxford: Pergamon Press.

Enteman, W. (1993) *Managerialism. The Emergence of a New Ideology*, Madison, WI: University of Wisconsin Press.

Foucault, M. (1970) *The Order of Things*, London: Tavistock.

—— (1979) *Discipline and Punish*, London: Penguin.

French, R. and Grey, C. (eds) (1996) *Rethinking Management Education*, London: Sage.

Furusten, S. (1995) *The Managerial Discourse: A Study of the Creation and Diffusion of Popular Management Knowledge*, Ph.D. thesis, Department of Business Studies, Uppsala University, Sweden.

Game, A. (1990) *Undoing Sociology*, London: Routledge.

Garsten, C. and Grey, C. (1997) 'How to become oneself: discourses of subjectivity in post-bureaucratic organizations, *Organization* 4: 211–28.

Giddens, A. (1974) *Positivism and Sociology*, London: Heinemann.

Grey, C. (1994) 'Career as a project of the self and labour process discipline', *Sociology* 28: 427–72.

—— (1996a) 'Critique and renewal in management education', *Management Learning* 27: 7–20.

—— (1996b) 'Towards a critique of managerialism: the contribution of Simone Weil', *Journal of Management Studies* 33: 591–611.

Grey, C. and French, R. (1996) 'Rethinking management education: an introduction', in R. French and C. Grey (eds) *Rethinking Management Education*, London: Sage.

Grey, C. and Mitev, N. (1995) 'Management education: a polemic', *Management Learning* 26: 73–90.

Grey, C., Knights, D. and Willmott, H. (1996) 'Is a critical pedagogy of management possible?', in R. French and C. Grey (eds) *Rethinking Management Education*, London: Sage.

Habermas, J. (1971) *Towards A Rational Society*, London: Heinemann.

—— (1987) *The Theory of Communicative Action (Lifeworld and System: A Critique of Functionalist Reason)*, vol. 2, Cambridge: Polity Press.

Heckscher, C. (1995) *White Collar Blues*, New York: Basic Books.

Heckscher, C. and Donnellon, A. (eds.) (1994) *The Post-Bureaucratic Organization: New Perspectives on Organizational Change*, London: Sage.

Hines, R. (1988) 'Financial accounting: in communicating reality, we construct reality', *Accounting, Organizations and Society* 13: 251–61.

Jackson, N. and Carter, P. (1995) 'The "fact" of management', *Scandinavian Journal of Management* 11: 197–208.

Jacoby, H. (1973) *The Bureaucratization of the World*, Berkeley, CA: University of California Press.

Jacques, R. (1996) *Manufacturing the Employee: Management Knowledge from the 19th to 21st Centuries*, London: Sage.

Kanter, R.M. (1977) *Men and Women of the Corporation*, New York: Basic Books.

Kay, J. (1994) 'Plenary address', British Academy of Management Conference, Lancaster University, September.

Kimball, B. (1992) *The 'True Professional Ideal' in America: A History*, Cambridge, MA: Blackwell.

Knights, D. (1992) 'Changing spaces: the disruptive impact of a new epistemological location for the study of management', *Academy of Management Review* 17: 514–36.

Kotter, J.P. (1982) 'What effective general managers really do', *Harvard Business Review* 60: 156–67.

Kramer, R. and Tyler, T. (eds) (1996) *Trust in Organizations*, Thousand Oaks, CA: Sage.

Kuhn, T. (1962) *The Structure of Scientific Revolutions*, Chicago: Chicago University Press.

Larson, M. (1977) *The Rise of Professionalism: A Sociological Analysis*, Berkeley, CA: University of California Press.

Leavitt, H. (1991) 'Socializing our MBAs: total immersion? Managed cultures? Brainwashing?', *California Management Review* 33: 127–43.

Littler, C. (1982) *The Development of the Labour Process in Capitalist Societies*, London: Heinemann.

Locke, R. (1984) *The End of Practical Man*, London: JAI Press.

—— (1989) *Management and Higher Education since 1940*, Cambridge: Cambridge University Press.

MacIntyre, A. (1981) *After Virtue*, London: Duckworth.

Mant, A. (1977) *The Rise and Fall of the British Manager*, London: Macmillan.

Marcuse, H. (1964) *One-Dimensional Man*, London: Routledge & Kegan Paul (reprinted 1986).

Mintzberg, H. (1973) *The Nature of Managerial Work* , London: Harper & Row.

Mitroff, I. and Churchman, C. (1992) 'Debate', *Harvard Business Review* 70: 134–6.

Nyland, C. (1988) 'Scientific management and planning', *Capital and Class* 33: 55–83.

Pollard, S. (1968) *The Genesis of Modern Management*, London: Penguin.

Raelin, J. and Schermerhorn, J. (1994) 'A new paradigm for advanced management education: how knowledge merges with experience', *Management Learning* 25: 195–200.

Reed, M. (1989) *The Sociology of Management*, Hemel Hempstead: Harvester Wheatsheaf.

Reed, M. and Anthony, P. (1992) 'Professionalizing management and managing professionalization: British management in the 1980s', *Journal of Management Studies* 29: 591–613.

Ritzer, G. (1993) *The McDonaldization of Society*, Thousand Oaks, CA: Sage.

Rizzi, B. (1939) *La Bureaucratization du Monde*, Paris: Champ Libre.

Rose, N. (1989) *Governing the Soul*, London: Routledge.

Rueschemeyer, D. (1986) *Power and the Division of Labour*, Cambridge: Polity Press.

Sarfatti Larson, M. (1984) 'The production of expertise and the constitution of expert power', in T.L. Haskell (ed.) *The Authority of Experts*, Bloomington, IN: Indiana University Press.

Senge, P. (1990) *The Fifth Discipline: The Art and Practice of the Learning Organization*, New York: Doubleday.

Sikka, P. and Willmott, H. (1995) 'The power of "independence": defending and extending the jurisdiction of accounting in the United Kingdom', *Accounting, Organizations and Society* 20: 547–81.

Sinclair, A. (1995) 'Sex and the MBA', *Organization* 2: 295–317.

Smith, A. (1904) *The Wealth of Nations*, London: Methuen (originally published in 1776).

Stewart, R. (1967) *Managers and their Jobs*, London: Macmillan.

Thompson, J. and McGivern, J. (1996) 'Parody, process and practice: perspectives for management education', *Management Learning* 27: 21–35.

Townley, B. (1994) *Reframing Human Resource Management*, London: Sage.

Veblen, T. (1918) *The Higher Learning in America: A Memorandum on the Conduct of Universities by Business Men*, New York: Huebsch.

Watson, T. (1994) *In Search Of Management*, London: Routledge.

—— (1995) 'Management fads: their role in managers' lives', *International Journal of Human Resource Management* 5: 889–905.

—— (1996) 'Motivation: that's Mintzberg isn't it?', *Management Learning* 27: 447–64.

Weber, M. (1968) *Economy and Society. An Outline of Interpretative Sociology*, New York: Bedminster Press (originally published in 1922).

Weil, S. (1988) *Oppression and Liberty*, London: Routledge & Kegan Paul (originally published in 1933).

Whitley, R. (1984a) *The Intellectual and Social Organisation of the Sciences*, Oxford: Oxford University Press.

—— (1984b) 'The fragmented state of management studies: reasons and consequences', *Journal of Management Studies* 21: 331–48.

—— (1995) 'Academic knowledge and work jurisdiction in management', *Organization Studies* 16: 81–105.

Whitley, R., Thomas, A. and Marceau, J. (1981) *Masters of Business: The Making of a New Elite?*, London: Tavistock.

Whyte, W.H. (1956) *The Organization Man*, New York: Doubleday.

Wilensky, H. (1964) 'The professionalization of everyone?', *American Journal of Sociology* 70: 137–58.

Willmott, H. (1984) 'Images and ideals of managerial work: a critical examination of conceptual and empirical accounts', *Journal of Management Studies* 21: 349–65.

Winch, P. (1958) *The Idea of a Social Science*, London: Routledge.

Wren, D. (1994) *The Evolution of Management Thought*, New York: John Wiley.

4 American business school education and the revolution in interactive information technology

Robert R. Locke

Introduction

The French Foundation for Management Education (FNEGE) held a symposium (November 1998) charged with examining retrospectively the management education program in North America that the foundation had launched for French students three decades earlier. Believing then that America was the Mecca of management education, FNEGE had sent, between 1969 and 1975, hundreds of fledgling French management instructors to North American business schools to learn about management science. Whilst the FNEGE retrospective focused mostly on the experiences of French participants in this program, there was room, within its province, for reflection about another side of the story: to wit, did the education that the French students had received in American business schools actually prepare them managerially for the future?

Two significant managerial events can be used as reference points to measure this educational effectiveness. One is the quality revolution (QR), which one scholar has called the most significant development in American business and industry of the past fifty years.[1] The managerial procedures identified with the QR (quality circles; kanban – just-in-time; total quality management – (TQM); Kaizen; lean manufacturing) developed first in Japan and then spread to the United States. But the QR, although an important part of American management history, will be set aside here because people now generally acknowledge that American business schools made no significant contribution to its propagation. Professor Robert S. Kaplan pointed this out several years ago after reviewing articles published in leading operations management journals and examining research and teaching in top business schools. He found only 1–2 per cent of the schools had "truly been affected, as of early 1991, by the TQM revolution that has been creating radical change in many U.S. and worldwide businesses. [Business schools] completely missed the quality revolution in management."[2]

The second major managerial event is the revolution in information technology (IT). IT encompasses a highly diverse microelectronic industry which is too vast to be presented here. The following remarks therefore concentrate on the part of IT that brought interactivity into the world. Interactivity is the jacking of the human mind into virtual reality, which has permitted the extension of the intellect in most creative ways – in molecular biological research, in computer-aided design, indeed in the host of applications that has dramatically altered our home and work environments since the early 1980s.

The industry that created interactivity – semiconductor firms like Intel, computer manufacturers like Apple, software producers like Microsoft, and telecommunications giants like AT&T – had reinvigorated the American economy at the century's end, for unlike in the QR, American-founded and -managed companies and corporations led this global transformation. Since IT arose primarily within an American managerial context and since the subject of its interaction with business school education has not, as in the QR case, been a focus of attention, it is useful, then, to consider whether that education contributed significantly to this IT entrepreneurialism. The answer I give is that the American management education those French visitors received circa 1970 no more prepared them managerially for the challenges of IT over the next twenty-five years than it did for those of the QR.

Management and business school education in the U.S.: a topology

Since two factors are to be correlated, the state of each during the period of correlation has to be established. Let us begin with management education. In its origin and development American management education always reflected an organizational sociology. Paul Jeffcutt, quoting Michel Foucault, identified its source when describing the elitist function of the human sciences, as they emerged in the late 19th century. While intellectually they took up the pragmatic task of managing the border between theory and practice, of ordering the relations between human beings and their world, both in space and surface, sociologically they assigned this task to a particular group of experts who were closer to the science of ordering this relationship than most people (Jeffcutt 1996: 90–1). "With their assumed close association with the science of management," Michael Fores noted, "and with their presumed off-job preparation in being 'scientific' in some way," managers were more widely accepted by people as being more "rational" actors than most human beings (Fores 1996: 110). They were, accordingly, better able objectively to order the firm to optimize output.

Under this regime American firms became "modern," "scientifically managed" organizations, utopian moral and economic orders in which managers and managed were functionally divided and specialized in a pyramidal structure, their interactions scientifically regulated and harmonized on the principle of efficiency, progress, and reward. Within the pyramidal structure, the managers, with their specific knowledge and skills, function as thinkers, and the managed, the employees, as doers under management's command.

Just as the rise of management separated managers from workers, or rather brought them under management-specified forms of control, so it separated tacit from formal knowledge. Managers tried always to convert tacit into formal knowledge. Frederick Winslow Taylor's time studies and Frank Gilbreth's motion studies are early examples of such conversions; the Toyota engineers' transformation of the tacit-skill content of the kanban production system into a formally encoded one is a later instance. The emerging management profession aspired to reduce its work to a decontextualized, codified body or bodies of knowledge that could be formally learned and applied.

Meanwhile, the successful application of science to operations research problems during the Second World War led to a sustained attempt in American business schools to turn management into a sophisticated science that would serve a corporate world increasingly perceived as "predictable and locally (for the firm) plannable" (Eliasson 1998: 2). In post-war America, management and academia came together (see Locke 1989). The Swedish economist Gunnar Eliasson, after conducting 80 interviews in 60 US and European firms between 1969 and 1975, concluded that in them "it was all short-term and long-range *planning* and a strong belief in repetitive environment, forecasting and centralized leadership of standardized production" (Eliasson 1998: 2).[3] Business schools taught a standard curriculum (accounting, finance, marketing, decision theory, etc.) meant to serve the management elite operating in the knowable environment of Fortune 500 companies, which during the post-war economic expansion became the "toast of the business schools."

And they have continued to be so until today, for, as Jeremy Hope and Tony Hope remarked in a 1997 book:

> With the exception of a few top-flight business schools,... [w]hile they may talk about quality and knowledge and have suitably titled course options, the main thrust of their written material remains the hierarchical, production-driven model where the priorities are volume and scale, the management mentality is one of contract and control, and the way to compete is to lower unit costs by all means possible.
>
> (Hope and Hope 1997: 222)

Professor Eliasson, bolstering the judgement in his 1998 paper, comments that "the bulk of subjects on the teaching agenda of business schools, like investment calculation and financial economics rests on the assumptions of [a formal knowledge] model" (Eliasson 1998: 6).

Managing the IT revolution in interactivity

Professor Eliasson notes that "conventional economic theory sees capitalism as the administration of existing structures" (1992: 23). Since the issue in IT is technological innovation, a scheme necessary to explain its development must deal as much with the creation of new structures as the good administration of old ones. Inasmuch as Professor Eliasson has since 1975 been explaining why economics cannot explore the realities of a dynamic IT, while he has at the same time been searching for more convincing theoretical explanations, his views are a useful place to start.[4]

For success, Eliasson notes, the technological pioneers have to bundle together a number of interrelated competencies into a "competence bloc": "the total infrastructure needed to *create* (innovation), *recognize* (venture capital provision), *diffuse* (spillovers) and successfully *exploit* (receiver competence) new ideas in clusters of firms."[5] This "competence bloc" is embodied in educated and talented networks of people: technical specialists and entrepreneurs (who integrate the science and technical competencies under restrictions of economic criteria), venture capitalists, corporate managers, finance specialists, and market experts (Eliasson 1996b: 13). And so, following Eliasson, the question becomes: what contribution did American business school education make to the development of the IT "competence bloc"?

For historians, Eliasson's views help when answering this question because they bring us closer to actual events. But historians also find that even Professor Eliasson's explanations raise difficulties when telling the IT story. This happens perhaps because economists and historians work on different principles. Whereas the former attempt to elaborate general explanatory schemes, the latter are interested in describing specific historical situations. Hence, if the economists' schemes cannot explain events economists often tend to disregard the events and cling to the explanatory systems; historians tend to do the reverse.[6] Economists sometimes get upset with historians for introducing non-economic elements into an economic analysis, but they should not, for historians are not really trying to create an alternate explanatory model; they are only introducing ad-hoc explanations which they think the facts warrant. In another case, the non-economic elements previously used might not apply and would be discarded. This point is significant because in the IT story Eliasson's model is much more useful explaining IT development after 1970 than before.

Before 1970: the non-commercial nature of the breakthrough in IT

Eliasson's analysis is least applicable before 1970 because the intricate hardware, software, and telecommunication tools that went into IT then developed primarily "outside the restrictions of market criteria." They were a product of the exigencies of the Cold War. Not greed, not free-market demand, but fear, especially after the Soviet Union exploded atomic bombs and possessed the intercontinental missiles to deliver them (witness the launch of Sputnik in 1957), drove Americans decades long to pay the enormous costs of superpower rivalry. Most of that money went into conventional weaponry, but billions of dollars also went for scientific research in IT. Consequently, one group of scholars noted: "From the explosion of the first Soviet atomic bomb in 1949 until the mid-1960s, the driving force for science policy remained the military-technological competition with the Soviet Union" (Alic *et al.* 1992: 97).

This, for two reasons, is not a trivial point. First, most of the interactive IT exploited commercially after 1970 had its origins in this government-sponsored research. Indeed, without a long and expensive gestation period IT could never have been exploited commercially because it would not have existed. Examples of a government-created commercially useful technology are legion, but to make the case let one, familiar to us all, suffice. After Sputnik the government lavishly funded a new organization, the Advanced Research Projects Agency (ARPA) as part of a crash program to help America regain the initiative in science and technology. In 1964 a team of ARPA funders visited Douglas Englebart, whom the National Aeronautics and Space Administration (NASA) had supported in the creation of a Augmentation Research Center at the Stanford Research Institute, and gave him computer equipment plus $1 million a year to "create the mind-amplifying computers" he had been writing about (Rheingold 1991: 81). In 1968 the Englebart research team presented the fruits of their work at a computer conference:

> Sitting on stage with a keyboard, screen, mouse, and the kind of earphone-microphone setup pilots and switchboard operators wear, Englebart navigat[ed] through information space…. He called up documents from the computer's memory and displayed them on the big screen at the front of the auditorium, collapsed the documents to a series of descriptive one-line headings, clicked a button on his mouse and expanded a heading to reveal a document, typed in a command and summoned a video image and a computer graphic to the screen. He typed in words, deleted them, cut and pasted paragraphs and documents from one place to another….The assembled engineers, programmers, and computer scientists had never seen anything like it.
>
> (Rheingold 1991: 84)

Englebart's ARPA-supported center introduced the interactive features of the personal computer that Apple brought to market in the 1980s.

The networks which tie computers together, moreover, began as government projects, starting with SAGE (Semi-Automatic Ground Environment system), a computer-activated real-time continental air-defense system developed at the Massachusetts Institute of Technology's (MIT) Lincoln Laboratory under Air Force contract, continuing through ARPANET, a computer network that ARPA researchers created, exploited themselves in their research, and gave to the commercial world.[7] None of this technology was originally designed with commercial application in mind, but it happened that the tools needed to solve military information problems (the need, for instance, for real-time computer networks that could effectively counter a continental-scale incoming missiles attack while providing for instantaneous retaliation) could be readily adapted to civilian circumstance.

Second, this government-sponsored research produced the highly sophisticated core of scientists and engineers that got involved subsequently in commercial IT. In other words, not just products but the brains needed to continue the development process came out of government-sponsored research.

By the early 1960s the federal share of the nation's research and development (R&D) had reached 66 per cent, "with defense- and space-related work accounting for about 85 per cent of the federal total." The "huge buildup of U.S. military R&D in the 1950s and 1960s" provided "a larger stock of scientists and engineers than in any other Western country" (Alic *et al.* 1992: 114). By 1965 the percentage of the US workforce consisting of graduated scientists and engineers was at least three times that of our principal industrial rivals in the free world. Because government-sponsored IT transferred to the commercial firm, the presence of a large group of scientists and engineers working on government projects helped subsequently to develop market-driven firms.

Much indirect and direct evidence supports this claim. Joshua Lerner's survey of the 1980s provides indirect evidence. It shows that 24.2 per cent of scientists and engineers with defense-related positions in 1982 had shifted to civilian jobs four years later, but it also shows that 26.5 per cent of the scientists and engineers that had been in defense-oriented jobs in 1986 had been in non-defense positions four years earlier.[8] The data cited covers scientists and engineers generally and thus applies only by inference specifically to people in IT. But lots of direct evidence about the transferability of scientists and engineers in interactive IT points to the same conclusion. Space considerations allow only one example of direct transfer, among many possible ones, to be cited. XEROX's research unit at Palo Alto (PARC), which developed the technology that Steve Jobs copied for Apple's Mackintosh project, hired "hundreds of ARPA superstars" after 1970 (Rheingold 1991: 85).[9]

Thus, the rapid growth of defense IT during the Reagan years, coupled with a concomitant explosion of IT in the private sector during the same period, and the use of the same scientists and engineers in each sector indicate a good transferability of scientific knowledge and technical know-how. As Joshua Lerner concluded, "The impression that emerges from this analysis is one of rapid circulation between defense and nondefense jobs in industry."

Civilian employers sometimes did complain about the employability of scientists and engineers coming from the government sector, but the deficiencies pertained to the design, management, and marketing aspect of their work rather than to "technical training or knowledge." Apparently science and technology competence transferred rather easily between government project and commercial industry; the non-technical competencies that fostered government-sponsored IT posed the transfer problem. This, at least, is the judgement of the Alic *et al.* study: "[T]echnical skills transfer more easily [from defense to the commercial firm] than managerial ones" (Smith and Alexander 1988: 124). And AnnaLee Saxenian's evaluation of Route 128 IT firms that were heavily into defense contracting concludes much the same:

> By 1970...the nation's leading center of innovation in electronics...Route 128 producers focused on the technologically sophisticated components and military electronics that required high levels of skill and constant innovation.... [But] in the early 1970s, military contracts to the region fell

precipitously.... Many of these firms, which had grown accustomed to the low-risk, cost-plus world of defense contracting, discovered that they lacked the organization and skills needed in civilian markets.

(Saxenian 1994: 17)

None of the particular competencies Eliasson outlined, therefore, promoted IT before 1970. Entrepreneurship served military and government demand not the commercial market. Venture capital networks were not necessary. Only after 1970 did "venture capital replace the military as the leading source of financing for Silicon Valley start-ups" (Saxenian 1994: 17–18), and Silicon Valley firms were the most commercial, market-oriented in the US. Military procurement officers, lobbyists, politicians, and bureaucrats formed the non-technical "competence bloc" for the expansion of IT at NASA and the Department of Defense.

But the importance of pre-1970 IT history is not thereby diminished. Even though economists, including Eliasson, want to attribute America's IT leadership to the superiority of its market enterprise system, its "competence bloc," and to claim that it provided a better IT entrepreneurial springboard than that of the government-dominated, centrally planned European economic environment, the view is historically inaccurate.[10]

Ample evidence exists of the sort of entrepreneurialism in Europe that the free-market economists admire. There are, for example, the regionally based networks of small firms specializing in shoes, textiles, and leather goods in Italy, the mix of small and medium-size makers of machine tools, textile machines, and automobile components in coexistence with great firms in the state of Baden-Würtemburg in Germany, and similar regions of flexible industrial clusters in certain regions of Sweden, Denmark, and Spain (Pyke *et al.* 1990; Herrigel 1995; Pyke and Sengenberger 1992). There is no reason to believe that European or Japanese entrepreneurs would have failed to grasp the commercial possibilities of IT had IT reached the level of sophistication that it had in the United States in 1970.

For their part, American firms were themselves not particularly prescient: they did not invest heavily in R&D in interactive IT during the early phase; nor did American bureaucrats and generals perceive commercial opportunities that private firms did not. There is never a guarantee that huge amounts of money spent on defense R&D will have commercial spin-off, and, in any event, Americans were fighting the Cold War. From a commercial perspective, the connection between pre-1970 and post-1970 was largely an accident.

America's commercial lead arose from the massive head start in government-sponsored IT, not from superior American free-market enterprise. For this reason, we can conclude, with Rheingold, that,

if necessity is the mother of invention, it must be added that the Defense Department is the father of technology; from the Army's first electronic digital computer in the 1940s to the Air Force research on head-mounted displays in the 1980s, the US military has always been the prime contractor for the most significant innovations in computer technology.

(Rheingold 1991: 80)

After 1970: IT competence in the commercial phase

According to Professor Eliasson the non-technical capabilities of a "competence bloc" must be:

1 entrepreneurial awareness (realizing the marketability of a new product or technology);
2 acquiring the venture capital to finance the start-up firms;
3 managing the enterprise from start-up, through expansion, into maturity.

To investigate the importance of business school education in the commercial phase it is best to consider points 1 and 2 together, leaving number 3 for a separate discussion.

IT entrepreneurial start-up and venture capital after 1970

Broadly speaking, interactivity breaks down after 1970 into a software and a hardware industrial sector. The hardware industry dominated at first; from the pre-interactivity era of IBM mainframes, through the minicomputers launched by Digital Equipment Company, which became the second largest computer manufacturer, after IBM, in the 1970s, to the personal computer, which entered the market in 1974. Miniaturization was the key, made possible by the introduction of the computer chip, which progressively incorporated more circuit imprints. Intel's invention of the microprocessor in 1971 took hardware a significant step forward, with computing capacity now concentrated in a device that one person could operate from a workstation or a desktop. The microprocessor, combined with internet telecommunications, made the personal computer an integral part of our daily lives.

These semiconductor firms evolved from small producers of made-to-order military products to mass producers of standard chips. Saxenian characterizes the end result thus:

> Intel co-founder Andy Grove coined the phrase "high technology jelly beans" to describe the millions of integrated circuits that Intel produced annually. He claimed the firm's goal was to reduce the cost of solutions…to market pre-fabricated, mass produced solutions to users.
>
> (Saxenian 1994: 86)

The industry rapidly expanded capacity and became capital intensive and vertically integrated; by 1980 only a few American semiconductor producers (Fairchild, Intel, National Semiconductor, Advanced Micro Devices) counted in an industry that employed 200,000 people in Silicon Valley alone. A similar evolution happened in the minicomputer industry, with a number of vertically integrated firms, led by DEC, dominating this industry in the late 1970s.

Management in these mass-production semiconductor and minicomputer firms adopted the budgeting, the accounting-based financing reporting systems, and the cost-control instruments typically found in the large M-form corporations. Consequently, business school education seemed just as suited to the managerial needs of the rapidly growing, highly competitive semiconductor and minicomputer industries as to those of the automobile industry.

But then in the era of interactivity the unexpected happened.

First, the high-technology jelly bean producers suffered grievous losses because of Japanese competition. Between 1983 and 1990 their share of worldwide semiconductor revenues fell from 80 per cent to 33 per cent. Then the semiconductor business moved away from a commodity-driven business to one of high-valued-added specialist, chipmakers, and high-tech, customized semiconductors. Even more importantly, IT bred a new software industry in the 1980s. Before 1970 applications programs were built right into the hardware, which meant that the hardware had to be changed to change applications. For military operations, whose programs were customized and purpose built, this restriction did not pose too much of a problem. But for the commercial world the need to standardize and to make products generally available (non-proprietary) proved irresistible. So the non-proprietary-standardized software industry grew prodigiously; by the early 1990s over 5,000 software firms operated in the US.

Professor Eliasson claims that this new technological environment affected the constitution of the firm. When he interviewed managers in 50 firms between 1985 and 1995 and compared the results to what he had learned in the 1969–75 interviews, he discovered that "out [had gone] reliance on detached analytical thinking in executive quarters; [i]n [had come]…experimental behavior…, [the] distinction between uncertainty and risk" (Eliasson 1998: 3).[11] Eliasson calls the second environment, in which commercial interactive IT blossomed, that of the experimentally organized economy (EOE). It is experimental because entrepreneurs with several possible options never know them all:

> even though [they] have stumbled upon the absolute best solution [they] will never know [it because the knowledge base is always insufficient]….The business manager will never feel safe, and will have to recognize in his or her management practice the possibility of coming out as a loser.
>
> (Eliasson 1998: 3)

In this, EOE failure need not be attributed to managerial ineptitude, as it would in a "full information economy," but can come from unavoidable risk. Failure consequently had to be considered a normal business experience, one from which entrepreneurs learn, as in any experiment.

In the EOE, then, management behavior has changed from that which Eliasson encountered in firms during his first interviews. Not only do managers move from a "full information" economy to one of information "uncertainty," but the kind of knowledge used in entrepreneurial decisions is differently obtained. In the "full information economy" it is gained formally; in the EOE it is more tacit knowledge absorbed on the job.

The burgeoning software industry offers the best example of a tacit-knowledge work environment. Charles A. Zraket describes software's peculiarities in an article worth quoting *in extenso*, since it clarifies so well the knowledge-management issue:

In its initial conceptualization stage, software generation resembles other engineering design activities – open-ended, fluid, not heavily constrained. A near infinite number of alternative solutions exists, and the designer has little beyond intuition, experience, and whatever formal knowledge may be applicable as a guide to meeting the functional requirements. But in the later design and development stages, software differs. Analytical procedures can help in refining the design of a physical system, but not a software system.... After a general "script" for a piece of software has been established, individual programmers must turn that script into working code. Each programmer will express himself or herself differently, no matter the programming language and no matter how detailed the high-level script.... Software development depends more heavily on individual skill and endowments than most engineering tasks. Experienced managers know that software projects ultimately stand or fall not on the sophistication and power of the tools used by their development teams, but on the quality of the programmers in those teams. Case histories demonstrate this. Sometimes a company will assign two independent groups to a given project to minimize the chance of failure. Team A may use one set of tools, completing the task 20 percent faster than team B and producing better code. Then the teams switch tools, but Team A still comes in 20 percent faster and with fewer errors. Most software managers would agree that such experiences reflect the situation today.

(Zraket 1992)

Tacit skill and innate ability, therefore, are more pertinent components of the software programmer's competence than of the engineer's at work on hardware. The largest software firm in the world hires, as Daniel Ichbiah and Susan L. Knepper state, "people with no professional programming experience or formal training. After all, neither of its two founders obtained college degrees" (Ichbiah and Knepper 1991: 226).

Software programmers do need formal knowledge. Writing software is not a job for most liberal arts graduates because good programmers have a sound grasp of mathematics. But the legend of Silicon Valley hackers/entrepreneurs is not a myth; they learned about programming tacitly on the job. No start-up could have flourished without such workplace-acquired skills, for to succeed people had to know programming, to be able to recognize the commercial possibilities of a software product and to judge precisely the abilities of the program-mers, on whom the fate of the enterprise depended. That is why so many people who founded companies in Silicon Valley learned the business primarily working for others and often failed before they succeeded.

Thus – to return to Eliasson's "competence" scheme – start-up entrepreneurs (*innovation*) in interactive IT could not have gained their entrepreneurial insight in some MBA program. Consciousness about the market possibility of a technology or a product depended on a thorough grasp of IT acquired on the job. Much the same reasoning explains the capacity to recognize innovation, the venture capital provision. Regular banks and financial institutions are risk averse, partic-ularly when unproved new technologies are involved. They are not ready to risk money on entrepreneurial ventures that they scarcely understand. The venture capitalists who supported IT start-ups knew the technology well. AnnaLee Saxenian commented about the most dynamic of the venture capitalists, those in Silicon Valley: "[they] brought technical skills, operating experience, and networks of industry contacts – as well as cash – to the [IT] ventures they funded" (1994: 39). This very closeness to the local technological networks, she feels, explains the superiority of Silicon Valley venture capital formation to that of the East. To support this view she cites a former Wall Street executive:

> In New York, the money is generally managed by professional or financial promoter types. Out here [Silicon Valley], the venture capitalists tend to be entrepreneurs who created and built a company and then sold out. When problems occur with any of their investments, they can step into the business and help out.
>
> (Saxenian 1994: 39)[12]

Tacit knowledge about IT learned on the job made up venture capital compe-tence more than any finance or investment techniques learned at a business school.

Even within firms the same East–West management dichotomy affected interac-tive IT start-up. XEROX top management in the East ignored computer research in its Palo Alto Research Center. The firm's chief executive officers (CEOs) in the 1970s, one a Harvard MBA, the other a Stanford MBA, had recruited their management team from finance people at Ford Motor Company and marketing people at IBM. One of the two CEOs, Archie McCardell, installed a "phased program planning" process for project evaluation brought from Ford when he came to XEROX. He, like the members of his team, believed that "if you sat on something long enough and hard enough,…you could control the outcome" (Smith and Alexander 1988: 157). The Easterners were "so risk averse and numbers-bound that meaningful change seemed impos-sible. [They] had become nothing more than bean-counters bound to heartless formulas without factors for enthusiasm, faith, or finesse" (Smith and Alexander 1988: 33). In short, they were not managers who could appreciate the commercial possibilities of the personal computer developed at PARC and who would take the appropriate start-up decisions. The same entrepreneurial stodginess happened at IBM, whose MBA-diplomad CEOs and presidents missed the first bus to the personal computer revolution in the mid-1970s.[13] Managers fit for the "full information economy," they were reluctant to assume the start-up risks necessary for success in the experimentally organized economy.

Management education and building the mature IT organization

The idea advanced so far is that the competence acquired from a business school education did not prompt start-up entrepreneurialism or produce venture capital for innovative IT firms in the post-1970 commercial phase of development. But management educators have always considered established firms to be their province. And in recent years the evidence suggests that the skills taught in business schools have continued to have ready employment there. Jeremy Hope and Tony Hope observe that in a 1987 survey of 402 US firms 97 per cent reported using a formal budgeting program, focusing time on measured variables considered critical to management control (1997: 151). Dr. George Ritzer, in his book entitled *The McDonaldization of Society* (1995), describes how the end of the 20th century saw the triumph of Taylorization, not its disappearance in the American firm.

Orthodox American managers in the late 1970s expected their views to be just as useful in the mature IT firm as in low-tech enterprises. John Sculley, the Wharton MBA, certainly thought so when he decided to leave Pepsi-Cola for Apple in 1983. He told Steve Jobs:

> Just as Northern California is the "technology center" for innovation in computers,...the Northeast corridor was the "management center" for innovation in business. "There are a lot of exciting concepts and tools being developed by business schools, and consulting firms in the East... Make sure you are exposed to these leaders and their ideas."
>
> (Sculley 1987: 135)

Persuading these managers to abandon the ideas that have given them so much power would not be easy.

But software firms, since they do not manufacture tangible products, basically lack the production facilities typical of the large integrated manufacturing firm; consequently software firms never take on the organizational dimensions of large manufactories. Even the largest, Microsoft, only employed 700 people in its new facilities at Redmond, Washington, in the late 1980s. The core workers there, moreover, the programmers, required "a work environment," as Ichbiah and Knepper remarked, "with as few restraints as possible. At Microsoft, the company [chooses] the best, hardest-working people and [turns] them loose to prove themselves" (1991: 225). Because of how software is created, programmers could not be subjected to top-down, micro-management, decision-making using traditional surveillance and control mechanisms.

Much the same conditions prevailed within the specialist chipmakers, whose business by the late 1980s outpaced that of the commodity-driven, mass-production microchip-makers. The highly skilled engineers of specialist chipmakers did make products, but mostly customized ones, with low production volumes. These companies consciously avoided the "cumbersome" organizations of the mass-production commodity sector; they outsourced spun-off enterprises to avoid bigness. And hence they did not need the financial control management mechanisms of the big vertically integrated semiconductor firm. They discarded the control mechanisms learned in business schools for networked organizations, "where people teams, and sometimes whole organizations," as Saxenian's research discovered, "act as independent nodes, form multiple links across boundaries, support one another, share common values, and report to a matrix of leaders who act as coaches and mentors more than line managers" (1994: 90).

Firms involved with both software and hardware exhibited similar organizational characteristics. The best example of this perhaps is Apple Computer. John Sculley learned that Silicon Valley had as much to teach Easterners about management as about technology. "At Apple," he eventually wrote, "we promote "buy-in management," a group decision-making process that recognizes individuals regardless of where they reside in the company. This was quite a difference from the "top-down management" style of so many American corporations, that he had known at Pepsi-Cola and that he had naively thought on his arrival would be the East's contribution to management in Silicon Valley (Sculley 1987: 135).

Because management method and organizational dynamics differed in the newly established IT firms, a gap opened up between management education and management practice. Many people have commented about it. Christopher Bartlett and Sumantra Ghoshal, for example, write of the need for a new theory of the firm that, as Hope and Hope observed, would abandon the "old mechanistic model subject to mathematic formula" for one where "organizational success will be based on long-term relationships and the dynamics of human behavior" (Bartlett and Ghoshal 1995, cited by Hope and Hope 1997: 216). Others have attempted to accomplish this goal by redefining the purpose of the privately owned firm, and hence its constitution, from one that serves exclusively the interests of stockholders (the "proprietary concept") to one that serves all stakeholders (the "entity" view). Still others have concentrated on formulating a view that reflects the entrepreneurial realities of the new high-technology environment.

This is what Gunnar Eliasson has done because his ideas about the experimentally organized economy are rooted in studies of biotech and IT industries. The stakes for business schools are high, for without a new theory of the firm they will persist in teaching the old management science. Or, to use Eliasson's words:

The management teacher as well as the economic theorist needs a realistic model (method) of the firm to support teaching and thinking. Since no realistic theory of dynamic markets exists no good theory of the firm has been created. The moral, hence, is that so far we have excellent firms, not thanks to, but despite management teaching.

(Eliasson 1998: 9)

But could a call for reform just be an exaggeration? If 97 per cent of American firms are still using top-down management control systems, business schools obviously have a market for MBAs educated in the traditional curricula. Indeed, countervailing pressure works on the new IT firms, forcing them to pay attention to management orthodoxies. American capitalism operates in the interest of stockholders and top management. The more initial public offerings of IT stock on NASDAQ, the more the management of these firms find themselves pressured to employ conventional top-down managers, to contain wages, guarantee increased return on investment, and thereby keep up stock valuations. This management, so educated, if ideally suited to the profit-driven system of American finance capitalism, did not form the IT "competence bloc" during the last quarter of the 20th century, and, if the historical record is any indication, will therefore not establish any better entrepreneurial track record in the first quarter of the 21st.

Thus, the French students who crossed the Atlantic between 1969 and 1975 might have prepared themselves well in American business schools to operate a McDonald's franchise in their country, but what they learned scarcely could have fomented IT there. The issue, moreover, is not just curriculum content but what the American business school experience taught them about the sociology of management. The French system of management education is highly elitist. Usually those who graduate from the *grandes écoles* find themselves one day at the top of the corporate ladder; those who do not don't. The French CEO is a *chef de file*, power flows from the top down in a pyramidal organization. Since this has always been the case in France, the elitist American business school experience only reinforced it. Inasmuch as the new IT business culture experimented with matrix organizations, employee empowerment, diffused, decentralized decision-making, teamwork, etc., the traditional form of American business school education did not condition the French student to adapt to the sociological realities of the IT firm.

Does this mean that the decision to send these French nationals to America was a mistake? People living in a particular historical moment must make decisions based on the known facts. By the late 1960s, Europeans had lived for decades with the mystique of American management education. To send their young people to American business schools – the best in the world – made great sense. How were the policy-makers to know before our era of "incomplete" knowledge that their ability to foresee the managerial future could be so limited.

Notes

1   Robert S. Kaplan, "Quality in Business School Education and Research," a presentation to the annual meeting of the American Assembly of the Collegiate Schools of Business, St. Louis, MO, 22 April 1991; quoted in Johnson (1992: 176–7).
2   *Ibid.* Also see Locke (1996).
3   For the survey, see Eliasson (1976).
4   His papers are too numerous to mention, but see his critique of traditional economic theory (Eliasson 1992) and 'Spillover, integrated production and the theory of the firm' (Eliasson 1996c).
5   The quote is taken from Eliasson (1996b: 12), but he uses the "competence bloc" idea everywhere in his recent work.
6   The economist Erich Schneider described the formality of economics this way:

> Theoretical propositions are always conditional propositions of the form: If A, then B....The theoretical proposition always has the character of logical necessity and is according to the assumptions made either right or wrong. A theoretical proposition, like a dogma, cannot be denied. The most that can be said is that a theoretically correct proposition is not relevant because its assumptions do not apply to the present situation. That does not mean the proposition is wrong. It only means that the proposition does not apply to present circumstances [*ist nicht aktuell*].
>
> (Schneider, quoted in Locke 1989: 11)

Such thinking makes economists discard the facts rather than the theory.
7   A 1956 press release described SAGE thus:

> This extraordinary "electronic brain" will become the first of the giant computers to fit into the interrelated complex of radar, ships, jet aircraft, communications networks, missiles, and people that is rapidly taking shape as the supersensitive continental air defense system. This immense project is known as the Semi-Automatic Ground Environment (SAGE) system.... With a knowledge of flight plans of friendly planes available in the computer, hostile planes can be identified immediately and the most effective defense action taken.
>
> (quoted in Pugh 1995: 213)

SAGE was a remarkable achievement for the late 1950s.
8   Joshua Lerner, "The mobility of corporate scientists and engineers between civil and defense activities: evidence from the SSE database," Science, Technology and Public Policy Program Discussion Paper 90 102 (Cambridge, MA: John F. Kennedy School of Government, August 1990); cited in Alic *et al.* (1992: 113).
9   These include Bob Taylor, who had headed ARPA's computer research center (IPTO), hired at PARC "primarily to staff the Computer Science Laboratory" with ARPA people; Ivan Sutherland, who had preceded Taylor as head of IPTO; Alan Kay and Butler Lampson, who had worked on ARPA-funded projects; and a research group that PARC hired away from Englebart's Augmentation Research Center. Before taking the job at PARC, Taylor learned how to manage a research laboratory at ARPA, where "he typically monitored fifteen to twenty research projects across the country at a given time" (Smith and Alexander 1988: 78). Alan Kay said that PARC in the early 1970s had 76 of the 100 best computer scientists. Bob Taylor commented years later of one of the recruits, Butler Lampson, that "he had the best track record for innovation in computer science of anyone in the world" (*ibid.*: 67).
10 See this opinion in two papers by Gunnar Eliasson: "Competence blocs and industrial policy in the knowledge based economy" (Occasional Paper, Department of Industrial Economics and Management, Royal Institute of Technology, TRITA–IEO

R 1997–04) and "The venture capitalist as a competent outsider" (Occasional Paper, TRITA–IEO R 1997–06, Department of Industrial Economics and Management, Royal Institute of Technology, Stockholm, 1997).

11 Several of the interviews of the second period were conducted in firms whose managers were interviewed in the first; but 15 of the firms involved were IT start-ups of the 1980s. The results of the interviews are contained in Eliasson (1996a.)

12 Despite the greater availability of capital in the East, Silicon Valley always had more venture capital investments. In 1981, for instance, "Of the $1.4 billion in total venture capital investments,…12 percent went to Massachusetts-based companies and 38 percent went to California" (Saxenian 1994: 184; information taken from *Venture Capital Journal*, Needham, MA: Venture Economics Inc., 1982).

13 Frank T. Cary, MBA Stanford, President, 1971–74, Chairman 1973–83; John R. Opel, MBA Chicago, President, 1974–83, Chairman, 1983–86.

References

Alic, J.A., Branscomb, L., Brooks, H. and Carter, A. (1992) *Beyond Spinoff: Military and Commercial Technologies in a Changing World*, Boston, MA: Harvard Business School Press.

Bartlett, C. and Ghoshal, S. (1995) "Changing the role of top management: beyond systems to people," *Harvard Business Review*, 132–42.

Eliasson, G. (1976) *Business Economic Planning: Theory, Practice and Comparison*, London: Wiley & Sons.

—— (1992) "Business competence, organizational learning and economic growth: establishing the Smith–Schumpeter–Wicksell connection," in F.M. Scherer and M. Perman (eds) *Entrepreneurship, Technological Innovation and Economic Growth: Studies in the Schumpeterian Tradition*, Ann Arbor, MI: University of Michigan Press.

—— (1996a) *Firm Objectives, Controls and Organization*, Boston, MA: Kluwer.

—— (1996b) "The pharmaceutical and biotechnological competence bloc," Occasional Paper of the Royal Institute of Technology, Department of Industrial Economics and Management, Stockholm.

—— (1996c) "Spillover, integrated production and the theory of the firm," *Journal of Evolutionary Economics* 6: 125–40.

—— (1998) "The nature of economic change and management in the knowledge-based information economy," KTH Stockholm, Department of Industrial Management.

Fores, M. (1996) "The professional as a machine: the death of each day's life," in Ian Glover and Michael Hughes (eds) *The Professional-Managerial Class: Comtemporary British Management in the Pursuer Mode*, Aldershot: Avesbury.

Herrigel, G. (1995) *Reconceptualizing the Source of German Industrial Power*, New York: Cambridge University Press.

Hope, J. and Hope, T. (1997) *Competing in the Third Wave: The Ten Key Management Issues of the Information Age*, Boston, MA: Harvard Business School Press.

Ichbiah, D. and Knepper, Susan L. (1991) *The Making of Microsoft*, Rocklin, CA: Prima Publishing.

Jeffcutt, P. (1996) "Modernity, manageability and the development of the modern management," in Ian Glover and Michael Hughes (eds) *The Professional-Managerial Class: Comtemporary British Management in the Pursuer Mode*, Aldershot: Avesbury.

Johnson, H. Thomas (1992) *Relevance Regained: From Top-Down Control to Bottom-Up Empowerment*, New York: Free Press.

Locke, R.R. (1989) *Management and Higher Education since 1940*, Cambridge: Cambridge University Press.

—— (1996) *The Collapse of the American Management Mystique*, Oxford: Oxford University Press.

Pugh, E.W. (1995) *Building IBM: Shaping an Industry and Its Technology*, Cambridge, MA: MIT Press.

Pyke, F. and Sengenberger, W. (1992) *Industrial Districts and Local Economic Regeneration*, Geneva: International Institute for Labour Studies.

Pyke, F., Becattini, G. and Sengenberger, W. (1990) *Industrial Districts and Inter-Firm Co-operation in Italy*, Geneva: International Institute for Labour Studies.

Rheingold, H. (1991) *Virtual Reality*, New York: Summit Books.

Ritzer, G. (1995) *The McDonaldization of Society: An Investigation into the Changing Character of Contemporary Social Life*, Newbury Park, CA: Pine Forge.

Saxenian, A. (1994) *Regional Advantage*, Cambridge, MA: Harvard University Press.

Sculley, J. (written with John A. Byrne) (1987) *Odyssey: Pepsi to Apple...A Journey of Adventure, Ideas, and the Future*, New York: Harper & Row.

Smith, D.K. and Alexander, R.C. (1988) *Fumbling the Future: How Xerox Invented, then Ignored, the First Personal Computer*, New York: William Morrow & Co.

Zraket, Charles A. (1992) "Software: productivity puzzles, policy challenges," in J.A. Alic, L. Branscomb, H. Brooks, and A. Carter *Beyond Spinoff: Military and Commercial Technologies in a Changing World*, Boston, MA: Harvard Business School Press.

5 UK management skills and the future of management education

Ewart Keep

Introduction

The aim of this chapter is to identify some of the most important issues about potential future management education, training and development (METD) needs and how they might best be filled, trying to pose questions that require further thought.[1] The focus of these points for debate is generally at the level of policy and practice rather than theory. In particular, the chapter seeks to frame questions that those engaged in UK management education may need to address. Where possible, the chapter highlights areas that are sometimes neglected in the general debate about managerial skills.

Four potential pitfalls should be highlighted at the outset. First, the history of initiatives aimed at improving the quality and quantity of METD in the UK has often been characterised by special pleading and the influence of various interest groups – usually the providers (public and private) of METD. Management academics are not always dispassionate observers; they can be a producer interest as well. The Handy Report (Handy 1987) is a case in point. There has also been a dysfunctional tendency within public policy debates to equate METD with business schools and, even more narrowly, with MBAs.

A second problem is that the question of what skills managers will require in the future (and how they might best be developed) is clouded by the very strong tendency towards 'fad surfing' within Anglo-Saxon management. A recent visit to my university bookshop's 'management' section revealed the following (if partial) list of key approaches to competitive success – global strategic alliances, electronic commerce, in-company incentive structures and knowledge management. Each brings with it very different skill demands. The viability of these fads or trends is often extremely limited, perhaps five years to move from 'next big thing' status to the 'yesterday's news' category. Examples of recently eclipsed fads include business process re-engineering (BPR) and the learning organisation (now being replaced by knowledge management; see Scarbrough *et al.* 1999). The various management gurus seem to be in agreement with the broad generality that we will need more highly skilled and intelligent managers (Obolensky 1999), but there is little unanimity about the specifics of what will be required.

The specificity of national context poses other problems. Although internationalisation and globalisation are supposed to be transforming economic activity and management practice, it remains the case that different countries have quite varied approaches to the contents, institutional setting and modes of delivery for METD. The UK fits into what can broadly be defined as an Anglo-Saxon model. Other countries arrange things very differently (for a review of different national METD systems, see Handy *et al.* 1988; Locke 1996).

Of particular note is the fact that the structure of different national and organisational managerial labour markets (for example movement up through well-defined internal labour markets or use of external labour markets to move from company to company, and notions of general management or the use of functional 'chimneys') is central to determining the shape and form of METD (see, for example, Storey 1991). So too are different national conceptions of what the main focus of managerial activity (especially senior managerial work) and skill needs to be. In Germany, for example, technical mastery and leadership have been viewed as critical to senior management, and therefore a doctorate in science or engineering has been an important route to top management in the manufacturing sector. Thus in 1985 no less than 54 per cent of the management board members of Germany's top 100 companies held doctorates (Randlesome 1990: 48).

Finally, although this chapter focuses on the skill-creation aspects of METD, the activity serves a broader range of functions and purposes, some of which have relatively little to do with the creation of skills (Lees 1992; Antonacopoulou 1999). For example, METD can be used as a reward or perk, as an opportunity for managers from different parts of the organisation to network, and as an opportunity to identify talent and potential. However, probably its most important 'non-skills' function is to act as the means by which managers are socialised into a particular organisational culture or way of doing things. A great deal of METD, especially that taking place within organisations, is about creating shared assumptions, outlooks, behaviours and modes of thought rather than skills as traditionally conceived.

With these stipulations in mind, the structure of the chapter is as follows. The starting point is a review of the UK management population, including stocks, flows and qualifications held. Consideration then turns to the question of whether current METD provision is equal to the scale of the task, in terms of both volume and quality. Current changes in the business environment and the issues they pose for METD are then surveyed. In the light of these, the challenges faced by UK management education providers are reviewed and assessed. The chapter concludes with an overview of the points raised.

The UK management population: a large and moving target for upskilling

In thinking about management skill needs and how they might best be met, it is important to note that how we choose to define 'skills', 'management' and 'manager', and more generally how we conceive of the managerial population that might be the beneficiaries of METD activity, will skew both the type and potential volume of METD. Constraints of space forbid engagement with current complex debates that surround the nature and meaning of managerial skills (those interested in this topic are directed to Johnson and Winterton, forthcoming).

A generally less well-covered area is the size and composition of the UK management population. The UK's current official occupational classification system reveals itself as possessing a higher proportion of 'managers and administrators' than other European economies. The new occupational classification system is expected to reduce this population, perhaps by as much as one-third. Nevertheless, the term is still a catch-all. Even if we exclude supervisors, the range of activities, spans of control, levels of seniority, bodies of specialist expertise and knowledge, and broader managerial skills that are involved remains very wide. For example, a store manager in a large food retailer operates with very limited discretion – nearly every aspect of his or her work is controlled by a manual or guidance from head office. The purchasing, HRM and distribution experts in head office who devise and codify the policies the store manager implements are also termed managers. So too is the company's chief executive. The METD needs for the various levels and functions will vary enormously (Hirsch and Bevan 1988; Knights 1992). This breadth raises issues for attempts at the definition and operationalisation of generic approaches to managerial skill requirements (a point which will be returned to below).

The UK management population: stocks and flows

What is known about the potential audience for METD in the UK? Although much data exists, it is widely scattered and has only recently been drawn together and analysed (by Bosworth 1999) for the National Skills Task Force (NSTF). This section draws heavily on this work.

According to Labour Force Survey (LFS) data, in 1997, 16 per cent of individuals reporting an occupation indicated themselves to be managers or administrators. This means that there were 4.1 million managers and administrators out of the total of 25.5 million individuals reporting being in an occupational group (Bosworth 1999: 8). However, this may be an underestimate of the population potentially in need of management skills. A general trend within the economy is the diffusion of managerial-type activities among a wider population of employees. In recent times, many jobs have absorbed or are in the process of absorbing within them elements of what has traditionally been seen as management work, particularly in professional groups such as nurses, doctors and teachers (see, for example, Wise and Bush 1999).

Besides knowing the scale of the current managerial population, at least as important in assessing the current impact of METD is some idea of flows in and out of this population. Bosworth provides detailed data on this issue which indicates that, via a combination of occupational mobility, growth in managerial employment and retirement/mortality, on present trends about 1.4 million jobs will need to be filled (1999: 9–15). In many cases this will be done by people moving from one managerial post to another, but Bosworth estimates that over the period as a whole there will be a net inflow of new entrants to managerial work of just under 0.5 million. As he remarks, this implies a considerable need for METD to fit these individuals for their new jobs and roles (1999: 13).

The quality of the management population's skills

Data on the quality of the current UK stock of managers is very sparse. In the absence of any better measure, levels of educational attainment have been used as an indicator of the relative potential of the human capital being deployed. The results are not very encouraging.

Using the five-level qualification framework afforded by National Vocational Qualifications (NVQs) – and their academic equivalents – Bosworth shows that the average qualification attainments of managers and administrators was 'not only below that for professional occupations, but also for associate professionals and technical occupations. Indeed, the management and administrator result is only marginally higher than the overall average for all occupations' (1999: 21–2). Examination of the proportion of individuals in different occupations holding particular levels of qualification reinforces this gloomy picture. Managers and administrators as a group had a far higher proportion of its members with no qualifications than professional workers, and one in five managers and administrators either has no qualification at all or is only qualified to NVQ level 1 or its academic equivalent (Bosworth 1999: 22). F. Green *et al.*'s (1997) data from the Skills Survey confirms this rather gloomy picture. In 1997 the managers and administrators covered by the Skills Survey indicated that 78.9 per cent of them were in jobs that required some form of qualification and that 27.1 per cent were using high-level (anything above NVQ 3/A-level) qualifications in their work. By contrast the figures for professionals were 98.8 per cent and 71.1 per cent, respectively. For associate professionals and technicians they were 89.8 per cent and 43.1 per cent (F. Green *et al.* 1997: 30).

This situation suggests that if managers are in some respects now seen as the 'leaders' and assumed problem-solvers within modern society, in the UK at least their status as such may not rest on higher levels of intellectual ability. In terms of qualifications held and qualifications required to undertake the job, the intellectual elite of the UK's working population tends to reside in professional and associate professional occupations rather than management (though some sections of the management population may be very highly qualified).

There must also be grounds for concern at the ability of the managerial population as whole to grapple with the pace and scale of change that is taking place in the business environment. At the very least, the figures outlined above suggest that the scale of the potential market and need for METD in the UK is very considerable. Job growth in managerial work, retirements from the existing management population and inadequacies in their current levels of qualification imply a requirement for major attempts to boost the supply of METD. The next section examines how well provision is geared for meeting this potential demand, at least in terms of the volume of METD being supplied.

METD provision: adequate to the scale of the task?

Volume

In a country where the overall levels of qualification are rising, and where the qualifications held by new entrants to the labour force tend to be higher than those leaving the workforce due to retirement or mortality, it might be predicted that the overall qualification levels of the national stock of managers will also be rising. Bosworth's analysis of LFS data supports this projection, though it finds that measured in terms of a simple weighted average based on NVQ levels (or their academic equivalents) the change is relatively small year on year. If no qualifications equals 0, and NVQ 5 equals a score of 5, the overall average of the stock is 2.56, the outflow is at 2.44 and the inflow is at a level of 2.55 (Bosworth 1999: 33–4). Unsurprisingly, given the large-scale expansion of higher education in recent times, the main point of improvement is at NVQ level 4 (i.e. degree level).

Employer-provided training

In terms of employer-provided management training, the figures tell a less straightforward story. Bosworth's overview of LFS data suggests 'a generally upward trend over time, but with the main overall growth in 1986 to 1990' (1999: 25). Lack of formalised METD within UK companies was identified as a problem by Mangham and Silvers (1986) and the Constable Report (Constable and McCormick 1987), with more than half of all firms making no formal provision for training their managers. According to the Management Charter Initiative (1992) the position has improved somewhat, with 80 per cent of organisations with 500-plus employees reporting some form of formalised management training programme, but with still only half of all organisations surveyed and half that proportion of smaller firms (less than 100 employees) having similar arrangements. Thomson *et al.* (1997) indicate a further improvement, with only 4 per cent of larger companies and 20 per cent of small and medium-sized enterprises (SMEs) reporting undertaking no training in 1996. Average training days per manager in larger companies had risen from 3.1 in 1986 to 5.5 in 1996 (Thomson *et al.* 1997: 30).

METD provision within the SME sector has traditionally been a source of concern to policy-makers, and despite general signs of improvement in UK employers' management training provision the story with regard to SMEs is generally less encouraging (Gray 1997; Curran *et al.* 1996). At least in terms of formalised policies and provision, SMEs continue to trail larger employers.

Within the managerial population as a whole, the incidence of training appears to decline with age, but is positively correlated with the levels of qualification held by the individual (Bosworth 1999: 26–7). However, as with the overall levels of qualification held, managers and administrators trail professionals and associate professionals and technical occupations in terms of the incidence of training. Bosworth's data, taken from the 1996 LFS, suggests that male managers and administrators were less likely to receive training in the four weeks preceding the survey than were those employed in protective services or sales occupations (1999: 26). Overall, managers and administrators appear to receive only a little more training than the average for all employees. As Bosworth notes, 'this seems a surprising result, given the central importance of managers to organisational performance' (1999: 26).

In terms of the type of training that is being provided, although great play is made by employers of the issue of employability and of the shift in responsibility for METD from the organisation to the individual manager, in practice the reality may be a little different. Research by Antonacopoulou (1996, 2002) suggests that genuinely self-directed management learning is relatively rare and that the organisation continues to determine to a large extent how individuals should develop and what knowledge and skills are relevant. Very often, the skills and knowledge required are framed within short-term requirements and are narrowly conceived, task- or job-specific, and not necessarily highly transferable. The danger is that this approach pushes managers and their organisations down the road of more of the same and of incremental approaches to organisational change, rather than encouraging a freer redefinition of the managerial task and a more radical approach to organisational transformation.

The contribution made by business schools

Given its prominence in public debate about UK METD, what contribution does management education in the shape of the business schools make to the upskilling of the nation's stock of managers? Each year, undergraduate higher education in the UK is currently supplying around 20,000 business and management graduates. MBA provision for home students generates just over 6,000 MBA graduates per annum. This is after a period of very substantial expansion, with the number of business schools offering the MBA qualification rising from 26 in 1985 to 116 in 1998 and home student numbers increasing from 3,640 in 1990 to 6,095 in 1997 (Bosworth 1999: 32). In addition, the business schools produce about 2,000 other postgraduates in business and management studies.

Given the overall size of the UK management population, the conclusion must be that our higher education system's management education provision has only a relatively limited impact on the supply of managerial skills. In particular, the much-vaunted MBA, at present volumes, is making only very small inroads. As Bosworth remarks:

> If, as a ball-park figure, we say there are around 3.5 to 4 million managers in post, then clearly the 6000 or so individuals graduating each year with an MBA is just a drop in the ocean. To illustrate this point, if the stock

remained constant and infinitely lived, it would take at least 583 years to get everyone up to MBA standard.

(Bosworth 1999: 32)

An MBA would be inappropriate for a high proportion of the overall management population, but even if the MBA is only necessary for a subset of potential high-flyers, current levels of provision appear unlikely to be able to satisfy the underlying level of need.

Finally, the quality of some management provision may be open to question. By international standards, many UK business schools are relatively small and poorly resourced. Anecdotal evidence suggests wide variations in the quality of both the faculty and the students in some of these institutions of higher education. Figures generated by the 1996 research selectivity exercise and analysed by Bosworth indicate that of the 100 business and management schools identified in the exercise only 10 were rated at 5 or above, while 43 were rated at 1 or 2 (1999: 33). If high-quality research does have a symbiotic relationship with teaching, these figures are a cause for concern.

Varying forms of METD

Despite a tendency on the part of those who organise METD still to conceive of it in terms of 'courses' (Antonacopoulou 1996), most METD probably takes place on the job in the form of experiential and more formally structured learning experiences (Eraut *et al.* 1998), many of which would be unlikely to figure in the data on in-company management training provision. Indeed, METD covers a wide range of issues and activities, including succession planning, assessment and appraisal systems (including assessment centres), outdoor/outward bound 'training', job rotation and lateral moves, secondments, international placements, project work, and the use of business involvement in the community as a management development tool.

METD can be delivered via a variety of modes, including open learning (covering CD-ROM, computer-based training and more traditional workbooks) and in-company and external courses. In recent times a great deal of speculation and discussion has centred around the potential of new modes of delivery (computer-based training (CBT; CD-ROM) to revolutionise the delivery of METD. Interesting though this is, particularly for those organisations seeking to profit from the supply of METD or to promote a low-cost expansion of provision, the relative neglect of content and curriculum design issues is worrying. How the 'box' is delivered is undoubtedly important, but the issue of what is in the 'box' may be still more important. It is to this issue that the next section turns.

The changing business environment and major issues for management education

If the section above suggests that there are problems with the quantity of UK METD relative to the scale of the skill needs being generated by changes to the managerial stock, then what about the qualitative dimension? In thinking about the future of METD, it seems important to examine what new challenges managers are facing and how they might best be equipped to analyse and deal with these changes. Consideration of the business environment in the 1990s generally rounds up a predictable list of the usual suspects – globalisation, the impact of IT and the internet, increased competition, the management of change, the need for flexibility and adaptableness, and customer responsiveness. Rather than retread these well-worn paths, it seems more interesting to review a number of other fundamental choices and issues that are currently impacting on the management skills agenda:

- technological literacy;
- doing more with less;
- stakeholder- or shareholder-value models;
- sustainability and the broadening social responsibilities of business (public/private partnerships etc.);
- new models of management and the growing gap between leading- and trailing-edge practice;
- path dependency and new models of competition;
- the strategic capacity of senior management teams.

Technical/scientific literacy

The impact of scientific and technical advances on organisational structure and operation is a commonplace of modern life. IT and the internet, multimedia and opto-electronics, and new materials and biotechnology offer a few examples of technological changes that are having a profound impact on the way that business is conducted and competitive advantage developed and maintained (see Senker 1992). In order to function effectively in an environment where this type of change is occurring, it seems reasonable to assume that managers, especially senior managers charged with strategic decision-making, need to possess a reasonable degree of technological and scientific literacy. It is unclear whether in the UK this is in fact the case.

Doing more with less

A combination of cost-reduction strategies, downsizing and, in the public sector, 'efficiency gains' means that managers are constantly trying to do more with less. In many UK organisations this has meant work intensification and, perhaps more importantly, the longest working hours in Europe, with one-third of all workers undertaking more than a 48-hour week. Indeed, the UK is the only European Union (EU) member state in which the average length of the working week has increased since the early 1990s. It is unclear whether the UK's relatively weak approach to working-hours regulation will do anything to change a culture that seems to find it much easier to find ways of 'turning the wick up under people' than it does of helping them to work smarter (Kodz *et al.* 1998).

However, there are major long-term social and motivational costs associated with this strategy, not least in terms of the fact that long working hours render it difficult for staff to find the time and energy to learn (the more so in organisations where the current norm is for more and more learning to be undertaken in the employee's 'own time' rather than during working hours). It is also likely that sooner or later the laws of diminishing returns will start to bite on efforts to further intensify work. Therefore, many managers will be faced with looking for news ways of organising work (some of which are touched on below). Whether they, and the organisations that employ them, will have the attitudes, conceptual understanding and skills necessary to make these changes work is open to serious doubt.

Stakeholder- or shareholder-value models

There is a continuing debate about the range of interests that might have a legitimate stake in the management of any given organisation. Put crudely, there are two lines of thought. One argues that once whatever existing legal obligations have been met the shareholders represent the sole source of legitimate interest and that management acts as their agent. As such, management is a form of property right that cannot be shared with others. The opposing view suggests that organisations have a range of stakeholders – customers, shareholders, employees and suppliers – and that the needs of all these groups must be considered and balanced in formulating organisational strategies if the organisation is to achieve long-term success (Goyder 1998).

The UK debate on this issue has generally been muted and has failed to engage the attention of the vast majority of the managerial population. However, the government has signalled that this issue will not go away, not least in respect of pay deals for senior managers, but also more broadly in terms of different models of corporate governance that might embrace a wider set of interest groups. It seems important that managers have the information and intellectual tools to formulate coherent views on the issue and to contribute to the debate, as choice between these very different models of capitalism has profound implications for the content and outlook of METD and for the conduct of management as a whole – not least in respect of the issues discussed in the next section.

Sustainability and the broadening social responsibilities of business

A small number of UK companies (for example Tarmac and BAA) have come to see issues of sustainability, the environment and other aspects of the company's relationship with the wider community as key to long-term success. Thus, the chief executive of Tarmac plc, Sir Neville Simms, recently commented: 'I don't think that companies that don't embrace the wider community and consider the whole environment have any future – certainly not in the medium and longer term' (BBC/The Centre for Tomorrow's Company 1999). If this view is correct, many other UK firms are liable to be in serious trouble, as these issues appear not yet to have impacted upon their organisational and managerial consciousness.

More generally, debate about the social and political impact of economic activity and about the responsibilities that companies may need to face has been growing. For examples of significant contributions to this arena, see Korten (1995) and Logan (1998). A result has been the growing interest in the topic of business ethics, one expression of which is the Royal Society of Arts' Forum for Ethics in the Workplace (see Harries 1998, 1999).

At the same time, a crucial element of New Labour's 'third way' is the notion of public/private partnerships and the belief that private-sector organisations (and their managers) will be willing to share time, expertise and effort in order to tackle a range of broad social and economic issues that confront the country. The author's experience of teaching MBAs in a top UK business school suggests that this agenda has little resonance with the vast majority of high-flying middle managers, who see short-term profit maximisation and cost containment as what drives them and their organisations. Given their conception of the managerial task, the wider social agenda appears at best an irrelevance, at worst a distraction.

This disjuncture between the rhetoric of politicians and senior management figures and the reality faced by the future senior management cadre suggests problems ahead. Warwick Business School's BP Corporate Citizenship Unit is currently developing teaching materials that can be used to address these issues with a management audience, but the scale of the learning/skills needs may be considerable.

New models of management and the growing gap between leading- and trailing-edge practice

In recent years a great deal has been written about the emergence of new models of organisational and managerial structures. The overall thrust of this literature has been to argue that the nature of management and what it takes to be a manager is changing very radically (Institute of Management 1994; Prahalad 1997; Ghoshal and Bartlett 1999). An extremely lucid example from this school of thought is provided by the work of Guile and Fonda (1998, 1999) for the New Learning for New Work Consortium. In addition to clear exposition, their work has the benefit of being based upon research in organisations attempting to make a step-change towards the new model of management. They suggest that the strategies, structures and processes within organisations need to change radically to create a value-adding workforce, and that these shifts will, in turn, alter the nature of the managerial task, the required skills and what it means to be a manager. Traditional models of management have cast managers as policemen/women, spies, controllers, dispensers of reward and punishment, decision-makers, sources of wisdom and expertise, order givers, and arbitrators between competing claims. The new model of management tries to paint them as teacher, coach, mentor, facilitator, resource controller and 'servant' of the team.

Change of the type depicted by Guile and Fonda raises profound implications for METD. It is not obvious that the majority of the UK's current stock of managers, mainly selected and developed to perform the very different tasks of the old model, possess the skills, behaviours and attitudes required to perform these radically different new functions.

In particular, moving the people-management elements of managerial work centre-stage is liable to reveal major managerial attitudinal barriers and skill deficiencies. Despite the old chestnut that 'people are our most important asset', the weight of evidence suggests that many UK organisations continue to see their staff as a disposable commodity, or as a cost to be contained. In too many cases, the skills, commitment and latent ability of the workforce are not being harnessed to good effect.

The problem goes beyond the usually cited deficiencies in management's ability to develop and sustain people-management systems that can recruit, retain and motivate and also embraces product market strategies, work organisation and job design. Despite all the talk about empowerment, a recent study on job satisfaction in UK manufacturing firms concluded that

> the current managerial approaches to job design are counterproductive...the type of impoverished jobs we see in manufacturing organisations up and down the country represent waste, on an enormous scale, of the resources, intelligence, skills and energy of those required to perform them.
>
> (Patterson and West 1998: 5)

Work by Dench *et al.* (1998) among a wider group of employers arrived at broadly similar findings about the very limited discretion (and skill levels) being built into many jobs and suggests that managers continue to cling (in some cases ever harder) to a traditional, hierarchical model where managers do the thinking and the workforce concentrates on executing this grand design – carefully, consistently and mindlessly.

It can thus be argued that one of the largest skills gaps in UK management appears to centre on the ability of managers to handle people issues in constructive and innovative ways and to put to best use the skills of those they employ. This problem has become more acute with the move by many organisations to devolve responsibility for large areas of people management to line managers, many of whom have been singularly ill prepared to deal with these newfound responsibilities. If, as Guile and Fonda (1998, 1999) and the Institute of Personnel and Development (IPD) (1997) suggest, the new model of leading-edge management demands much more integrated, sophisticated and forward-thinking approaches to the motivation, deployment and development of employees, then there is plainly a serious problem. How the new type of approach is to be fostered on a large scale is unknown. A major reskilling of the managerial workforce would be a necessary but not sufficient prerequisite.

The difficulties this situation poses for those trying to design and deliver management education are all the greater because, in terms of competitive and product market strategies and management systems, values and structures, the UK has become an extremely diverse economy. As suggested above, many large organisations, especially in the service sector, appear to be locked into price-based strategies; Tayloristic work practices; hierarchical command-and-control management structures; low-trust employee relations systems; high levels of surveillance, not least of managers (see Collinson and Collinson 1997); limited employee discretion, and an underlying belief that managers do the thinking and then direct and control its implementation (Dench *et al.* 1998). As the author and others have argued, such responses may reflect, in the short term at least, a rational market-segmentation strategy response to the structure of domestic demand (Keep and Mayhew 1997).

At the same time, other companies are seeking competitive advantage through moves to higher value-added goods and services, genuine teamworking, a more highly skilled and autonomous workforce, and a shift in the functions of management towards the roles of facilitator, enabler and coach. The battle between these two opposing visions, a battle often being fought out within individual organisations, is of fundamental importance to the future shape, purpose and skills profile of UK management as it enters the 21st century. Although management gurus and futurologists imply that the triumph of empowerment and creativity over command and control (theory Y as opposed to theory X) is inevitable, the match remains too close to call.

For as long, however, as there is this polarisation (and a range of points in between), UK METD has to cater for a very diverse audience with radically different conceptions of what management is there to do, how it should do it and what skills it needs to fulfil its allotted role. These divergent demands raise major issues for the providers of METD in terms of defining workable curricula, and for any qualification structure that tries to offer generic management qualifications.

Path dependency and the new models of competition

A related point follows on from that above, and concerns the ability of organisations to make the jump to the new model. The government's recent White Paper on competition (Department of Trade and Industry 1998) urged the need for a 'knowledge driven economy', while the Organisation for Economic Co-operation and Development (OECD) and the European Commission have argued for the adoption of radically different models of work organisation and the creation of the 'high-performance workplace'. Research suggests, at least in the area of people-management systems, that to be effective such change needs to be 'bundled' – that is, comprised of a broad set of intermeshing, mutually reinforcing policies which are implemented as a coherent package (Pil and MacDuffie 1996). Unfortunately, the same research suggests that such change is inherently risky (as it may disrupt organisational performance) and requires high levels of managerial skills and commitment to work. Yet it is precisely this kind of step-change that is required if more organisations are to adopt the new model.

This suggests that one of the keys to good economic performance and the renewal of organisational capability in the UK will be the managerial ability to design and implement wide-ranging, coherent and co-ordinated programmes of organisational change embracing product market strategies, management structures, control systems, work organisation, job design and people-management systems. As argued above, it is unclear how many UK organisations have current competitive strategies that require or signal the need for such transformation, or the managerial vision, capacity and skills to superintend this level of change.

In part, our slowness to make the jump to the new paradigm or model may reflect the problem of 'path dependency' – the tendency for past choices to mould or 'imprint' the way an organisation will act in the present and future, not least by setting management skills or 'core organisational competences' within a narrow band. A prime example would be cost-containment strategies. The danger for organisations that go down this route is that, after a while, their managers may not have the incentives, vision or skills to implement any other form of strategy. All the organisation can then do is more of the same, but harder.

Modern managerial recruitment systems based on psychometric testing often reinforce this tendency through 'cloning'. These selection systems are geared to recruiting managers who display the same behaviours, thought patterns, aptitudes and outlook as a profiled selection of current high-performing managers in the organisation. Marks & Spencer is a good example of a company that has utilised this system, and it might be argued that some of their current problems stem from narrowing the corporate 'gene pool'. The system works well until the external environment undergoes radical change, at which point the range of ideas and approaches that management can deploy to meet the challenge posed by the change is very limited and locked into a model that was specifically designed to address a now vanished world.

The strategic capacity of senior management teams

An overarching concern is the strategic-management capabilities of UK senior management teams and their ability to analyse and respond to the challenges outlined above. There are a range of issues for concern, which cannot be reviewed here. Instead, what follows focuses on a single area: recourse to mergers and acquisitions as a source of competitive advantage.

There is a wealth of academic research from both sides of the Atlantic now available on this topic. The overall message of recent work is fairly straightforward. In general, mergers and acquisitions fail to produce the expected improvements in business performance (Dickerson *et al.* 1995; Franks and Mayer 1996; Carper 1990). They also appear to reduce long-term profitability (Dickerson *et al.* 1995) and frequently appear to reduce innovation and research and development (R&D) (Hitt *et al.* 1991a, 1991b; Hitt *et al.* 1996). Mergers will only work within particular, fairly tightly bounded circumstances (Hitt *et al.* 1998).

Unfortunately, UK senior managers appear to discount these findings and to continue to rely very heavily upon merger activity as a source of competitive advantage. As a proportion of gross domestic product (GDP), UK merger activity generally outstrips that in the USA, and at present UK companies are the most acquisitive in the world, having spent $139 billion in the second quarter of 1999 on buying up foreign rivals (*Guardian*, 19 July 1999).

This behaviour may reflect a number of things: the triumph of hope over experience; the influence of an incentives structure that provides large financial rewards for the leaders of newly merged companies and for legal and financial firms that act as advisors and brokers for such deals; a need for quick fixes and more rapid expansion than organic growth can deliver; or a belief that in a globalising size economy, market share and associated economy-of-scale advantages outweigh any risks. What it does demonstrate is that research findings have a limited impact on the perceptions and behaviours of senior managers. We may be entering a knowledge-driven economy, but some forms of knowledge can apparently be easily discounted if they clash with other priorities. Besides raising questions about the wisdom and calibre of senior management teams willing to invest so much in what is, at best, a risky strategy, this situation also illustrates one major problem that management educators face – how to influence practice by the deployment of research and reasoned argument.

Having examined the broad canvas of UK METD and outlined some of the strategic issues it faces, we now turn to examine the challenges which this environment poses for UK management educators.

The challenges for UK management education

The section above indicated a range of trends and issues that pose large questions, both for those running businesses and for those who seek to educate managers. The question is whether those supplying management education are reacting with sufficient vigour and rigour to these challenges. There are some grounds for arguing that they are not.

At present, in contrast to many other areas of educational provision, the effort put into curriculum design and innovation is limited, and the standard model still relies on non-integrative, compartmentalised knowledge heavily skewed towards the areas of marketing and finance. New areas have been tacked on via additional course options, but the design of a curriculum and learning style that would encourage integrative, analytical thinking remains limited, and management education's ability to engage with the concepts discussed by Guile and Fonda (1998, 1999) is also sometimes limited. Moreover, although there are exceptions, in general the curriculum being offered across the different institutions appears surprisingly standardised. There may be differences in quality and mode of delivery, but content is generally broadly similar.

In trying to move forward from this position to address the many changes that are undermining the validity of the current management education pedagogy and curriculum, a range of issues need to be addressed. Some of the more important are reviewed below.

Technicism or radicalism and creativity

An unresolved tension within many management education institutions is the nature of their role and relationship with business. Are management educators there to act as cheerleaders for, or handmaidens to, capitalist enterprises and current management practices, or are they there to act as pearls in the oyster, represent and investigate wider interests (such as those of society, workers and trade unions, consumers), offer radical criticism, or develop and popularise alternative approaches?

These debates raise many large questions, which there is not the space to debate here. A single, limited facet of these debates will serve as an example. On the one hand, a significant strand of current thought suggests that the organisations that will be successful in the future will be those that can harness the creativity, innovation and tacit knowledge of their employees. Such organisations will be innovative, risk-taking, non-hierarchical and able to operate outside the constraints of traditional management-control systems. At the same time, a countervailing set of developments and trends can be observed, whereby organisations are in effect revitalising Taylorism and Fordism (particularly in the mass markets of the service sector) in moves driven by a search for certainty, measurability, control and a form of monolithic consistency of delivery that they equate with quality. These tensions are crystallised very clearly within current debates about knowledge management (see Scarbrough *et al.* 1999; Scarbrough and Swan 1999).

How should business schools react? In many ways, the ethos of much management research is supportive of the technicist search for certainty (Fox 1998), but there are other strands of work, for example organisational behaviour (OB) and organisational development, that are more interested in pursuing the search for creativity. Whatever balance or compromise might be arrived at in terms of relative emphasis within management courses, it still begs the question of how students can be sensitised to the need to choose between competing solutions within the varying contexts of very different individual organisations.

A toolkit for Action Man / Woman or analytical training for the reflective practitioner?

In thinking about reinventing their offerings, management educators face a market which has fairly clear views about what it wants and which embodies a strong strand of short-termist instrumentalism in its conception of the value of management learning. These in turn reflect organisational and individual concepts of the nature of the managerial task – that is, of what it means to be a manager and of what it is that a manager actually needs to know and do – which exert a very powerful influence over the shape of skill requirements. As has been suggested above, different national cultures embody different conceptions of the managerial task. At the same time, new models of management in the UK suggest the need for a very radical realignment of managerial values and skills towards a more sophisticated and broadly focused conception of what is required to be a good manager.

Unfortunately, the prevailing practitioner conception and practice of management in the UK sees the manager as primarily doer, firefighter and 'Action Man/Woman', rather than as an analyst or reflective practitioner. In part, this orientation reflects the problems which analysis and reflection by subordinates pose to senior managers. As one MBA student once remarked to the author, '[W]hat would my organisation want with reflective practitioners? What would we reflect upon, perhaps critically, except the decisions taken by our senior managers. They wouldn't like that.'

More broadly, as suggested above, firms tend to see their own management training as needing to be about meeting narrow, short-term, task-specific requirements. This approach inhibits questioning and experimentation and provides limited freedom to unlearn and rethink (Antonacopoulou 2002; see also Dearden 1992).

The difficulty for management educators is the gulf between what managers do and are required to do by the organisations that employ them, and what theory or even best practice models say they ought to be doing. Attempts to shift the focus of management away from doing towards reflection and analysis, or to direct attention towards leading-edge practice, for example in the shape of learning organisations (see Keep and Rainbird, forthcoming), are open to the criticism that they are not relevant to the current needs of managers or able to address the organisational contexts and realities that most managers face. Within a national business cultural heritage that champions the cult of the practical man, charges of abstraction, irrelevance and an overly academic approach have a strong resonance. This problem affects many of the issues discussed below.

Universal prescriptions and internationalisation

Despite constant talk about the need to internationalise approaches to METD, in the US and the UK much of the 'management guru' and producer-led literature on METD stresses the utility of approaches based around broad, generic skills or competencies and competences, and upon the universality (cultural and technical) of particular management systems and techniques. Often what is on offer is a 'one-size-fits-all' toolkit which can supposedly be applied in any circumstances (organisational or national). This reflects a brand of Anglo-Saxon imperialism of thought whereby instead of territory it is a worldwide empire of managerial attitudes, techniques and systems upon which the sun is expected never to set. The drive towards universality is also motivated in no small part by the desire of those selling nostrums (be they management textbooks, airport bookstall management best-sellers, MBA courses or competence frameworks) to maximise the size of their potential audience or market. There are strong reasons for doubting the validity of this approach.

As both the National Health Service (NHS) and the newly privatised rail industry have demonstrated, sector-specific knowledge is still crucial to success. Few of the managers imported into the NHS from the outside world in the 1980s and early 1990s have survived. In the privatised rail industry, the vast majority of senior managers running the train operating companies (TOCs) are old British Rail (BR) managers, as the new owners of the train companies (mainly bus operators) simply lack the know-how to operate effectively in a railway environment.

The impact of specific contexts and cultures (organisational and national) also undermines the ability of generic 'answers' to produce the expected results. What works in an Anglo-Saxon business environment may play out less well in Japan or Scandinavia, for example in terms of the meanings and values attached to a particular managerial competency framework, which, as Trompenaars and Woolliams point out, 'owes its origins to observations of business practice in Anglo-Saxon or US studies, and is often ethnocentric' (1999: 30). A wide range of research, both in business subjects and economic geography, underlines the continuing importance of particular institutional settings and the absence of convergence towards some homogeneous norm (A. Green *et al.* 1999; Maskell *et al.* 1998; Gospel 1999; Kohler and Woodard 1997).

At a broader level, business schools tend to celebrate the inevitable triumph of the Anglo-Saxon model of capitalism. While acknowledging the need to undergo adjustment and refocusing, policy-makers in Germany and Japan are by no means minded to accept that the abandonment of their systems and the adoption of a full-blown Anglo-Saxon model of corporate governance and management are by any means inevitable.

Rather than simply assuming that our model for organising business is inherently superior and will triumph, perhaps a more sophisticated comparative approach to the study of management in other countries and cultures might be productive, not least in acting as a mirror wherein both the strengths and weaknesses of the Anglo-Saxon model of management and the skills it prizes can be examined. Looked at from this perspective, it can be argued that, at least in part, other cultures' conception of the managerial task and required skills may chime more readily with the leading-edge model outlined above. One example would be the stress placed within Japanese management on the development of subordinates as a key element of the managerial task (Koike 1997).

The gap called business ethics

Although UK management education has largely been modelled on the US business school model, there are differences. One would be the perhaps greater emphasis placed in the US on people-management issues within the MBA curriculum. The other would be the contrast in the relative importance attached in US and UK business schools to the issue of business ethics. In the US, this is regarded as an important element in management education. In the UK, with a few exceptions (London Business School being one), the issue is often treated as marginal and comparatively little time or energy is devoted to it. As has been suggested above, calls for a widening of the range of social and environmental issues that business needs to address, coupled with an increasingly complex array of legislative requirements and the interplay within a global economy of very different national approaches to the conduct of business affairs, suggest that equipping managers with a better understanding of the issues and the intellectual and moral tools to dissect these issues will be important (see Kidder 1999 for an accessible and interesting discussion of the issues).

METD for SMEs: who, why, what, how? The $64,000 questions

The mass provision of METD to SMEs represents a challenge to business educators which has not been resolved. The goal is desirable, but is extremely difficult, perhaps impossible, to achieve. The vast majority of the literature and prescription on METD focuses on the needs of large organisations, which can employ a critical mass of often specialist managers. The world of the SME is very different and calls for radically different types and methods of METD.

Unfortunately, although there has been much experimentation with different curricula, learning methods and modes of delivery, METD for SMEs remains an unresolved problem in the UK. There appears to be broad agreement that much of what has been offered in the past has been ill focused, poorly targeted and hence relatively ineffectual, and that in future more and better focused provision is required. At present, the expectation is that the University of Industry (UfI) will take the lead in resolving this weakness. Given that UfI is not supposed to be in the business of providing courses itself, and must rely upon other organisations to deliver the learning, it will be interesting to see what progress it can make and to what degree business schools will be willing or able to help it.

The MBA: overplayed and overvalued?

Are business schools putting too many eggs in the MBA basket? At one level it seems hard to question the value of MBAs. The fact that they achieve an average 27 per cent rise in salary on graduation (*People Management*, 4 December 1997: 12) would appear to suggest that the employers and the labour market value this form of METD highly and that the rate of return on investment in MBAs must be strongly positive. Nevertheless, there are grounds for questioning the heavy emphasis that is placed on MBAs whenever METD is discussed as public policy.

To begin with, we have little idea whether the skills and knowledge being imparted by these courses are actually put to good use. Individuals benefit in terms of subsequent salary, but whether their employers secure a return on investment is generally taken as an act of faith. We do know, via research by the Association of MBAs (AMBA), that around 40 per cent of MBAs leave their employers within one year of graduating, often because they feel that their newfound skills are not being used (*People Management*, 4 December 1997: 12).

Furthermore, one of the traditional arguments deployed about British (particularly English) education is that it is good at dealing with a small elite but does little for those at the middle or bottom. The MBA fits this pattern of criticism, in that it targets a relatively 'select' subsection of the managerial workforce (supposedly the potential high-flyers, though the evidence to support the supposition that those sent on MBAs really are the most talented in their cohort is almost wholly absent). It is open to debate whether some of the resources currently targeted at the MBA might not more productively be allocated to other types of management training and other segments of the managerial population.

It can also be argued that the MBA represents a remedial model of METD, in that much of what is taught on an MBA concerns the basic building blocks and tools of management, which one might have expected to be reasonably fully developed before embarking on what purports to be a master's-level postgraduate qualification. In part, this problem reflects the fact that too many students enter MBA programmes with insufficiently wide or deep managerial experience, but it may also indicate weaknesses in the METD processes in many large UK organisations, in that high-flying managers in their mid-30s have yet to acquire a basic grounding in what many might regard as the essentials of management.

Non-MBA management education: a relatively neglected resource?

The MBA tail very often appears to wag the management education dog, despite the fact that MBAs represent only one segment of the output of UK management education. Much activity exists in the shadow of MBAs:

- undergraduate business studies courses and joint honours degrees (e.g. business and engineering, and business and a foreign language);
- a huge range of specialist master's programmes in areas such as finance, human resource management (HRM) and industrial relations;

- various postgraduate diplomas and certificates covering the broad spectrum of management disciplines;
- short courses;
- seminars and lectures;
- business and management research provision (including Ph.D. and doctor of business administration (DBA) and consultancy activities.

Perhaps greater effort needs to go into promoting and developing these rather than an over-concentration on the MBA as the 'flagship' offering. In terms of meeting the potential volume of demand for management updating and reskilling, it is many of these activities, rather than the MBA route, that could arguably make a significant difference.

The need for product development and innovation in management education

Leaving to one side the intellectual or moral arguments for a new approach to management education in the UK, the challenges outlined in this chapter suggest that, at a practical level, those running UK management education need to think long and hard about future directions. There are many fundamental and difficult choices to be made. In a world where the gap between best and worst practice widens, where and at whom should management education's output be pitched? Should the focus be on a technicist, toolkit approach or on generating radical critiques of existing practice, or a mixture of both? Should the time and space currently devoted to strategic marketing (to pick a random example) instead be turned over to courses addressing issues such as business ethics or the social accountability of business and environmental issues, or can both be fitted within course structures? Is there an over-concentration on the MBA and a relative neglect of other offerings and types of activity? What is management education doing to address the scale of need for more and different management education in the UK? Is it neglecting large parts of its potential market?

In trying to grapple with these questions and issues, those working in business schools, the majority of which are located within a university environment, find themselves under multiple pressures. Their host institutions generally see them as an earned-income-generating cash cow, and want to maximise short-term profits. The reward structures and personnel-management systems offered by higher education militate against their ability to recruit, retain and motivate suitably qualified and enthusiastic faculty. Customers, whether students or organisations, are ever more demanding and assertive. In terms of their own internal management structures and systems, the gap between what business schools practice and what they teach is probably widening.

The great danger must be that faced with pressures of time and resources, and with currently buoyant market demand for the existing product range, the business schools will invest too little time, thought, energy and resources in reinventing themselves and in curriculum development to meet future needs. More of the same is highly marketable at the moment, but to pursue this as a long-term strategy may be to risk running down a cul-de-sac. The scale of this risk is all the greater because technology appears to be lowering the barriers to entry in the management education market, making it easier for private providers, not least corporate universities and large publishing and media companies, to enter the field.

Final thoughts

As this chapter has sought to demonstrate, although there have been improvements in the position since the identification of a major weakness in UK METD in the mid-1980s, the providers of METD face major challenges in terms of both the volume and the contents and nature of what is being provided. Moreover, in terms of the educational base of the UK management population relative to professional and associate professional groups, managers are currently trailing quite markedly.

Much of the METD system (both in-company and external-provider provision) appears to be centred on the delivery of elements of task-, function- and company-specific skills. It also acts as an important means of socialising staff into particular patterns of organisational thought and behaviour. What seems to be less strong is the current system's ability to deliver broader, integrative and strategic management skills or to tackle the new and much wider business agenda that has started to emerge. We may be in danger of expanding the supply of METD to meet yesterday's skill needs, rather than confronting the requirement for radically different conceptions of the managerial task, for deconstructing orthodoxies in management thinking and practice, and for a step-change in analytical, integrative and strategic management skills. Following yesterday's path can be dangerous. As US business guru Gary Hamel recently remarked, 'those who live by the sword...will be shot' (*People Management*, 12 November 1998: 10).

Within this overall tableau, business schools, as the purveyors of high-level management education, currently play, at least in terms of volume, a fairly marginal role, though they can claim to be catering for a relatively lucrative and strategically important segment of the management cohort. In sustaining and perhaps expanding their position within the METD system, management educators within the business schools face a range of substantial challenges, some of which have been outlined above. Their capacity to respond to these challenges is unclear. Finding themselves in much the same situation as UK car manufacturers in the 1950s – able to sell everything they can produce – the necessity of business schools to invest in R&D, product redesign and quality enhancement may be neglected, with results that may parallel what happened to the domestic car producers. The old maxim that, in the long run, nothing fails like success may yet come to haunt the UK's management educators.

Finally, it is startling to note that in overall terms we have little or no idea if the METD system is creating the skills that are really needed or which produce useful long-term results. Despite the believed importance of management skills to organisational performance, the more so because they are the chief source of ideas and leadership in organisations located within a society that has no formalised notions of social partnership or co-determination, there have been very few systematic or rigorous attempts to evaluate the effectiveness of different forms of METD, their impact on organisational behaviour and effectiveness, or the public and private rates of return that accrue to investment in METD activities (see Bosworth 1999 for a review of what is available). As the DfEE/Cabinet Office's *Skills Audit* report observed:

> We are led therefore to the somewhat paradoxical conclusion that although our management skills may be no better than our competitors' we have created and are continuing to create a system of competence-based training and qualifications which is unique to the UK, together with a Business Schools system based largely on the US model. Yet, while there is much research into UK management, none has established to what extent good training contributes to good management, and good management to good company performance.
>
> (Department for Education and Employment/Cabinet Office 1996: 43)

Notes

1   This chapter springs from an issues paper which the author was asked to prepare for the UK Department for Education and Employment's (DfEE) National Skills Task Force (NSTF).

References

Antonacopoulou, E.P. (1996) 'A study of interrelationships: the way individual managers learn and adapt and the contribution of training towards this process', unpublished Ph.D. thesis, University of Warwick, Warwick Business School, Coventry.

—— (1999) 'Individuals' responses to change: the relationship between learning and knowledge', *Creativity and Innovation Management* 8(2): 130–9.

—— (2002) 'Revisiting the what, how and why of managerial learning: some new evidence', *SKOPE Research Paper* No. 25, Coventry: University of Warwick, SKOPE.

BBC/The Centre for Tomorrow's Company (1999) *Building Tomorrow's Company: The Community Relationship*, London: BBC (video).

Bosworth, D. (1999) 'Empirical evidence on management skills in the UK', paper prepared for the DfEE workshop on Management Skills, 5 July, Manchester, UMIST (mimeo).

Carper, W.B. (1990) 'Corporate acquisitions and shareholder wealth: a review and explanatory analysis', *Journal of Management* 16: 807–23.

Collinson, D.L. and Collinson, M. (1997) ' "Delayering managers": time–space surveillance and its gendered effects', *Organization* 4(3): 375–407.

Constable, J. and McCormick, R. (1987) *The Making of Managers*, London: British Institute of Management.

Curran, J., Blackburn, R., Kitching, J. and North, J. (1996) *Establishing Small Firms' Training Practices, Needs, Difficulties and Use of Industry Training Organisations*, London: DfEE.

Dearden, R. (1992) 'Education and training', in G. Esland (ed.) *Education, Training and Employment: The Educational Response*, UK: Addison-Wesley/Open University.

Dench, S., Perryman, S. and Giles, L. (1998) 'Employers' perceptions of key skills', *IES Report 349*, Sussex: Institute of Employment Studies.

Department for Education and Employment /Cabinet Office (1996) *The Skills Audit: A Report from an Interdepartmental Group*, Competitiveness Occasional Paper, London: DfEE.

Department of Trade and Industry (1998) *Our Competitive Future: Building the Knowledge Driven Economy*, Cm4176, London: Stationery Office.

Dickerson, A.P., Gibson, H.D. and Tsakalotos, E. (1995) 'The impact of acquisitions on company performance: evidence from a large panel of UK firms', *Studies in Economics* No. 95/11, University of Kent, Department of Economics.

Eraut, M., Alderton, J., Cole, G. and Senker, P. (1998) 'Learning from other people at work', in F. Coffield (ed.) *Learning at Work*, Bristol: Policy Press.

Fox, S. (1998) 'UK management and human resource management', in S. Fox (ed.) *The European Business Environment: The UK*, London: International Thomson.

Franks, J. and Mayer, C. (1996) 'Do hostile takeovers improve performance?', *Business Strategy Review* 7(4): 1–6.

Ghoshal, S. and Bartlett, C.A. (1999) *The Individualised Corporation: A Fundamentally New Approach to Management*, London: Heinemann.

Gospel, H. (1999) 'Nations, firms and their workers', *Centre Piece* 4(2): 18–22.

Goyder, M. (1998) *Living Tomorrow's Company*, London: Gower.

Gray, C. (1997) 'Management development and small firm growth', paper presented to the 20th Small Firms National Policy and Research Conference, Belfast.

Green, A., Wolf, A. and Leney, T. (1999) 'Convergence and divergence in European education and training systems', *Bedford Way Papers*, London: Institute of Education.

Green, F., Ashton, D., Burchell, B., Davies, B. and Felstead, A. (1997) 'An analysis of changing work skills in Britain', paper presented to the Low Wage Employment Conference of the European Low Wage Employment Research Network, Centre for Economic Performance, London School of Economics, 12–13 December.

Guile, D. and Fonda, N. (1998) *Performance Management through Capability*, London: Institute of Personnel and Development.

—— (1999) *Managing Learning for Added Value*, London: Institute of Personnel and Development.

Handy, C. (1987) *The Making of Managers: A Report on Management Education, Training and Development in the United States, West Germany, France, Japan and the UK*, London: Manpower Services Commission/National Economic Development Office/British Institute of Management.

Handy, C., Gordon, C., Gow, I. and Randlesome, C. (1988) *Making Managers*, London: Pitman.

Harries, S. (1998) 'Working ethics', *RSA Journal* vol. CXLVI, no. 5486: 24–8.

—— (1999) 'Programme report: forum for ethics in the workplace', *RSA Journal* vol. CXLVII, no. 5489: 40–1.

Hirsch, W. and Bevan, S. (1988) 'What makes a manager?', Report No. 144, Brighton: Institute of Manpower Studies.

Hitt, M., Harrison, J., Ireland, R.D. and Best, A. (1998) 'Attributes of successful and unsuccessful acquisitions of US firms', *British Journal of Management* 9(2): 91–114.

Hitt, M., Hoskison, R.E., Ireland, R.D. and Harrison, J.S. (1991a) 'Effects of acquisitions on R&D inputs and outputs', *Academy of Management Journal* 34: 693–706.

—— (1991b) 'Are acquisitions a poison pill for innovation?', *Academy of Management Executive* 5(4): 22–34.

Hitt, M., Hoskison, R.E., Johnson, R.A., and Moesel, D.D. (1996) 'The market for corporate control and firm innovation', *Academy of Management Journal* 39: 1084–119.

Institute of Management (1994) *Management Development to the Millennium: The Cannon and Taylor Working Party Reports*, London: Institute of Management.

Institute of Personnel and Development (1997) *Employee Relations into the 21st Century: An IPD Position Paper*, London: IPD.

Johnson, S. and Winterton, J. (forthcoming) 'Management skills', *National Skills Task Force Research Project Report*, Sheffield: DfEE.

Keep, E. and Mayhew, K. (1997) 'Was Ratner right? – Product market and competitive strategies and their links with skills and knowledge', *EPI Economic Report* 12(3), April: 1–15.

Keep, E. and Rainbird, H. (forthcoming) 'The learning organization', in S. Bach and K. Sisson (eds) *Personnel Management*, 3rd edition, Oxford: Blackwell.

Kidder, R. (1999) 'Global ethics and individual responsibility', *RSA Journal* vol. CXLVI, no. 5488: 38–41.

Knights, S. (1992) 'Changing spaces: the disruptive impact of a new epistemological location for the study of management', *Academy of Management Review* 17(3): 514–36.

Kodz, J., Kersley, B. and Strebler, M. (1998) 'Breaking the long hours culture', *IES Report 352*, Brighton: Institute of Employment Studies.

Kohler, C. and Woodard, J. (1997) 'Systems of work and socio-economic structures: a comparison of Germany, Spain, France and Japan', *European Journal of Industrial Relations* 3(1): 59–82.

Koike, K. (1997) *Human Resource Management*, Tokyo: Japan Institute of Labour.

Korten, D.C. (1995) *When Corporations Rule the World*, West Hartford: Kumarian Press/San Francisco: Berrett-Koehler.

Lees, S. (1992) 'Ten faces of management development', *Management Education and Development* 23(2): 89–105.

Locke, R.R. (1996) *The Collapse of the American Management Mystique*, Oxford: Oxford University Press.

Logan, D. (1998) 'Corporate citizenship in a global age', *RSA Journal* vol. CXLVI, no. 5486: 65–71.

Management Charter Initiative (1992) *Management Development in the UK 1992*, London: MCI.

Mangham, I. and Silvers, M.S. (1986) *Management Training: Context and Practice*, London: Economic and Social Research Council.

Maskell, P., Eskelinen, H., Hannibalsson, I., Malmberg, A. and Vatne, E. (1998) *Competition: Localised Learning and Regional Development*, London: Routledge.

Obolensky, N. (1999) 'The death of the traditional CEO', *News from the Centre* 5, spring: 4.

Patterson, M. and West, M. (1998) 'People power', *Centre Piece* 3(3): 2–5.

Pil, F.K. and MacDuffie, J.P. (1996) 'The adoption of high-involvement work practices', *Industrial Relations* 35(3), July: 423–55.

Prahalad, C.K. (1997) 'The work of the new age manager in the emerging competitive landscape', in F. Hesselbein, M. Goldsmith and R. Beckard (eds) *The Organisation of the Future*, San Francisco: Jossey-Bass.

Randlesome, C. (1990) 'The business culture in Germany', in C. Randlesome, W. Brierley, K. Bruton, C. Gordon and P. King *Business Cultures in Europe*, London: Butterworth Heinemann.

Scarbrough, H. and Swan, J. (eds) (1999) *Case Studies in Knowledge Management*, London: Institute of Personnel and Development.

Scarbrough, H., Swan, J. and Preston, J. (1999) *Knowledge Management: A Literature Review*, London: Institute of Personnel and Development.

Senker, P. (1992) 'Technological change and the future of work', *Futures*, May: 351–63.

Storey, J. (1991) 'Do the Japanese make better managers?', *Personnel Management*, August: 24–8.

Thomson, A., Storey, J., Mabey, C., Gray, C., Farmer, E. and Thomson, R. (1997) *A Portrait of Management Development*, London: Institute of Management.

Trompenaars, F. and Woolliams, P. (1999) 'First class accommodation', *People Management*, 22 April: 30–7.

Wise, C. and Bush, T. (1999) 'From teacher to middle manager: the role of the academic middle manager in secondary schools', *Educational Research* 41(2): 183–95.

Part II

Management knowledge and the challenge of learning

6 Situated learning theory and underpinning disputes in management learning[1]

Stephen Fox

To turn mainstream theories into objects of analysis and critique, while accounting for their crucial role in organising and justifying numerous Euro-American social practices, is to take on the culture more broadly.

(Lave 1993: 30)

Introduction

Formal management education, and education more widely, is the tip of a learning iceberg. Most research on learning is focused on the tip of the iceberg. Managers, like other people, learn in everyday practice as well as in formal education. People without the title 'manager' learn to manage all kinds of situations and events and manage to learn as they go (Fox 1994a, 1994b). Management learning, as a research field, studies the management of learning and the learning of management (Fox 1994a, 1994b). The former is very general, covering the formal and informal management of all areas of knowledge production and learning in practice, whereas the learning of management is more specific, asking how do people learn management? There are three main routes:

* management practice itself – learning by doing management work, often in an organisational context;
* engaging in management development and training, often, though not always, organised by the employer;
* engaging in management education, usually leading to an accredited qualification, such as an MBA or a professional diploma (see Fox 1994a and 1997 for discussion).

Historically, management learning has researched all of these routes for learning management.

In the 1970s management learning researchers focused on the learners' experience of business school (Burgoyne 1973) and the management teacher's preferred teaching methods and implicit theories of learning (Burgoyne and Cooper 1976; Burgoyne and Stuart 1977). These studies drew attention to the issue of the learning experience, in formal settings (Boot and Reynolds 1980). In the early 1983s phenomenological and qualitative studies of managers in the workplace setting produced accounts of managers learning to manage by practising their work (Burgoyne and Hodgson 1983, 1984; Davies and Easterby-Smith 1984). These accounts emphasised the social dimension to managers' learning to manage in practice, and influenced my ethnomethodologically informed ethnographic study of executive MBA students (Fox 1987, 1990a, 1990b) and subsequent evaluation research (Tanton and Fox 1987). The sociology of business school classrooms derived its methods from the sociology of education more widely, especially the classroom interaction studies of Delamont (1977), Woods and Hammersley (1977), and Woods (1980a, 1980b, 1983). Subsequent ethnographic studies of management-in-practice have focused on the significance of career, self-management and forms of social exchange amongst managers in workplace settings from an increasingly critical viewpoint (e.g. Grey 1994; Watson 1994; Brewis 1996).

From the brief history above we can see that management learning has been characterised by studies of learning through management education and through management practice. In the 1990s educational psychologists and sociologists more widely began to take an interest in the implications of social learning in practice for learning and cognitive theory in general (see Augoustinos and Walker 1995 for a broad introduction). Resnick, Levine and Teasley edited a book called *Perspectives on Socially Shared Cognition* (1991), which showed that the social dimension could no longer be simply an extra factor or variable modifying a basically functionalist psychological theory of cognition. In the same year Lave and Wenger published a book called *Situated Learning: Legitimate Peripheral Participation* (1991), which summarised several anthropological studies of learning through situated practice and drew together a general theoretical account of mind-in-lived-in-world. The studies spanned communities of practice ranging from naval quartermasters, through Mayan midwives and Goan tailors, to members of Alcoholics Anonymous, and established situated learning theory (SLT) as a principled alternative to traditional cognitive theory. A brief account of SLT drawing implications for the study of management learning can be found in Fox (1997).

The significance of SLT theory is that it offers a critique of traditional cognitive theory and marks a wider shift towards the study of situated practice in occupational and workplace settings. When it does the latter, however, it encounters the wide range of theoretical and methodological disputes which characterise contemporary social and cultural studies. The present chapter offers an overview of the main differences between traditional cognitive theory (TCT) and SLT in the next section, and then proceeds to offer a discussion of some of the key difficulties with SLT. These difficulties turn on SLT's treatment of social and material context. Basically it argues that we understand more about learning when we study it happening in everyday practice in social contexts other than formal educational ones. However, different perspectives see context differently. Some see it as a pre-given container, like a stage, which contains the action, whereas other perspectives see context as emergent in the course of the action.

This debate is not simply a rerun of determinism versus voluntarism, but concerns the methods of ordinary practice, science and narrative.

Traditional cognitive theory and situated learning theory

Traditional cognitive theory (TCT) dominates thinking about learning and the practice of education. In management studies, TCT has been influential in 'upper echelon theory', which applies cognitive psychology to top management's perceptions of the environment (Hambrick and Mason 1984). TCT has been influential in the field of managerial and organisational cognition, for example in Daft and Weick's (1984) 'model of organisations as interpretation systems'. Schwenk has applied TCT to the theory of escalating commitment to a course of action (1986) and to strategic decision-making (1988). More recently the approach has been modified to incorporate a 'political' dimension (Schwenk 1989) and to develop the idea of 'congregate' cognitive maps (Bougon 1992) and 'shared' cognitive maps (Langfield-Smith 1992). Organisations themselves are seen as possessing 'knowledge structures' on the model of individualist cognitive theory (Lyles and Schwenk 1992).

Work in the the field of managerial and organisational cognition tends to apply the suffix 'social-' to its cognitive theory and proceed as normal. But, as Jean Lave says:

> It is not enough to say that some designated cognitive theory of learning could be *amended* by adding a theory of 'situation' for this raises crucial questions about the compatibility of particular theories.
>
> (Lave 1993: 7)

As we will show in the following section, SLT is in several ways incompatible with TCT.

TCT

We first outline the main characteristics of TCT as SLT portrays it and then contrast the main features of SLT. We note that whenever one characterises a theory one does so from a vantage point; in this case we view TCT from the standpoint of SLT and doubtless focus on aspects of TCT which the latter does not recognise in itself as well as some which it does:

1   TCT sees learning as a process that takes place inside the head or mind. It has a 'mentalistic' conception of learning consistent with the longstanding mind–body duality of Euro-American culture.
2   TCT sees learning as an individual's problem, with which professional educators, learning theorists, psychologists, therapists and education

researchers all assist. It regards the individual as morally responsible for his or her own learning achievements.

3   TCT assumes that most culturally significant learning takes place within the formal education system ('schooling' of various kinds: from kindergarten to graduate school). It is within the institutions of formal education that the professionals mentioned above provide their help and assistance. Such institutions and professional practices are functionally designed in the light of the best research and within budgetary considerations to optimise the conditions in which individuals may learn and be helped to learn.

4   Much of the research done under the auspices of TCT has been oriented to improving professional practices in formal educational settings. Sometimes TCT has included the social-psychology of learners, as in the tradition of Vygotsky (see Wertsch 1985, 1991 for good discussions; and see Blackler 1992, 1993 for useful applications of activity theory to management and organisation studies). But although TCT allows the social dimension a role through activity theory, its focus remains *within* the formal education system and, regardless of the sociological theories, treats learning as an individual accomplishment.

5   TCT problematises the learning process, which it sees primarily as a *process of acquisition*, within formal education contexts. Consistent with TCT's mentalism, learning is regarded as a process of internalisation in which learners memorise, understand and are able to reproduce on demand the contents of the syllabus which they have been taught. This is also consistent with 'the banking system of education' originally critiqued by Freire (1968) and more recently and succinctly characterised by bell hooks as being 'based on the assumption that memorising information and regurgitating it represented gaining knowledge that could be deposited, stored and used at a later date' (1994: 5).

The metaphor of acquisition, internalisation, storage and retrieval reinforces TCT's institutionalisation of a discrete boundary between the inside and the outside of the individual learning mind.

6   The metaphor of mind as mental container of knowledge also *presumes* an ontology of knowledge which is seldom articulated by TCT. It sees knowledge as freestanding, decontextualised stuff which the learner simply has to acquire or appropriate. Knowledge is taken to be unproblematically and appropriately preclassified by the existing academic disciplines, taxonomies and library classifications. In these forms it constitutes the bodies of knowledge which learners should consume, internalise and inwardly digest. There are three further features of TCT that are enmeshed with this presumption about freestanding knowledge which are also seldom discussed within TCT itself but which SLT turns into significant critical issues, as follows:

7   By problematising the individual learning process within formal education, TCT takes for granted a particular view of knowledge, i.e. that it is 'professionally produced' stuff. This entails the assumption that 'knowledge' is subject to appropriate quality-control procedures by the research communi-

ties which produce it and the teaching communities which distribute, disseminate and transmit it. It further assumes that there is a discrete difference between professionally produced and lay knowledge. The former is scientific, disciplined, theoretical, systematic and general; the latter is commonsensical but limited, undisciplined, based in narrow experience, anecdotal and ad hoc – 'particular' rather than 'general', contextual not transcendent of this or that local context.

8   TCT itself is one category of professionally produced knowledge; it shares with all the other research communities a professional status and it occupies a strategically significant site within the entire educational system, for it legitimises the professional structures and practices of the teachers who seek to fulfil the learning needs of their students.

9   Educational research and theory applies TCT along with most university disciplines. As the study of teaching, educational research is often dismissed by other disciplines because teaching is seen as of secondary importance, the primary business of the academic community being the production of new knowledge. Teaching is seen as a derivative or supplementary activity. In her recent book on teaching, hooks notes that her

> [p]ublic seemed particularly surprised when I said that I was working on a collection of essays about teaching. This surprise is a sad reminder of the way teaching is seen as a duller, less valuable aspect of the academic profession.
>
> (hooks 1994: 12)

Radical pedagogues such as hooks (and Giroux 1983; Freire 1968) spiritedly seek to reinvigorate 'the classroom excitement about ideas and the will to learn' with the concept of 'learning community', for example (hooks 1994). However, perhaps for reasons of vested interest, TCT does not doubt or question the received wisdom that there is an insurmountable gulf between professional and lay knowledge which teaching as a whole reinforces. It has been left to SLT and the sociology of scientific knowledge to critique the knowledge-production process of specific communities of practice, as we shall see in the next section.

It is the last four points to which TCT may be most blind, but they are entailed in the first five points. We now characterise SLT, point by point, contrasting its position or viewpoint with the nine points above.

SLT

1   SLT seeks to overcome the mind–body dichotomy and attempts 'to construct a theory that *encompasses* mind and lived-in-world, treating relations among person, activity, and situation, as they are *given* in social practice, itself viewed as a "single encompassing theoretical entity"' (Lave 1993: 7). Unlike 'mentalism', it sees mental phenomena as occurring socially

in relation to a social and material situation. The 'social' here is not reduced to interactions between independent individual minds; nor is it separate from its material context.

2   Accordingly SLT does not see learning as an individual's problem, but sees phenomena like 'failure to learn', as it occurs within formal education systems, as a product of such systems and the social practices of its educational professionals. The educational system assigns individuals to categories which become 'socially arranged' identities for people (Lave 1993: 16). For example, Mehan (1993) gives a detailed account of how individuals are provided with an identity by virtue of 'possessing' a learning disability. For SLT, TCT in educational practice operates with unquestioned assumptions about 'consensus' of interests, ignoring the possibility that social conflict may be inherent in learning. For SLT the meaning of error or failure can depend upon 'whose socially positioned point of view is adopted' and upon 'historically and socially situated conceptions of erroneous action and belief' (Lave 1993: 16). SLT sees the moral responsibility of the learners for their own learning as an expression of TCT's presumed individualism, institutionalised by formal education.

3   SLT does not assume that formal educational contexts are necessarily the site of the most culturally significant learning processes. SLT directs the research attention of learning theorists away from the sites of formal education towards everyday settings, in particular to 'communities of practice' based upon formal or informal apprenticeship practices (Lave and Wenger 1991; cf. Orr 1990; Latour 1987; Suchman 1987; Lave 1988).

4   SLT's research is not necessarily directed towards improving the practice of educationalists, trainers and developers, therapists, etc., since it is not necessarily directed at the formal institutional sites of learning which they occupy and where they practice their professional interventions and build up their repertoires.

5   SLT does not problematise the learning process as a process of mental acquisition. It does not see 'mind' as a container waiting to be filled up, but sees mind-in-action in the everyday world, creating knowledge and learning simultaneously in interaction with the social and material aspects of the lived-in-world. The products of learning are as likely to be 'contained' in artefacts, writing and other material traces of action in the world as in individual memories. This is in stark contrast to the banking model of education, summarised by hooks (1994) above.

6   Relatedly, SLT does not regard knowledge as decontextualised, freestanding, ahistorical, asocial, apolitical, objective, disinterested stuff standing ready to be acquired by individual minds within the distributive formal education system. Instead SLT sees the learning process as a generative process of knowledge production which is *indissociable* from a situated, contextual, social engagement with the material lived-in-world.

7   Accordingly, SLT questions the widespread presumption in Euro-American culture that professionally produced knowledge is necessarily of superior

quality to lay knowledge and that there is always a discrete boundary between the two. Rather, SLT sees professionally produced knowledge to be rooted in socially, materially situated contexts just as much as lay knowledge. This does not devalue scientific knowledge but it does remove the discrete boundary between it and everyday knowledge. For SLT, professionally produced knowledge never *reaches* the objective, decontextual general law-like status which TCT, along with many scientific disciplines, claims for it, but remains a temporary, provisional, attached and contingent accomplishment. This is not to deny the possibility of replicating experimental results, but it is to place the emphasis upon the necessary engagement with different contexts which is involved in such a 'dissemination' of ideas. For SLT, there is no impermeable boundary between contextual and decontextual knowledge; 'abstractions' exist only in concrete formulations, not in 'ideal form'.

8   SLT is, like TCT, a species of professionally produced knowledge, but with a difference. SLT does not attempt to legitimate the structures and practices of professionalised teachers and their 'ministry' to students and the educated public at large (see Fox 1992 for a discussion of the pastoral power of the professional). Rather, SLT questions the relations among institutionalised research, teaching, education and learning, and questions their 'legitimacy'. This has the potential to unravel the legitimate role and function which these professions occupy within society, but it also has the potential to unravel the legitimacy with which these professions provide that society. Thus SLT offers a critique of the political-economy of education, research and learning.

9   SLT is not necessarily applicable, although it is *teachable*, within educational research. However, SLT's emphasis on learning as an everyday social practice indissociable from other practices raises questions over the value of teaching decontextualised knowledge as if it were freestanding stuff within the sequestered spaces of the formal education system. This does not imply that SLT would recommend the closure of all schools, but that the relations between the theory and practice of learning should, if anything, be reworked. As Lave remarks,

> Conventional theories of learning and schooling appeal to the decontextualized character of some knowledge and forms of knowledge transmission, whereas in the theory of situated activity 'decontextualized learning activity' is a contradiction in terms.
>
> (Lave 1993: 6)

For SLT, theory is always a situated, practical accomplishment, rather than a transcendental account of reality decontextualised from the social and material practice which produced it. In the traditional 'opposition' between theory and practice, practice is regarded as the more encompassing term.

In the next section we discuss TCT and SLT in the light of the debate on modernism and postmodernism. The question of interpretation (and representation) is pivotal to the difference between modernism and postmodernism. Interpretation is also central to the difference between SLT and TCT: for the former it is a social process dependent upon a community of practice, whereas for TCT it is an individual process. For SLT interpretations are always context-bound, while for TCT interpretations can be abstracted.

Modernism–postmodernism

This section does not try to be an overview of modernism and postmodernism; it simply homes in on those aspects of that debate which are relevant to the difference between SLT and TCT. Suffice to say that I do not here buy into the idea that postmodernism is a period of history which follows modernism, or that modernism has died. Rather, I draw on Lyotard's conception that postmodernism is modernism in its nascent state and that what characterises that state is 'experimentation' in all fields, from the arts to the sciences (1984: 79). I also accept Lyotard's point that scientific knowledge is, largely, a modernist variety of knowledge, not so much in the sense that scientific method marks any great difference from other practical methods of knowledge production, past and present, but in the sense that, for modernism, *it is hoped that* the knowledge produced by scientific methods cumulatively adds up to something universally true or at least consistent. Scientific knowledge is modernist to the extent that it labours to represent or exactly correspond to the 'real world', as it presumes that world looks like, from a unified transcendent, or objective, viewpoint.

Where postmodernism does mark a break with modernism is regarding the metanarratives of legitimation (knowledge for knowledge's sake, emancipation's sake, etc.) that sustain modernism. For Lyotard, these metanarratives were eroded in the course of the 20th century. If postmodernism marks a rupture with modernism it is with the ideology or metanarrative behind the practice of experimentation, not the practice of experimentation itself. In this light, the present section will argue that TCT can be read as a thoroughly modernist approach and that SLT can be read more equivocally. SLT does not claim to be either modernist or postmodernist. The main point of introducing the modernist–postmodernist debate is in order to critique SLT in regard to a specific ambiguity in its treatment of the idea of contextual knowledge, which reflection on the modernist–postmodernist debate highlights.

Modernism regards the social and material context as the natural environment or container from which knowledge can be abstracted or extracted; such knowledge is the pearl in the oyster. The oyster itself, its position on the seabed and the difficult work of its discovery are like so many impurities or irrelevancies surrounding the pearl. As Jeffcutt puts it, for modernism

> the essential truth of the world is understood as underlying and hidden, the essential focus of modernism becomes, the revelation of that truth through rational processes of uncovering (interpretation). Here a complex surface that appears incoherent, contradictory and unstable (the symbolic world) is

able to be understood, ordered and co-ordinated (rationalised) at theoretically submerged levels of unity ('reality').

(Jeffcutt 1994: 236)

The 'complex surface' is the context; the underlying and hidden truth, unity and 'reality' are abstract knowledge revealed, by a process of *rational* interpretation, and decontextualised. Such pearls of knowledge once removed can be commodified as propositional or denotative knowledge which claims to correspond to an aspect of the underlying real world. For TCT, knowledge is a decontextualised entity: it circulates as a nugget of truth in a distribution system of facts and theories – the banking system of knowledge. TCT has a view of 'knowledge as a collection of real entities, located in heads, and of learning as a process of internalizing them' (Lave 1993: 12). In this system, abstract knowledge has value because it is taken accurately to represent a part of the hidden, underlying unity of the world. In this view the interpretation process is ultimately impersonal, detached, asocial, ahistorical and apolitical. Although particular scientists or researchers are credited with 'discovery' or 'invention' at particular times and places (as the citations of every academic paper testify and as is documented by the history of science), the findings or results themselves are held to be generalisable – that is, true beyond the local site of production or discovery.

A major feature of abstract denotative knowledge is that it has been shorn of its original context and recontextualised within the banking system of knowledge for ease of retrieval. Comparable to retailing, the abstract knowledge, like any retailed commodity, is now 'merchandised' by the education system, which packages it as part of a course or module and gives it a particular place on the syllabus, just like goods on a supermarket shelf. Some goods are placed at eye level to catch the shopper's eye. Others are placed at hand level for ease of picking up. Other products are placed in less advantageous positions. The retailer decides how to position the product in relation to all the other goods on display, not in relation to the original site from whence the goods came. The knowledge, packaged in reading lists and lecture materials, is positioned in either a first-year or second-year course, or maybe given a special place in the first-year taught element of a doctoral programme, according to the 'retailing' decisions of the academic staff.

There is a difference between kinds of knowledge, however, which is broadly encapsulated in the division between the arts and sciences. Foucault distinguished between 'interpretations of things' and 'interpretations of interpretations':

Language contains its own inner principle of proliferation. There is more work in interpreting interpretations than in interpreting things; and more books about books than on any other subject. 'We do nothing but write glosses on one another.'

(Foucault 1970: 40)

However, one feature of postmodernist thinking is that the boundary between the interpretation of things and of interpretation itself is permeable. For example, Ilya Prigogine notes that 'science is a cultural phenomenon, formed in a cultural context' (1989: 397), and that

> science today introduces a narrative element. The former dichotomy between the social sciences, based on a narrative element and the pure sciences, based on the laws of nature, is breaking down.
>
> (Prigogine 1989: 400)

Modernist science seeks to synthesise all the propositions from all the fields into one complete picture of the world (the laws of nature) which truly represents the presumed unified underlying nature of the world. It presumes that the (imagined) transcendent eye of an objective (omniscient) observer would see the world as it really is. Each study, descriptive, explanatory and predictive, seeks to simulate that viewpoint while minimising contradictions with all other studies, working within the constraints of imperfect information and limited practical understandings. In this sense, science continues to subscribe to what Lyotard calls the 'speculative' metanarrative of science (1979: 33). It justifies its experimental practice in the name of a horizon which is never reached, the myth of which nonetheless warrants the search for a set of propositions which agree with each other in total consensus and which also truly represent the real world. TCT is a theory of learning which complements that modernist quest for consensus amongst theories. It suggests that decontextualised facts, and theories about facts, which circulate in the knowledge-distribution system which is 'education', in all its diverse institutions, are capable of being mentally internalised and thus synthesised in one unity. Although modernism long ago lost the ideal of *Homo universale*, the all-round general intellectual who could internalise the sum total of contemporary knowledge (Fox 1989a), its apologists still harbour the hope that the university institution, run as a democracy of the disciplines, can still accomplish the grand synthesis (Habermas 1988). Given that the individual mind can never grasp the totality of all knowable facts, the functioning of the knowledge-distribution system is institutionally crucial to the modernist project of combining all the abstractions in the right way, not just arbitrarily. Thus, TCT studies the learning process within the contexts of 'schooling', where the world's vast knowledge reserves are being recontextualised and recombined within curricula, degrees and disciplines. Its conception of this activity is that it is working toward's an overarching theoretical synthesis.

In contrast, SLT draws our attention away from the classrooms and formally schooled settings, suggesting that our understanding of learning as an everyday phenomenon is severely limited if we disregard learning taking place in situated practice. In common with postmodernism, it doubts that modernist teaching practice will ever construct a perfect abstract map of the real world. It sees knowledge arising indissociably within social and material contexts. SLT presents itself as a theory of learning arising from the comparable study of diverse anthropological case studies (Lave and Wenger 1991). Therefore, it is itself a form of decontextualised knowledge, abstracted from a range of specific contexts by the craft methods of ethnography – from fieldwork to storytelling. But when we look at the ways SLT treats 'context' we find it varies depending on the theoretical perspective of the ethnographer supplying the case study. In itself, the mere fact of theoretical dispute about the nature of social and material context does not hold the project of SLT back; rather, it provides many useful lines of research. But for those who wish to pursue the research SLT advocates, in the field of management learning for instance, the alternative theorisations of social and material context need to be addressed.

SLT offers one view of context which is very close to modernism, namely that *context is pre-given* and harbours 'historically emerging contradictions that characterise all concrete social institutions and relations' (Lave 1993: 17–18). Unlike some Marxist ideas, this first view of pre-given context, when SLT draws on *activity theory*, emphasises the 'non-determinate character of the effects of objective social structures' (Lave 1993: 18). However, it does see social differences and the related possibilities for action as 'real', restricting some people more than others, determining who can legitimately find or produce knowledge in the contemporary society. Activity theory sees that

> *differences in the social location of actors are inherent in political economic structures*, and elaborated in specific sociocultural practices. Differences of power, interests and possibilities for action are ubiquitous. Any particular action is socially constituted, given meaning by its location in societally, historically, generated systems of activity. Meaning is not constituted through individual intentions; it is mutually constituted in relations between activity systems and persons acting, and has a relational character.
>
> (Lave 1993: 18)

This view of context emphasises that knowledge, as a form of meaning, arises from interactions and relations between socio-culturally differentiated persons and their activities within a material situation. It does not prevent the decontextualisation of knowledge, but it does point to all kinds of situations in which meaning and knowledge are constituted which are not recognised by existing professional (disciplinary) producers of knowledge, and it looks outside formal education for these situations. This is a view of context which is perhaps consistent with critical theory (cf. Habermas 1988; Outhwaite 1994).

SLT's second view of context is derived from the phenomenological perspective. Rather than regarding context as *pre-given*, it regards context as *emergent*. That is, situations create their own context:

> Situations are constructed as people organize themselves to attend to and give meaning to figural concerns against the ground of ongoing social inter-

action. Silence, erasure, and the construction of boundaries, and collusion constitutive here.

(Lave 1993: 19)

Context is less a social category or identity in which people are positioned and more 'an order of behaviour of which one is a part' (Lave 1993: 19). In this sense, 'activity is its own context' (Lave 1993: 17); moment-by-moment interaction changes the context, again indeterminately from the outset, and meaning or knowledge arises in the process. This view of context sees all 'entities' of knowledge as provisional and highly locally dependent on the interpretations made by the specific personnel on hand in specific situations in the course of emergent action. It is this more phenomenological perspective on context which most challenges TCT's conception of freestanding decontextualised knowledge which can be readily abstracted. The phenomenological variant of SLT is more consistent with some accounts of ethnomethodology and conversation analysis where decontextualisation by abstraction is criticised, as Lee makes plain:

> If the data of sociology, for example, the speech acts of respondents in an interview situation, is always the product of a practical methodology and is always dependent upon its specific context for its sense, then how could it *ever* be decontextualized or translated into the context of sociological research without the destruction of natural significances.

(Lee 1987: 24)

SLT seems inconsistently to work with a model of context as both *pre-given* and *emergent*. The first model raises questions of a critical, political and moral nature, an agenda it shares with critical theory. But the second model raises questions concerning the nature of abstract general knowledge *per se* and the very possibility of practically decontextualising it, an agenda it shares with ethnomethodology and conversation analysis (see Lee 1987, cited above).

Whereas TCT is clearly a body of modernist theory, SLT is ambiguous. The ambiguity in SLT concerns the two conceptions of context, pre-given and emergent, discussed above. When SLT treats context as pre-given, it adopts a realist theoretical position; when it treats context as emergent, it adopts an interpretative analysis more commensurate with ethnomethodology. In both cases, SLT places *more* analytical emphasis on the social context of learning than TCT. A consequence of this is that research attention is focused on knowledge production in communities of practice *in situ* rather than the transfer of knowledge in educational settings. For that reason, in order to examine SLT it is instructive to draw upon the sociology of science literature, which supplies a further set of case studies describing how scientific knowledge itself is produced socially. Such studies make the postmodern insight clear: that the modernist concern with the interpretation of things is already embedded in a wider cultural narrative concerning the interpretation of interpretation.

Postmodernism prioritises the interpretation of interpretation, less as an act of revolution and more as a reframing of modernism (Fox 1996). Interpretation itself is seen as a textually mediated process, even a textually dependent process, rather than a mental operation. Jeffcutt cites Derrida's phrase, 'There is nothing beyond or outside of the text', and concludes:

> Consequently, the hierarchies formed by modernism's articulation of the material–textual interrelationship become overturned and imploded by postmodern textuality...by asserting that no text can exist as a self-sufficient whole, or function as a closed system.
>
> (Jeffcutt 1994: 23)

To illustrate this we can look at the scene of scientific knowledge production exemplified by the laboratory (but similarly the questionnaire survey, the ethnography). Here the researcher encounters 'the real' in a methodical manner and exits the scene with an account (descriptive/explanatory/predictive).

For Jeffcutt, discussing organisational research:

> Organisational interpretation has typically been practised as a skill of translation, whereby textual data (a rich plethora of organisational, verbal and non-verbal symbolism, such as artefacts, stories, etc.) has been extracted from a particular setting, disaggregated, re-categorised and recombined in the construction of a 'meaningful account' of that setting.
>
> (Jeffcutt 1994: 235)

While this process may be characteristic of social, cultural and organisational research, it is less often seen as characteristic of natural science because laboratory work is not regarded as dealing with 'texts'; yet, as Lynch and Woolgar describe:

> Manifestly, what scientists laboriously piece together, pick up in their hands, measure, show to one another, argue about, and circulate to others in their communities are not 'natural objects' independent of cultural processes and literary forms. They are extracts, 'tissue cultures' and residues impressed within graphic matrices ordered, shaped, and filtered samples; carefully aligned photographic traces and chart recordings; and verbal accounts...they are more than simply representations of natural order.
>
> (Lynch and Woolgar 1990: 5)

Matter is not confronted directly but through 'graphic matrices', 'filtered samples', 'photographic traces' and such like. Even before the selection of 'material', these materials have already been 'textualised'; they have been classified by earlier generations of researchers. Farber (1982), for instance, describes the 18th-century naturalist Brisson, who developed a taxonomy of birds by creating a meticulous museum of stuffed specimens filed away in museum drawers. Star and Griesemer (1989) discuss a similar process of classification with respect to 'vertebrate zoology'. Latour (1988) provides a similar account of the classification underpinning microbiology, and Rudwick (1985) examines the classification underpinning geology. All of these examples are cited by Lynch and Bogen, who comment that

> The natural science that developed was inseparable from the organised methods for collecting, preserving, circulating and arranging specimens, along with the literary conventions for composing and juxtaposing pictures and descriptions.
>
> (Lynch and Bogen 1994: 87)

All of these examples illustrate the *textuality* of science's matter. It is the textured scientific account which *constructs* the 'real' rather than *finds* the real. Instead of an 'extraction' process we find a textual translation which constructs the 'real'. Latour and Woolgar argue that it is not simply that facts are socially constructed but that the 'craft' basis of scientific production is forgotten or repressed: 'The process of construction involves the use of certain devices whereby all traces of production are made extremely difficult to detect' (1979: 250). As Cooper and Fox discuss, two steps are responsible for this mental sleight-of-hand:

1   the splitting of the statement – the statement is a set of words (text) which represents a statement about an object;
2   on the other hand, the statement corresponds to the object in itself, which takes on a life of its own – 'It is as if the original statement had projected a virtual image of itself which exists outside the statement'.

(Cooper and Fox 1989: 250)

Material reality is never encountered except inside a set of words, text and numerous other traces. It is not that the (secondary) interpretation of interpretation is prioritised over the (primary) interpretation of things; it is that the latter are textually produced through the invisible (tacit) practical skilled craftwork of the researchers.

For postmodernism the depth–surface model of the world is seen as an effect of textuality: 'All we have is textuality' (Jeffcutt 1994: 238). As Cooper and Fox put it, 'the key to understanding texture is the idea of "connectedness-in-action"' (1990: 576). Pepper describes the structure of texture thus:

> As we analyse a texture, we move down into a structure of strands and at the same time sheer out into its context. A bottom is thus never reached. For the support of every texture lies in its context.
>
> (Pepper, cited by Cooper and Fox 1990: 576)

In the postmodern view, 'context' is no longer 'out there' in the messy, complex surface of an objective world; rather, that very surface complexity and confusion is a projection of language itself, the inconsistencies of its classifications, taxonomies, dichotomies and more. Modernist science hides or represses the socially skilled craftwork producing the 'real' with textual materials and accounts. SLT's valorisation of emergent context is consistent with postmodern understandings of textuality, especially in the material and social context of scientific communities of practice, where practitioners work textually to fabricate the 'real world'.

SLT has an uneasy relationship with postmodernism; as Chaiklin says of contributions to SLT, 'One does not find any explicit appeal to postmodern themes as the central motivation' (1993: 384). SLT's two versions of context, however, suggest different relations with postmodern ideas. The view of social context as pre-given is basically modernist and realist, while the view of social context as emergent in social action is commensurate with postmodernism. The former emphasises the interpretations of things, whereas the latter emphasises the interpretation of interpretations.

To summarise this section, we might say that in modernism context is 'out there' in the real world, whereas for postmodernism context is always 'in here' within the cultural map of that world. Different versions of SLT can accommodate the differences between modernism and postmodernism. However, by its focus on context and its problematisation of decontextualised knowledge, SLT comes closer to a postmodern recognition of textuality and texture than to sustaining the depth–surface model of the world basic to modernism.

Conclusion

The study of management learning faces the same theoretical and methodological disputes as SLT, since it is also concerned to study learning in situated practical action. Our discussion of SLT highlights some of the failings of TCT and conventional education. It is worth noting that 'experiential' approaches to management education involve reflection upon experience, rather than the internalisation of abstract knowledge. Such work, like the skills training involved in workplace management development, works with the nature of practice. The critique SLT levels at TCT does not automatically apply in such cases, but further work is needed which examines skilled interventions into ongoing management practices and designs for learning in light of the insights that SLT provides into situated communities of practice. Wenger (1998) offers some suggestions in this regard. However, the deeper problems concerning how any social research should account for action-in-context, exposed in this chapter, await further developments in the sociology of science, which could benefit from SLT. The disputes between ethnomethodology and more voluntaristic versions of social constructionism, and between postmodern and modern legitimations of science, are perhaps most suggestive of the more fruitful lines of enquiry.

Notes

1   This is a modified version of a paper which previously appeared in *Systems Practice* 10(6): 727–47.

References

Agouistinos, M. and Walker, I. (1995) *Social cognition: An Integrated Introduction.* Sage Publications, London.

Berger, P. and Luckmann, T. (1966) *The Social Construction of Reality*, Harmondsworth Penguin.

Blackler, F. (1992) 'Formative contexts and activity systems: postmodern approaches to the management of change', in M. Reed and M. Hughes (eds) *Rethinking Organization: New Directions in Organization Theory and Analysis*, London: Sage.

—— (1993) 'Knowledge and the theory of organizations: organizations as activity systems and the reframing of management', *Journal of Management Studies* 30(6): 863–84.

Blumer, H. (1969) *Symbolic Interactionism: Perspective and Method*, Berkeley, CA: University of California Press.

Boot, R. and Reynolds, M. (1983) *Learning and Experience in Formal Education*, Manchester: Manchester Monographs.

Bougon, M.G. (1992) 'Congregate cognitive maps: a unified dynamic theory of organization and strategy', *Journal of Management Studies* 29(3): 367–89.

Brewis, J. (1996) 'The "making" of the "competent" manager: competency development, personal effectiveness and Foucault', *Management Learning* 27(1): 65–86.

Burgoyne, J.G. (1973) 'An action research experiment in the evaluation of a management development course'. *Journal of Management Studies,* **10**(1), 8-14

Burgoyne, J.G. and Cooper, C.I. (1976) 'Research on teaching methods in management education: bibliographical examination of the state of the art', *Management International Review* 16(4): 95–102.

Burgoyne, J.G. and Hodgson, V.E. (1983) 'Natural learning and managerial action: a phenomenological study in the field setting', *Journal of Management Studies* 20(3): 387–99.

—— (1984) 'An experimental approach to understanding managerial action', in J.G. Hunt, D.M. Rosking, C.A. Schriesheim and R. Stewart (eds) *Leaders and Managers: International Perspectives on Managerial Behaviour and Leadership*, New York: Pergamon Press.

Burgoyne, J.G. and Stuart, R. (1977) 'Implicit learning theories as determinants of the effect of management development programmes', *Personnel Review* 6(2): 5–14.

Chaiklin, S. (1993) 'Understanding the social scientific practice of understanding practice'. In Chaiklin, S., and Lave, J. (eds.) (1993). *Understanding Practice: Perspectives on Activity and Context,* Cambridge University Press, Cambridge.

Chaiklin, S. and Lave, J. (eds) (1993) *Understanding Practice: Perspectives on Activity and Context*, Cambridge: Cambridge University Press.

Cooper, R. and Fox, S. (1989) 'Two modes of organization', in R. Mansfield (ed.) *Frontiers of Management: Research and Practice*, London: Routledge.

—— (1990) 'The texture of organizing', *Journal of Management Studies* 27(6): 575–82.

Daft, R.L. and Weick, K.E. (1984) 'Toward a model of organizations as interpretation systems', *Academy of Management Review* 9(2): 284–95.

Davies, J. and Easterby-Smith, M. (1984) 'Learning and developing from managerial work experiences', *Journal of Management Studies* 21(2): 169–83.

Delamont, S. (1976). *Interaction in the Classroom*. Methuen, London

Farber, P. (1982) *The Emergence of Ornithology as a Scientific Discipline: 1760–1850*, Dortrecht: D. Reidel.

Foucault, M. (1970) *The Order of Things*, London: Routledge.

Fox, S. (1987) 'Self-knowledge and personal change: the reported experience of managers in part-time management education', unpublished Ph.D. thesis, University of Manchester.

—— (1989a) 'The panopticon: from Bentham's obsession to the revolution in management learning', *Human Relations* 42(8): 717–39.

—— (1989b) 'The production and distribution of knowledge through open and distance learning', *Education Training & Technology International* 26(3): 269–80.

—— (1990a) 'The ethnography of humour and the problem of social reality', *Sociology* 24(3): 431–46.

—— (1990b) 'Becoming an ethnomethodology user: learning a perspective in the field', in R.G. Burgess (ed.) *Studies in Qualitative Methodology, Vol. 2: Reflections on Field Experience*, Greenwich, CT: JAI Press.

—— (1992) 'What are we? The constitution of management in higher education and human resource management' *International Studies of Management & Organization* 22(3): 71–93.

—— (1994a) 'Debating management learning: I', *Management Learning* 25(1): 83–93.

—— (1994b) 'Debating management learning: II', *Management Learning* 25(4): 579–97.

—— (1996) 'Viral writing: deconstruction, disorganization and ethnomethodology', *Scandinavian Journal of Management* 12(1): 89–108.

Fox, S. (1997) 'From management education and development to study of management learning'. In Burgoyne, J. and Reynolds, M. (eds.) (1997) *Management Learning: Integrating Perspectives in Theory and Practice*. Sage, London

Freire, P. (1968) *Pedagogy of the Oppressed*, New York: Seabury Press.

Giroux, H. (1983) *Theory and Resistance in Education: A Pedagogy for the Opposition*, London: Heinemann.

Grey, C. (1994) 'Career as a project of the self and labour process discipline', *Sociology* 28(2): 427–72.

Habermas, J. (1988) *The Theory of Communicative Action: Reason and the Rationalization of Society*, vol. 1, Cambridge, MA: Polity Press.

Habermas, J. (1989) *The New Conservatism*. Polity Press, Cambridge

Hambrick, D.C. and Mason, P.A. (1984) 'Upper echelons: the organization as a reflection of its top managers', *Academy of Management Review* 9(2): 193–206.

hooks, b. (1994) *Teaching to Transgress: Education as the Practice of Freedom*, New York: Routledge.

Jeffcutt, P. (1994) 'The interpretation of organization: a contemporary analysis and critique', *Journal of Management Studies* 31(2): 225–50.

Langfield-Smith, K. (1992) 'Exploring the need for a shared cognitive map', *Journal of Management Studies* 29(3): 349–68.

Latour, B. (1987) *Science in Action: How to Follow Scientists and Engineers Through Society*, Harvard University Press. Cambridge, MA:

—— (1988) *The Pasteurization of France*, Cambridge, MA: Harvard University Press.

Latour, B. and Woolgar, S. (1979) *Laboratory Life: The Social Construction of Scientific Facts*, London: Sage.

Lave, J. (1988) *Cognition in Practice: Mind Mathematics, and Culture in Everyday Life*, Cambridge: Cambridge University Press.

—— (1993) 'The practice of learning', in S. Chaikim and J. Lave (eds) *Understanding Practice: Perspectives on Activity and Context*, Cambridge: Cambridge University Press.

Lave, J. and Wenger, E. (1991) *Situated Learning: Legitimate Peripheral Participation*, Cambridge: Cambridge University Press.

Lee, J.R.E. (1987) 'Prologue: talking organisation', in G. Button and J.R.E. Lee (eds) *Talk and Social Interaction*, Clevedon, Avon: Multilingual Matters.

Lyles, M.A. and Schwenk, C.R. (1992) 'Top management, strategy and organizational knowledge structures', *Journal of Management Studies* 29(2): 155–74.

Lynch, M. and Bogen, D. (1994) 'Harvey Sack's primitive natural science', *Theory, Culture and Society* 11: 65–104.

Lynch, M. and Woolgar, S. (1990) 'Introduction: sociological orientations to representational practice in science', in M. Lynch and S. Woolgar (eds) *Representation in Scientific Practice*, Cambridge, MA: MIT Press.

Lyotard, J.F. (1984). *The Postmodern Condition: A Report on Knowledge*, trans. G. Bennington and B. Massumi, Manchester: Manchester University Press.

Mehan, H. (1993) '(Beneath the skin and between the ears: a case study in the politics of representation'. In Chaiklin, S., and Lave, J. (eds.) (1993). *Understanding Practice: Perspectives on Activity and Context*, Cambridge Universtity Press, Cambridge.

Orr, J. (1990) 'Sharing knowledge, celebrating identity: community memory in a service culture', in D.S. Middleton and D. Edwards (eds) *Collective Remembering: Memory in Society*, Beverley Hills, CA: Sage.

Outhwaite, W. (1994) *Habermas: A Critical Introduction*, Cambridge, MA: Polity Press.

Prigogine, I. (1989) 'The philosophy of instability', *Futures*, August: 396–400.

Resnick, L.B., Levine, J.M. and Teasley, S.D. (eds) (1991) *Perspectives on Socially Shared Cognition*, Washington, DC: American Psychological Association.

Rudwick, M. (1985) *The Great Devonian Controversy: The Shaping of Scientific Knowledge Among Gentlemanly Specialists*, Chicago: University of Chicago Press.

Schwenk, C.R. (1986) 'Information, cognitive biases, and commitment to a course of action', *Acad. Manage. Rev.* 11(2): 298–310.

—— (1988) 'The cognitive perspective on strategic decision making', *Journal of Management Studies* 25(1): 41–55.

—— (1989) 'Linking cognitive, organizational and political factors in explaining strategic change', *Journal of Management Studies* 26(2): 177–87.

Shapin, S. and Schaffer, S. (1985) *Leviathan and the Air-Pump: Hobbes, Boyle, and the Experimental Life*, Princeton, NJ: Princeton University.

Star, S.L. and Griesemer, J. (1989) ' "Translations" and boundary objects: amateurs and professionals in Berkeley's Museum of Vertebrate Zoology, 1907–39', *Social Studies in Science* 19: 387–420.

Suchman, L. (1987) *Plans and Situated Actions*, Cambridge: Cambridge University Press.

Tanton, M. and Fox, S. (1987) 'The evaluation of management education and development: participant satisfaction and ethnographic methodology', *Personnel Rev.* 16(4): 33–40.

Watson, T.J. (1994). *In Search of Management: Culture, Chaos and Control in Managerial Work*, London: Routledge.

—— (1991) 'A sociocultural approach to socially shared cognition', in L.B. Resnick, J.M. Levine and S.D. Teasley (eds) *Perspectives on Socially Shared Cognition*, Washington, DC: American Psychological Association.

Wenger, E. (1998) Communities of Practice: Learning, Meaning and Identity. Cambridge University Press, Cambridge.

Wertsch, J. (ed.) (1985) *Culture, Communication, and Cognition: Vygotsyian Perspectives*, New York: Cambridge University Press.

Woods, P. and Hammersley, M. (eds.) (1977) *School Experience*. Croom Helm, London

Woods, P. (eds.) (1980a) *Pupil Strategies*. Croom Helm, London

Woods, P. (eds.) (1980b) *Teacher Strategies*. Croom Helm, London.

Woods, P. (eds.) (1983) *Sociology and the School: An Internactionist Perspective*. Routledge & Keegan Paul, London.

7 Making learning critical

Identity, emotion and power in processes of management development[1]

Hugh Willmott

> Management development is largely done to managers rather than done by them, socializing them into the existing norms, practices and values, and treating them very much as 'patients' rather than 'agents'.
>
> (Pedler 1998, cited in McLaughlin and Thorpe 1993: 21)

Introduction

Established approaches to management education have tended to treat students and practitioners as comparatively passive receptacles into which knowledge – of theory, techniques and values – is poured. Action learning, in contrast, is founded upon the view that effective management development and practice relies not only, or even primarily, upon the possession of a body of knowledge. More fundamentally, it relies upon the personal problem-solving capacities of embodied individuals. In action learning, learning processes are more directly connected to personal experience.[2]

In this chapter I explore some affinities as well as divergences between action learning and critical pedagogies (e.g. Freire 1972), each of which espouses a shift to a model of learning in which 'the teacher is no longer merely the-one-who-teaches, but who is himself [*sic*] taught in dialogue with the students' (Freire 1972: 53). They are each critical of the established approach to education, in which there is an emphasis upon the memorizing and regurgitation of seemingly factual bodies of knowledge, abstracted from the concerns and struggles of individual students or practitioners. Where they differ is in the value placed upon 'theory'. Action learning equates 'theory' with the accumulation of programmed knowledge (Willmott 1994a, 1997a). The contribution of 'theory' is effectively marginalised on the grounds that it is the stuff of educational methods dedicated to the accumulation of programmed knowledge abstracted from personal experience, 'practice'. Action learning is a priori unreceptive to the possibility that 'critical thinking'[3] might be applied to analyse and address problems thrown up in the action learning process. What this blanket devaluation of theory ignores is the variety of (critical) social theory – from Marx to Foucault and Derrida – that directly challenges and subverts the idea of theory as something which purports to stand outside or above the social relations that it seeks to understand and change. Action learning's antagonism to 'theory', based upon its persuasive critique of traditional educational methods, inhibits an appreciation of its affinities with other, critical, pedagogies that, in common with action learning, advocate a different, practically engaged kind of theory.

The chief purpose of this chapter is to put some flesh on the claim that the potential of action learning is impeded by its indiscriminate devaluation of 'theory', which it equates with programmed knowledge. I will argue that critical social theory[4] can make an important contribution to management education by exposing and redressing shortcomings in action learning associated with its blanket devaluation of theory.[5] Equally, although not the focus of this chapter, action learning's challenge to traditional management education, and, in particular, its methods of connecting learning processes to learning-set members' experience, can begin to redress the scant consideration of how critical knowledge of management and organisation is to be applied and disseminated (see Alvesson and Willmott 1996).[6] I begin by summarising some key differences between traditional management education and action learning. I then illustrate these differences by reference to a case study presented by Pedler (1996), a leading advocate and exponent of action learning (Pedler 1991, 1996). My purpose in giving detailed consideration to this case study is to embed my analysis in an example of action learning that has been identified and discussed by one of its more prominent advocates. By taking this example, it is possible to move beyond an abstract critique of action learning (e.g. Willmott 1994a) to give a concrete illustration of how critical thinking has relevance for identifying and illuminating issues thrown up in action learning processes.

Traditional management education, action learning and critical action learning

McLaughlin and Thorpe (1993) differentiate action learning from traditional management education along the lines summarised in the *first two* columns of Table 7.1.[7]

Traditional management education invites students and practitioners to acquire knowledge of relevant facts and techniques that, in principle, have universal relevance. The world is assumed to have the status of an exterior, independent object about which knowledge can be accumulated, and increased control of this world can thereby be secured. By acquiring this knowledge, the student or practitioner becomes an expert who can better use, manipulate and control human and material resources.

Action learning, in contrast, emphasises the contiguity of learners and their knowledge of the world: knowledge is always embodied in the lived experience of the learner (see also Fox's discussion of situated learning in Chapter 6). The value of expertise is not entirely denied, but action learning seeks to increase the capacity of individuals to deal with their lived problems instead of evaluating what they learn in terms of their acquisition and accumulation of facts about the world. Experts are viewed with some caution as the value of knowledge is

Typology of approaches to management education

	Traditional management education	*Action learning*	*Critical action learning*
World-view	The world is an exterior 'object' to be learned about	The world is a contiguous 'subject' to act upon and change	The world is a contiguous psycho-political field of action and change
	Self-development is unimportant Some notion of correct management practice, established by research, defines the (formal) curriculum	Self-development is very important Content and/or delivery of learning are defined by the organisation and/or the learners	Self-development and social development are interdependent Interdependence of human beings militates against any individual or group gaining monopoly control of the curricula
Modus operandi	Managers should learn theories or models derived from research	Learners should be facilitated by a tutor to solve problems	Learners are potentially receptive to, and facilitated by, the concerns of other groups, in addition to individual tutors, when identifying and addressing problems
	Experts decide on what should be learned, when and how much	Experts are viewed with caution	Received wisdom, including that of experts, is subject to critical scrutiny through a fusion of reflection and insights drawn from critical social theory
	Models, concepts and ideas are provided to offer tools for future thinking and action	Models, concepts and ideas are developed in response to current problems	Models, concepts and ideas are developed through an interplay of reflection upon practice and an application of ideas drawn from critical traditions

Source: adapted from McLaughlin and Thorpe (1993).

appraised primarily in relation to its practical relevance for tackling live problems. As Thomas (in Chapter 2) notes, Revans, the founder of action learning in the context of management education, was highly sceptical about the relevance and value of courses comprising lectures on a variety of subjects – such as 'economics, sociology and mathematical bric-a-brac'. This approach to education, he contended, was not founded upon any defensible belief that they are 'essential to the prosecution of better management', but was taken because programmed knowledge of these subjects was 'all they had to offer' (Revans 1980: 194–5; cited by Thomas in Chapter 2). Action learning, in contrast, encourages participation in sharing knowledge and constructively criticising others' diagnoses and prescriptions. Learning is thus directed to, and guided by, a process of self-development rather than by a concern to acquire abstract bodies of knowledge.

In principle, then, action learning depends upon, and actively contributes towards, a process of self-reflection and learning, as ignorance, confusion and uncertainty *encountered in the practical activity of managing* are acknowledged and worked through with fellow learners in action learning groups or 'sets'. These 'negative' elements, as they are routinely represented by traditional management education (and, incidentally, by most of the contemporary gurus of management), are identified as a valuable stimulus and resource for becoming better informed, gaining greater clarity of understanding, coming to terms with uncertainties, and thereby identifying and developing less self-defeating solutions to actual, live problems. In the example of an action learning set discussed in a later section, the adoption of a more cost-effective system of inventory control is seen to depend upon learning-set members' willingness to address and work through the threat that this innovation poses to their role and identity within the company.

Critical action learning shares the emphasis of action learning upon embodied practice and self-development but situates this within a broader social and institutional context. It shares action learning's criticism of the established approach to management education, in which 'the teacher talks about reality as if it were motionless, static, compartmentalized and predictable. Or else he expounds on a topic completely alien to the existential experience of the students' (Freire 1972: 45). However, in critical action learning, social development and self-development are understood to be mutually constitutive. This understanding is reflected in its conception of social reality as a psycho-political field of action and change in which tensions and inconsistencies repeatedly stimulate conflicts, debates and learning processes. As noted earlier, a major difference between action learning and critical action learning concerns their attitude to 'theory'. Suspicious of theory, action learning is unreflective about its own theoretical assumptions and about the inescapable engagement of lay theories by learning-set members. It assumes that problems can be adequately surfaced, diagnosed and addressed within learning sets without reference to 'theory'. Action learning does not pay attention to how the (theory-dependent) process of defining and addressing problems in learning sets is constrained as well as enabled by relations of power (e.g. ownership, patriarchy, expertise, etc.) that condition both the contents of lay theory and the scope and depth of learning. In contrast, critical action learning highlights and explores the interdependence of personal learning and social development. It demonstrates the relevance of ideas drawn from critical traditions for exposing the power-invested limits of received wisdom in ways that are also personally meaningful for the lived experience of those involved in learning processes (see Grey *et al.* 1996).

Action learning in practice

To appreciate more fully what action learning means and how it is accomplished, I now draw upon a case study of action learning presented by Mike Pedler, a leading advocate and exponent of action learning (see Pedler 1991, 1996). This case provides a vehicle for illuminating some of the key differences between action learning and critical action learning. It is worth emphasising that it is offered by Pedler (1997) as an *exemplary case* of action learning – not in the sense that it is a pure or perfect case, but that it is typical of the processes and the kind of learning that occurs. Pedler (1997) discusses this case in response to a series of criticisms that have been levelled against action learning – notably its incorporation into unquestioned management agendas, its atheoretical approach, its excessive attention to individuals as agents of change and its degeneration into inward-looking support groups rather than learning processes. 'A response to the critique', he writes, 'demands a deeper look at action learning' (*ibid.*: 6), to which the present chapter is intended to make a contribution.[8] I will return to these elements of Pedler's critique in my discussion of the case.

The David Docherty case

Pedler's (1997) case focuses upon the experience of one member of a learning set: David Docherty, a director of Harbourne Engineering, a company employing about 60 people. The interested reader may wish to consult Pedler's work (1991: 65–7; 1997: 6–8), where the case is presented in some detail. I make reference to much of this detail in my discussion of the case, but, for the moment, it may be helpful to summarise its central elements:

- David Docherty is 29 and is a director of Harbourne Engineering, which he formed five years ago with his two fellow directors. He is mainly responsible for site work and equipment. He has no formal management training.
- Harbourne Engineering has tripled its turnover in every year of its five-year existence. It has about 60 employees.
- Harbourne Engineering does all its work on other people's premises. At any one time, it may be working on 30–40 jobs throughout the UK and abroad.
- David's boss, Bill Harbourne, is concerned about the time spent by David chasing equipment and men. He initiated David's participation in the action

learning set. Other members of this learning set are engineers from big companies.

Pedler describes how, at an early meeting of the learning set, David was asked how many items of equipment were owned by his company. He could only give an estimate of 800. He then reluctantly agreed to compile a record for a later meeting. This yielded an incomplete list of over 2,000 items. Members of David's learning set identified as a problem his ignorance of his equipment and the associated absence of a system for recording its existence and monitoring its use, not least because it emerged that David was regularly working 60 or 70 hours a week, including 12 hours on Sundays[9]. His fellow set members then proceeded to make numerous suggestions about how 'David's equipment problem' might be solved. David always found reasons for rejecting their proposals on the grounds that the solutions were inappropriate for the particular circumstances of his company. Nonetheless, several weeks later he announced to the set that he had developed a solution. This involved creating an information system based upon a simple form, a paper filing system and the employment of a part-time pensioner. All the elements of this solution, Pedler (1997) reports, had been proposed earlier by the members of the learning set. As David Docherty stonewalled suggestions made by fellow learning-set members about how to solve 'his problem', he initially maintained a calm distance, arguing that their prescriptions were inappropriate. He remained calm even when, after five hours of tiring discussion, one of them aggressively accused him of not really wanting to solve 'his problem'. Only as David was repeatedly pressed to provide an account of his work – first by telling them how much equipment the company owned and then by having to justify his working methods – did he become 'ruffled and rather angry' (*ibid.*: 8). His calm defence began to collapse and he was eventually led (or perhaps forced) to confront how he was spending his time; and, more specifically, to acknowledge how much time he was spending in keeping tabs on the existence, location and use of equipment, which, *inter alia*, was placing considerable strains on his marriage.[10]

An initial assessment of the case

I suggest that this case illustrates a number of the strengths but also reveals a number of the limitations of action learning. Positively, it demonstrates how learning can occur when members of learning sets are pressed to reflect upon and account for the value and defensibility of their actions. This can be productive of discussion as set members encourage each other to focus upon a particular live problem. Action learning can reveal how the recognition and solution of a problem can be conditional upon a shift in awareness and self-understanding. Simply possessing knowledge of possible solutions (which in the David Docherty case other set members provided in profusion) is not necessarily sufficient. Before David could change his methods of working he had first to confront his resistance to taking on new responsibilities.

In the case of its limitations, it is noteworthy how in response to David's vagueness about the amount of equipment owned by his company the other members of his learning set immediately treated this as a *discrete, technical problem* that could be solved by introducing a new system for recording its acquisition and use. So, although the form of action learning may depart from traditional management education, the process may continue to be dominated by a model in which, in the guise of set members, the task of the educator is:

> to 'fill' the students with the contents of his narration – contents which are detached from reality, disconnected from the totality that engendered them and could give them significance.... Education thus becomes an act of depositing, in which the students are the depositories and the teacher is the depositor.
>
> (Freire 1972: 45)

On Pedler's account, no member of the set sought to understand how or why the situation in which David Docherty found himself had arisen. Nor, relatedly, did any member of the set seek to explore the particular circumstances of Harbourne Engineering as a small but rapidly growing capitalist enterprise or David's position within it. Yet arguably these were conditions of possibility for the emergence and continuation of the practices which drew sustained criticism from David's set members (to be discussed below).

The other set members were seemingly unaware of the limits of their managerially common-sense way of identifying and analysing 'David's problem' as a (technical) matter which could be solved by replacing an amateurish approach with a rational system. So far as they were concerned, the nature of David's problem was self-evident: the absence of an inventory system – an absence which 'amazed' members of the set employed by big companies (Pedler 1997: 7). This amazement is perhaps unsurprising. Nonetheless, it speaks volumes about the other set members' taken-for-granted understanding of business organisation; and, more specifically, their very limited knowledge (and dismissive view) of small business practice.[11] More generally, the amazement of the big-company engineers indicates a resistance, or trained incapacity, to appreciate how the use of such systems is a contingent rather than a natural feature of organising activity.

David's vagueness about the inventory and his admission of the hours spent tracking its use did not serve to open up a discussion about the specificities and practicalities of his work. Any such discussion was displaced by a focus on the techniques that would enable David to solve a discrete problem. Many hours were spent by the set exploring the relative merits of alternative inventory systems without apparently any effort to appreciate the distinctive history of the company or of David Docherty's position within it. Set members were seemingly oblivious to how their contributions were governed by a narrow, instrumental rationality – a rationality preoccupied with acquiring and applying the relevant technique, to the exclusion of any discussion of the history and development of

David's positioning and participation within the particular structure of social relations at Harbourne Engineering. In short, the set members proceeded by abstracting 'his (technical) problem' from the social relations of production in which, arguably, David's routines were embedded.

This initial assessment of action learning indicates that it subverts the tendency to 'dichotomise reflection from action' (Freire 1972: 56) but is ill equipped to challenge, and is even perhaps content to endorse, an approach to learning in which processes of self-development are, at best, limited to the removal of psychological impediments to the performativity of individuals. And, at worst, it results in discrete problems being identified and fixed without addressing these psychological impediments directly, preferring instead to rely upon peer pressure from other set members to shame a target individual into reforming his or her ways.

Action learning on reflection

In his own commentary upon the David Docherty case, Pedler considers three possible interpretations of how the principles of action learning are illustrated by it. First, the case may be interpreted as exemplifying Revans' concern to change the world: set members enabled David Docherty to confront the reality of 'the external world' and thereby develop a more effective way of managing it (Pedler 1997: 8–10). Second, the case may be interpreted as nurturing a process of self-development: David comes to face 'the self-deceptions which have so far made the many previous sensible suggestions for action unworkable' (*ibid.*: 11). Or, thirdly, it may be viewed as a combination of 'external change' and 'self-development' (*ibid.*: 12). However, as Pedler acknowledges, action learning's emphasis upon self-development means that 'external change', such as the introduction of a new inventory system, is generally connected to the learning of *the individual*.[12]

Responding to criticisms of action learning's focus upon individual rather than collective or organisational learning, Pedler suggests a fourth possibility for interpreting the case: as *a process of social construction* in which 'new social meanings and realities' are produced (*ibid.*: 12 et seq.). The focus then shifts to the development of *collective* capacities to construct meanings and realities in new ways rather than 'external change' or 'self-development', so that action learning is understood as a process which 'allows for new thoughts to be thought, new words to be spoken, new perspectives, possibilities and worlds to be glimpsed' (*ibid.*: 16).

It is difficult, Pedler acknowledges, to find support for this understanding of action learning in Revans' writings because an attentiveness to the process of social construction 'frees us from the limitations of individual action and learning' (*ibid.*: 16). It is also difficult, I suggest, to see how the David Docherty case illustrates the capacity of action learning to foster collective learning, as there is no indication of other members having learned anything from their attempts to address and explore 'David's problem'. Nonetheless, as Pedler argues, a social-constructionist conception of action learning is potentially helpful for addressing two of the four criticisms levelled against action learning identified earlier. Most obviously, it involves a shift away from a concern with the individual as agent and the associated 'cult of the self' (*ibid.*: 17). Second, a focus upon collective learning, which in principle extends beyond the boundaries of the learning set, also lessens the likelihood of action learning sets turning into inward-looking support groups for their members. However, this leaves the other two criticisms of action learning – namely the criticism that action learning is 'atheoretical' and the related objection that it has become increasingly incorporated into management agendas.

Beyond action learning

The difficulty with action learning's rejection of 'theory' is that it admits only the theory which set members bring to the articulation and discussion of problems; and, as Pedler observes, this is 'usually an inadequate basis on which to critique their own practice' (1997: 17). As a consequence, action learning is inherently limited and conservative in the learning which it facilitates. Access is denied to ideas that might challenge or clarify whatever stocks of knowledge and understanding happen to be available to members of the learning set. As a consequence, to the extent that learning-set members stay 'in role' as 'managers' and/or embrace common-sense thinking infused by managerialist values, action learning processes are placed, by default, in the service of managerial agendas.

I suggest that the heavy reliance upon set members' lay theories can limit the possibilities and processes of learning, just as these can be impeded by an excessive dependence upon some external theory or authority. Disaffection with the accumulation of programmed knowledge provided the very impetus for Revans' advocacy of action learning. As was also argued earlier, the action-centred philosophy favoured by Revans is not incompatible with critical knowledge or 'theory' which challenges a dualistic conception of the relationship between action and theory, the knower and the known, and the teacher and the taught. However, the move away from this 'banking concept of education' is likely to be partial and limited if lay theories of learning are unchallenged by critical thinking. In the David Docherty case, other set members assumed the adequacy of their definition and diagnosis of 'David's problem' and endeavoured to 'fill' him with their 'deposits' (Freire 1972: 45). To be clear, the 'reality' from which such 'deposits' become 'detached' (*ibid.*) is not the reality ascribed to organisations by authors of Harvard Case Studies or by David's set members. Nor is it the reality implied by the anecdotes and heroic exploits or 'war stories' told by business leaders. These are simply other kinds of 'deposits', albeit less static and dry, which are also invariably 'disconnected from the totality which engendered them' (*ibid.*: 45). Rather, the 'reality' refers to the lived experience of students, or, in the context of action learning, to the lived experience of set members when at work as managers or in sets. This 'reality' is understood to encompass, but also to *extend well beyond*, the contents of functions ascribed to (aspiring) executives by management textbooks, cases and guru guides; for the representations of managerial work contained in these sources tend to reduce the lived experience of social practices to a technical activity impersonally performed by soulless functionaries (see Knights and Willmott 1999). These practices are most fully portrayed in ethnographies of organisational work informed by critical social theory (e.g. Kunda 1992; Collinson 1992), where it is shown how work, as a 'lived experience', is made possible by, and embedded within, social relations.

The psycho-political field of managerial work is powerfully conveyed by Watson, who notes:

> The more I saw of the managers at Ryland, the more I became aware of the extent of human angst, insecurity, doubt and frailty among them.... Managers not only have to 'manage people' (customers, bankers, suppliers, and so on, as well as employers), they have to manage themselves, too...there is a significant emotional dimension to managerial work.
>
> (Watson 1994: 178, 179)

It is this dimension, Watson observes, 'which normal organizational and administrative discourse suppresses or marginalizes' (*ibid.*: 180). As he also shows, expressions and repressions of this 'emotional dimension' are conditioned by managers' positioning with a hierarchy of social relations where they are under increasing pressure to divest themselves of established practices and benefits, including their job security (*ibid.*: 64 et seq.). The key point to be grasped is that, in contrast to other, highly influential representations of managerial work, ethnographies informed by critical social theory are attentive to 'existential experience', the contents of which are understood to be engendered by the wider totality. In the absence of such theory, learners are more likely to fall back upon received wisdom, which in the case of managers is likely to associate expertise with a technocratic approach to problem identification and diagnosis. This is clearly evident in the Docherty case, where, paradoxically, members of the action learning set proceed to act in a way that parallels the kind of approach and prescription advocated by traditional management education. That is to say, David is defined as a 'student' who must be 'filled' with knowledge-deposits about inventory systems in a way that entirely detaches his experience from the totality of social relations which arguably engendered his time-consuming routines and fuelled his resistance to pressures to change his ways.

Towards critical action learning

Despite its limited capacity to depart from the understandings and insights provided by traditional management education, action learning's attentiveness to lived experience means that it can nonetheless throw up issues and problems that are amenable to illumination by critical social theory. As McLaughlin and Thorpe have observed:

> At the level of their own experience, managers undertaking Action Learning programmes...*can become aware of the primacy of politics, both macro and micro, and the influence of power on decision making and non-decision making, not to mention the 'mobilization of bias'.*
>
> (McLaughlin and Thorpe 1993: 25; emphasis mine)

As the references to 'the primacy of politics' and 'the "mobilization of bias"' imply, there is the *possibility* of linking the embodied insights generated by action learning with the theoretical contributions of diverse traditions of critical social theory which have explored how agendas and decisions are conditioned by the differential access of individuals and groups to scarce material and symbolic resources. In practice, however, the link between (1) the capacity of action learning to expose 'the primacy of politics' in the lived experience of set members and (2) traditions of critical analysis which illuminate this experience may be more tenuous on account of the antipathy of action learning to 'theory' of all kinds.

In Pedler's account of the David Docherty case there is little evidence of action learning actively generating an awareness of 'the primacy of politics', even though, arguably, this 'politics' was rarely far from the surface of its account of events. First, David is pressured by Bill Harbourne, the most senior of the three directors, to review his methods and to participate in the action learning set. David then faces pressures from his fellow set members to overcome his resistance to their diagnosis and solutions to 'his problems'. David's reluctance to introduce a new system can be interpreted as symptomatic of a comparative lack of resources (e.g. qualifications), including a positive self-image, which might have allowed him either to leave the company or positively to relish the challenge of undertaking new responsibilities. In the meetings of David's learning set, the other members repeatedly impress upon him the truth of their (self-evidently superior) big-company knowledge of inventory systems. In effect, they can be heard mobilising their bias towards an instrumental rationality that is preoccupied with devising more technically sophisticated methods of working irrespective of the context and is largely oblivious to the practical rationality (however perverse or distorted, in their eyes) which informed David's approach to his work.

Such mobilisation of 'biases', as Pedler's discussion of the social-construction perspective reminds us, is not coherently viewed as the activity or property of individuals. Rather, this mobilisation is articulated through social relations wherein individuals and groups are identified and positioned as 'possessors' of valued material and symbolic resources. Those who have very limited access to valued resources (e.g. savings, salaries, qualifications) are routinely involved in supporting or actively producing the material and symbolic goods which are disproportionately allocated to others in a systematic way. Although accomplished by human agents, biases and resources are articulated through social relations. It is precisely an appreciation of the presence of *systemic domination and exploitation* in mundane social and organisational practices that is lacking in action learning. If this understanding is to be incorporated, a shift in world-view is required, from one which regards organisational work as a continguous 'subject' to act upon and change, to one which regards it as a contiguous psycho-political field of action and change (see Table 7.1).

Towards a critical analysis of management

It has been argued that a shift from action learning to critical action learning necessitates a critical analysis of management which provides an alternative framework for exploring the issues and problems thrown up within learning sets. This framework, I will now argue, differs from both rationalist and post-rationalist theories of management, each of which preserves the separation between action and theory and between the knower and the known.

Traditional management theory understands managerial work as an (instrumentally) rational activity which is directed towards the more effective and/or efficient means of securing collective goals. What this means, according to Drucker, is 'management grounded in a discipline and informed by the *objective needs* of the organization and of its people, rather than management based upon ownership or political appointment' (1977: 33; emphasis mine). Attaining this 'discipline' is a matter of acquiring a knowledge of 'the objective needs' and then applying this knowledge in an impartial way. The following typifies this conception of how to identify and satisfy such 'needs':

> Managers are concerned with efficient operation…. The knowledge produced in organization studies may sometimes imply that the policies and procedures employed by the management of a particular organization are ineffective. In this way the analysis constitutes a critique of current affairs.
>
> (Donaldson 1985: 93)

Rationalist theory assumes that objective needs can be unproblematically identified and satisfied through the provision of knowledge which serves to correct ineffective policies and procedures. *Post-rationalist* management theory, in contrast, understands managerial decision-making to be *inescapably* conditioned, guided and restricted by managers' particular allegiances, preoccupations and hunches (e.g. Pettigrew 1973). From this perspective, conceptions of 'efficiency' and how to secure it are indelibly coloured by considerations of organisational politics and occupational culture. Or, as Child puts it, managerial work is 'an essentially political process in which constraints and opportunities are functions of the power exercised by decision-makers in the light of ideological values' (1972: 16). Non-rational elements are understood to subvert all attempts to establish the kind of 'discipline' commended by rationalists such as Drucker.

The post-rationalist understanding of management offers a valuable counterbalance to an over-rationalised conception of management. Potentially, it opens up a space which enables managerial work to be analysed as the medium and outcome of the contradictory pressures that constitute its practice. However, the attribution of deviations from rational decision-making to the values of occupational cultures into which managers are assimilated or to departmental politics in which there are interpersonal struggles over material and symbolic resources abstracts the organisational politics of managerial work from the historical structures of social relations (e.g. patriarchy, capitalism) through which such politics are played out. Post-rationalist analysis identifies nothing that is fundamentally problematical or contradictory in the organisation of managerial work. It remains preoccupied with 'trumping' traditional management theory rather than transcending or transforming its technocratic, managerialist agenda. Post-rationalist theory is commended by its advocates as a means of *smoothing* processes of *top-down* reforms whose purpose is to further secure the status quo by alerting change agents to the role of political processes and ideological values in securing corporate objectives.[13] In this sense, post-rationalist analysis has been commended or enlisted to facilitate a situation in which

> technique and procedure tend to become ascendant over substantive reflection about organizational goals.... *Even at higher levels of management, one sees ample evidence of an over-riding emphasis on technique rather than on critical reasoning.*
>
> (Jackall 1988: 76; emphasis mine)

I suggest that this 'over-riding emphasis upon technique', to which post-rationalist theory contributes as it translates a way of debunking rationalist theory into a means of management control, is itself a product of power relations in which managers and academics are trained and feel obligated, as salaried employees, to establish and defend their authority and privileges by presenting themselves as neutral experts who develop and apply 'technique and procedure'. What is often overlooked or forgotten is that an espoused logic of neutrality and impartiality renders managers vulnerable to the demand that their work be subjected to the same rationalising processes that this logic visits upon others (Fletcher 1973; Smith 1990; Willmott 1997a). Managers become steeped in and disciplined by 'technique and procedure' and are obliged to account for and prescribe their actions in these terms. They are ill prepared to make (critical) sense of, let alone resist, the contradictory operation of the technocratic 'logic' of rational and post-rational management theory. This is not to deny that privately managers talk critically and ethically about their work, especially when their established practices and values are perceived to be threatened (Watson 1998). However, as Anthony has observed, the absence of any well-developed counter-discourse means that managers

> are more likely to be the unwitting victims of reorganization (more and more frequently); transferred, retrained or dismissed at the behest of organizational plans drawn up by distant consultants; regarded as human resources, shuffled and distributed by specialists in management development and planning.
>
> (Anthony 1977: 310)

In this respect, as Grey (in Chapter 3) argues, management education operates to police the potentially wayward inclinations of managers who might be tempted to develop and pursue their own agendas instead of acting 'responsibly' as trustworthy and predictable agents of the owners of corporate assets. Still, managers are not organisational dopes.[14] As employees, they are not necessarily unreservedly willing to assimilate and implement rational or 'post-rational' principles of work organisation, though they may pay eloquent lip-service to their efficacy. The findings of critical ethnographies have disclosed how the principles and logics of organisation are interpreted and enacted in relation to perceived opportunities for securing or advancing a mêlée of identity-securing concerns and values. These include the expansion of a specialist area, preserving a sense of integrity or dignity, achieving speedy promotion, pursuing the chance of more challenging work, the continuation of a quiet life, etc., etc.

It has been noted how a post-rational perspective conceptualises such identity-securing concerns as expressive of allegiances to occupational cultures or other affiliations. In contrast, a critical perspective on managerial work understands these as stratagems for coping with a division of labour which pulls managerial work in contradictory directions. As employees, managers are hired primarily to advance the interests of those who own corporate assets. But when performing this role they experience the oppression as well as the privileges associated with the controls to which they are subjected (e.g. budgets, appraisals, targets, etc.). Obliged to sell their labour to provide for themselves and their dependants, managers find themselves positioned in a hierarchical relationship where they are not infrequently required to act, and to make demands upon others, in ways that are felt to be personally unpalatable, disadvantageous, distasteful or compromising (see Willmott 1997a).

Tensions between the values and priorities of managers as persons and the demands of their work roles present managers with repeated opportunities for critical reflection upon their experience. The difficulty, as noted earlier, is that 'substantive reflection' and 'critical reasoning' are frequently displaced or indefinitely postponed by 'an over-riding emphasis on technique' (Jackall 1988: 76). In principle, action learning can provide an opportunity to explore dilemmas and issues in a way that is less tied to the identification of technical solutions for discrete problems. However, as the David Docherty case indicates, it is not necessarily easy for managers to question the coherence and ethics of techniques and procedures from which they derive a measure of authority and security (see Knights and Morgan 1991). In order to break out of a narrow, common-sense approach to problem diagnosis and prescription it is necessary to draw upon theory which, by looking beyond the formulae for fixing problems devised by 'rationalist' and 'post-rationalist' gurus, can provide personal and collective insights into the tensions, dilemmas and paradoxes which are a recurrent feature of the lived experience of managerial work of the kind performed by David Docherty.

Power and identity in managerial work and action learning

In the light of the preceding discussion, I now reinterpret Pedler's example of action learning by focusing upon some issues of power and identity (Knights and Willmott 1983, 1985, 1989). The issue of *identity* is most explicit in David Docherty's resistance to giving up a role that made him feel 'important and indispensable' (Pedler 1997: 8). A connection between issues of *identity* and *power* can be made through a consideration of his gendered way of doing his job and his responses to questions from other members of his learning set. The practical consciousness exemplified in these dealings, I suggest, is expressive of a masculinist identity in the sense that David Doherty seems to have been motivated by a desire to exercise sovereign control over his responsibilities at work and to reject all suggestions about how to resolve his inventory problem (Seidler 1989).[15] In this respect, David's attitude would seem to confirm what Watson observed of the managers he studied:

> The managerial role puts a lot of normal and vulnerable human beings in a position where they are expected to be fully 'in control'... They are expected to be in full possession of all 'the facts' of situations, and in the case of the great majority of them, to 'be men' – strong, confident, masculine individuals who can 'hack it'.
>
> (Watson 1996: 339)

It would appear that David Docherty had not raised or discussed his problems with his fellow directors. Significantly, the problem of inventory did not surface in the learning set on his initiative. Rather, it was identified only when a member of the learning set asked him how many pieces of equipment his company owned. By rejecting the group's proposals and then later assembling them into his 'own' system, David preserved his masculinist sense of being 'in control'.

Both David Docherty and the members of his learning set abstract *'his problem' and capacities from the wider social division of labour in which he works*. This abstraction is reflected in the assumption that members of learning sets meet as equals, whereas, arguably, every learning experience is mediated by social relations of power between learners as well as between them and their teachers/facilitators. For example, it may not be too fanciful to suggest that David was positioned by other members of the learning set as a comparatively young, inexperienced manager. This construction of identity positioned him unequally in relation to the other set members, who deployed it when making and imposing their diagnosis of and technical solutions to 'his problem' in a way that offered little insight into the wider institutional dimensions of his difficulties. What Vince bitingly characterises as 'the pervasive humanist myth' of learning sets (1996: 127) operates to place a taboo on the discussion and analysis of relations of power as enablers and inhibitors of individual actions. This myth also makes it more likely that emotional conflicts, frustrations and insecurities associated with relations of subordination and subjugation are silenced; or, that when they surface, such conflicts are interpreted as problems of individual immaturity and adjustment. In this sense, there is a politics of learning in operation where *within* learning sets a mobilization of bias acts to suppress recognition and discussion of how people are 'positioned unequally in and by organizations and groups as a consequence of social constructions of their identity' (*ibid.*: 124).

Although not the declared intent of action learning, a focus upon the problems of *individual* learners, combined with (1) an embrace of the idealistic notion that learners meet as equals and (2) a resistance to the use of theory other than the ideas generated by set numbers, conspires to support and promote a narrow, task-oriented focus for learning. In Pedler's example, David's difficulties are interpreted exclusively as *his* problems and these problems are addressed purely in terms of the tasks that *he* must undertake to resolve them. David's stonewalling and his eventual 'breakdown' are taken to be symptomatic of nothing but his own resistance to learn. As Vince observes of action learning, feelings generated in action learning sets, 'which might produce learning and change *if they were acknowledged and worked with*, instead become detached or 'split' from the objectives of the group' (1996: 124; emphasis mine). In the absence of a theory that situates problems of learning in a broader context – and, in doing so, understands how emotional experience is generated and suppressed within power relations – action learning tends to reflect and reproduce, rather than challenge and subvert, the operation of power relations in work organisations wherein expressions of emotion are generally discouraged or suppressed, or alternatively are carefully regulated and marketed (Van Maanen and Kunda 1989).

As emphasised in the previous section, the social relations in which David was positioned at work were not simply patriarchal but also, and relatedly, *politico-economic*. Although comparatively little contextual information is provided by Pedler (1991, 1996), who typically concentrates upon interpersonal dynamics, it seems reasonable to assume that Harbourne Engineering was a capitalist enterprise. Pedler's account suggests that within this enterprise there was a basic division of labour between the fitters, who used the inventory to perform the work undertaken by the company, and the three directors, who took responsibility for winning the business, for managing the work of the skilled labour, and, in David's case, for site work and equipment. I suggest that this division of labour between fitters and directors cannot be entirely explained in terms of rational or functional necessity. More fundamentally, this technical division of labour articulates, and serves to maintain, a social difference of ownership. More specifically, it is a manifestation of the imperative for the owners of the business to control the labour of others in ways that secure and sustain the private accumulation of capital. If left to their own devices, it cannot be assumed that the fitters would privilege the accumulation of capital over their own job security or the improvement of their wages and working conditions. For this reason, responsibility for the conception of work is guarded by the owners and their agents, while execution is undertaken by employees whose ownership of the business is at best minimal. This social division operates to inhibit or circumscribe the involvement of employees in decisions which nonetheless affect their work – such as the availability and safety of equipment.

Had the fitters themselves owned the company as a co-operative, it is certainly possible, and perhaps probable, that the need for a system to track *their* inventory would have been identified and developed by them. However, given a social division of labour at Harbourne Engineering which reflected the estrangement of the fitters from the means of production (e.g. the equipment that they used), they were not empowered to introduce such a system. The system accommodated considerable inefficiency and ineffectiveness precisely because one of the directors was in a position, until challenged by Bill Harbourne and members of the learning set, to develop and maintain practices on the basis of his personal preferences or capacities. Relations of ownership and power meant that David Docherty was accountable primarily to Bill Harbourne, not to the fitters. The pressure on David to participate in the learning set was a product of Bill Harbourne's concern that David was 'spending far too much time on the equipment side of his job' (Pedler 1997: 7) when his time could be more effectively and profitably employed doing something else, such as winning more business and meeting clients. From this perspective, Bill Harbourne's decision to arrange for David to participate in the action learning set was seemingly informed by the assessment that David's labour was yielding sub-optimal returns – a view subsequently echoed by other 'professional' managers at the learning set, and later vindicated by David's own decision to replace his working methods with an inventory system. In effect, then, David's participation in the learning set can be seen as a comparatively subtle means of management control applied by Bill Harbourne in an effort to increase the additional value yielded by the application of his (managerial) labour.

So, in addition to issues of identity, to which Pedler makes reference but which he does not elaborate, it is relevant to locate pressures upon David Docherty to introduce an inventory system and his reluctance to do so within the broader context of capitalist relations of production. Within these relations, David was simultaneously an employee and a company director. His reluctance to introduce an inventory system can be related to his insecurities about his capacity to undertake other kinds of tasks, and ultimately about retaining his employment, given his lack of 'formal management training' (Pedler 1997: 7), which would seriously disadvantage him in the market for an equivalent position.

Conclusion

Traditional management education is currently being criticised by practitioners for abstracting knowledge from the practical realities of managerial work (*Harvard Business Review*, September–October and November–December 1992; see also Chapter 2). Action learning and critical action learning are each concerned to address these 'practical realities' in a way which departs from traditional management education.

Action learning contributes the insight that an exchange of ideas, and even the acceptance of intellectual insights (espoused theory), does not of itself necessarily produce equivalent transformations in practice (see Fay 1987; Willmott 1994b).[16] In common with action learning, critical action learning understands that the transformation of students and practitioners into active learners demands a radically different orientation to practitioners' experience of ignorance, uncertainty, confusion, ambiguity, etc. from that favoured by more established approaches to management education. Fundamental to critical action learning is the understanding that embodied reflection upon problems experienced in everyday practice, guided by critical theory, must be encouraged and supported if personal and social transformation is to be accomplished.

Given the resistance to 'substantive reflection' and 'critical reasoning' Jackall 1988: 76) illustrated by participants in the David Docherty case, it would be perverse to anticipate a warm reception from either practitioners or teachers for critical action learning. Even when the relevance and value of its critical insights are tacitly or partially recognised, a degree of selective and instrumental appropriation is to be expected (see Nord and Jermier 1992). Nonetheless, in a world where received truths are being questioned, traditional divisions are being eroded and continuous learning is being encouraged, the conditions are not entirely inauspicious for soliciting interest in alternative approaches to forms of learning, including critical action learning.

Notes

1 This is a modified version of a paper that previously appeared in *Systems Practice* 10(6): 749–71.
2 In this respect at least, action learning resonates with contemporary concerns and calls amongst mass management education providers, often stimulated by expediency as resources are cut, to shift from a pedagogy based upon teaching ('the sage on the stage') to one based upon learning ('the guide at the side').
3 The placing of scare quotes around 'critical thinking' is judicious because, of course, it can be ascribed to a wide diversity of discourses and practices. For example, critical thinking may be attributed to those who challenge received wisdom as they develop novel recipes for improving organisational performance. Total quality management (TQM) and business process re-engineering (BPR) may be described as 'critical' in the sense that they question the rationality and effectiveness of established production methods. However, such claims assume the rationality of existing ends, for which they propose improved means. In contrast, the term 'critical thinking' is used here to identify forms of analysis which question the value-rationality of established ends as well as the instrumental rationality of the means of their attainment (see Alvesson and Willmott 1996: ch. 2).
4 The term 'critical social theory' is deliberately used to indicate a 'broad church' that is not confined to a single 'school' or 'paradigm'. One commentator on this chapter took the view that 'the author is arguing for a critical learning theory based upon radical-structuralist ideas', and then noted that Table 7.1 'tends to [lean] more or as much toward the radical-humanist' approach before expressing the view that 'the radical structuralist approach is inadequate for the aims of the paper' and then concluding that the paper 'should address the tension between a structuralist and a humanist analysis and be clear what [the author] is opting for'. Needless to say, I contest this reading and its associated advice. Supposing for a

moment that the conveniently neat pigeonholing of work into different paradigms is accepted, even for the political purpose of resisting the hegemony of functionalist analysis (see Willmott 1993), this division ignores the obvious concern in this chapter with processes of interpretation and negotiation ('the interpretive paradigm'). I believe it possible that there are things in this chapter that people of very different 'critical' persuasions – Foucauldian, critical theoretic, poststructuralist, Marxist – would find that they agree, and disagree, with. But I refuse to accept that a choice has to be made between a structuralist/determinist(?) and humanist/(voluntarist?) analysis. This choice must be made only if the structuralism–humanism dualism is reified rather than deployed heuristically to appreciate how human action is simultaneously partially conditioned and partially indeterminate.

5 Of course, critical thinking can be packaged and presented as a commodity to be 'banked' as programmed knowledge, as can action learning. But this, I suggest, runs directly counter to the challenge of critical pedagogy to the (idealised) separation of 'theory' from 'practice'.

6 To the extent that critical knowledge of management becomes disseminated, the risk is that it is simply substituted for the contents of traditional management education, in which case critical management academics set themselves up (or are set up) as an alternative set of experts who provide a new body of programmed knowledge that continues to represent the world as an exterior 'object' and is 'banked' as a commodity by students for whom it has minimal personal relevance or significance beyond providing them with a valued qualification. In principle, the philosophy and practice of action learning question and disrupt this tendency to divorce learning from (engaged) action. The adoption of its educational methods is more consistent with critical educational practice, in which 'teacher–student and the students–teachers reflect simultaneously on themselves and the world *without dichotomizing this reflection from action*' (Freire 1972: 56; emphasis mine). See Grey *et al.* (1996) for a discussion of this issue.

7 The paragraphs which follow have been extracted and revised from Willmott (1994a).

8 All page numbers for Pedler (1997) are taken from the final version of the manuscript submitted for publication.

9 Although Pedler does not provide us with a list of criticisms made by members of the learning set, it can be surmised that, in addition to soaking up much of David's time on matters that were routine and, in principle, could be achieved by other, cheaper and more effective means, the lack of a system rendered the company's assets unnecessarily vulnerable to theft or loss.

10 Perhaps David already had a tacit, practical awareness of the pressures upon him and/or an intuitive sense of the difficulty of indefinitely sustaining his established ways of working. But if David had privately developed this consciousness, this had not been translated into a discursive consciousness of his situation and he was disinclined to share this understanding with others. The distinction between practical and discursive consciousness is derived from Giddens (1984; see especially pp. 41 et seq.). In his commentary, Pedler (1997: 13) notes how, in his original write-up of the case (Pedler 1991: 65–7), he omitted his knowledge that David had two failed marriages behind him and was under pressure from his third wife. From a critical perspective, social institutions – such as the bourgeois, individualised nuclear family – are understood to be important because pressures emanating from them (e.g. responsibilities upon individuals to be 'breadwinners' as well as 'family wo/men') engender resistance to personal and social change.

11 More surprising is the seeming reluctance of the learning-set facilitator to draw the attention of set members to *how they* were identifying and addressing David's vagueness about the amount of equipment for which he was responsible.

12 This tendency is illustrated by Pedler's (1991: 65–7; 1997: 6–8) presentation of the case, in which the focus is upon the removal of resistances to change in David: replacing his time-consuming routines required David to acknowledge, learn about and deal with the feelings of insecurity about his ability to undertake new tasks such as selling and meeting clients.

13 Traditional depictions of management are, in effect, criticised for being *imperfectly* managerial because they fail to grasp the importance of managing and exploiting 'irrational' elements more effectively. If only other managers would learn to become more aware of the role of values in shaping their perceptions, 'post-rationalist' analysis suggests, they would appreciate the nature and significance of organisational cultures and their politics. Many current difficulties and dysfunctions could then be directly addressed and attenuated, if not avoided (see, for example, Pettigrew 1985b: 314–16).

14 The allusion here is to Garfinkel's (1967) notion of the 'cultural dope' – a phrase that he coined to characterise the tendency of functionalist analysis to disregard the role of human agency in the reproduction of social institutions.

15 It is relevant to stress that this interpretation of David's behaviour in terms of patriarchal relations that are constitutive of a particular, controlling sense of masculinity is not being equated with his male sexuality. Rather, the suggestion is that David's practical, gendered consciousness of himself as a man informed his way of addressing a mundane managerial problem. In this case, the patriarchal values embodied in David's orientation to his work and his response to other members of the learning set seemed to condition his approach to diagnosing and solving problems. Of course, women can also acquire this practical consciousness, although their positioning within patriarchal relations, as more receptive and submissive, tends to make it more likely that problems will be shared with others and that they will be less preoccupied with controlling outcomes in a way that enables them to believe that they alone produced an effective solution.

16 The insights of critical theory may do little more than fuel cynicism and/or guilt. Critical theory may itself become commodified as just another interesting set of ideas that competes for attention in the mall of social and management theory. See also note 2 .

References

Alvesson, M. and Willmott, H.C. (1996) *Making Sense of Management: A Critical Introduction*, London: Sage.

Anthony, P. (1977) *The Ideology of Work*, London: Tavistock.

Child, J. (1972) 'Organizational structure, environment and performance: the role of strategic choice', *Sociology* 6(1): 1–22.

Collinson, D. (1992) *Managing the Shopfloor*, Berlin: de Gruyter.

Donaldson, L. (1985) *In Defence of Organization Theory: A Reply to the Critics*, Cambridge: Cambridge University Press.

Drucker, P. (1977) *Management*, London: Pan.

Eccles, R.G. and Nohria, N. (1992) *Beyond the Hype: Rediscovering the Essence of Management*, Cambridge, MA: Harvard Business School Press.

Fay, B. (1987) *Critical Social Science*, Ithaca, NY: Cornell University Press.

Fletcher, C. (1973) 'The end of management?', in J. Child (ed.) *Man and Organisation*, London: Allen & Unwin.

Friere, P. (1972) *Pedagogy of the Oppressed*, Harmondsworth: Penguin.

Garfinkel, H. (1967) *Studies in Ethnomethodology*, Englewood Cliffs, NJ: Prentice-Hall.

Giddens, A. (1984) *The Constitution of Society*, Cambridge: Polity.

Giroux, H. (1983) *Theory and Resistance in Education: A Pedagogy for the Opposition*, London: Heinemann.

Grey, C., Knights, D. and Willmott, H.C. (1996) 'Is a critical pedagogy of management possible?', in R. French and C. Grey (eds) *Rethinking Management Education*, London: Sage.

Jackall, R. (1988) *Moral Mazes: The World of Corporate Managers*, Oxford: Oxford University Press.

Kjonstad, B. and Willmott, H.C. (1994) 'Business ethics: restrictive or empowering?', *Journal of Business Ethics* 13: 1–20.

Knights, D. and Morgan, G. (1991) 'Corporate strategy, organizations and subjectivity: a critique', *Organization Studies* 12(2): 251–73.

Knights, D. and Willmott, H.C. (1983) 'Dualism and domination', *Australian and New Zealand Journal of Sociology* 19(1): 33–49.

—— (1985) 'Power and identity in theory and practice', *Sociological Review* 33(1): 22–46.

—— (1989) 'Power and subjectivity at work: from degradation to subjugation in social relations', *Sociology* 23(4): 535–58.

—— (1999) *Management Lives!*, London: Sage.

Kunda, G. (1992) *Engineering Culture: Control and Commitment in a High-Tech Corporation*, Philadelphia: Temple University Press.

McLaughlin, H. and Thorpe, R. (1993) 'Action learning: a paradigm in emergence: the problems facing a challenge to traditional management education and development', *British Journal of Management* 4(1): 19–27.

March, J.G. and Simon, H.A. (1958) *Organizations*, New York: Wiley.

Nichols, T. and Beynon, H. (1977) *Living With Capitalism*, London: Routledge.

Nord, W.R. and Jermier, J.M. (1992) 'Critical social science for managers? Promising and perverse possibilities', in M. Alvesson and H. Willmott (eds) *Critical Management Studies*, London: Sage.

Pedler, M. (1988) 'Self-development and work organizations', in M. Pedler and T. Boydell *Applying Self-Development in Organizations*, Englewood Cliffs, NJ: Prentice-Hall.

—— (ed.) (1991) *Action Learning in Practice*, Aldershot: Gower.

—— (1996) *Action Learning for Managers*, London: Lemos.

—— (1997) 'Interpreting action learning', mimeograph.

Pettigrew, A. (1973) *The Politics of Organizational Decision-Making*, London: Tavistock.

—— (1985a) *The Awakening Giant: Continuity and Change at ICI*, Oxford: Basil Blackwell.

—— (1985b) 'Examining change in the long-term context of culture and politics', in J.M. Pennings (ed.) *Organizational Strategy and Change (MA) or Strategic Decision-Making in Complex Organizations*, San Francisco: Jossey-Bass.

Pfeffer, J. (1981) *Power in Organizations*, London: Pitman.

Revans, R. (1980) *Action Learning: New Techniques for Management*, London: Blond & Briggs.

—— (ed.) (1982) *The Origins and Growth of Action Learning*, Bromley: Chartwell-Brat.

Roberts, J. (1996) 'Management education and the limits of technical rationality: the conditions and consequences of management practice', in R. French and C. Grey (eds) *Rethinking Management Education*, London: Sage.

Seidler, V. (1989) *Rediscovering Masculinity*, London: Routledge.

Smith, V. (1990) *Managing in the Corporate Interest: Control and Resistance in an American Bank*, Berkeley: University of California Press.

van Maanen, J. and Kunda, G. (1989) '"Real feelings": emotional expression and organizational culture', in L.L. Cummings and B.M. Staw (eds) *Research in Organizational Behaviour* 11: 43–104, Greenwich, CT: JAI Press.

Vince, R. (1996) 'Experiential management education as the practice of change', in R. French and C. Grey (eds) *Rethinking Management Education*, London: Sage.

Watson, T. (1994) *In Search of Management: Culture, Chaos and Control in Managerial Work*, London: Routledge.

—— (1996) 'How do managers think? Identity, morality and pragmatism in managerial theory and practice', *Management Learning* 27(3): 323–42.

—— (1998) 'Ethical codes and moral communities: the Gunlaw temptation, the Simon solution and the David dilemma', in M. Parker (ed.) *Ethics and Organizations*, London: Sage.

Willmott, H.C. (1993) 'Breaking the paradigm mentality', *Organization Studies* 14(5): 681–719.

—— (1994a) 'Management education: provocations to a debate', *Management Learning* 25(1): 105–36.

—— (1994b) 'Theorising agency: power and subjectivity in organization studies', in M. Parker and J. Hassard (eds) *Towards a New Theory of Organizations*, London: Routledge.

—— (1997a) 'Analysing management as a labour process: capitalism, control and subjectivity', *Human Relations* 50(11): 1329–60.

—— (1997b) 'Critical management learning', in J. Burgoyne and M. Reynolds (eds) *Management Learning*, London: Sage.

8 Management learning as a critical process

The practice of storying

David Sims

Introduction

The centrality of learning in management is now widely accepted. The practical and theoretical enthusiasm for this has been enormous and the importance of learning is usually not so much demonstrated as asserted. We are not shown evidence to support the idea that everybody is suddenly engaged in learning, but simply told that this must be the case because it is the only way that an organisation can survive in 'today's fast-moving business environment' (or some such phrase). In this chapter I shall suggest a different way of thinking about learning which may provide us with a more effective analytic tool for understanding how learning takes place and for considering how managers may come to act as natural critical theorists. And from this basis, I will enable responses to questions such as: Why do managers not learn what others often would like them to learn? How do they keep some control of their learning despite the presence of powerful others who would like to influence or control their learning for them?

In the context of a book on 'the foundations of management knowledge', my interest is in the knowledge of the manager. Other forms of management knowledge, such as the statements that we can make about the generality of managers and management, I would take to be based on the knowledge of the manager, and in some way to be a generalisation of the knowledge of particular managers. The knowledge of the manager, however, is usually an apparently disordered collection of the tacit, the rule of thumb, the explicitly theorised, and various hybrid states such as ideas that have been explicit at an earlier point in time but which have now sunk into the subconscious. Into this collection comes learning, the change in knowledge, the way that new knowledge comes about for the manager.

The thinking of managers is notoriously done in short bursts (Mintzberg 1973; Weick 1984). Short attention spans are part of the package of managerial life. How do managers learn, given that they are faced with the twin problems of a continuous bombardment of the urgent and a ragbag of theoretical fragments with which to understand what is happening around them?

Hearing, learning and remembering

Let us first look more fundamentally at the question of how things come to be within the manager's awareness, and thus available as the raw material for learning. What do we hear, and specifically in the context of managers in a chronically overloaded and over-rich environment, what do they hear? The extent of selective perception in such an environment will be clear to anyone who has ever heard a tape recording made in an office. Numerous sounds are audible that no one noticed at the time. Physical hearing may be challenged in some managerial environments, but the major issue is usually that attention is grabbed by some sounds and not others.

Organisations are theatres in which there is continuous competition for the attention of others. The literature on agendas is full of cases of competing issues and champions, and of commentary on the competing demands among many issues which might be seen as worthy in their own right, but which will never command an audience unless someone actually works on their behalf (Dutton 1997).

How does anybody hear anything?

So how do some things come to be heard? It is clear that the interest has to be engaged. The actual means of doing this may vary, but I argue that this variety only reflects the variety of ways in which people tell – and hear – stories. To be heard a story needs the fundamental story properties of a setting, a build-up, a crisis, learning and new awareness (Davis 1993). Let us consider an example.

Peter was new to the board of a medium-sized company within a well-known group of companies. He had taken a risk to join them; his old organisation was better known and more established. But he had liked the style, the very unstuffy way in which these people went about their business, and he was tired of his old place. It was not long after he moved that he realised that there were an awful lot of things going on that nobody could explain; some crazy purchasing decisions were being made – and repeated – and when he asked why, no one could give him an answer. Most of these things were related to problems at the level of the group rather than of his particular company, but there seemed to be no way of isolating the company from the problems created at group level. The corporate finance department was months and sometimes years behind with its figures, and hours were spent chasing money that seemed to go astray in the system. Some smaller businesses had been acquired for what he had assumed, before joining, were good reasons, but on closer inspection those reasons evaporated and he was left to conclude that the group had been collecting for the sake of it. Worse still, they had given no consideration to the consequences of their acquisitions for internal working. One of the companies they had acquired was in direct competition with his own company.

The time came when he had to decide whether to start getting involved in the management of his new company or whether to concentrate on exercising and developing his professional skills. The arguments for staying out of the thick of the action were strong. He had been brought in to give an independent view and for his contacts and networking skills. Surely he owed it to his new colleagues not to get embroiled in their day-to-day management? On the other hand, he had joined at a senior level and there were very few others in the firm at his level. There was a lot of pressure on those few to get involved in the wider group of companies rather than to stay within the confines of the firm, and this could clearly benefit his firm. But this could only happen if Peter was prepared to roll his sleeves up, drop his professional pretensions and get involved in helping to run the place.

Peter went to a meeting with Andrew, chief executive of his own company, and Stephen, the group managing director. Andrew was needed for a post at group level, and Stephen was offering the two of them control over the competitor company they had acquired and the chance to merge it into their own company in return for Andrew taking on the group role. Of course Stephen never actually said that this was the deal. The conversation proceeded from Stephen saying what he needed and leaving Andrew and Peter to bid for what they wanted in return. Taking over their competitor was what they sensed would be the best deal they could get in return for their co-operation.

But, for this to work, Peter had to agree to take on the job of merging the two companies. This was the last thing he had wanted to do when he joined the company, but now he found his view had changed without his having realised it. The wish to make things turn out right (as he saw it) for his new colleagues was stronger than his old professional orientation. He hoped that he would be able to get back to his professional work at a later stage, and even took steps to get more heavily involved with his professional body and to develop closer links with it. However, he knew that he was setting off on a path that did not take him towards professional respect.

So why are you doing it, his old friends would ask him? Peter could only conclude that, without his noticing it, his intentions and values had changed. He liked Andrew, and thought it would be good for him to develop a new role in the group. He could not help wanting to impress Stephen and demonstrate to him that he was capable of managing the merger. And he had started to care about the company itself, and his colleagues there, and wanted a successful future for them.

This story will be used to illustrate a framework from Davis (1993) for viewing stories, and then throughout the chapter it will be used and elaborated to illustrate the practice of storying in management learning in several different ways. Davis offers a five-stage model of storytelling:

1 setting
2 build-up
3 crisis or climax
4 learning
5 new behaviour or awareness.

In Peter's story, the first paragraph gives the setting of the story (Peter has joined a new company). The second paragraph begins the build-up (Peter begins to find himself caught between the objectives with which he had originally joined the company and new ones that are emerging in his work). The third and fourth paragraphs contain the crisis or climax, where Peter is confronting Stephen's offer and deciding where to take his future. The fifth paragraph comments on Peter's learning and the new behaviour and awareness that he had reached. Those last two of Davis's stages are often inseparable.

Peter's experience in this story is already mediated by the stories into which he has cast himself. When he moved to his new company he extracted himself from the continuing soap opera of his previous company – often one of the strongest disincentives to moving job. A whole lot of stories that he had seen developing were left behind, and he never knew how most of them turned out. Also, if he had not been ready to recast himself for a new story he would not have put himself into a position to hear Stephen's offer. Something in Peter has prepared him to see himself as a deliverer. He will deliver Andrew from continuing the role that he has been playing for the past few years. He will also deliver his company from the threat of unmanaged merger or, worse, of merger managed by the competitor. The way that Peter perceives the offer is affected by the way that he places himself in such stories. What you hear depends on who you take yourself to be.

How do we learn and remember?

In narrative literature the point has often been made that we learn and remember through narrative. Hardy says:

> We dream in narrative, daydream in narrative, remember, anticipate, hope, despair, believe, doubt, plan, revise, criticise, construct, gossip, learn, hate and love by narrative.
>
> (Hardy 1968: 5)

Widdershoven argues that 'experiences have little value as long as they are not connected to, or as Proust says, fused with stories' (1993: 6–7). He argues that everything that we can remember is cast in narrative form, that narrative is sensemaking and vice-versa, and that if we do make any sense at all without narrative, it is not memorable. In the words of Weick:

> The requirements necessary to produce a good narrative provide a plausible frame for sensemaking. Stories posit a history for an outcome. They gather strands of experience into a plot that produces that outcome. The plot follows either the sequence beginning-middle-end or the sequence situation-transformation-situation. But sequence is the source of sense.
>
> (Weick 1995: 128)

When we speak of learning, we are always looking two ways. What is it that we are learning, and who is learning it? Only by understanding who we take ourselves to be can we understand what we are interested in learning. If Peter thinks of himself primarily as a professional, he will learn quite different things than if he understands himself as a manager, or as a manager in the making. The narratives that he sees himself as a part of, that he writes himself into, will reflect his identity. Funkenstein says:

> The identity of an individual and the identity of a group consists of the construction of a narrative, internal and external.
>
> (Funkenstein 1993: 23)

Funkenstein also argues that where people have been unable to construct a narrative account of what they are doing their lives have been robbed of meaning and purpose. If we are to see our lives as meaningful and purposeful, we will only do so by having a story into which our thoughts and actions can be fitted.

Many of the techniques that are used to help people remember are based on stories. A well-known way of remembering the sequence of the planets in orbit around the sun is to construct a story which includes a car (Mercury), a beautiful woman (Venus), a chocolate bar (Mars) and a small dog (Pluto). For most people, propositions are difficult to remember without some connecting storyline. History becomes easier to remember when it becomes detailed enough to start discussing the causal links that connect facts and people that might otherwise be all too easy to forget, or, in other words, when it becomes a story. Similarly, modern methods of teaching chemistry enable pupils to find a story in the atomic series and the ways that elements react, where a previous generation had to struggle to remember these as propositions.

Events only become meaningful and memorable when they form part of a story. It is hard to find an exception to this, although many of us can remember musical melodies or harmonic sequences without a story. Perhaps the sense of sequence in a melody or harmony can be argued to be the same as a narrative structure, as implied by the language of musical analysis (perfect, imperfect or interrupted cadences, strong or weak melodic endings, etc.). Even accountants and financial managers, who are engaged in what is often seen as one of the most propositional and rational of activities, seem in practice to make sense and to remember that sense through stories rather than through ratios (Birts *et al.* 1997).

Peculiarities of the organisational setting

The argument so far has been in terms of personal sensemaking, and has been conducted in terms of individuals regardless of where they are. To what extent might this be applicable to organisational life?

Organisations as arenas for stories have received considerable attention lately (Boje 1994: Gabriel 1991). For example, O'Connor says this about them:

> To discover how anything happens in an organization, we ask people to tell us stories. To convince others that we know something about how things happen in organizations, we construct and tell stories about those stories. As others react to our stories, they tell stories about the stories we have told — and so on.
>
> (O'Connor 1997: 304)

Elmes and Kasouf describe how this process worked in their research on biotechnology organisations:

> We discovered two contrasting and, we believe, competing narratives: a) learning as a process of rational, scientific inquiry and action to identify and develop effective new products and b) learning for the purpose of survival in a hostile economic and regulatory climate.
>
> (Elmes and Kasouf 1995: 418)

Particular forms of story are regarded as acceptable in particular organisations. As with most forms of culture, these are invisible to the extent that they are embedded, and only become visible in times of change. For example, the absence of stories about competition, efficiency and budgetary control in public-sector organisations only really became visible when it was under challenge from the new right in the 1980s. The absence only became visible when it was starting to be filled.

It would be possible to retell many stories of organisational change as being stories of a change in the dominant mode of storytelling. An important part of what managers spend their time doing is telling stories to one another and developing stories together to explain and understand what they are trying to do. Some of the published accounts of organisational change show the agent of change deliberately affecting the stories that are being told, or deliberately planting the raw material for storytelling. For example, Lee Iacocca tells of how he gave himself a salary of $1 per year when he took over at Chrysler, to give a lead to his new subordinates in seeing what he was prepared to do to save their company. This would work through spreading stories along the lines of 'look what the chief executive was prepared to do to give us a future'.

Organisations are complicated places, and the more we are faced by complexity and confusion the more we need to hear and to tell stories to cope with all that is going on. It seems reasonable to take it that storytelling is at least as important for hearing, making sense and remembering in an organisational setting as it is anywhere else.

Listening to stories

Storytelling is only part of the story. The role of the listener is also important. Listening to stories can be quite an active process. Stories are not necessarily passively received. The listener responds to some stories with enthusiasm, to some with disbelief, to some with excitement and to some with boredom. What are the characteristics that make the difference between stories that are influential and those that are dismissed?

There are some sources that are taken more seriously than others. This is not necessarily because they are believed to be truthful. If you asked Peter, in the story above, about his previous company, he would tell you about Alan.

> Of course Alan was always the most influential character there, and the funny thing was, however many times he let you down, you still believed him. Everybody wanted to believe him; that was the key. He would always talk to you as if you were his best and oldest friend, and before you knew where you were you found yourself warming to his story. Later on you found that he had given someone else the opposite story, and then you would find yourself trying to make excuses for him!

So credibility is important, and that is not the same thing as having a record of truthfulness. Other people may have a good record of telling the truth and never be able to get anyone interested in their stories. So the criteria on which stories do or do not have influence with those who hear them suggest that the critical faculties at work in judging them are complex. Here we can get help from Bruner, who discusses a view of narrative truth which he derives from Spence (1984):

> Spence addressed the question of whether a patient in analysis *recovered* the past from memory in the sense in which an archeologist digs up artifacts of a buried civilization, or whether, rather, analysis enabled one to *create* a new narrative that, though it might be only a screen memory or even a fiction, was still close enough to the real thing to start a reconstructive process going. The 'truth' that mattered, so went his argument, was not the historical truth but the *narrative* truth.

(Bruner 1990: 111)

So the issue is about which stories are taken as having narrative truth, enough internal strength and texture to come over as convincing, whatever their historical status may be. For the purpose of our argument in this chapter, the point is that storytelling is the means of exercising critical judgement on the part of both tellers and listeners, and that people will learn critically from the stories they come across. This critical learning will be based not on historical truth, but on narrative truth.

I also want to introduce a distinction which comes from Barthes (1974) between readerly and writerly stories.

Writerly stories

When you hear a story, what response is expected from you? Barthes (1974) differentiated between *scriptible* texts and *laisible* ones, translated by Roe (1994) as, respectively, 'writerly' and 'readerly'. The differentiation is about the recipient of the story, not the teller. When you hear some stories they invite you to put yourself in the position of a writer. The response they seem to require is active. They invite you not simply to sit back and listen, but in some sense to join in the storytelling, to respond as a writer or co-author of the story. To take Peter's story above, to the extent that you felt the story was complete in itself it was readerly, and to the extent that you were drawn into an act of contributory imagination, building up aspects of the story not touched on for yourself, it was writerly.

A particular variant of this is Boje's (1991) notion of multi-authored stories. Often in organisations a story is not told by one person but by several people in collaboration. One person will begin a story and someone else who was present at the event being discussed will bring in some point that was particularly salient for them. Someone else breaks in with their gloss, or with a phrase that was used (perhaps by someone not now present) when they first heard the story, and so it goes on. This is often very satisfying in itself; the production of a co-authored story can give the authors some of the same satisfaction as might be gained from the improvisation of a good jazz performance or a convincing piece of street theatre.

In the same way, writerly stories draw in and excite their hearers much more than would a story for which you are expected to remain passive. A writerly story gives the listener a considerable amount of freedom about what lessons they shall learn from it. Indeed, they may write into the story aspects of their own thinking and experience which give the story a meaning quite different from the one which the teller had originally intended to convey. Writerly stories do not offer much control to their tellers. They build in the opportunities for active critical response from listeners.

Readerly stories

Stories that are told in a more 'readerly' fashion (expecting the listener to behave in a more passive manner) do not invite a critical response so positively. These are stories that are told so as to cover the ground carefully, stories that have been carefully prepared, stories that have been designed to take the listener clearly in the direction desired by the storyteller.

If we take the story of Peter, when Stephen wanted him to get involved in the merger of the companies he engaged in a form of storytelling which was supposed to encourage him to take on the task. However, Stephen cannot really imagine that there are people in his group who would not like to be chief executive, so the storytelling was all on the assumption that Peter would like to have a job like Stephen's. The storytelling was intended to be readerly; the only interpretation was intended to be the one which showed the desired course of action as leading to power and glory. Peter took the story in a writerly fashion. He was not much interested in the picture that Stephen was painting of the possible future, but he was interested in seeing what he could get out of Stephen's need of him which would further the interests of his company.

A readerly story is an attempt to persuade the listener to behave in a passive way. It will not necessarily be successful as such. The listener may, like Peter, take his/her own meaning from the story and rewrite it in his/her own fashion. In this case the storyteller may be the only person who is convinced by the single interpretation of his/her own story, and may find him/herself cut off from later attempts to influence the way that the story is understood by his/her own clear interpretation of it. The only person constrained by readerly storytelling may be the storyteller.

Retelling stories

In the general commerce and dealing of organisations, there is not one teller and one hearer. Many stories are trafficked at some length. Like Boje's multiple authors, many people have a hand in their construction. Stories are traded; if someone tells you a really interesting and revealing story about what is happening in the organisation they may well expect one in return.

With storytelling, there is an expectation that it will not simply be a recitation of supposed facts. It is also expected to cohere, to have the properties of narrative truth and to entertain. As stories are retold they are also connected with other stories. Sometimes a composite story is formed. For example, when Peter tells his story about how he came to be managing the merger there is a story he tells about the opportunity to create a major player in the field of operation of the merged company. This is a compilation of Stephen's story to him and of various stories that Peter and Andrew have concocted over time to explain what they are doing. The retelling of stories bears in mind the new audiences for those stories, and may concoct something which is quite freestanding of the original story.

Stories and a critical stance

It is my contention in this chapter that it is reasonable to look at storytelling as a major managerial activity, and that if we do so we begin to understand how managers are able to act as natural critical theorists in their everyday managerial life. By means of hearing stories critically they are able to distance themselves from many attempts at influence and to evaluate how well founded they think the management knowledge they are being offered is. But how does this evaluation take place?

Testing stories

It has been said that drama as a representation of social life can be better tested than most social scientific theories on the grounds that a play has to withstand the scrutiny of an audience night after night. If the audience does not find narrative truth in what it is watching, the willing suspension of disbelief on which theatre depends will not be forthcoming.

So just what are the tests that are applied by a listener to a story? We have already discussed the question of whether they are prepared to credit it. It should be remembered that this is independent of whether the listener believes the story to be true. Another tests will be: what do they think the teller is up to in telling the story? That it is an innocent story being told to pass the time will not cross the minds of most managers. Storytelling is taken to be purposeful, and a lot of judgements are made about people on the basis of what you believe they are trying to do in telling you a particular story. For example, Peter had a highly discrediting story that he could have told Stephen about Tom, the chief executive of the competing company with which he was to merge. However, he dared not risk telling the story, not because he had any doubt as to whether he could demonstrate that it was true, but because he could not manage the impression that Stephen would have of his (Peter's) motives in telling it. So he told the story to some other colleagues who he thought could be trusted to pass it on to Stephen in due course.

Other tests will be: What can you do with the story? Is it interesting enough or revealing enough to give you credit in other circles? Is the story of any use to you? What can you trade for it? What can you understand with it that you could not understand beforehand? If stories are often told as an exercise in influence, what influence does the story give you? Alternatively, what does it tell you about the person who is trying to influence you?

I am not trying to suggest that these tests are explicit. Managers are rarely to be heard speaking directly along the lines of the ideas presented here. However, they are quite often to be heard passing comments which are consistent with what I am saying. I am offering an interpretive, not a grounded, theory of managers' response to stories.

Editing stories

The retelling of stories is always an act of authorship. That is not to say that it is a deliberate, instrumental activity. Like other forms of authorship it is prone to revealing unintended features of the author, and to the inclusion of errors. However, there is a considerable component of conscious editing, as we decide what versions of stories to pass back to whom, and how.

For example, in his new role Andrew gets to hear a lot of stories that would be of interest to Peter in his attempts to develop his newly merged company. He does not, however, pass many of these on. In some cases he feels they might be hurtful to Peter or be taken by him as negative feedback. In other cases he cannot rely on what Peter might do with them. It would be damaging to Andrew if he were seen to be feeding Peter preferential information within the group. Andrew edits with care the stories that he tells Peter, and tries not to tell him stories that would damage Andrew, either in Stephen's eyes if he were later to discover that Andrew had told them or in Peter's eyes when he is looking to Andrew for help and support.

Equally, Peter is careful about the editions of stories about Tom that he passes on to different colleagues. For consumption in his own company, he will make them as negative as possible, because Tom has long been seen as a scoundrel there and stories that confirm this view are popular. They also demonstrate that Peter has not been infected by the world-view of the other party in the merger – a widespread fear of his longer-serving colleagues in the company he came from. On the other hand, he will also tell stories about Tom in Tom's old company which show that, while Tom may have been misguided and not very clever, he is not being persecuted or hounded for his past actions. Peter needs to keep the show on the road in Tom's company and not suggest the possibility of mass executions, which might have Tom's colleagues leaving the ship to sink or staying only to sabotage.

Stephen, meanwhile, has a different style again of editing. He appears to be a very straightforward character who has no need to edit stories before use. The main clue to his highly active and selective editing probably lies in the rapid movement of his eyes during meetings, where he can be seen to spend all the time when he is not talking looking around very actively watching the effect of what is being said on all colleagues. This gives him the data he needs for editing stories later.

Recognising the character of the storyteller

People edit stories because of their awareness of the judgements that will be made of them by their audience. Why do we expect people to judge us on the basis of the stories we tell? Principally this is because any story which reflects a situation that we are connected with will reveal something of the way that we characterise ourselves. Many stories are told about the way that people place themselves in stories (also known as their managerial role identities; Pitt and

Sims 1998). For example, if your stories include references to the many important people that you have been talking to recently, stories will be told about your
name-dropping. If your stories are full of the plots against you and how you are
managing to survive them, you probably want people to tell stories about what
an effective fighter and survivor you are, but they may instead tell stories about
your paranoia. You may tell stories to show how busy you are, how effective you
are or how fallible you are; this last category is popular with managers who want
their employees to be able to own up to mistakes and learn from them.

We live our lives as characters in a plot. In our imaginations we see the character that we are enacting and script the reactions of other characters. We say
things to convey messages about the character that we are enacting, as well as for
all the other well-worn purposes. So when Peter sends a memo to Tom calling
him to account for some apparent acts of minor rebellion, Peter is not only
demanding explanations for particular pieces of behaviour but also telling Tom
that he intends to be seen as a strong and definite person, and one whom it
would be better not to treat badly. Behind the memo is a character statement
which says, ' You have already stepped over the mark, and I am ready to punish
any further transgressions' (Mangham and Overington 1987; Bolman and Deal
1994).

From the point of view of the hearer, the ability to hear what character the
storyteller wishes to be taken as is very important. It is not the basis of a good
relationship if this is misunderstood. For example, Peter and Andrew will take
great care when talking to Stephen to take account of his world-view and to edit
their stories so that he sees their characters as they (Peter and Andrew) would like
to be seen. But when they listen to Stephen's stories they are busy trying to
understand what character he would wish to be seen as. Is he being a friendly
helper? An avuncular supporter? A debt collector? A macho manager? Such
questions as to how to read the behaviour of the boss are regular topics of
conversation after meetings. It can be difficult to change character because of
the assumption on the part of listeners that you are still the same person. For
example, anyone who presents him/herself as the organisational joker may have
difficulty being taken as a serious character, even if s/he thinks s/he has something important to say.

Character is taken as continuous. The wish to play different characters in
different situations may be seen by others as a sign of unreliability or of a lack of
integrity. The person who has a rich repertoire of roles may give him/herself a
more exciting life, but does so at the cost of being seen as unreliable or 'lacking
character' by others.

Managers as natural critical theorists

As we have said, managers interpret the stories they are told. They interpret
them in the light of other stories they have heard, in the light of their view of
the character of the storyteller, in the light of the coherence of the story and so
on. They take on a function not unlike that of the reader of a novel or theatre-

goer in hearing the story and choosing to what extent to believe what they hear. They are not easily swayed to believe a story by the organisational power of the storyteller, although they may not display their disbelief so publicly in the face of a powerful teller.

The distance which managers get from events by their critical appreciation of stories is very much parallel to the distance achieved by critical theorists by a more propositional route. The project of the critical theorist has been described as allowing 'members of a society to alter their lives by fostering in them the sort of self-knowledge and understanding of their social conditions which can serve as the basis for such an alteration' (Fay 1987: 23, cited in Alvesson and Willmott 1992). There has been a tendency in some parts of critical theory to assume that the inhabitants of power structures may not be able to take a critical stance. My argument is that, while power relationships may certainly challenge such a stance, it is quite possible to achieve elements of a critical approach through the careful appreciation and criticism of the stories that are heard. It may be that we have a capacity for remembering and working with more complexity with stories, so that criticism becomes possible within a richer framework. Just as storytelling is the natural application of phenomenology in everyday life (Wallemacq and Sims 1998), so it is the natural means of critical knowledge in organisational life.

The achievement of critical learning

The foundations of management knowledge, as known and employed by managers, depend on a body of critical learning assembled over time. This cannot be expected to be gained easily. There will always be some uncritical acceptance of current norms, some collusion with current power structures, some mouthing of current clichés. However, there will also be subversion of the norms, covert or overt resistance to the power structures and rejection of cliché. Managers do not always learn what powerful figures would like them to learn. How is this achieved?

The argument of this chapter has been that it is achieved through the power of stories to handle complexity and ambiguity. When a story is being told, the possibility of several different things going on at once, of several different – and possibly apparently contradictory – interlocking modes of understanding coexisting, means that complex and ambiguous situations do not have to be reduced to unitary propositions. Such complexity and ambiguity are seen as of the essence of storytelling, rather than as annoying by-products. Managers understand, learn and remember through stories. They develop their questioning and their listening through stories. They have been listening to stories, and evaluating them, throughout their life. They therefore have had considerable experience as critical listeners to propositions, much longer than they have as critical listeners to propositional arguments. If we want to understand how managers achieve some degree of critical independence in their thinking and learning, storytelling gives us the best means of doing this.

The practice of storying: spoken 'tacit' knowledge

In this chapter I have argued that managers engage in a lot of storying, both as tellers and as listeners. The format of the story is well understood and well recognised, and leaves participants in little doubt as to the characters in the plot. Stories offer ways of communicating with far more complexity than most other available means.

This has implications for the old division between tacit and explicit knowledge (Polanyi 1967). If tacit knowledge is that which is left unspoken, what is a story? It is spoken or in some way communicated, it carries learning and knowledge, but the knowledge which is taken from it, especially for a 'writerly' story, is outside the control of the storyteller. Also, it is not explicit what the knowledge content of the story is supposed to be. Similarly, if it is true that our remembering takes place in stories, do those stories constitute tacit knowledge? In a sense they do, because the content of the knowledge is tacit. Nothing is said which tells you what is learned or remembered from the story.

It is therefore my proposition in this chapter that stories are the means by which tacit knowledge is held and stored, and are the means by which tacit knowledge is transferred from one person to another, and this is true however explicit the story may be. This transfer is an encouragingly critical process, because people are better able to hear stories critically than less narrative forms of communication.

References

Alvesson, M. and Willmott, H. (1992) 'On the idea of emancipation in management and organization studies', *Academy of Management Review* 17(3): 432–64.

Barthes, R. (1974) *S/Z*, trans. Richard Miller, New York: Hill & Wang.

Birts, A., McAulay, L., Pitt, M., Saren, M. and Sims, D. (1997) 'The expertise of finance and accountancy: an interdisciplinary study', *British Journal of Management* 8: 75–83.

Boje, D. (1991) 'The storytelling organization: a study of story performance in an office-supply firm', *Administrative Science Quarterly* 36: 106–26.

—— (1994) 'Organizational storytelling: the struggles of pre-modern, modern and post-modern organizational learning discourses', *Management Learning* 25(3): 433–61.

Bolman, L. and Deal, T. (1994) 'The organization as a theater', in H. Tsoukas (ed.) *New Thinking in Organizational Behaviour*, Oxford: Butterworth-Heinemann.

Bruner, J. (1990) *Acts of Meaning*, Cambridge, MA.: Harvard University Press.

Davis, D. (1993) *Telling your Own Stories: For Family and Classroom Storytelling, Public Speaking and Personal Journeying*, Little Rock, AR: August House Publishers.

Dutton, J. (1997) 'Strategic agenda building in organizations', in Z. Shapira (ed.) *Organizational Decision Making*, New York: Cambridge University Press.

Elmes, M. and Kasouf, C. (1995) 'Knowledge workers and organizational learning: narratives from biotechnology', *Management Learning* 26: 403–22.

Fay, B. (1987) *Critical Social Science*, Cambridge: Polity Press.

Funkenstein, A. (1993) 'The incomprehensible catastrophe: memory and narrative', in R. Josselson and A. Lieblich (eds) *The Narrative Study of Lives*, Thousand Oaks, CA: Sage.

Gabriel, Y. (1991) 'On organizational stories and myths: why it is easier to slay a dragon than to kill a myth', *International Sociology* 6(4): 427–42.

Hardy, B. (1968) 'Towards a poetics of fiction: an approach through narrative', *Novel* 2: 5–14.

Mangham, I. and Overington, M. (1987) *Organizations as Theatre: A Social Psychology of Dramatic Appearances*, Chichester: Wiley.

Mintzberg, H. (1973) *The Nature of Managerial Work*, New York: Harper & Row.

O'Connor, E. (1997) 'Telling decisions: the role of narrative in organizational decision making', in Z. Shapira (ed.) *Organizational Decision Making*, New York: Cambridge University Press.

Pitt, M. and Sims, D. (1998) 'Preparing for novel situations: evoking managerial role identities', *Journal of Management Education* 22: 6.

Polanyi, M. (1967) *The Tacit Dimension*, New York: Doubleday.

Roe, E. (1994) *Narrative Policy Analysis: Theory and Practice*, Durham, NC: Duke University Press.

Spence, D. (1984) *Narrative Truth and Historical Truth: Meaning and Interpretation in Psychoanalysis*, New York: Norton.

Wallemacq, A. and Sims, D. (1998) 'The struggle with sense', in D. Grant, T. Keenoy and C. Oswick (eds) *Discourse and Organization*, London: Sage.

Weick, K. (1984) 'Managerial thought in the context of action', in Suresh Srivastva (ed.) *The Executive Mind*, San Francisco: Jossey-Bass.

—— (1995) *Sensemaking in Organizations*, Thousand Oaks, CA: Sage.

Widdershoven, G. (1993) 'The story of life: hermeneutic perspectives on the relationship between narrative and life history', in R. Josselson and A. Lieblich (eds) *The Narrative Study of Lives*, Thousand Oaks, CA: Sage.

Part III
Re-situating management knowledge

9   The shaping of dominant modes of thought

Rediscovering the foundations of management knowledge

Robert Chia

In each period there is a general form of the forms of thought; and, like the air we breathe, such a form is so translucent, and so pervading, and so seemingly necessary, that only by extreme effort can we become aware of it.

(Whitehead 1933: 20)

Introduction

The historical processes of human evolution through natural selection and creative adaptation have generated the necessary conditions for basic survivalist patterns of thinking to emerge, be developed, preserved and passed on. Humans have, as a consequence, become ingeniously adaptive in coping with the vagaries of life. The elemental responses which have precipitated this adaptive pattern of thinking have become internalised to such an extent that they almost form a part of what we call human nature. Thus, the almost instinctive predisposition to observe, classify, typologise and thereby to create an inventory of categories of experience from which we are able to draw causal inferences is part of what McArthur calls our primordial 'taxonomic urge' (1986: 32). This basic human impulse to impose some systematic order on our lived experiences fuels the almost insatiable need for further *clarification*, the search for *causal explanations* and the accompanying attempt to *predict* future courses of events so as to be able to act advantageously therefrom. These cerebral predispositions have become the defining characteristics of the prevalent mode of thought especially dominant in the developed West. It is by now a well-documented fact that the ability to ask questions relating to these three key domains of concern is what accounts for the impressive artefacts of modern civilisation and underpins almost all of its outstanding discoveries and achievements. What is less well understood is the fact that the basic principles of modern organisation and management, formulated and developed within the context of contemporary preoccupations, are inextricably linked to these wider-ranging survivalist patterns of thought, which have continued to be adapted and refined to accommodate ever newer local experiences. Managing and organising are, therefore, fundamentally reality-constituting and world-ordering activities intrinsic to the survivalist instincts of the human species and not just techniques applicable to economic activities designed to achieve profits, growth, market share or global dominance.

The purpose of this chapter is to trace the foundational roots of modern principles of organisation and management and to relocate their origins in the broader civilisational processes that have taken place especially in the last three millennia. In particular, it will be shown that contemporary management thinking owes much to two major transformational events occurring in the history of Western civilisation – namely the alphabetisation of the world beginning some 3,000 years ago and the rapid rise of the printed word from the latter half of the 15th century. These two civilisational milestones irretrievably changed the course of human history in that they precipitated the necessary asymmetries in our *sense-ratios* for Euclidean thinking, with its attendant emphasis on abstraction, individuation, linearity and fixity in dealing with social and material phenomena, to rise to the level of prominence it holds today. These intellectual orientations and predispositions have, in turn, fundamentally shaped contemporary attitudes towards management knowledge-creation and hence the priorities and practices of management. It is argued here that without such a historical appreciation of the material events in human history and their effects on contemporary modes of thought the foundational principles of modern management knowledge and, more importantly, their hidden limitations cannot be fully appreciated. As the mathematician-turned-philosopher Alfred North Whitehead (1933) reminds us, the history of thought cannot be properly understood unless we critically examine and render more transparent the achievements and limitations of both the observational order and the conceptual order we have inherited from our forbears. This chapter seeks to make a small contribution towards this deeper understanding of the foundational forces shaping management thought and hence to reframe it in terms of the wider historical-shaping of modern civilisation.

The alphabetisation of the world

> By the meaningless sign linked to the meaningless sound we have built the shape and meaning of Western man.
>
> (McLuhan 1967: 50)

Any understanding of Western cultural evolution and change is impossible without a prior appreciation of the fundamental changes in *sense-ratios*, and hence attitudes of *observational discrimination*, brought about by the invention of the alphabet, the rapid spread of the printed word and the more recent discovery of the theory of relativity in the 20th century. Together, the first two constitute the defining moments shaping the very ground of possibility for the rise of the Cartesian/Newtonian world-view, which lasted till the latter half of the 19th century. This has now been superseded by the more recent momentous discovery of the theory of relativity and the quantum view of reality deriving therefrom. Our current heightened awareness of the severe limitations of classical scientific knowledge in general, and management knowledge in particular, owes much to the penetrating insights achieved at the dawn of the 20th century. However, to begin fully to appreciate how the mechanistic world-view first became possible, and how far-reaching its effects remain in contemporary management theorising, we must begin with the preliterate world of tribal cultures in which the 'multisensory void was an animate, pulsating, and moving vibrant interval, neither container nor contained – acoustic space penetrated by tactility' (McLuhan and McLuhan 1988: 34). For this autopoietically closed tribal world, thinking occurred without any systematic separation of sight and sound and without any need for abstract framing, so much so that these preliterate tribes 'scan objects and images as we do printed pages, segment by segment. Thus they have no detached point of view; they are wholly *with* the object. They go empathetically into it. The eye is used, not in perspective but tactually' (McLuhan 1967: 37; emphasis in original). Preliterate communities use their senses as prosthetic devices rather than as mechanisms for framing experience. The idea of abstract frames of meaning is alien to preliterate cultures.

This concrete predisposition was very vividly demonstrated by Wilson's (1961) discussion of an experience in which he attempted to use an educational film to teach African natives about basic hygiene and sanitation. To their amazement, Wilson and his team discovered that all the natives had picked up from viewing the film was a chicken running across the bottom frame of the film. After much bewilderment Wilson concluded that the natives had not develop the ability to see the picture frame as a whole and to follow the intended storyline. Instead they had inspected the frame for details only and the accidental occurrence of the chicken running across during filming provided the only bit of information they could relate to. Non-literate societies such as this African tribe cannot see films or photos without much training in literacy. This is because in learning the alphabets and the construction of words we also intuitively learn to attend to the frames of reference in relation to the details contained. The phonetic alphabet first translates images into arbitrary consonants and sound syllables which by themselves are meaningless. These are then mentally reassembled back into the form of words, from which meaning is then extracted. Meaning then only becomes possible at the operative level of words and not at the level of the individual alphabet. Literacy training, therefore, systematically develops the ability to construct meaningful frames out of otherwise meaningless consonants and sound syllables. As a result the capacity for framing is internalised. Literacy thus gives us the capacity to interpret meanings for the whole frame rather than the isolated details. It thereby affects the physiology as well as the psychic life of a people. This means that non-literate people have to be 'prepared' through literacy to develop an abstractive and purposive mindset. Hence, they cannot be straightforwardly 'managed' performatively, in the sense we conventionally understand, because the framing of what constitutes right and wrong, desirable and undesirable outcomes, and, more crucially, the notion of causality and its consequences has not yet been established and internalised. This is something which alphabetisation accomplishes. As McLuhan cryptically points out, 'Nobody ever made a grammatical error in a non-literate society' (1967: 238).

Alphabets transformed acoustic sound into visual terms and by so doing gave 'the barbarian or tribal man an eye for an ear' (McLuhan 1967: 26). The interiorisation of the technology of the phonetic alphabet 'delivered' man (*sic*) from the magical acoustic world to a world dominated by vision and abstract visual space. As Carothers points out:

> When words are written, they become, of course, a part of the visual world. Like most of the elements of the visual world, they become static things and lose, as such, the dynamism which is so characteristic of the auditory world in general, and of the spoken word in particular, in the sense that the heard word is most commonly directed at oneself, whereas the seen word most commonly is not.... Thus, in general, words by becoming visible, join a world of relative indifference to the viewer – a world from which the magic 'power' of the word has been abstracted.
>
> (Carothers 1959: 311)

The tonal inflections and emotional emphases accompanying the spoken word are inevitably lost in the translation into written form.[1] The sound heard and the word seen are distinctly different experiences. In the former, like listening to a continuous melody, the individual sounds melt into one another and there are no clear distinctions separating each note of the music. On the other hand, the phonetically based alphabet clearly delineates one syllable from another, one word from another and one sentence from another, and each is treated as a distinct entity to be manipulated and dealt with in isolation. This attitude is analogous to that form of thinking which developed in primitive life when hunting and gathering food was the major preoccupation. As McArthur argues:

> Just as, long ago, we learned to cut up the carcasses of animals and name the varieties of plants, just as we acquired the ability to make shapes out of pieces of skin sewn together, so we transpose 'ideas' from the physical world and 'cut up' and 'stitch together' parallel artefacts inside our heads, creating mental dissections, mental classifications, mental frames and mental bags or containers. Language was the midwife in this transfer from worldscape to mindscape.
>
> (McArthur 1986: 4)

Whilst language as speech developed secondarily from primary physiological apparatuses such as lungs, larynx, pharynx, mouth, nose, teeth and lips, which were all intended for the more primary purposes of breathing and eating, the shift to writing changed the focus from mouth and ear to hand and eye. This shift dramatically affected the secondary use of the senses. McLuhan suggests that it is this shift in sense-ratios from an overwhelming reliance on mouth and ear to hand and eye that generated the abstractive and detached attitude necessary for precipitating the opening up of otherwise closed preliterate societies (1967: 8). Likewise, Evans insists that the invention of writing 'was the most revolutionary of all human inventions, for in one great blow it severed the chains which tied an individual and his limited culture to a finite region of space, to a restricted slice of time' (Evans 1979: 104). Henceforth, man (*sic*) could preserve the richest fruits of his brainpower and stockpile them indefinitely for the benefit of future generations. This idea is reminiscent of Karl Popper's (1972) idea of World 3, which is a cumulative result of human interactions. World 3 is the whole cultural heritage comprising ideas, art, science, language, ethics, institutions and so on, which has acquired a reality of its own and which has become a part of the public domain. In short, it is only through the invention of writing that it has become possible systematically to accumulate what we now call knowledge and information to such an extent that humankind has become almost absolutely the dominant creature on this planet.

Invented some 3,000 years ago by the Phoenicians and appropriated and modified by the Greeks some three centuries later, alphabetic writing paved the way for the detribalising of ancient Greece and its subsequent rise into prominence in the first millennium BC. Through the newly systematised alphabetic script, the Greeks created, from the fifth and fourth centuries BC, one of the richest literatures of all times, including poetry, drama, epics, history and philosophy – so much so that we have today inherited much of this literature and wisdom, just as we have inherited the writing system in which it was recorded.

The advantage of the alphabetic system over previous forms of scribal writing lay in its startling economy and flexibility of use in communication: as an achievement it has often been compared to the invention of the wheel and the domestication of the horse. Henceforth, instead of having to deal with hundreds of distinct pictograms (picture signs), ideograms (idea signs) and logograms (word signs), between 20 and 30 quasi-phonetic symbols could now be used to portray an infinity of words and hence afford a much wider variety of expressions. This breakthrough in streamlining an otherwise unwieldy mess of previously disorderly signs gave language an overall orderly shape and made it much more manageable than before. It eventually led to the almost obsessive labelling, classification and thematisation of material and social phenomena so as to create order and predictability in an otherwise amorphous and fluxing life-world.

Writing in general, and alphabetic writing in particular, is inextricably linked to the systematic ordering and organisation of society. Thus, 'Communities developed ranks, casts and guilds, armies their divisions, priesthoods their hierarchies, merchants their inventories and farmers their fields and boundaries' (McArthur 1986: 32). As Goody (1986) perceptively points out, modern nations are highly dependent on writing for their legislatures and for their systems of governance. For Goody, 'the desk and the bureau' (1986: 90) are critical to Weber's concept of bureaucracy. Likewise, Green argues that:

The emergence of a large-scale, centralized, bureaucratic institution...might itself have been a consequence of the creation of tools which empowered its functioning. Certainly writing enabled the administration to grow and, through written liability, to maintain direct authority over even the lowest levels of personnel and clientele.

(Green 1981: 367)

Moreover, as McLuhan and McLuhan (1988) convincingly demonstrate, prolonged mimesis of the alphabet produced a dominant mode of perception which was overwhelmingly visual and which elevated the universal, the abstract and the static. Carothers (1959) reiterates that Western thought, because of its overwhelming influence by the alphabet, has developed a high degree of visual shaping of spatio-temporal relations, which, in turn, has led to the prevailing mechanistic understanding of causality that is so fundamental to our understanding of modern life. Likewise, Popper (1966) devoted a substantial section of the influential work *The Open Society and Its Enemies* to an analysis of the 'detribalisation' of ancient Greece effected by phonetic literacy and the opening up of these previously 'closed' societies. In sum, the alphabet is, as McLuhan puts it, 'an aggressive and militant absorber and transformer of cultures' (1967: 48). It precipitated the abstraction, isolation, objectification and linearising of phenomena for the purpose of analysis, and, by reducing all our senses into visual and pictorial or enclosed space, precipitated the rise of the Euclidean sensibility which has dominated our thought processes for over 2,000 years.

From copyist manuscripts to the printed word

Along with their civilisation, the Romans left us their language, Latin, and, with it, their writing system, which they had, in turn, borrowed from the Greeks. From around the third century BC an alphabet consisting of 19 letters emerged, and in the centuries following this lapidary script flourished on the monuments of the Roman Empire. With some small additions, this legacy of the Latin alphabet remains the basis for modern writing in Europe. However, writing, as a skill, remained confined to the 'men of letters'. These were, first, the scribes who copied the biblical texts onto rolls of papyrus and then subsequently the monks in the monasteries, who saw it as their duty to preserve the words of Christianity so that they could be passed on to the generations to come. But whilst the scribes used the cumbersome papyrus for keeping their records, the introduction of a new medium, parchment – made of sheepskin or calfskin that did not soak up ink or paint in the same way as the papyrus did and so was able to preserve the original colours better – revolutionised the process of copying and decorating. This discovery of parchment as a much better alternative rendered obsolete the use of papyrus and precipitated the binding together of sheets of folded parchment in the form of a 'codex' or book. Thus, by the 9th and 10th centuries each abbey and monastery had its own scriptorium where manuscripts were copied, decorated and bound. The art of copying using goose-quill pens became the major preoccupation of monastery life. Flawless organisation and a rigorous division of labour lay at the root of manuscript production. This de-secularising of writing in abbeys and monasteries gave rise to a new class of monastic artisans who jealously guarded their calligraphic secrets. Moreover manuscripts and books were mainly issued to the nobility and the clergy; for the former they were luxury pieces of work, for the latter they provided the necessary missals and theological manuals to perform their religious duties.

In around the year 1447, Johannes Gutenberg of Mainz became the first in the West to mechanise printing. The Chinese had used moveable characters since the 11th century AD and the screw press had also been known for some centuries before the time of Gutenberg, but they had been primarily used for pressing grapes and creating patterns on textiles, not for the purpose of producing the printed word. Initially, printing appeared to complement manuscript writing, which was increasingly in demand by the upper and middle classes, and the demand for which the monastic scribes had become increasingly unable to cope with. The printer's main purpose was to provide an alternative to scribal manuscript in producing decorated volumes that were as luxurious as the calligrapher's work. For this reason, large areas of the printed page were left blank to enable the decorations to be put in by an illuminator so that the final product could be as close as possible to the handwritten page. Soon, like the cottage industries of more recent times, the slow and laborious process of producing the written word gave way to printing. This marked a significant moment in the modification of the visual/tactile/audible *sense-ratios* that had first been rendered apart by the introduction of the alphabet. For whilst manuscript culture is effectively *conversational* in that 'the writer and his audience are physically related by the form of *publication as performance*' (McLuhan 1967: 84), the print culture created the distinction between authors and the consuming public. The invention of typography 'extended the new visual stress of applied knowledge, providing the first uniformly repeatable *commodity*, the first assembly-line, and the first mass-production' (McLuhan 1967: 124). Typography as the first mechanised handicraft altered the use of language and utterance as a means of tactile exploration and perceptual shaping (i.e. uttering as 'outering') to a portable commodity distinct from the producer. Whilst scribal culture was concerned with throwing light on the world *through* the manuscript form, typography threw light *on* the surface print itself. Its emergence radically shaped not only private sense-ratios but also the prevailing 'patterns of communal interdependence' (McLuhan 1967: 164). *Uniformity, quantification and measurability, individualism,* and *centralised control* became important priorities in the management of economic and social life.

Uniformity and quantification were important because print made it possible to produce almost identical copies in increasingly larger quantities. And this, in turn, created a larger appetite for more of the same. For the first time ever, mass production, as we understand it today, became possible. Print, in facilitating the translation of the vernacular into a mass media, initiated the demand for uniformity and standardisation, and hence inspired the homogenising forces of modernity. Likewise, individualism was accentuated because print emphasised the discrete and infinitely manipulable character of the individual alphabet, so much so that it became clear that an increasingly complex pattern of combinations may be rendered possible by an initially small number of constituent parts. As Rescher observes, even if the number of constituents of a system are small, 'the ways in which they can be combined to yield products in space-time might yet be infinite' (1996: 79). In the case of the alphabetic system, we are able to produce, from the initial 26 characters, impressive combinations of syllables, words, sentences, paragraphs, books, genres and so on to create the seemingly inexhaustible libraries of books we find around us. This rapid proliferation of the printed word to almost every corner of the earth testifies to the potency of print in radically extending the scope of the alphabetic system as the most powerful communicational medium civilisation has ever had.

This sense of incredible potentialities was first noticed, not so much by the scholars, but by the compositors working on the printing presses. They were constantly reshuffling the letters of the alphabet around as small hard metal objects in trays and in composite form. As a consequence they and their associate writers became

> increasingly at home with the convenience that the alphabet offers as an invariant series. Where scholars and copyists had previously been unaccustomed even to think of words and parts of words alphabetically, printers were now spending a greater part of their time doing nothing else. *Sheer familiarity with hard physical objects in a very practical craft appears, therefore, to have promoted interest in ABC order in other, related but more abstract fields.*
>
> (McArthur 1986: 77; emphasis mine)

Linear ordering of discrete and individualised items became a common feature in almost every activity in the world of affairs.

Centralised control and a linear, hierarchical order were also accentuated through the print culture because the latter provided possibly the first truly economical means significantly to overcome the hitherto troublesome limitations of space and time in terms of communication and influence. For print made it possible to achieve widespread communication at a distance and across time, for the literate masses to be reached directly, thereby influencing their attitudes, cultural habits and lifestyles. It is this principle of extension and intensification of communicational channels which made possible the kind of large-scale, centralised and bureaucratic institutions that Green (1981) referred to in his perceptive analysis of the organisation of society. Without the written word, communication would have to be passed on 'by word of mouth', thereby incurring inevitable distortions. Without the printed word, communication would have been restricted only to the privileged few and not to the critical masses required to produce revolutionary changes in the priorities and mindsets that paved the way for the Enlightenment to take place. The dramatic transformations and breakthroughs achieved in the West over the last 500 years especially would not have been possible.

Unbridled rationalism and the triumph of modernism

> A civilisation which cannot burst through its current abstraction is doomed to sterility after a very limited period of progress.
>
> (Whitehead [1926] 1985: 73)

The Enlightenment, as Gergen and Thatchenkery (1998) argue, was a historical watershed because of the emphasis it gave to four key ideational imperatives which continue to dictate much of contemporary management theorising. First, there is the unquestioned commitment to individualistic rationalism, the idea that individual agents are the ultimate unit of social reality and hence the most convenient unit of analysis. Such agents are deemed to be capable of exercising rational choice in any given situation. The result is that individual identities, actions and intentions provide the basis for description and classification as well as causal explanations. Henceforth, all phenomena were construed as discrete and independent entities, 'simply located' (Whitehead [1926] 1985: 61) and hence susceptible to causal analysis. This breaking-up of experienced phenomena into discrete manageable pieces and the fixing of these in space-time rendered them more amenable to cognitive manipulation and causal investigation. Such a strategy of analysis replicates the typesetting mindset associated with the invention of printing. It has also been discussed at some length by Philip Fisher (1991), who perceptively traced the origins of the idea of commodification and mass production to the basic activity of mining. In Fisher's view, the mining industry provided us with the first examples of the idea of deconstituting and reconstituting the natural world into a 'resource' for our use. As he points out, 'it is in mining that the world first appears as broken lumps of pure matter' (Fisher 1991: 223). For Fisher, the modern mass economy is best understood in terms of a series of stages beginning with the conversion of the mute and mutable mass into a useable resource by breaking it down and converting it into repeatable part elements. These are then reassembled back into an aggregate assemblage that is able to perform a function that satisfies the needs of modern society. In this way an initially intractable and amorphous mass (whether material or otherwise) is made more amenable to the demands of modern living. In a similar manner, individualistic rationalism can be understood as the result of a convenient habit of analysis inspired by the same principles underlying mass production. Just as the print typesetters dextrously shuffled individual alphabetic letters around to produce the desired combinations, the breaking-up and simple locating of human experiences to create clear-cut, definite things occupying clear-cut, definite places in space and time reinforced the underlying principle of individualistic rationalism.

Second, with the Enlightenment came the increasing emphasis on the observation of both natural and social phenomena and their location and classification in typological schemas. Vision and observation became central to our forms of knowing. Berger (1972), for example, shows convincingly how the Enlightenment systematically transformed our way of seeing from one of involved engagement to one of passive objectification. With the Enlightenment came the overpowering desire to scan, document, classify and sort out objects of interest, and to attribute causal powers to these artificially isolated objects of analysis. Through such careful observation and painstaking differentiation and classification of phenomena, it was believed that our knowledge of the universe could be systematically documented and the underlying natural order revealed. Linnaeus's *Systema Naturae*, written in the early 18th century, provides one of the clearest examples of this obsession with observation and classification. It precipitated the emphasis on what we now call 'systematic empiricism', the second ideational imperative associated with the advent of the Enlightenment. Initiated by Aristotle's call for grounding our knowledge in observations and inspired by Descartes' rigorously logical method of doubting, systematic empiricism surfaced most prominently in the kind of logical positivism which held sway in intellectual circles for the best part of the earlier half of the 20th century. It is within this theoretical soil, as Gergen and Thatchenkery (1998: 19) put it, that contemporary management and organisation theory took root.

Third, for Gergen and Thatchenkery (1998) the triumph of Enlightenment knowledge brought with it the idea that language was primarily a medium designed to enable us accurately to represent linguistically our visually perceived reality. This representationalist view of language derives from the Cartesian split between mind and matter. The purpose of the Cartesian mind is to mirror accurately the nature of matter existing externally to itself. Thus, to claim to possess knowledge, in the Cartesian sense, is to be able accurately to describe and explain things and events occurring outside the mind. In Rorty's (1980) terms, the picture used to ideologically captivate the Western world for over three centuries is the image of the mind as a mirror, containing various linguistic representations of the world. Thus:

> The picture...is that of the mind as a great mirror, containing various representations – some accurate, some not.... Without the notion of mind as mirror, the notion of knowledge as accuracy of representation would not have suggested itself. Without this latter notion, the strategy common to Descartes and Kant – getting more accurate representations by inspecting, repairing and polishing the mirror so to speak – would not have made sense.
>
> (Rorty 1980: 12)

For Rorty, it is this representationalist world-view which has provided the fundamental premises for the legitimation of modern knowledge. Knowledge is only deemed true and acceptable if it is able accurately to represent external reality as it is in itself. Such a view implies that language is seen as merely the medium of communication and that it does not play an active and constitutive role in the production of social reality. This belief about language has led to the commonplace insistence on literal precision and parsimony in the theory-building process in general and organisational theorising in particular (Pfeffer 1993).

Finally, Gergen and Thatchenkery (1998) maintain that the *narrative of progress* is also a key ideational imperative of modernity. For, if reason and observation were to work in harmony with language to give us an unmediated access to an objective reality, it would be possible objectively to validate and assess the status of any truth claims. This would, in turn, mean that an inexorable march towards a complete and ultimate truth was possible. The result would be the systematic application of this established knowledge to produce absolute predictability and the total elimination of any surprises in all facets of our lives. Our world would then be increasingly subjected to our absolute control, and this, in turn, would be a desirable outcome for mankind. It is the inherent attractions of the narrative of progress that drive the still-unabated search for a 'theory of everything'. These four ideational imperatives provide the intellectual cornerstones of modern thought in general and management thought in particular. Together, they serve as the recursive leitmotif underpinning the apparent diversity of ideas, concepts and theories generated over the past three centuries or more.

As in the natural sciences, so it has also been in management and organisation studies. The ultimate aim in these still-fledgling disciplines is to attain a respectable academic status and the accompanying recognition that the ideas, concepts and theories they produce are universally applicable because of their explanatory power, and, more importantly, because of their powers of prediction. To do this, management theorising has had to embrace the four ideological imperatives of modernism identified in this section. Yet the very epistemological templates for the natural sciences themselves have been radically revised ever since the momentous discovery of the principle of relativity and the more recent vindication of quantum views of reality. The very foundations of classical knowledge, including modern management knowledge, have, thereby, been dramatically challenged and undermined. Yet within the field of management and organisational theorising there has been relatively little attempt to incorporate these insights into contemporary modes of analysis. It is not within the scope of this chapter to delve into the complex transformational effects of these recent discoveries and their wide-ranging implications. However, it is the intention here to identify a number of key features which resonate with the concerns and preoccupations of this New Physics, and which have led to a call for a reappraisal of our understanding of science and the re-enchantment of nature (Bohm 1980; Prigogine and Stengers 1984; Ray Griffin 1988).

New metaphysical foundations for management knowledge: heterogeneous becoming, multi-locationalism, hybrid identities and informational flows

> Time is the substance I am made of. Time is a river which sweeps me along, but I am the river; it is the tiger which destroys me, but I am the tiger.
>
> (Borges 1970: 269)

A number of discernible theoretical initiatives, each recursively resonating with the others and hence loosely clustered together for conceptual convenience here, make up the emergent ideational orientations for a post-Newtonian view of reality. They also provide the necessary conceptual grounding for reformulating the foundations of management knowledge as we begin the new millennium. For the purpose of this chapter, I shall only deal with four of these interrelated epistemological strategies arising from the contemporary critique of modernist knowledge.

First, our understanding of change must be drastically revised. Instead of the still-dominant emphasis on 'things changing', thereby giving implicit priority to an entitative view of reality, what we have been made aware of through these newfound insights is that at the most fundamental level reality does not possess thing-like characteristics. Instead it is an undifferentiated, fluxing and amorphous whole indifferent to our causes. Events and experience, not things, are the ultimate units of reality. Thus for Whitehead (1929) the most basic unit is 'an atom of experience'. For him, the new outlook brought about by the quantum requirements of post-Newtonian physics is

> [the] displacement of the notion of static stuff by the notion of fluent energy. Such energy has its structure of action and flow.... Mathematical physics translates the sayings of Heraclitus, 'All things flow', into its own language. It then becomes, 'All things are vectors'.
>
> (Whitehead 1929: 437)

Hence, if we are to go back to that ultimate pristine realm of pure experience unwarped by the sophistication of theory, it is flux, change and transformational energy which prevail. Likewise, for the French philosopher Henri Bergson ultimate reality is 'global and undivided growth, progressive invention, duration' ([1946]/1992: 95). Time and temporality, flux and change precede substantive existence, as the Nobel laureate Ilya Prigogine (1996: 163) astutely observed. Order and stability, and hence form, substance and existence, are exceptional states rather than common conditions. Stability, locatability and identity are only possible because of acts of human intervention which operate to slow down, arrest and conceptually fix the incessant flux and flow of reality. What we call 'things' or 'entities', such as 'individuals' and 'organisations', are merely the 'material manifestation points' (Ford and Ford 1994) of an underlying implicate order (Bohm 1980). Or, as the process theologian Charles Hartshorne puts it, '[t]he point is not that individual identity is an illusion, but that it is abstract' (Hartshorne, in Browning 1965: xii). What is more concrete than the concept of an individual is the actual history, the succession of experiences and 'states' which constitute the reality of the individual through time. This means that the stabilities and regularities that we find in social reality must be understood as islands of artificially constructed order in a sea of ceaseless change. The image of how such apparent stability is achieved is best captured by the idea of two trains travelling on parallel tracks in the same direction and at the same speed. For passengers in each of the two trains, the other train is effectively stationary. This clearly *exceptional* situation is what allows the travellers in the two trains to hold out their hands to one another or talk to each other, since they are 'stationary' in this special sense. Our mistake in academic theorising has been to take this eminently familiar 'stationary' situation as the rule rather than as an exception and to then weave our system of comprehension around it. What the principle of relativity and quantum theory reasserts is the primacy of flux, change, movement and spatio-temporal interpenetration. Things, entities and apparently solid substances are but the temporal coalescence of matter-energy, and the actual world is a ceaseless process involving the *becoming* of such event-entities.

Moreover, becoming and change are always heterogeneous, other and surprising. Change does not occur in a linear manner or in the form of an incremental, homogeneous unfolding. Instead, change is multiple, complex and heterogeneous. It is the 'perpetual unification of a pluralistic reality which, as fast as it gets unified, becomes pluralistic again, and so can never be finally unified' (Hartshorne, in Browning 1965: xviii). Thus, as Bergson describes it, when we think about change around us we must be aware that

> That which goes from yellow to green is not like that which goes from green to blue: they are different *qualitative* movements. That which goes from flower to fruit is not like that which goes from larva to nymph and from nymph to perfect insect: they are different *evolutionary* movements. The action of eating or drinking is not like the action of fighting: they are different *extensive* movements. And these three kinds of movement themselves – qualitative, evolutionary, extensive – differ profoundly.
>
> (Bergson 1911: 321; emphasis in original)

In our thinking about change, however, we tend to conceptualise a change that is 'everywhere the same and invariably colourless' (Bergson 1911: 321), a change devoid of this richness and multiplicity. Change, flux and heterogeneity are fundamental features of ultimate reality. The social reality that we find so immediately familiar and necessary is in fact an abstraction and stabilisation of this underlying heterogeneous change process.

Second, because all social and material phenomena we subconsciously experience are temporarily stabilised and delineated by our very act of perception, experienced phenomena cannot be simply taken to be made up of discrete, identifiable elements or objects external to us and identifiable in space-time. This creates an insurmountable problem for traditional casual analysis, which relies on the notion of the simple locatability of the causal element and its effects. As Whitehead clearly demonstrates, the concept of an ideally isolated system, simply locatable in space-time, was a necessary precondition for Newton successfully to formulate his first law of motion ([1926]/1985: 58). It is this ontological assumption that reality is made up of a 'succession of instantaneous configurations of matter' (Whitehead [1926]/1985: 63) that the 17th-century thinkers gave as an answer to the ancient Ionian question: what is the world made of? This is the ontological premise which provides the basis for the orthodox creed of modern scientific thought. It is this very premise which has been challenged and undermined by new developments in physics which reject the possibility of simple location even for material phenomena. As Prigogine explains, acceptance of the primacy and necessity of flux and instability implies that 'We can no longer prepare a single trajectory, as this would imply infinite precision [in terms of location]' (1996: 37). This is because '[t]he initial condition is no longer a point in space but some region described by ρ... We thus have a *nonlocal* description. There are still trajectories, but they are the outcome of a stochastic, probabilistic process' (Prigogine 1996: 37; emphasis in original), not trajectories of identifiable particles. What Prigogine and others are pointing out to us is that in post-Newtonian physics we no longer deal with simply located or locatable phenomena, but with phenomena which are essentially dispersed and *multi-locational*. This is a point reiterated by McLuhan and McLuhan when they maintain that 'Relativity theory forced the abandonment of absolute space and time' (1988: 43), thereby creating the necessary conditions for an indeterminacy resulting from the incongruity between 'the visual bias of classical science and the new acoustic sensibilities' (*ibid.*: 44) to arise. This understanding has inspired the experimental arts to 'paint as if you held, rather than as if you saw, objects' (*ibid.*: 54). Cubism, for example, exemplifies this painterly form of 'multi-locational' experimentation brought about by the advent of post-Euclidean acoustic space in physics.

These insights go entirely against the grain of the still-dominant reductionistic and *centred* attitude of analysis (what Derrida (1977) calls 'logocentrism' or the metaphysics of presence[2]) that we find so difficult to overcome in our habits of thought. Yet it is this call to embrace a *decentred* approach to phenomenal analysis that underpins the metaphysical project of Whitehead, Bergson, Prigogine and a number of other significant contemporary postmodern writers, including especially Serres (1982), Deleuze and Guattari (1988), and Cooper (1998). Such a decentred approach to the analysis of organisation and management would open up entirely new avenues of enquiry, in that it would eschew simple causal explanations for a far more complex and dispersed as well as historically informed understanding of how events take shape, develop and realise themselves in the unpredictable flux of life. It would sensitise us to the multifaceted becoming of events and happenings, 'with all the accidents, the minute devia-tions – or conversely, the complete reversals – the errors, the false appraisals, and the faulty calculations that gave birth to those things that continue to exist and have value' (Foucault, in Rabinow 1984: 81). It is this deeper appreciation of the genealogical traces immanent in the formation of things that has been generally overlooked in the ideological imperatives of modernism.

Such a sensitivity also enables us to recognise that, especially in the world of social reality, there are no 'pure' identities, no clear lines of demarcation, no 'a priori' justifiable imperatives we can conveniently make or rely upon in our attempts to understand and evaluate the complex of situations we regularly find ourselves in. Instead, much of what constitutes our late-modern social identity are loosely clustered tendencies assembled and precariously held together momen-tarily to achieve a desired response or outcome. *Hybrid identities* better characterise those precarious 'assemblages' we call individuals, social systems, objects and things at the beginning of this new millennium as we begin to take stock of the wide-ranging effects of the internet, mass media and communica-tion, and genetic engineering on our lives. This is the point Cooper and Law (1995) make in their reference to the term 'cyborganisation': a hybridisation of bodies and technologies in informational fields. The cyborg is a hybrid of machine and organism whose ambiguous constitution relativises the differences between human and mechanical systems. It expresses itself through the 'plas-ticity of informational patterns' (for example databases, electronic money, etc.), thereby enabling and facilitating the 'combinatorial play of matter and thus the continuous disassembly and reassembly of new forms and patterns' (Cooper and Law 1995: 268). Cyborganisation stresses *information in the process of forming, infor-mation on the move*, so to speak, thereby giving priority to the

> translation of patterns, ideas, programmes *between* systems rather than the individual systems themselves. For, in cyborganization, it's not the system – the individual, the organization, the society – that count [*sic*] but the patterns of information that move between them and which constitute them.
>
> (Cooper 1998: 139)

Identities are the after-effects of information and translation.

In an interesting paper discussing the impending virtualisation of the organi-sational subject, Sotto (1998) maintains that the grammatical habit of putting an 'I' at the origin of any activity in order to attribute to it some causal powers may very soon be rendered obsolete by the advent of computerised information tech-nology. For Sotto, the rise of computers and information technology offers wide-ranging ramifications for the 'virtualisation' and 'decentring' of individual subjectivities. First, the embodiment of the subject in a material body is chal-lenged. This is because human actors, in their interface with computer technology, invariably need to acquire an *online persona* and adopt a 'terminal' identity instead of being secured and simply locatable in a single physical body. Moreover, consciousness in this context is redefined as the temporal and spatial 'arresting' and 'suspension' of the never-ending flow of worldly events, rather than as an internal state of mind. Correspondingly, agency is not simply locatable but instead distributed in the temporary intertext of informational flows. The decentred subject thus becomes a kind of open-ended field providing a topos for the exchange of discourses. This precarious networked identity is a far cry from the self-secure and easily identifiable individual agent that modernism constructed, which, at the beginning of the new millennium, has now run its course.

Finally, the postmodern world unleashed by seminal events at the turn of the 20th century, but relatively unnoticed until recently by management and organisation theorists, is one in which *informational flows* and nodal points of interaction dictate possibilities and outcomes. In his massive trawl of contemporary economic, societal and cultural trends, the sociologist Manuel Castells (1996) impressively charted the emergent dynamics of the information age. For Castells, the information age is marked by the rapid rise and ceaseless proliferation of social networks. Such a relationally networked society no longer rests upon fixed realities circumscribed by time and space. Instead, networks are nodal clusters of relationships through which information flows, and in that very process they help temporarily secure the transient identities that transcend space and time. As is now well known, the internet, for instance, allows us to establish and sustain close friendships across many thousands of miles. Surfing the internet opens up infinite possibilities for engagement with other network identities, often creating totally unexpected outcomes. More relevantly for the world of management, financial transactions in the global economy take place seemingly without much concern for national boundaries, geographical distance or relational familiarity. Its substance consists of endless complex ebbs and flows from one part of the world to another, oftentimes causing acute local instabilities and disruptions, as witness the case of the Asian financial crisis. As with financial flows, so also with *informational flows* and image flows. Knowledge and information as well as visual images flow to wherever advantage can be momentarily gained and immediate gratification achieved. There is a relentless transgression of local priorities, cultures, lifestyles and modes of thought. As a result, the ability to 'manage' local resources, aspirations and work attitudes, for example, is seriously undermined by the infinite possibilities created by informational flows through the internet. The almost inexorable outcome seems to be a determined homogenising of ideals, aspirations, strategies and practice, and the eventual tyranny of the universal over the particular. Yet such informational flows also precipitate an awareness of the transient nature of events and situations, the particular and the here-and-now where local experimentation and novelty-creation become evermore urgent. Thinking in terms of informational flows allows us to recognise the fleeting nature and infinite brevity of contemporary human experiences.

Our far too brief discussion of heterogeneous becoming, multi-locationalism, hybrid identities and informational flows provides a glimpse of the kind of intellectual orientation needed for rebuilding the foundations of management knowledge. Thinking heterogeneous becoming orients us to understanding 'how things become' rather than specifying the characteristics of 'how things are'.

According to this view, 'how an entity *becomes* constitutes *what* that actual entity *is*; so that the two descriptions of an actual entity are not independent. It's "being" is constituted by its "becoming". This is the principle of process' (Whitehead 1929: 28; emphasis in original). Events and entities must not be viewed in isolation, but rather seen as part of an ongoing process of creative evolution. Multi-locationalism points us to the need to develop a decentred approach to analysis where attention is shifted from the centre or core of a problematic to the peripheral and the marginal. It encourages the development of a kind of scattered vision that enables us to detect the tangential unfolding of events occurring outside the central focus of attention. Hybrid identities alert us to the transience of seemingly present phenomena and their intrinsic precariousness, whilst informational flows direct us to look for pattern formations rather than established stabilities as the starting point for our analytical investigations. Together these four intellectual orientations serve as intellectual orientations for guiding us in revising our understanding of the problematic of contemporary management and for laying the foundations for a new epistemology of management consistent with the metaphysics of our time.

Conclusion

Modern management knowledge relies overwhelmingly on the written word and is disseminated through print. Writing in general and alphabetic writing in particular facilitated the development of abstract thinking and the capacity for purposeful framing of individual activities. In so doing it encouraged the necessary goal-orientation required for a rudimentary form of organisation and management to emerge. However, these organisational forms were confined to local orderings, and this state of affairs did not substantially change until the invention of the printing press enabled the printed word to reach far beyond the spatial confines of a particular established order. Through the printed word, the aspirations, cultural attitudes and lifestyles of those both far and near, and across time, could be influenced and shaped. Printing thus freed thought and aspirations from the shackles of local knowledge.

Contemporary management knowledge has only become possible for two interconnected reasons. First, the practice of management as a technique for constituting, ordering and controlling 'resources' is only possible because of the development of an analytical attitude based upon the alphabetisation of the world and the advent of typography. Second, the systematic accumulation of knowledge *about* management (i.e. management knowledge) as a reality of World 3₁ is only possible because such knowledge relies upon the stockpiling of the written word. In this sense, as I have attempted to argue throughout this chapter, modern management knowledge would not have been possible without the alphabetisation of the world and its systematic dissemination through the printed word. However, it is clear that we are now entering a realm of reality in which wisdom, knowledge and information can no longer be simply understood in commodified and identitarian terms. Instead, instability and 'noise', informational fluxes, dispersions and transient configurations of relations are what characterise the phantom-like qualities of postmodern management knowledge, an elliptical form of knowledge in which the 'in-betweens', the opportunistic 'conquests', the restless expansions and sudden offshootings are accentuated and celebrated. Such knowledge-forming is often subtle, agglomerative, subterranean and heterogeneous in nature, spreading like oil patches rather than following any particular pre-established order. This is the new mode of thought to cultivate at the beginning of this new millennium.

Notes

1   This is much less the case in the Chinese language, which is ideographic in character and which allows for tonal inflections in its written form.
2   'The metaphysics of presence' is a term used to describe the overwhelming tendency to believe that things can be presented to us in their pristine immediacy through language without language itself becoming an obstacle in that process. It is this metaphysics of presence which justifies a representationalist view of knowledge.

References

Berger, J. (1972) *Ways of Seeing*, London: Penguin.
Bergson, H. (1911) *Creative Evolution*, London: Macmillan & Co.
—— ([1946]/1992) *The Creative Mind*, New York: Citadel Press.
Bohm, D. (1980) *Wholeness and the Implicate Order*, London: Routledge & Kegan Paul.
Borges, J.L. (1970) *Labyrinths: Selected Stories and Other Writings by Jorge Luis Borges*, ed. D.A. Yates and J.E. Irby, Harmondsworth: Penguin.
Browning, D. (1965) *Philosophers of Process*, New York: Random House.
Carothers, J.C. (1959) 'Culture, psychiatry and the written word', *Psychiatry*, November: 18–34.
Castells, M. (1996) *The Information Age*, vol. 1, Oxford: Basil Blackwell.
Cooper, R. (1998) 'Assemblage notes', in R. Chia (ed.) *Organized Worlds*, London: Routledge.
Cooper, R. and Law, J. (1995) 'Organization: distal and proximal views', *Research in the Sociology of Organizations*, vol. 13, Greenwich, CT: JAI Press.
Deleuze, G. and Guattari, F. (1988) *A Thousand Plateaus*, London: Athlone Press.
Derrida, J. (1977) 'Limited Inc.', in S. Weber and H. Susman (eds) *Glyph 2*, Baltimore, MD: Johns Hopkins University Press.
Evans, C. (1979) *The Micro Millennium*, New York: Viking.
Fisher, P. (1991) *Making and Effacing Art*, New York: Oxford University Press.
Ford, J.D and Ford, L.W. (1994) 'Logics of identity, contradiction and attraction in change', *Academy of Management Review* 19(4): 756–85.
Gergen, K.J. and Thatchenkery, T.J. (1998) 'Organizational science in a postmodern context', in R. Chia (ed.) *In the Realm of Organization*, London: Routledge.
Goody, J. (1986) *The Logic of Writing and the Organization of Society*, Cambridge: Cambridge University Press.
Green, M. (1981) 'The construction and implementation of the cuneiform writing system', *Visible Language* 15: 345–72.

McArthur, T. (1986) *Worlds of Reference*, Cambridge: Cambridge University Press.

McLuhan, M. (1967) *The Gutenberg Galaxy*, Toronto: University of Toronto Press.

McLuhan, M. and McLuhan, E. (1988) *Laws of Media*, Toronto: University of Toronto Press.

Pfeffer, J. (1993) 'Barriers to the advance of organizational science: paradigm development as a dependent variable', *Academy of Management Review* 18(4): 499–520.

Popper, K.E. (1966) *The Open Society and Its Enemies*, Princeton, NJ: Princeton University Press.

—— (1972) *Objective Knowledge: An Evolutionary Approach*, Oxford: Oxford University Press.

Prigogine, I. (1996) *The End of Certainty*, New York: Free Press.

Prigogine, I. and Stengers, I. (1984) *Order Out of Chaos*, London: Fontana.

Rabinow, P. (1984) *The Foucault Reader*, Harmondsworth: Penguin.

Ray Griffin, D. (1988) *The Reenchantment of Science*, New York: State University of New York Press.

Rescher, N. (1996) *Process Metaphysics*, New York: State University of New York Press.

Rorty, R. (1980) *Philosophy and the Mirror of Nature*, Oxford: Basil Blackwell.

Serres, M. (1982) *Hermes: Literature, Science, Philosophy*, Baltimore, MD: Johns Hopkins University Press.

Sotto, R. (1998) 'The virtualization of the organizational subject', in R. Chia (ed.) *Organized Worlds*, London: Routledge.

Whitehead, A.N. ([1926]/1985) *Science and the Modern World*, London: Free Association Books.

—— (1929) *Process and Reality*, New York: Free Press.

—— (1933) *Adventures of Ideas*, Harmondsworth: Penguin.

Wilson, J. (1961) 'Film literacy in Africa', *Canadian Communications* 1(4), summer: 1–38.

10 Hybridisation and dis-identification

Fatal modernisation strategies in organisations

Willem Koot

Introduction

In the early 1990s my longstanding anthropological interests took me in the direction of cultural and identity processes in organisations. My previous research had been mainly on migration and ethnicity. This interest in organisations initially had a very negative colouring, for I was extremely irritated by the way organisational analysts, followed by managers and consultants, handled the concept of culture. The dominant view at the time was that culture was a manager's plaything. You could direct it and change it in this or that direction as you chose. Culture was identified with shared values, rituals and symbols. It was supposed to be the cement of the organisation and decisive for its success or failure. Following authors like Peters and Waterman (1982), every effort went into finding out the characteristics of the ideal culture so that those characteristics could be implemented as quickly as possible. Notions of so-called excellent organisational cultures were presented as universally applicable. There was little or no interest in diversity or interpretations by the members of the organisation itself, and no links were made between the attribution of meaning and power. There was absolutely no concern about the situational use of cultural elements and the shifting of ethnic and cultural identities depending on the context, which had been familiar in anthropology since Barth's publications in the 1960s (see in particular his standard work from 1969). In short, the dominant conception of organisational culture was too instrumentalist, mechanistic, static, uniform, top-down oriented and atomistic (for an extensive critique, see, for example, Koot and Hogema 1990).[1]

Ten years later, the present situation looks much more favourable, with some encouraging developments taking place in practice and in organisational theory.

First of all, during the last few years organisational analysts and management specialists have begun to take a real interest in self-management, empowerment and trust. This seems to mark a departure from the desire to control processes of sensemaking in organisations and the top-down approach to cultural change. The notion of uniformity appears to have gone out of currency as well. Terms like 'management of diversity' and 'pluralism of norms and values' repeatedly crop up in various places (not only in academic discourse but in magazines that are popular among consultants and managers and, subsequently, in management training courses). Indeed, almost every large consultancy in the Netherlands is currently engaged in setting up a division to deal with issues of social responsibility, sustainability, integrity and trust. An interest has even emerged in non-Western views of management and organisation.

At first sight, then, there is much to welcome in these changes. Many of these developments can be directly or indirectly derived from the basic principles of postmodernism, which has pronounced the death of truth and reason, with the consequent vigorous opposition to absolutism, universalism and monoculturalism. These concepts have been replaced by others, such as ambiguity, paradoxicality, multiperspectivism, pluralism, hybridity, and the situational switching and strategic deployment of identities. We seem to have been liberated from the constrictions of Enlightenment principles like rationalisation, control and standardisation. Any opinion seems to go. Representatives of ethnic minorities in the West and residents in non-Western countries should take advantage of the situation. After all, their views (not only of time or of interaction with nature, but also of organisation and management) are not only tolerated, but incorporated and hybridised in the cultures of the West. Moreover, with the emphasis on empowerment, reflexivity and self-management, more attention seems to be being paid to strengthening the autonomy of the individual and with it the power of other members of staff. The ideal that many strove and fought to achieve in the 1960s, but which was rejected after a while as unfeasible and bad for the economy, now seems to be actually developing: a global society in which no single culture is dominant and all cultures are allowed, in which organisations delegate authority far away and individuals take their fate in their own hands and determine their own course. The 'reflexive modernisation' so dear to Beck *et al.* (1994), in which modal citizens detach themselves from the experts, 'place active trust' in the other and become aware of the 'side-effects' of modernisation, seems on the point of becoming reality.

Upon closer inspection, however, the principles of the Enlightenment and Western ethnocentrism still seem to persist. It is only that they are now more veiled and complex (because of being mixed with other principles) than they were in the 1980s and early 1990s. Situational behaviour is also displayed much more than in the past, and different discourses are employed in different contexts by the same persons or groups, entirely in accordance with the principles of postmodern society. People change their identity and opinions, combine one opinion with another, present the non-authentic as authentic, and in the course of time they come to believe it themselves (Baudrillard 1994). Simulations and hybrid models are particularly well represented in the world of management and organisation.

In this chapter I shall try to throw light on this position, and also go into the possible negative and positive effects of the trends outlined above. I shall also attempt to present alternatives.

The first stage is to analyse the currently dominant theory and practice of change in organisational culture (especially concerning the implementation of self-management in the organisation and the operationalisation of the 'management of diversity') and of cross-cultural co-operation in Western (mainly Dutch) organisations in the light of a changing global cultural order. I shall start with the latter aspect.

The growing significance of ethnicity in a globalising and fragmenting world[2]

Since the late 1980s events have become highly intertwined at a global and local level. Local events are increasingly being influenced by events that take place thousands of miles away and vice-versa. Intertwining of local and global issues also applies to organisations that can be seen as hybrids that have resulted from the interaction of global and local factors. Hannerz (1992) draws attention to present-day hybridisation, but mainly concentrates on processes that take place on the periphery (a term he uses for the former Third World countries). In this connection he has introduced the concept of 'creolisation'. By means of extensive and detailed empirical material, Hannerz illustrates that this so-called periphery does not take up all kinds of cultural elements from the centre indiscriminately, but selects and fits them with care. The periphery, partly due to the use of technologies and organisational forms identical to those of the centre, increasingly talks back. In other words, more and more often cultural elements are being supplied to the centre and even offered for sale, or 'commodified', as Giddens (1991) and Appadurai (1986) have put it. This applies not only to music, clothing, literature and art but also to the know-how of organisations, for example. According to Hannerz, the supremacy of the so-called First World is diminishing, and one could imagine that the periphery of today will be the centre of tomorrow (1992: 226).

The worldwide proliferation of knowledge and technology, and also of cultural elements, has in some respects led to unification, homogenisation and standardisation, in others to differentiation and fragmentation. The latter notably apply to the question of ethnic identities. It is precisely the process of globalisation that has made people aware of differences in opinion but also in status, power and the possession of scarce commodities. This in turn has led to a stronger sense of identity and the significance of it. For affective reasons (a desire for security and safety in the growing massiveness, loneliness and vagueness of our individualised world), but also for reasons of strategy and self-interest, people are standing up for their own region and are desperately seeking roots. Phenomena such as ethnic revitalisation, cargo cults, and the invention and reinvention of traditions are frequently occurring in our globalising world. This concerns not only the periphery but also the centre. The two processes, globalisation and localisation, go hand in hand. They cannot be seen separately. Globalisation leads to anti-globalisation and particularisation, which is why several authors (e.g. Ohmae 1990; Robertson 1995) use the term 'glocalisation'.

These cultural and ethnic processes cannot be understood without a profound analysis of the attendant oppositions in power of the different ethnic groups, regions and nations involved. Cultural imperialism, minority formation and emancipation are causally interconnected with social identity formation processes such as ethnicisation (e.g. Koot and Rath 1987). In that respect, the general growth in the importance of ethnicity is not a mere coincidence, but rather a derivative of a changing world order (cf. Friedman 1994).

The radicalisation of the principles of modernisation such as individualisation, rationalisation, differentiation (the division of the totality into smaller components) and domestication has directly and indirectly contributed to a significant extent to such processes of emancipation. Individualisation, after all, has in practice not only led to an expansion of the autonomy of the individual in general and underprivileged groups in particular, but also brought about feelings of the growth of dependence on experts and specialists in all kinds of areas. One of the consequences of rationalisation has certainly been that we have obtained more of a grip on nature and more insight into the operation of all kinds of chemical, physical and economic processes. On the other hand, as a result we have increasingly lost our view of the totality, and, also in part through the quest for increase of scale, uniformity and standardisation, feelings of blurring have arisen. Nature is talking back, insecurity has increased, and we live more and more in a risk society (Beck 1992). In combination with the process of globalisation sketched above, all of these factors have contributed to a demand for distinction.

Regionalisation and ethnicisation are the logical consequence. Since Barth (1969) we also know, however, that ethnicisation is often a reaction to feelings of oppression, making it a weapon in the hands of those wishing to emancipate. Ethnic minorities in Western Europe and the United States defend their rights, and Third World countries increasingly resist the economic and military dominance of the West and what they regard as the associated cultural imperialism. It is logical, therefore, that the resistance is strongest against those elements on which Western culture is based. These are in particular the principles of modernisation such as individualisation, rationalisation and differentiation, and probably include hybridisation as well (in the view of Baudrillard (1990) hybridisation is the logical consequence of the radicalisation of the principles of modernisation). This means a threat to Western culture and society from within and without: through the resistance of ethnic minorities and Third World countries, but also through the fact, as Baudrillard (1990) indicates, that the trend towards hybridisation marks the fact that modernisation has gone to the limits. The paradoxes in Western culture become stronger and stronger, the anchorpoint seems increasingly to disappear, rhetoric assumes alarming proportions and there is a threat of implosion. Let us see the effects of all this on Western models and practices of organisation and management. How do they deal with the increasing cultural and ethnic complexity?

The dominant 'theory' of the management of diversity and cross-cultural co-operation

Ever since the early 1980s, when the focus on organisational culture resurfaced in organisational theory and practice, there has been an ambiguity in the mainstream approach to this concept. After all, it was intended as a reaction to the failure of the rational systems approach, in which the key words were efficiency, planning and manipulability. The majority of organisational theorists at the time were influenced by two main sources of inspiration: the publications of Peters and Waterman (1982) and Ouchi (1981). Both books attempted to make it clear that success in organisations is in the last resort dependent on commonality in the views of organisations and management (the corporate culture), in which the core of the culture has to be formed by values like flexibility, striving for quality, customer orientation and outward orientation. The success of Japanese industry and commerce, with its hybrid organisational culture of traditional Confucian views – holistic, non-linear, cyclical and collectivist – and certain aspects of recent American approaches to management (especially those of Juran), was the model for Ouchi and Peters. The importance of the human factor and of the role of interpretation in organisations was at least recognised again, and organisational culture became a buzzword. The rational systems approach was declared dead, and every self-respecting manager and consultant gave organisational culture a dominant place in his vocabulary. Training courses were offered everywhere, and the number of publications expanded exponentially. Since organisational culture was linked with economic success (and this in itself came to assume increasing importance in the 1980s), every manager wanted to create such a successful culture in his organisation as quickly as possible. The implicit assumption behind this was that cultural change could be managed too: the attribution of meaning could be manipulated and planned independently of the existing culture. The logical consequence was universalism: successful cultures can (and must) be implemented everywhere. In fact, this trend was the classic example of a contradiction in terms: the programmed changing of the attribution of meaning (arising from the idea that the rational systems approach did not work and that more attention should be paid to irrational organisational processes). All the same, there were criticisms of this popular approach to culture at the time. Critics like Smircich (1983) and Van Maanen (1985) pointed out that members of an organisation are more than role-players and adherents to values. Those members of an organisation continually define and redefine situations, and they do so per department, sector, stratum, ethnic group, etc., so that differences in interpretive processes and symbols (i.e. in subcultures) arise within organisations. Moreover, we experience and 'make' reality in accordance with how we picture it, they argued. It is the task of the researcher to find out which pictures (or cultural maps) are important for which people in their thinking, acting and communication with others. People themselves attribute meaning and significance to their lives, and they determine themselves to what extent they accept new conceptions of reality and values as relevant to their behaviour.

This immediately indicates the restrictions on planned cultural change: take the existing culture and cultural differences in organisations into account, and be wary of the idea that the members of the organisation will immediately follow a manager's new slogan or mission.

Managers and consultants were also warned in another way. In 1980 Hofstede published his famous dissertation on the significance of differences in national culture for the management of an international organisation. He provided a convincing[3] account of how dangerous it is to assume that success models are universally applicable. In the course of time, under the influence of Hofstede's work large international corporations did start to organise brief preparatory training courses for prospective expatriates, but hardly anybody drew the consequence that the idea of a universally applicable success culture should be abandoned. The projects for large-scale cultural change in organisations were simply continued, and the mainstream of organisational literature on culture and cultural change still clings to the idea of a static, monolithic and manipulable culture. Even today, little has essentially changed in that situation (see, for example, Tennekes 1995; Hope and Hendry 1996; Koot and Van Marrewijk 1997), despite the fact that many a large-scale change has not produced the desired result (or has even produced the opposite effect, such as holding the organisation up to ridicule and creating opposition to change) and the criticism of the dominant uniform approach to organisation culture has grown sharply (see, for example, Martin 1992; Cox 1993).

However, there have been changes in the characteristics of the ideal organisational culture over the years. For some time now the list of corporate identity, quality, flexibility and customer orientation has been expanded to include management of diversity, chaos, trust, empowerment, self-management and social responsibility. These characteristics are borrowed by consultants and the writers of popular management from debates that are conducted by more serious organisational analysts, who in turn often derive their ideas from theoretical sociologists, anthropologists and philosophers (of science). Important intellectual sources of inspiration for organisational analysts are scholars like Giddens (1991), Beck (1992) and Luhmann (1991). Let us now see how the ideas of the latter group have been transposed to organisations.

If we follow Giddens (1991), the increasing attention that is being focused on trust can be explained from the fact that we live in a society that it characterised by great insecurity. That insecurity has arisen not only because all kinds of traditions, kinship networks, local communities and religious associations have decreased in importance through the individualisation process, leading to a less normative creation of order and a less unquestioned and predictable form of behaviour. Insecurity has also arisen because, as a result of the growth of specialisation, we are no longer able to grasp all the economic, social, legal and technological processes. At most we may have a thorough knowledge of a few subsidiary fields, but as far as the other fields are concerned we have to trust in the expertise of others. This entails risks. Furthermore, we are increasingly aware of those risks thanks to the process of informatisation and globalisation. It does not take us long to know when and where unplanned and surprising events with negative effects take place. In the case of these events, it is also clear that knowledge about nature and improved technology leads in a number of cases to aggressive 'talking back' by nature and thus to undesired side-effects of modernisation. Risks linked to technological interventions prove to be taken into account less and less in practice (Beck 1992). Giddens even considers that the fears which are connected with the realisation of the unpredictability and capriciousness of the natural and social environment can lead to existential insecurity.

Organisational analysts (like In't Veld (1991) and Stacey (1996) talk about the developments in and connected with organisations in similar terms. The world of the modern manager, they believe, is complex and full of uncertainties. He or she must know how to survive in a turbulent setting where new rivals are perpetually emerging, stakeholders are becoming more and more critical, other organisations are behaving alternately as partners or as rivals, and mergers and takeovers are common events. They consider that the organisation has increasingly become an open network with entering, exiting and re-entering individuals who change identity situationally, display commitment to a number of different sides and engage in temporary alliances. Besides, organisations are becoming increasingly multicultural and multi-ethnic, so that employees experience increasing difficulty in knowing how to act. After all, there are no fixed frameworks or procedures. Finally, through the confrontations with others, individuals in contemporary organisations are increasingly prompted to reflect on their own culture. It is argued that cultural-ethnic diversity and the phenomena of multiple commitment and shifting alliances thereby increase the risk of doubts and insecurity. Trust in the other, self-management and self-confidence are thus recommended as ways of dealing with that insecurity. Reflection leading to openness to and trust in the other and in oneself not only reduces insecurity, but also, some scholars argue, acts as a social lubricant between groups in our modern, fragmented and unpredictable society, and thereby creates a kind of order (see, for example, Gambetta 1988; Putnam 1993).

Trust promotes co-operation, according to Gambetta, because it implies a sort of precommitment, 'a device, whereby we can impose some restraint on ourselves and thus restrict the extent to which others have to worry about our trustworthiness' (1988: 221). In fact, by trusting in the other we involve ourselves in fewer transactional costs in the sense of regulations, contracts, etc. Besides, as has been shown by numerous experiments on the prisoner's dilemma, trust in the other and co-operation on the basis of it are the only ways to solve a clash of interests created by third parties between two individuals or groups. Centrally imposed co-operation between parties, at any rate, does not offer a sufficient guarantee of co-operation in practice (Putnam 1993). According to Pascale (1990), the management of the organisation must not rigidly try to create unity in a differentiated organisation. On the contrary, it must cherish diversity and stimulate constructive conflict, while naturally striving for coherence and cohesion. This hybridisation of unity and difference leads to a complex situation which should not be avoided. After all, he argues, it is the motor of change.

Stacey (1996) is also enthusiastic about the increase in insecurity and complexity arising from the collapse of traditions and the relinquishing of the related group identities. In his view, this insecurity has positive effects on the creativity of employees in the organisation. However, this is only the case when the individuals concerned do not rigidly try to gain control of the uncertain situation, when they trust in themselves, and when the organisation provides positive feedback, not only formally but also informally, and dares to bring existing rules of behaviour up for discussion (by the way, the latter comes close to the ideas promoted, above all, by Senge (1990) in organisational analysis of the 'learning organisation' and 'double-loop learning'). According to Stacey, an organisation must continually balance 'at the edge of chaos, that is the edge of system disintegration' (1996: 242). That status, he claims, is 'a paradoxical one, that is both stable and unstable at the same time, driven by contradictory dynamics of both competition and co-operation, both amplification and constraint, both exposure to creative tension and protection from it' (*ibid.*). In the last resort, Stacey's thesis boils down to a plea for a self-organising organisation that continually and deliberately alternates between destruction and reconstruction in order to survive.

How does a leader manage to secure a central position for trust in the organisational culture? Most theorists who have tackled this question consider that it requires 'inspiring' or 'transformational' leadership, and that 'transactional' leadership is not enough (see, for example, Bass 1985; Den Hartog *et al.* 1997). Transactional leadership, they believe, is based on a relationship of exchange between leader and employee in which mutual efforts and rewards cancel one another out and a sort of contract determines internal labour relations. The aim is to motivate employees to perform by creating good (above all material) conditions in exchange for (direct and tangible) remuneration. Leadership can be called transformational when a leader is able to expand and deepen the needs of employees and to point them towards the aims of the organisation. A transformational leader displays trust in himself and his subordinates, is reliable, imposes high demands on his own and others' performance, behaves creatively and innovatively, formulates targets and tasks in ideological terms, and displays strong commitment and conviction. Trusting in the other and oneself and displaying reliable behaviour elicit trust, according to Bass and others.

The idea of opening oneself up to the other to avoid psychological collapse in the capriciousness of the modern organisation can also be found in Giddens (1991: 121). He considers that people should open themselves up through a process of self-reflection. This should lead them to a clear picture of their own identity and insight into their own successful survival strategies. In the end this will facilitate self-management, Giddens believes. Merry (1995) even considers that people in 'tomorrow's organisation' must entirely shake off constricting ties caused by traditions, loyalties, norms and group identities. They should strive, he claims, for a 'mutual self' and 'dis-identification' in order to become genuinely free and to create good chances of survival in the postmodern, fragmented world. He understands 'mutual self' in the sense of a view of self by an individual in which s/he is receptive to every possible (contradictory) experience, wish and capacity of the self and also knows how to integrate them. Dis-identification means the stripping of unconscious identifications. Time and again, an individual must learn deliberately to opt for a specific identity and not feel that any identity is imposed by tradition or norms. The result is self-mastery. Choices resulting from this process of dis-identification will always be situational, options will always remain open and solutions will always have a hybrid character.

These insights of Merry, Stacey and others have in practice led to a massive supply by trainers and consultants of management training courses in self-management and personal coaching. Similar views are expressed on cross-cultural management. Here too various leading scholars (Hannerz 1992; Trompenaars 1994; Fung 1995, for example) opt for chameleon-like approaches to make the modern complexities of international co-operation manageable.

Fung distinguishes three strategies for cross-cultural co-operation: the ethnocentric, the polycentric and the geocentric. The first is characterised by the pursuit of unity, efficiency and strong appreciation of the culture of the home, country and of the organisational culture of the headquarters or parent company. Monitoring from above or from the centre is very strong. Cultural diversity is seen as a threat instead of as an opportunity. The risk of this ethnocentric approach is the failure to achieve cross-cultural co-operation or its collapse through a lack of understanding of one another and feelings of resistance towards the alleged superiority of the dominant (usually Western) partner. For the latter reason, a polycentric approach is to be preferred (as recommended by a number of well-known scholars, such as Adler (1991) and Hofstede (1992). This strategy starts out from the idea that a universal strategy is not possible and that international business enterprises should accommodate to the local situation: when in Rome, do as the Romans do. Diversity is allowed plenty of room, and monitoring from above is replaced by the relative autonomy of local branches. The corporate culture is seen as a melting pot of cultures. The risk of this strategy, according to Fung, is that the local partner hardly pays any heed to the headquarters, which is a serious risk to co-operation.

To find a good balance between integration and differentiation, Fung (and others, such as Trompenaars) advocate what he calls a hybridisation strategy, the so-called 'geocentric strategy'. This is characterised by the fact that a limited number of central corporate values are followed, which have a powerful radiatory force. In other respects the local branches are autonomous. The local manager (who may be of local origin, but should preferably come from elsewhere) must identify strongly with his branch but not get bogged down in parochialism. He must remain outward looking and have a cosmopolitan, globalist approach ('think globally, but act locally'). The corporate culture must not be based exclusively on the values of the headquarters and be fixed for a long time, but it should be the result of ongoing negotiations between the headquarters and the local branch. In the end it is a question of achieving cultural synergy in which both partners make certain accommodations and engage in a reciprocal relationship. A crucial role in this process is played by the cosmopolitan local managers: they are the bridgehead, but at the same time they are the engine of cultural innovation in the central and local branches. Hannerz too attributes a creative role in cultural processes to the so-called cosmopolitans. He defines a cosmopolitan as someone with a 'willingness to engage in the other, an intellectual and aesthetic stance of openness toward divergent cultural experience', but also someone who 'does not negotiate with the other culture but accepts it as a package deal' (1992: 252–3). The ideal cosmopolitan picks things up all over the place, does not tie himself down personally to a particular culture, and can adapt to any situation. This ideal type of a cosmopolitan comes close to Merry's (1995) 'dis-identified' individual with a 'mutual self'.

To what extent do managers conform to these models and ideal types, and do they always do so, or only under certain conditions? What are the causes and consequences of this behaviour? Let us try to answer these questions as a first step towards a critical evaluation of the dominant models of the management of cultural differences.

A critical evaluation of the dominant models of diversity and cross-cultural management

Let me begin by relating a recent personal experience. A year ago, a colleague, Ida Sabelis, and I started research on the everyday lived experience of top-level managers. The main question of the research was how they dealt with the cultural complexity that many have supposed to exist. We have made use of various techniques for collecting data, including biographical conversations and focused interviews lasting several hours, the 'shadowing' of top-level managers, and interviews with members of the inner circle of the persons involved. Some months ago I related this to a very experienced organisational consultant friend of mine. On this basis I was invited to join an organisational innovation network with two other senior consultants and a number of top-level managers that would focus not on the familiar management and organisation models but on the practicalities of everyday experience. I was very struck by this initiative and decided to take up this opportunity. Five top-level managers were selected and invited to a preliminary meeting from Friday evening to Saturday afternoon in an attractively situated conference centre in Belgium that belonged to one of the initiators. The list of participants included several chief executive officers from large companies, the chairperson of the governing body of a large merged polytechnic, and a general and secretary-general of a ministry. The arrivals in the conference centre, situated on the edge of a simple rural village in the Ardennes, were eye-catching, to say the least. Almost all of the managers arrived in chauffeur-driven limousines and after getting out of their cars they tried in all sorts of ways to attract as much attention as possible. It looked like a procession of film stars at a première. After cocktails and a lavish dinner the working conference got under way.

The arrangement was that I would 'kick off' on Friday evening with a brief summary of the research results to date. During the presentation I showed them a sheet with two columns. The first contained terms like 'scoring', 'achieving targets', 'control' and 'planning', 'achieving a corporate identity', while the second contained terms like 'self-management', 'empowerment', 'the learning organisation' and 'diversity'. The two columns were more or less diametrically opposed to one another, but they both played an important part in the life of a top-level manager, I argued. The difference between them, however – to borrow the terms of Goffman (1971) – was between 'frontstage' and 'under the stage'. This opposition entailed tensions, to which the informants in my research had applied various coping strategies. I had hardly finished speaking when one of the members of the audience, a person who assumed a very macho role in the group, reacted very negatively. How could I imagine that top-level managers displayed paradoxical behaviour? Scoring, planning and self-management can easily be reconciled with one another, and they are in the everyday practice of a top-level manager, he added, with the approval of some other members of the audience. He became more and more worked up, and I could see that my fellow initiators began to be concerned about how the rest of the weekend would proceed. I therefore proposed to postpone the discussion until the following morning.

On Saturday morning one of my colleagues began by saying that there was now an opportunity for the participants to come forward with their everyday problems as top-level managers. They were then asked to form subgroups, draw up a list of the major dilemmas and present these through a spokesperson to the whole group later on with specific cases. The first spokesperson was the top-level manager who had attacked me so violently on the previous evening. The main problems, he said, lay in the difference in information level between the manager and his organisation, and the fact that you cannot always be open towards your organisations. He is the general manager of a large international clothing company with many branches in Germany, the Netherlands and other countries. The main shareholder, the original founder of the concern, had asked him some time before to rationalise the company and to introduce profound changes in the organisational culture. On the basis of a preliminary analysis, he had formed a picture of which branches were to be expanded, reduced or closed down. 'My problem now,' he continued, 'is that I cannot be open about these plans to the people in the organisation. At the same time, I'm telling them that a new culture of openness and integrity has to be introduced into the organisation.' I asked him to explain his problem in more detail, and after some hesitation he stated that he was afraid to be open for fear of a further drop in results, the risk of being called to account by the major shareholder, and possibly even of being sacked. 'In fact, I'm also a person who likes harmony,' he concluded. Later on others came up with similar problems. Loneliness, fear, doubt, impotence and insecurity were the commonest topics of discussion for the next few hours. On Saturday afternoon, at the end of the session, most of them, including my earlier opponent, returned to the debate of the previous evening. What had at first been denied was now confirmed: the two columns of management ideals were diametrically opposed to one another, and this opposition led to serious professional and personal problems among top-level managers – problems, they added, which are not taken into account in the conventional management models. Their conclusion at the end of the meeting was thus that there was good enough reason to meet on a regular basis for an exchange of dilemmas by analysing the specific everyday practice of management.

I believe that this is a good illustration of what is at stake at the moment in management practice. Managers announce with plenty of rhetoric and bombast (prompted by organisational 'experts') to the stakeholders (customers, clients and shareholders) that their organisation has introduced or will shortly introduce the latest management catchphrases: hence, empowerment, self-management, ethics, integrity, trust, sustainability, social involvement and tolerance of other cultures are presented as the characteristics of 'the new organisation'. Until recently they were the ideals of left-wing groups, of what the average manager regarded as environmental activists, Third World specialists, the trade unions, and those representing ethnic minorities. Now these values are embraced by the top level of the world of industry and commerce. The organisational 'experts' stimulate this process with wonderful accounts of the fantastic objectives which will eventually be attained in this way. Emancipation of the ordinary average employees will be brought about by them opening themselves up and by self-management. They will become more creative. Their fears will be drastically reduced. The application of 'management of diversity' and of a pluralistic, geocentric and cosmopolitan attitude in international management will lead to equality and the emancipation of women, immigrants and Third World countries. Paying systematic attention to integrity and trust will result in a high level of cohesion and bonding in the organisation. The environment will stand to gain as well if sustainability is set high on the list of priorities. Finally, for some, society will even achieve a higher social order through the growth of complexity (see, for example, Merry 1995). The new insights are presented by managers as a gift to the organisation and as an appreciation of people and the environment.

At the same time, however, a different discourse is used among managers and stakeholders (cf. Watson 1994).[4] It is a discourse in which the dominant values are scoring, planning, programming, settling accounts, achieving targets, displaying decisiveness, running and, above all, looking forwards and not backwards. The contradictions between the central frames of cultural standards in the two discourses are responsible for what Beck has called 'undesirable side-effects of modernization'. New fears have emerged and organisations 'talk unexpectedly and loudly back' (1992: 20). Stress among employees has increased (Schaufeli 1995; Reuters Business Information 1996) and social cohesion has dropped sharply. The press contains an increasing number of reports of companies where the employees on the shop floor are terrorised by certain individuals and mutual solidarity has disappeared. The organisation demands total commitment to the company, and at the same time it calls for the employees to be increasingly emancipated from the restrictive ties of traditions and frames of cultural norms through the process of opening themselves up and of flexibilisation. The new frames of norms and the demand for total commitment place demands on employees that are much heavier, both physically and psychologically, than the old ones. This is particularly true for the upper-level functions, where working hours are long and personnel have to show that they have a flexible, 'modern', path-breaking mind and body. It is partly as a result of this that sports centres are packed and there is a gigantic interest in spiritual, 'mind-reinforcing' sessions led by some guru or other (Hogema 1995).

The 'gift' of trust, empowerment and self-management by the organisation to employees is probably one of the most far-reaching forms of 'colonization of the way we live and work by the system', as Alvesson and Willmott (1996: 106) also suppose. The system seems to cater more and more for the individual with the slogans of emancipation and the opening up of self, but the reverse is the case. The individual has probably never been under such a threat as s/he is today. Personal emancipation is instrumentalised and has now acquired a function within the rational management of organisations. The individual must conform to a certain picture of emancipation and must show that s/he always exerts self-control. A deliberate choice has to be made for specific cultural behaviour and an identity in the face of each situation, and strategic, temporary, professional and commercial alliances have to be entered into (incidentally, companies in the high-tech sector are in the front line when it comes to determining this frame of cultural norms). Long-term, 'unmotivated', unprofitable and unfashionable alliances are taboo. Ideally, the individual is a sort of sponge that absorbs all kinds of influences, a chameleon that can easily adjust to the most bizarre and extreme situations. Particularity, recognisability and predictability for others have disappeared, s/he has no continuity for him/herself. There is no clear beginning or end, now that history and the future hardly play a part any more. Only today counts. To have an awareness of identity, a person must not only know who s/he is, but also who s/he is not. In the hybrid organisation, however, people are everybody (self and other) and thus nobody. To live without a sense of continuity is 'to be faced with one's own death' (De Vos and Romanucci-Ross 1995: 357). Long-term alliances and traditions, no matter how few they may be, and contrasts and confrontations are necessary to survive as a person and as a group. There is hardly any other situation in which so much negative and positive energy is released as in processes of emancipation and ethnicisation resulting from feelings of relative deprivation (Koot and Rath 1987; and Koot 1997).

Ethnicity can also offer great advantages in situations of non-relative deprivation because it entails communality, recognisability, solidarity and trust between people from different backgrounds. Kotkin (1993) has clearly demonstrated the power and cohesion of the networks of Chinese commercial concerns with branches all over Southeast Asia, those of Indians in the United States, and those of Libyan businessmen all over the world. Of course, processes of ethnicisation also have their risks, as a result of the dominance of a specific group. After all, this can lead to a simplification, narrowing down and silting up of the vision of (historical) reality, and thus in the longer term reduce the internal variation which is necessary for creativity and dynamics (cf. Said 1993). Besides, there is a danger that the ethnic struggle will be deployed by individuals with purely personal interests who want to impose their will on others. In the short and medium term, however, ethnicity can be a good weapon enabling the non-dominant party to resist and emancipate.

In my opinion, at any rate, it is clear that the present trend towards dis-identification, hybridisation and cosmopolitan behaviour on the part of organisational analysts and the consultants and mangers who follow in their wake is not a good response to the increasing turbulence and ethnic-cultural complexity in Western organisations.

The same doubts can be raised with regard to the current 'theory' and practice of cross-cultural management. Here too the designers of the models emphasise that, with the present emphasis on hybridisation, tolerance and pluralism, the era of Western domination and the desire for standardisation and uniformity are definitively behind us. Every culture, it is argued, is now appreciated in some way or other; there is no fundamental difference between 'us' and 'them'; 'the other' has been incorporated into our system; and the world has become one big bazaar of lifestyles where everyone can shop: hybridisation as the ultimate emancipation, resting on the intellectual foundations of postmodernism. But to what extent is this a Euro-(American-)centric view that is imposed on the non-Western countries, as Sadar (1998) supposes? Moreover, does postmodernism, a 'discovery' of the West, not completely absorb and cannibalise 'the other', swallowing it up within the dominant system? The particularity of the other is fragmented through the drive towards hybridisation, and the strength that is radiated by particularity is in danger of being lost. It is as if everyone at the moment has equal access to the world of the conferment of meaning but that access has its price, thereby excluding many non-Western countries. Furthermore, the media, which shape the conferment of meaning, are in the hands of the West. Models of hybridisation emphasise the inclusion of foreign, exotic cultural elements in 'our' postmodern organisations, but it is questionable whether the exclusion and oppression of the Third World and the ethnic minorities in our own Western societies (including the organisations in them) have not thereby become complete and reached their ultimate stage. For Sadar, at any rate, postmodernism, with its opposition to uniformity and its plea for pluralism, is 'the master alibi for the continued exploitation and oppression of non-western cultures' (1998: 36). Perhaps this goes too far (partly because it suggests a deliberate conspiracy), but in my view its critical attitude is entirely justified. As in the case of the terms 'empowerment' and 'self-management', pluralism and management of diversity leading to emancipation are advocated by dominant partners who have lost their control over and hold on society and organisation. The dependence of the non-dominant partner is increased and 'the (social, economic and political) system' increasingly colonises the life of the individual and 'the other'. It is not only logical that ethnic and nationalist movements are currently making headway in a large number of non-Western countries as a reaction to the growing cultural domination of the West, but – in the short term – it may even be a good thing. Exclusion by non-Western countries ('the periphery talks back', as Hannerz (1992) put it) is necessary if Europe and the

United States are to realise that the drive for standardisation and uniformity has to be dropped.

In everyday practice, too, the modern manager is confronted by contradictory frames of norms, rationalities and ideologies. S/he has to satisfy the picture of the self-confident cosmopolitan who has all social, political, technical and cultural processes under control and also allows pluralism, is a knowledge broker, is a coach for his fellow employees, deals openly, gives a high priority to communication and is successful. As one of my informants from the research on top-level managers put it: 'an impossible task! Take the question of combining corporate identity and local identities. How can that be done in practice? The management of identity processes has grown way above our heads.' Moreover, top-level managers are increasingly expected to provide 'impression management' and to be convincing in public. They must show that they can manipulate the media and public opinion. They can do so by suggesting self-confidence, self-control and control of the organisation. Their body language, outfit and office interior must therefore be carefully selected (my informants gave me numerous examples of how they use their bodies to exercise power in confrontations with others, and of how they prepare themselves to do so). At the same time, they know that at innumerable points they hardly have a grip on the cultural and identity processes in and around the organisation. The stakeholders are constantly breathing down their neck. There is hardly any time to calm down or to engage in some simple activity. Every activity has to be (made to seem) important. The manager's assistants are pleased to co-operate, because, as everyone knows, the more status they receive, the more importance they assume. Most of them find that this pressure always to act importantly can be a burden at times. Sometimes they try to escape by secretly doing so-called unimportant things. For instance, one of our informants keeps a pencil sharpener in his desk. Every day he tries to sharpen his pencil without being seen: 'I need that, a moment for myself.'

It is debatable who is restrained or (following Foucault 1977) disciplined and imprisoned in himself the most: the manager or his fellow employees. The power of the manager is often more an illusion than a reality. At any rate, my research regularly came up with the picture of the manager as a relative puppet in the hands of the shareholders. Unlike the managers, the latter are not in search of publicity. Constantly on the alert, they remain in the background and exert their influence from behind the scenes.

By the way, it is sometimes suggested that it is the experts who increase dependence, discipline others, and in the final analysis are in control of the (post)modern society (see, for example, Giddens 1991; Beck 1992), but they are objectively and subjectively trapped too. During a study session recently organised by the Netherlands Order of Organisational Consultants on the prison as an organisational metaphor, most of the consultants spontaneously indicated that they felt trapped. They claimed that they have to satisfy political demands, the urge to score, the instinctual need to be in control and the rational instrumentalist views of the manager if they are to make the business profitable. Fundamental criticism is inappropriate and unacceptable. Organisational and management models that are followed in recommendations must be in tune with social trends, be above all aimed at success, and precisely indicate how the manager must act in order to achieve that success. The organisational recommendations must be drawn up in the same words and jargon as that of the models and main concepts. There is no opportunity to stop and reflect on the causes of the present-day culture of an organisation. The behaviour of managers and their consultants thus forms a closed circuit. They join in sharing a large number of values, symbols and rituals. Their language, body language, culinary habits, external status symbols (outfit, car), the look of their office interior and other cultural aspects are often identical. The two groups constantly influence one another in all kinds of spheres of everyday life, and are completely intertwined. As a result, fear, loneliness and insecurity are rampant at the top levels of contemporary organisational life.

Concluding remarks

The question thus arises of how this paradoxicality, hybridisation and ambiguity in management models and practice is to be explained. There seem to be arguments to be adduced that see these processes as fatal strategies of modernisation, as Baudrillard (1983, 1990) has described them – with a good deal of plausibility. According to Baudrillard, late modernism or hyper- or postmodernism has brought us to a disastrous but inevitable point. In order to get some grip on the turbulence and capriciousness in society, the economy and nature that modernism itself has created, everything is mixed with everything else: evil with good, truth with untruth, reality with fiction, freedom with unfreedom, masculinity with femininity. Every activity tends towards homogenisation, synthesisation, synchronisation and synergetisation.[5] Nothing seems to have value or meaning any more, because everything has meaning. As Baudrillard put it: 'When everything is political, nothing is political any more, and the word has no meaning. When everything is sexual, nothing is sexual any more, and sex loses all determination' (1990: 17). Boundaries no longer exist and oppositions are suspended. No choice is final or almost final – every decision is serial, partial, fragmentary and situational. Freedom, which everyone pays lip-service to today, has therefore become an empty concept. After all, there is nothing left to choose now that everything is possible. Dreams and myths have become hollow phrases, because in theory every real or virtual dream can be made to come true. Every thing, every phenomenon loses its particularity, its unique character. The result, in Baudrillard's vision, is a total confusion and damming of creativity, energy and the will to fight. Baudrillard's view of the future is thus pessimistic: 'Everything that loses its idea is like a man who has lost his shadow – it falls into delirium or loses itself' (1990: 14). All the same, there does not seem to be any escape from this course because the phenomenon is actually a logical stage in the process of modernisation: the Enlightenment ideals of individualisation and rationalisation that we have all appropriated and that have become an integral part of all kinds of institutions are simply being taken further and radicalised. He thus sees the strategy of hybridisation as fatal.

The current trend in the Western theory and practice of management to learn how to cope with paradoxes, to turn individuals into cosmopolitans with a 'mutual self', and to strive for a combination of global and local views of management and organisation in international co-operation thus seems to correspond exactly to the fatal strategies described by Baudrillard. Every manager wants an excellent (and thus in fact a unique) organisation, but what he really wants is to conform as much as possible to the ideal organisation that the 'organisational experts' have produced. The rhetoric is one of excellence, but the practice is aimed at clones. Particularity is not only hard to find at the organisational level, but even at the individual level there is a trend towards formlessness, hollowness, superficiality and emptiness. Flexibilisation and self-management irrevocably entail interchangeability and situational adaptation. In that case, alliance and identification are temporarily and predominantly motivated by the expected personal advantages, such as material gain, 'professional surroundings' and career opportunities. The rhetoric is about 'corporate identification', trust and integrity, but the practice reveals the opposite: a large degree of legalisation and a growth of distrust. As suggested earlier in this chapter, the terms 'management of diversity', 'plurality of cultures' and 'self-managing teams' suggest that differentiation is the goal, while in fact what is sought are integration and homogenisation. After all, the entire organisation is dragged through the mill of consultants and trainers, who want to spur the employees on towards self-management and 'empowerment' in an unequivocal and centrally managed way. It is not that 'everything is allowed', but that 'everything is compulsory' – a contradiction in terms, as much as self-management and 'empowerment' imposed from above or an orchestrated emancipation of the individual (or the emancipation of non-Western countries by Europe and the United States). The organisation as prison, as Foucault (1977) described it, now seems to have reached a final stage. The disciplining has become almost perfect.

Are there signs of hope on the horizon? Can we reverse certain processes? I see very little of the growing mistrust of experts and the increase in critical reflection, as presented by Beck *et al.* (1994, as a logical consequence of the 'risk society' and as a positive characteristic of our late-modern era), in management and organisational practice. Management slogans – provided they are conveyed with plenty of public relations – are still followed and copied pretty uncritically. As I was able to observe in my own research, there is a growth of self-reflection among top-level managers, but it is fairly narcissistic and is primarily motivated by fear and insecurity.

However, there are signs that, as Maffesoli (1996) indicates, the process of individualisation in our modern society is not going so far that in a short while there will no longer be any informal social ties at all. He argues that we are witnessing the emergence of more and more 'new, modern tribes' – temporary but very intense social ties with which people can satisfy their fundamental need to share. We can also witness the emergence of these 'new, modern tribes' in organisations, but I doubt whether this is the answer to what Baudrillard sees as the total waning and damming of creativity and the will to fight. After all, these are very temporary choices, and ties change on the basis of calculations and purely consumerist considerations.

Perhaps the largest sign of hope is that, if we follow Turner (1974), the present situation of paradoxicality and hybridisation can be seen as the transitional phase towards a fundamental U-turn in our Western society. At any rate, all of the features that he lists seem to be present: fear, insecurity, doubt, ambiguity, vagueness and fragmentation. In addition, the former 'periphery' is talking back: it is slowly becoming clear in non-Western countries that modernisation (and thus organisation and management in accordance with North American models) is not always successful and that the development of their own locally developed management and organisational models is to be preferred. Emancipation, the will to fight and innovation, as I see it, are directly linked to the striving for particularity.

Notes

1   Among the well-known critics from the late 1980s and early 1990s are Smircich (1983), Frost *et al.* (1985) and Sackmann (1991). Although their theories were more profound and were more in line with recent developments in anthropology, sociology and psychology on culture and identity, their voices were virtually if not totally ignored by the mainstream of organisational analysts and management specialists.

2   This section is a revised version of part of my contribution to *Cultural Complexity in Organizations* (Sackmann 1997).

3   There have been justified criticisms of his methodology and of his definition of culture. Surveys among IBM personnel that are confined to city branches simply are not the best way to penetrate to the deeper strata of a culture and cultural differences, so there is a lack of precision. Nevertheless, in a general sense he has convincingly demonstrated that there are significant differences in views of organisation and management.

4   Following Watson (1994: 113), I would define a discourse as a connected set of statements, concepts, terms and expressions which constitute a way of talking or writing about a particular issue, thus framing the way people understand and act with respect to that issue.

5   Elsewhere (Koot 1997) I have tried to demonstrate that a good deal of the rhetoric of a dominant party who wants to retain power is latent in the concept of synergy.

References

Adler, N. (1991) *Organizational Behavior*, Belmont: Wadsworth Publishing Company.

Alvesson, M. and Willmott, H. (1996) *Making Sense of Management: A Critical Introduction*, London: Sage.

Appadurai, A. (1986) *The Social Life of Things*, Cambridge: Cambridge University Press.

Barth, F. (1969) *Ethnic Groups and Boundaries: The Local Organization of Cultural Difference*, Oslo: Universitatslaget.

Bass, B.M. (1985) *Leadership and Performance Beyond Expectations*, New York: Free Press.

Baudrillard, J. (1983) *Les Strategies fatales*, Paris: Grasset.

—— (1988) *Selected Writings*, Oxford: Polity Press.

—— (1990) *La Transparance du mal*, Paris: Galilee.

—— (1994) *Simulacra and Simulation*, Ann Arbor, MI: University of Michigan Press.

Beck, U. (1992) *Risk Society*, London: Sage.

Beck, U., Giddens, A. and Lash, S. (1994) *Reflexive Modernization: Politics, Tradition and Aesthetics in the Modern Social Order*, Cambridge: Polity Press.

Cox, T. (1993) *Cultural Diversity in Organizations: Theory, Research and Practice*, San Francisco: Berrett-Koehler Publishers.

de Vos, G. and Romanucci-Ross, L. (1995) *Ethnic Identity, Creation, Conflict, and Accommodation*, 3rd edition, London: Sage.

den Hartog, D., Koopman, P. and Muyen, J. (1997) *Inspirerend leiderschap in organisaties*, Schoonhoven: Academic Service.

Foucault, M. (1977) *Discipline and Punish: The Birth of the Prison*, Harmondsworth: Penguin.

Friedman, J. (1994) *Cultural Identity and Global Process*, London: Sage.

Frost, P.J., Moore, L.F., Louis, M.R., Lundberg, C.C. and Martin, J. (eds) (1985) *Organizational Culture*, Beverly Hills, CA: Sage.

Fung, R. (1995) *Organizational Strategies for Cross-cultural Cooperation*, Delft: Eburon.

Gambetta, D. (1988) *Trust: Making and Braking Cooperative Relations*, Oxford: Basil Blackwell.

Giddens, A. (1991) *The Consequences of Modernity*, London: Sage.

Goffman, E. (1971) *Relations in Public*, New York: Colophon Books.

Hannerz, U. (1992) *Cultural Complexity*, New York: Colombia University Press.

Hofstede, G. (1980) *Culture's Consequences*, London: Sage.

—— (1992) *Cultural Constraints in Management Theories*, lecture for the Annual Meeting of the Academy of Management, Nevada, Las Vegas/Maastricht: IRIC.

Hogema, I. (1995) 'Op zoek naar spiritualiteit en management', in I. Weeda (ed.) *Spiritualiteit en wetenschap*, Amsterdam: Anthos.

Hope, V. and Hendry, J. (1996) 'Corporate cultural change, is it relevant for the organizations of the 1990's?', *Human Resource Management Journal* 5(4): 61–73.

In 't Veld, R. (ed.) (1991) *Autopoiesis and Configuration Theory: New Approaches to Societal Steering*, Dordrecht: Kluwer.Koot, W. (1993) 'Ambiguity and changing identities', in W.A. Shadid and P. Nas (eds) *Culture, Development and Communication* 17: 92–110, Leiden: CNWS Publications.

—— (1997) 'Strategic utilization of ethnicity in organizations', in S. Sackmann (ed.) *Cultural Complexity in Organizations. Inherent Contrasts and Contradictions*, London: Sage.

Koot, W. and Hogema, I. (1990) *Organisatiecultuur. Fictie of werkelijkheid?*, Bussum: Coutinho.

Koot, W. and Rath, J. (1987) 'Ethnicity and emancipation', *International Migration* 25(4): 426–40.

Koot, W. and van Marrewijk, A. (1997) 'Cultuurverandering bij politieorganisaties', *Handboek voor politiemanagement*, Alphen aan de Rijn: Samsom.

Kotkin, J. (1993) *Tribes*, New York: Random House.

Luhmann, N. (1991) *Soziologie des Risikos*, Berlin: Springer.

Maffesoli, M. (1996) *The Times of the Tribes*, London: Sage.

Martin, J. (1992) *Cultures in Organizations: Three Perspectives*, Oxford: Oxford University Press.

Mbigi, L. (1997) *Ubuntu. The African Dream in Management*, Randburg, South Africa: Knowledge Resources (PTY) Cultural Ltd.

Merry, U. (1995) *Coping with Uncertainty*, Westport, CT: Praeger.

Ohmae, K. (1990) *The Borderless World*, London: Fontana.

Ouchi, W.G. (1981) *Theory Z: How American Business Can Meet the Japanese Challenge*, Reading: Addison-Wesley.

Pascale, R.T. (1990) *Managing on the Edge: How Successful Companies Use Conflict to Stay Ahead*, London: Penguin Books.

Peters, T.J. and Waterman, R.J. (1982) *In Search of Excellence: Lessons from America's Best Run Companies*, New York: Harper & Row.

Prud'homme van Reine, P. (1996) 'Globalization and the local development of models for management and organization: the periphery talks back', in W. Koot, I. Sabelis and S. Ybema (eds) *Contradictions in Context, Puzzling over Paradoxes in Contemporary Organizations*, Amsterdam: VU University Press.

Putnam, R.D. (1993) *Making Democracy Work*, Princeton, NJ: Princeton University Press.

Reuters Business Information (1996) *Dying for Information: An Investigation into the Effects of Information Overload in the UK and Worldwide*, London: Porto Bello Press.

Robertson, R. (1995) 'Glocalization: time–space and homogeneity–heterogeneity', in M. Featherstone, S. Lash and R. Robertson (eds) *'Global Modernities*, London: Sage.

Sackmann, S. (1991) *Knowledge in Organizations: Exploring the Collective Mind*, Newbury Park, CA: Sage.

—— (ed.) (1997) *Cultural Complexity in Organizations, Inherent Contrasts and Contradictions* London: Sage.

Sadar, Z. (1998) *Postmodernism and the Other, the New Imperialism of Western Culture*, London: Pluto Press.

Said, E.W. (1993) *Culture and imperialism*, London: Chatto & Windus.

Schaufeli, W. (1995) *Burnout: Dwaallicht of Lichtpunt?*, inaugural thesis, Utrecht.

Senge, P.M. (1990) *The Fifth Discipline: The Art and the Practice of the Learning Organization*, New York: Doubleday Currency.

Smircich, L. (1983) 'Concepts of culture and organizational analysis', *Administrative Science Quarterly* 28(3): 339–58.

Stacey, R. (1996) *Complexity and Creativity in Organizations*, San Francisco: Berrett-Koehler Press.

Tennekes, J. (1995) *Organisatiecultuur, een antropologische visie*, Leuven: Garant.

Trompenaars, F. (1994) *Riding the Waves of Culture*, London: Nicholas Brealy Publishing.

Turner, V. (1974) 'Cycles of social change', in Dranaz (ed.) *Fields and Metaphors*, Ithaca, NY: Cornell University Press

van Maanen, J. (1985) 'Cultural organization: fragments of a theory', in P. Frost, L. Moore, M. Lewis, C. Lundberg and J. Martin (eds) *Organizational Culture*, London: Sage.

Watson, T. (1994) *In Search of Management: Culture, Chaos and Control in Managerial Work*, London: Routledge.

Zegers, R. (1997) 'Angst en zelfsturing in organisaties', *Management en Organisatie* 6: 60–91, Alphen aan de Rijn: Samsom.

11 The politics and ethics of knowledge construction in corporations

Dialogic interaction and self–other relations

Tanni Haas and Stanley Deetz

Introduction

The concept of 'informed decision' is central to organisational legitimacy and power relations. Organisational scholars, however, have long known that decisions are only partly knowledge based. Decisions are frequently made in conditions of considerable uncertainty. Thus, many decisions are driven by politics, values and decisional routines. Rationality is always 'bounded'. Most of these conceptions have looked at processes that complement or supplement knowledge in decisional processes.

More recent analyses, often following Foucault, have begun to explore the politics and values present 'in' knowledge rather than those which stand alongside it (e.g. Townley 1993). The concept 'informed' is increasingly problematic as information and knowledge are more clearly seen as resources in, and products of, active political processes. In these analyses experience and truth claims are seen more as artefactual than factual (more textual than referential). To the extent that we accept these insights, we have a new sense of how knowledge is, and might be, negotiated in communication processes without recourse to foundations or privileges. Such negotiations are part of the micro-politics of everyday life, which can be called an 'in-formational politics' (see Deetz 1995a for development).

If such negotiations are central to organisational life and decisions, active stakeholder involvement in the construction of knowledge is critical for the representation of diverse values and for the legitimacy of the knowledge produced. Stakeholder involvement can lead to more creative communication, providing a kind of knowledge which enables organisations to better adapt to changing environments and meet diverse social needs. Unfortunately, many of our everyday conceptions of communication are not sufficiently rich to explicate the way communication processes work in knowledge construction. The prevailing communication conceptions take for granted 18th-century conceptions of self, other and interaction which fail to problematise routine views of knowledge. Most everyday conceptions of communication are grounded in informational/expressionist/liberal-democratic theories which see communication as the process of knowledge exchange and distribution but fail to see the processes of communication in the social construction of knowledge. As such, they fail to provide adequate descriptive or normative guidance. Here we wish to pursue the normative dimension. Can we develop a conception of 'good communication' adequate to consider knowledge-construction activities and guide the reformation of discourse in corporations? We will claim that the conception of 'good communication' in regard to knowledge construction is fundamentally an ethical question rather than an epistemological one.

Whilst issues of epistemology are clearly important to consider, it is our contention in this study that the question of how the corporation ought to construct knowledge should be considered not only an epistemological issue but also, and perhaps more fundamentally, an ethical issue. It is in this important respect that our approach represents an attempt to develop the conceptual foundation for an ethic of knowledge construction in corporations. In particular, we will argue, the corporation should consider not only upon what methodological bases and through which means it constructs knowledge of central constituencies within its external environment; but also, and perhaps more fundamentally, whether these reflect an ethically sound stance towards them. Importantly, to assume a sound ethical stance is not only an important end in itself, but is also likely to be associated with positive epistemological consequences and corporate responsiveness to changing environments.

Central to the question of what constitutes a sound ethical stance, we will argue, is the question of how the corporation (as a self) conceptualises and relates to central constituencies within its external environment (as others). While these constituencies by definition represent others, in the sense that they are situated conceptually external to the corporation, certain ways of conceptualising and relating to them as others represent more or less sound ethical stances. It is in this important respect that the writings of three influential moral philosophers, Jürgen Habermas, Seyla Benhabib and Emmanuel Levinas, become relevant to consider. What has come to be known as the question of the other – that is, how to conceptualise and relate to the other as other – represents in different ways one of the most central of questions in their respective thought. Their writings are of particular interest as they have developed different, and in important respects conflicting, yet significant, conceptions of self–other relations. We thus aim to incorporate different aspects of their respective thought in the development of a conceptual foundation for an ethic of knowledge construction in corporations. We will conclude by showing that a conception of 'radical otherness' is essential for an adequate conception of democratic knowledge construction.

Stakeholders' knowledge construction and ethics

The construction of knowledge arguably represents one of the most important activities in any corporation. For a corporation to function adequately, it needs to construct knowledge of central constituencies and its external environment – that is, of those groups of people and processes that affect and/or are affected by actions taken by the corporation. As such, the corporation needs to reflect upon what methodological bases and through which means it constructs knowledge – in other words, issues of epistemological character.

The initial recognition that the construction of knowledge in the corporation raises not only epistemological but also (and perhaps more fundamentally) ethical issues may be attributed to the development of a theoretical perspective within organisation studies under the name of stakeholder theory (see, for example, Freeman 1984; Freeman and Gilbert 1988, 1992; Carroll 1989; Deetz 1995a, 1995b). Central to this theoretical perspective is the recognition that the modern corporation is responsible for the satisfaction of the interests of a multiplicity of central constituencies (or stakeholders) other than those of its owners/stockholders. A central corollary of this responsibility concerns the construction of knowledge in the corporation. If the corporation is to satisfy the different and potentially conflicting, yet legitimate, interests of a multiplicity of stakeholders other than the (primarily economic) interests of its owners/stockholders, it needs to provide these stakeholders with genuine representation rights within its internal knowledge-generating processes. Without genuine stakeholder representation, the corporation is unlikely to develop the necessary knowledge of their interests which subsequently will enable it to satisfy them.

Communication and ethical interaction

The question of how the corporation may facilitate genuine stakeholder representation within its internal knowledge-generating processes has benefited considerably from attending to Habermas' (1979, 1984, 1987, 1990, 1993) influential discourse ethics, and especially the ideal speech situation (Habermas 1973). Central to Habermas' discourse ethics is, from an organisation-theory perspective, the argument that the interactions between the corporation and its stakeholders ought to be radically reciprocal and symmetric. Only when the force of the better argument, rather than various types of systematic distortion in the form of discursive closures, governs their interactions does the corporation facilitate genuine stakeholder representation within its internal knowledge-generating processes. However, Habermas' discourse ethics is based upon a conception of self–other relations which, due to the unique historical context in which the modern corporation operates, limits its potential scope of application considerably. Most importantly, Habermas' discourse ethics is based upon a narrow conception of the moral point of view, associated with a distinction between moral-practical discourses (about normative questions of justice and rights), which are amenable to rational-critical discourse under conditions stipulated by the ideal speech situation, and ethical-existential discourses (about evaluative questions of the good life), which are only amenable to rational-critical discourse within the unproblematic horizon of a concrete historical form of life.

The distinction between moral-practical discourses, to which Habermas' discourse ethics applies, and ethical-existential discourses, to which it does not, is appropriate for traditional homogenous societies, characterised by considerable value consensus among different societal (and stakeholder) groups. However, it is problematic in modern heterogeneous societies, such as the United States, characterised by considerable, and increasing, value dissensus among different societal (and stakeholder) groups. In particular, the distinction between moral-practical and ethical-existential discourses implies that both the corporation and its stakeholders ought to assume the standpoint of the generalised other, which requires them to bracket rather than thematise differences in the values which underlie their respective knowledge-claims during communicative interaction. This way of conceptualising the ethical basis upon which knowledge ought to be constructed in the corporation, we will argue, is not only ethically problematic, but also likely to be associated with negative epistemological consequences.

Some of the problems with Habermas' discourse ethics, and especially the problematic conception of self–other relations, may be addresses by attending to Benhabib's (1992; see also 1985, 1986, 1987, 1990) reconsideration thereof. Through a distinction between assuming the standpoint of the generalised other (*à la* Habermas) and the concrete other, Benhabib attempts to transcend the problematic distinction Habermas draws between moral-practical and ethical-existential discourses. Benhabib's argument that one ought to assume simultaneously the standpoint of the generalised other and the concrete other in an open-ended, moral conversation is important to organisation theory. In particular, we will argue, it provides for a universalistic, yet contextually sensitive, mode of interaction between the corporation and its stakeholders in which differences in the values which underlie their respective knowledge-claims ought to become thematised rather than bracketed. This way of conceptualising the ethical basis upon which knowledge ought to be constructed in the corporation, we will argue, not only represents an ethically more sound stance towards its stakeholders than the one advanced by Habermas, but also is likely to be associated with positive epistemological consequences.

Despite important differences between the discourse-ethical approaches of Habermas and Benhabib, they share certain similarities. Both contend that the interactions between the corporation (as a self) and its stakeholders (as others) ought to be radically reciprocal and symmetric (the responsibility of the self as being-with the other). Levinas' (1969, 1981) approach to ethics, however, differs fundamentally. For Levinas, the relationship between self and other is characterised by the non-reciprocal and asymmetric responsibility of the self for the other (the responsibility of the self as being-for the other). This implies not only that the responsibility of the corporation (as a self) towards its stakeholders (as others) is antecedent to its (self-)conscious (or freely determined) choice to engage in ethical relationships with them, but also that the question of how to conceptualise and relate to them as others in an ethically sound manner is not adequately resolved by arguing that their interactions ought to be based upon the ethical ideals of reciprocity and symmetry which underlie, respectively, the ideal speech situation (Habermas) and the moral conversation (Benhabib). Furthermore, we will argue, since the otherness of the other rests in the fact that he or she is by definition un-thematisable, not only should the corporation engage in a thematisation rather than bracketing of the values which underlie the knowledge-claims of its stakeholders (Benhabib), but rather should facilitate their perpetual thema-tisation/de-thematisation.

Yet for the corporation to facilitate a perpetual thematisation/de-thematisa-tion of the values which underlie the knowledge-claims of its stakeholders is not adequate in a Levinasian perspective. An ethically sound relationship between the corporation (as a self) and its stakeholders (as others) may only be established, we will argue, if the corporation self-deconstructs in the face of its stakeholders, followed by an ethically charged self-construction. This implies that the corpora-tion ought to transcend its fixed subjectivity by recovering latent, yet legitimate, conflicts between its multiplicity of potential selves. If the corporation does not attempt to recover its own internal conflicts, it is unlikely that it will be able to help recover and recognise those of its stakeholders. The importance of providing the corporation's stakeholders with representation rights within its internal knowl-edge-generating processes thus rests upon the opportunity not for successful self-expression, but rather for self-deconstruction in the face of the other. The interactions between the corporation and its stakeholders ought to be potentially productive rather than reproductive, aimed at producing what neither of the participants had access to prior to their interactions rather than successfully repro-ducing either or both of their respective values and knowledge-claims.

The ideal speech situation

The ideal speech situation provides a useful conceptual entrance for appreciating Habermas' (1979, 1984, 1987, 1990, 1993) discourse ethics. It is based upon the underlying assumption that every speech act functions during instances of inter-action only by virtue of certain presuppositions made by participants. Even when these presuppositions are not honoured by the participants, they serve as the basis of appeal as failed instances of interaction turn to rational-critical discourse concerning the disputed validity-claims. The basic presuppositions and validity-claims arise out of four domains of reality: the external world, human relations, the individual's internal world and language. The claims raised in each validity-claim are, respectively, truth, correctness, sincerity and intelligibility. Every instance of interaction thus presupposes the representation of facts (the external world), establishes legitimate social relations (human relations), discloses the speaker's point of view (the individual's internal world) and is understand-able (language). Any validity-claim which may not be disputed by the participants through the application of rational-critical discourse serves as a basis for what Habermas (1970) has described as systematically distorted communication. A communication situation in which these validity-claims are honoured by the participants, however, represents an ideal speech situation (Habermas 1973); or what Habermas (1990) has subsequently termed the universal and necessary communicative presuppositions of argumentative speech.

Moral-practical versus ethical-existential discourses

The ideal speech situation thus represents a communication situation in which potential conflicts of interest (and knowledge-claims) ought to be rationally evaluated by the participants through a mode of interaction which is free of manipulation and in which only the force of the better argument prevails. The participants are guaranteed the reciprocal and symmetric opportunity to apply all types of speech acts during interaction. It thus stipulates certain ethical ideals upon which knowledge ought to be constructed during interaction between the corporation and its stakeholders. Only when the force of the better argument, rather than various types of systematic distortion in the form of discursive closures, governs the interactions between the corporation and its stakeholders does the corporation facilitate genuine stakeholder representation within its internal knowledge-generating processes (see Deetz 1992, esp. ch. 7, for development).

The ideal speech situation is, however, based upon a narrow conception of the moral point of view which limits its potential scope of application considerably. Most importantly, Habermas' discourse ethics is based upon a conception of the moral point of view associated with a razor-sharp distinction (1990: 104) between moral-practical discourses (about normative issues of justice and rights), which are amenable to rational-critical discourse under conditions stipulated by the ideal speech situation, and ethical-existential discourses (about evaluative questions of the good life), which are only amenable to rational-critical discourse within the unproblematic horizon of a concrete historical form of life. It is for this reason, Habermas argues, that his discourse ethics may more accurately be characterised as a discourse theory of morality, than a discourse ethics proper (1993: vii).

The standpoint of the generalised other

Habermas' reason for distinguishing between moral-practical and ethical-existential discourses is that in modern heterogeneous societies, characterised by considerable (and increasing) value dissensus among different societal groups, to achieve a consensus about underlying values (such as what constitutes the good life) has become problematic. Under such circumstances, Habermas argues, the ethical basis for social interaction may only be located in the structure of interaction itself through rational-critical discourse about generalisable interests: '[Moral-practical] reason is thereby transformed from a context-dependent faculty of prudent deliberation that operates within the horizon of an established form of life into a faculty of pure reason operating independently of particular contexts' (1993: 120). The emphasis placed upon generalisable interests is significant for the present purposes. For an interest (or knowledge-claim) to qualify as generalisable it, needs to be abstracted from the concrete identities and motivations of the participants. It is thereby associated with a conception of self–other relations in which others ought to be conceptualised and related to as generalised others (a term originating with Mead (1934)), in that the participants ought to assume a standpoint of impartiality as concerns the values which underlie their respective interests or knowledge-claims. This may be accomplished, Habermas argues (following Mead), by engaging in a mode of ideal role-taking, 'which requires everyone to take the perspective of all others' (1993: 174). To view something from the moral point of view, Habermas thus argues, 'means that we do not elevate our own understanding and worldview to the standard by which we universalise a mode of action but instead test its generalizability also from the perspective of all others' (1993: 174–5). The moral point of view thereby privileges moral-practical discourses as the type of discourse which ensures the impartiality of moral judgement.

Paradoxically, Habermas' reason for excluding issues of ethics proper (evaluative issues of the good life) from his discourse ethics arguably ought to have led him to the exactly opposite conclusion. It is precisely in a situation of considerable and increasing value dissensus among different societal groups that a discourse ethics is needed which provides a mechanism for the rational-critical mediation of the different, and potentially conflicting, yet legitimate values of different societal groups.

The distinction Habermas draws between moral-practical discourses, to which his discourse ethics applies, and ethical-existential discourses, to which it does not, is problematic. From an organisation-theory perspective, to assume the standpoint of the generalised other requires that both the corporation and its stakeholders bracket, rather than thematise, differences in the values which underlie their respective knowledge-claims during interaction. This bracketing of differences in their underlying values would not represent a problem in a traditional homogeneous society, characterised by considerable value consensus among different societal (and stakeholder) groups. But in a modern heterogeneous society, such as the United States, characterised by considerable, and increasing, value dissensus among different societal (and stakeholder) groups, it becomes problematic. In particular, it is likely to result in interactions between the corporation and its stakeholders associated with various types of systematic distortion in the form of discursive closures. If both the corporation and its stakeholders must bracket rather than thematise the values underlying their respective knowledge-claims, it becomes possible for the corporation to contend that its knowledge-claims are value-neutral (a form of discursive closure known as neutralisation; see Deetz 1992, esp. ch. 7, for development). Similarly, it becomes possible for the corporation to dismiss the knowledge-claims of its stakeholders as not being amenable to rational-critical discourse on the basis that these concern evaluative issues of the good life which may be rationally evaluated only within the unproblematic horizon of a concrete historical form of life that differs fundamentally from that of the corporation. When the knowledge-claims differ radically among the corporation's different stakeholder groups internally, it thus also becomes possible for the corporation to contend that it is problematic to identify a common ground for their rational-critical evaluation. This becomes especially problematic if the corporation's stakeholders attempt to introduce knowledge-claims of a non-economic character into the corporation's internal knowledge-generating processes. In need of seemingly value-neutral (or impartial) means of conflict resolution, the corporation may be provided with the opportunity to reduce non-economic conflicts of interest to questions of economic character in ways which further the (primarily economic) interests of its owners/stockholders.

The distinction between moral-practical and ethical-existential discourses is thus associated with a problematic conception of self–other relations. Within the logic of Habermas' discourse ethics only gereralisable interests (or knowledge-claims) – that is, those which may be abstracted from the concrete identities and motivations of the participants – qualify for rational-critical discourse through the application of ideal role-taking. This implies that the participants ought to conceptualise and relate to one another as generalised others, in the sense that what they have in common is rendered more significant than what differentiates them from each other. Again, this would be relatively unproblematic in a traditional homogeneous society characterised by considerable value consensus among different societal (and stakeholder) groups, where commonalities tend to overshadow salient differences in underlying values, but it becomes problematic in a modern heterogeneous society characterised by considerable and increasing value dissensus among different societal (and stakeholder) groups. By requiring the participants to bracket rather than thematise differences in their underlying values, the conditions for various types of systematically distorted communication rather than genuinely open and reflexive interactions are made possible. This way of conceptualising the ethical basis upon which knowledge ought to be constructed in the corporation is thus not only ethically problematic, but is also likely to be associated with negative epistemological consequences. If the nature of knowledge-claims deemed amenable to rational-critical discourse is determined in advance of interaction, important types of knowledge-claims are likely never to enter the corporation's internal knowledge-generating processes.

The generalised and the concrete other

Benhabib's (1992; see also 1985, 1986, 1987, 1990) reconsideration of Habermas' discourse ethics represents an attempt to transcend his narrow conception of the moral point of view the associated distinction between moral-practical discourses (about normative issues of justice and rights), to which his discourse ethics applies, and ethical-existential discourses (about evaluative issues of the good life), to which it does not. While Benhabib's reconsideration is not motivated by purely conceptual concerns, but, rather, has been developed in terms of a feminist emancipatory agenda (see Haas and Deetz, 2000 for development), we will primarily focus attention here upon the aspects which appear most salient from an organisation-theory perspective. Most importantly, Benhabib (1992) argues that Habermas' conception of the moral point of view is associated with a problematic conception of self–other relations (the other as a generalised other), which limits its potential scope of application considerably.

A broadened conception of the moral point of view

A broadened conception of the moral point of view may be developed, Benhabib (1992) argues, by attending to two distinct conceptions of self–other relations which delineate both moral perspectives and communicative structures: respectively, the standpoint of the generalised other (*à la* Habermas) and the concrete other. These two conceptions of self–other relations, Benhabib argues, reflect traditional dichotomies between autonomy and nurturance, independence and bonding, the public sphere and the private sphere, and, more broadly, between normative issues of justice and rights and evaluative issues of the good life. For Benhabib, to assume the standpoint of the generalised other

> Requires us to view each and every individual as a rational being entitled to the same rights and duties we would want to ascribe to ourselves. In assuming this standpoint, we abstract from the individuality and concrete identity of the other. We assume that the other, like ourselves, is a being who has concrete needs, desires and affects, but that what constitutes his or her moral dignity is not what differentiates us from each other, but rather what we, as speaking and acting rational agents, have in common. Our relation to the other is governed by the norms of formal equality and reciprocity: each is entitled to expect and to assume from us what we can expect from him or her. The norms of our interactions are primarily public and institutional ones.
>
> (Benhabib 1992: 158–9)

To assume the standpoint of the concrete other, on the other hand,

> Requires us to view each and every rational being as an individual with a concrete history, identity and affective-emotional constitution. In assuming this standpoint, we abstract from what constitutes our commonality, and focus on individuality. We seek to comprehend the needs of the other, his or her motivations, what he searches for, and what s/he desires. Our relation to the other is governed by the norms of equity and complementary reciprocity: each is entitled to expect and to assume from the other forms of behaviour through which the other feels recognised and confirmed as a concrete, individual being with specific needs, talents and capacities. Our differences in this case complement rather than exclude one another. The norms of our

interactions are usually, although not exclusively, private, non-institutional ones.

(Benhabib 1992: 159)

The moral conversation

For Benhabib (1992), a broadened conception of the moral point of view requires that one simultaneously assumes the standpoint of the generalised other and the concrete other, which entails a shift from a substantial to a discursive understanding of communicative rationality. This may be accomplished, Benhabib argues (following Habermas), by engaging in an open-ended, moral conversation which requires the adherence to two underlying principles: (1) the principle of universal moral respect (the recognition of the rights of all beings capable of speech and action to be participants in the moral conversation); and (2) the principle of egalitarian reciprocity (the recognition that within such conversations each has the same symmetrical rights to various speech acts, to initiate a new topic, to ask for reflection about the presuppositions of the conversation). These principles are derived, of course, from Habermas' discourse ethics, but the approach is no longer general and universal, but rather concrete and contextual. The purpose of engaging in the moral conversation, Benhabib argues (in a critique of Habermas), is not to reach a rationally motivated consensus among the participants concerning their respective interests or knowledge-claims. Rather, the objective is 'the anticipated communication with others with whom I must finally come to some agreement' (Benhabib 1992: 158–9). The moral conversation thus does not guarantee that a consensus may ultimately be reached among the participants. Rather, to engage in the moral conversation 'demonstrates the will and readiness to seek understanding with the other and to reach some reasonable agreement' (*ibid.*). A moral conversation which is genuinely open and reflexive and does not operate upon the basis of certain epistemological limitations may thus lead to a mutual understanding of the otherness of the participants. It actualises a moral dialogue between different selves who are considered to be generalised others, in the sense of equal moral agents, and concrete others, in the sense of individuals with irreducible, yet legitimate, differences.

This way of conceptualising the moral conversation, Benhabib argues, represents a transcendence of the distinction Habermas draws between moral-practical discourses (about normative issues of justice and rights) and ethical-existential discourses (about evaluative issues of the good life): 'If in discourses the agenda is radically open, if participants can bring any and all matters under critical scrutiny and questioning, then there is no way to predefine the nature of the issues as being public ones of justice versus private ones of the good life' (Benhabib 1992: 110). A distinction that, such as between moral-practical and ethical-existential discourses, is therefore 'subsequent and not prior to the process of discursive will formation' (*ibid.*).

Behabib's (1992) reconsideration of Habermas' discourse ethics is significant to organisation theory. The aforementioned thematisation, rather than bracketing, of differences in the values which underlie the knowledge-claims of (respectively) the corporation and its stakeholders and between the corporation's different stakeholder groups internally may arguably only be achieved by conceptualising and relating to others as generalised others and concrete others simultaneously. From the perspective of the corporation (as a self), this ought to imply conceptualising and relating to each stakeholder group as a concrete other with irreducible, yet legitimate, differences while conceptualising and relating to the individual members of a stakeholder group as generalised others – that is, as similar representatives of a stakeholder group. While it may be ethically worthwhile ideally to assume the standpoint of the concrete other towards the individual members of a stakeholder group, it is clearly problematic to do so in practice. Oftentimes, stakeholder groups are comprised of so many members that it becomes practically unfeasible to attend to differences among the individual members.

Only by assuming the standpoint of the generalised other and the concrete other simultaneously may the corporation thus recognise that its multiplicity of stakeholders may have different and potentially conflicting, yet legitimate, knowledge-claims worthy of representation within its internal knowledge-generating processes. This way of conceptualising the ethical basis upon which knowledge ought to be constructed in the corporation not only represents an ethically more sound stance towards its stakeholders than the one advanced by Habermas, but also is likely to be associated with positive epistemological consequences since it is not associated with epistemological limitations as to the types of knowledge-claims deemed amenable to rational-critical discourse.

It should be considered, however, that Habermas has responded directly to Benhabib's (1992) contention that to assume the standpoint of the concrete other becomes problematic in terms of his discourse ethics. In a recent interview, Habermas argued that the impression that his discourse ethics renders the assumption of the standpoint of the concrete other problematic is associated with a one-sided preoccupation with questions of justification: 'the Unique disposition of a particular case that calls for regulation and the concrete characteristics of the people involved, comes into view only after problems of justification have been resolved' (Habermas 1993: 153–4). Consequently, Habermas argues, '[moral-practical] reason is not fully realised in discourses of justification. Whereas in justifying norms [Moral-practical] reason finds expression in the principle of universalization, in the application of norms it takes the form of a principle of appropriateness' (*ibid.*: 154). However, the distinction Habermas draws between a decontextual justification of norms and a contextually sensitive application of norms does not adequately resolve the issue. Simultaneously to assume the standpoint of the generalised other and the concrete other requires that one thematises (or contextualises) individuating characteristics of the other right from the outset, rather than introduces their thematisation during the subsequent decision on how to relate to the other in an ethically sound manner. In contrast, Habermas' approach requires an initial bracketing of individuating characteristics of the other (during the justification of norms) which makes it problematic to introduce their subsequent thematisation (during the application of norms). In this important respect, Habermas' approach is associated with the problematic contention that one ought initially to assume the standpoint of the generalised other and then follow this by assuming the standpoint of the concrete other. In other words, there is a problematic two-step process: 'In justificatory discourses it is necessary to abstract from the contingent contextual embeddedness of a proposed norm only to ensure that the norm, assuming it withstands the generalisation test, is sufficiently open to context-sensitive application' (*ibid.*: 58).

Despite important differences between the (discourse-theory) approaches of Habermas and Benhabib, they share certain conceptual similarities. Both contend that the interactions between the corporation (as a self) and its stakeholders (as others) ought to be radically reciprocal and symmetric (the responsibility of the self as being-with the other). However, Levinas' (1969, 1981) approach to ethics differs fundamentally, since the relationship between self and other is characterised by the non-reciprocal and asymmetric responsibility of the self for the other (the responsibility of the self as being-for the other).

Ethics as first philosophy

Levinas' (1969, 1981) approach to ethics differs fundamentally from the approaches of Habermas and Benhabib. It does not represent an attempt to develop ethical ideals for the relationship between self and other based upon an account of a less than ideal present, such as through an ideal speech situation (Habermas) or a moral conversation (Benhabib). Because for Levinas the relationship between self and other represents a priori an ethical relationship from which certain ethical ideals may subsequently be deduced, it represents a transcendence of the traditional moral philosophical distinction between questions of factuality (what is) and normativity (what ought to be). It is for this important reason, Levinas argues, that 'morality is not a branch of philosophy, but first philosophy' (1969: 304;). In so arguing, Levinas' objective is to establish the 'primacy of an irreducible structure upon which all other structures rest' (*ibid.*: 79).

Since Levinas' approach to ethics is both far-reaching and complex, we will primarily focus attention here upon three closely interrelated aspects of the relationship between self and other which appear most salient to organisation theory. These include: (1) the non-reciprocal and asymmetric responsibility of the self for the other; (2) the problems with thematising the other; and (3) the concepts of self-deconstruction/construction in the face of the other. In so doing, we hope to provide an overall presentation of Levinas' approach to ethics without doing excessive violence (incidentally a key concept in Levinas' terminology) to its integrity.

The non-reciprocal and asymmetric responsibility of the self for the other

Levinas argues that the relationship between self and other represents the primordial ethical relationship – that is, the relationship upon which all ethics is and ought to be based. The self, Levinas argues, is responsible for the other, even before his or her own freedom; it belongs to (or is invested with) responsibility rather than chooses to be responsible. This responsibility, which Levinas (1996) refers to as an election, implies the obligation to serve the other as a being-for the other. Levinas is thus critical of the ethical ideals of reciprocity and symmetry because, he argues, they imply that human beings are interchangeable, that one may substitute one human being for the other. Rather, Levinas argues, the self is unique in its responsibility for the other. The uniqueness of the self does not rest in its self-assertion, but rather in its answering the calling of the other which appoints it as unique. The self is the only human being who may respond to a responsibility which is so personal that it arises directly from its orientation towards the other, from its position in the relation. The relationship between self and other thus characterised by the non-reciprocal and asymmetric responsibility of the self for the other is prior to the relationship – before the 'I am' – for which reason the self may not escape its orientation.

The self is, in Levinas' terminology, a being delivered to the other as a hostage, an other which comes from a dimension of height (1969) or reaches the self through proximity (1981) without achieving unity. The freedom of the self, Levinas thus argues, does not rest in being-for itself, but rather in being-for the other. Contrary to the traditional view of freedom, Levinas argues that ethics is based upon a fundamental heteronomy of which the other is the origin: 'Freedom would therefore signify the acceptance of a vocation to which I alone can respond, or again, the power to respond to it when called. To be free is only to do what nobody else can do in my place' (1994: 172).

The response of responsibility, Levinas argues, is thus a response which 'answers, before any understanding, for a debt contracted before any freedom and before any consciousness and any present' (1981: 12). A radical passivity of the self (or subjectivity as a passive subjection to the other) lies at the centre of this responsibility, which precedes the ontological subjectification of the self in any traditional sense. Yet this passivity implies not apathy on the part of the self, but rather the self's ability to be moved by what happens to the other, to respond to the other when called upon. The self is thus in a position neither freely to accept nor reject its responsibility for the other. It is impossible freely to accept or reject responsibility, Levinas argues, when it arises in advance of the freedom of the self: 'As soon as I acknowledge that it is "I" who am responsible, I accept that my freedom is anteceded by an obligation to the other' (1986: 27) Consequently, Levinas argues,

> Even if I deny my primordial responsibility to the other by affirming my own freedom as primary, I can never escape the fact that the other has

demanded a response from me before I affirm my freedom not to respond to his demand.

(Levinas 1986: 27)

The responsibility for the other thus arises not from the ontological universality of reason which discloses to the self criteria for (self-)conscious (or freely determined) action, but rather from the uniqueness of its responsibility for the other.

In a reversal of the traditional order of privilege which promoted speculative reason on the part of the self, responsibility is thus not first disclosed to the self in its universality. On the contrary, responsibility binds the self since it takes hold immediately, before any understanding or (self-)conscious choice on the part of the self. The ethical terminology of which Levinas makes use thus does not point towards a system of ethical commands and prohibitions, as it is based upon a conception of responsibility which precedes every ethics, a responsibility which subjectivises the self even before he or she may ask the question how should I conduct myself towards the other?

Levinas' approach to ethics thus differs fundamentally from the approaches of Habermas and Benhabib in two important respects. First, while Habermas and Benhabib contend that the choice to engage in an ethical relationship with the other is based upon voluntary on the part of the self, since no external constraints may force the self to adhere to the ethical ideals which underlie the ideal speech situation (Habermas) or the moral conversation (Benhabib), Levinas disagrees fundamentally. For Levinas, the self has no choice but to engage in an ethical relationship with the other since the responsibility of the self for the other precedes his or her own freedom to choose. Second, while Habermas and Benhabib contend that the ethical relationship between self and other ought to be radically reciprocal and symmetric, Levinas disagrees fundamentally. Since the self is responsible for the other even before his or her own freedom, the relationship between self and other is characterised by the non-reciprocal and asymmetric responsibility of the self for the other.

These two sources of conflict between the approaches to ethics of, respectively, Habermas/Benhabib and Levinas are significant to organisation theory. Without choosing sides on these complex issues, Levinas' approach to ethics arguably draws attention to aspects of the relationship between self and other which are not well captured by Habermas and Benhabib. First, Levinas' view that the self has no choice but to engage in an ethical relationship with the other (since the responsibility of the self for the other precedes his or her freedom to choose) draws attention to an important feature of the relationship between the corporation and its stakeholders. When a corporation is initially established, it is likely to be immediately immersed in a multiplicity of relationships with stakeholders, of which at least some are not the result of its (self-)conscious (or freely determined) choice. That is, actions taken by the corporation right from its initial establishment are likely to have significant, often unintended, consequences for a multiplicity of stakeholders. Under such circumstances, the responsibility of the corporation towards these stakeholders may be concluded to be antecedent to its freedom to exercise its responsibility. It is likely to be immersed in a multiplicity of ethical relationships even before its own acknowledgement of them. Similarly, the corporation's subsequent actions, once established, are likely to have significant consequences for a multiplicity of stakeholders, of which at least some are not the result of its (self-)conscious (or freely determined) choice.

Second, and perhaps more important, is Levinas' argument that the relationship between self and other is characterised by the non-reciprocal and asymmetric responsibility of the self for the other. This argument implies that the question of how to conceptualise and relate to the other in an ethically sound manner is not adequately resolved by arguing that the interactions between the corporation (as a self) and its stakeholders (as others) ought to be based upon the ethical ideals of reciprocity and symmetry, which underlie the ideal speech situation (Habermas) or the moral conversation (Benhabib). Language, Levinas argues, represents a relational medium which facilitates contact between self and other, but it does not facilitate contact in the Habermasian or Benhabibian sense of the establishment of a common ground for rational-critical discourse. To establish a common ground in order to achieve consensus (Habermas) or mutual understanding (Benhabib) between self and other would be to thematise the otherness of the other, which is equal to enacting his or her violation. While for Habermas and Benhabib the ethical ideal for interaction between self and other is to achieve an intersubjectivity free of any form of domination, for Levinas the 'inter' of intersubjectivity represents (a priori) a violation of the otherness of the other. In a Levinasian perspective, the interactions between self and other ought rather to be concerned with disrupting a subjectivity which permits the 'inter' of intersubjectivity to be subsumed under a single thematic rubric. To assume that the otherness of the other may be subsumed during rational-critical discourse is thus problematic in a Levinasian perspective. The responsibility to which the self is to respond transcends the reciprocal and symmetric relationship between self and other of discourse ethics – that is, the kind of ethics based upon participation in a common reason (Habermas) or an explicit contract of reason (Benhabib).

For Levinas, language does not represent a potential source of unity between self and other, but rather the very impossibility of unification: 'Language accomplishes a relation between terms that break up the unity of genus' (1969: 194). It is this relationship, prior to thematic unity, which represents the ethical dimension of the relationship between self and other: 'Conversation from the very fact that it maintains the distance between me and the Other...cannot renounce the egoism of its existence' (1981: 10). But, Levinas argues,

> The very fact of being in a conversation consists in recognising that the Other has a right over this egoism, and hence in justifying oneself. Apology, in which the I at the same time asserts itself and inclines before the transcendent, belongs to the essence of conversation.

> (Levinas 1981: 10)

The activity of communicating thus displaces the self from its central position in the relationship with the other. The communicating self is no longer by and for itself; it is for the other.

The important question is, then, whether it is possible to deduce ethical ideals for the relationship between the corporation (as a self) and its stakeholders (as others) which transcend the ethical ideals of reciprocity and symmetry which underlie the ideal speech situation (Habermas) and the moral conversation (Benhabib). This is a complex issue, since it requires a conception of interaction which facilitates contact between self and other while avoiding an ethically problematic thematisation of the otherness of the other.

The problem of thematising the other

The relationship between self and other is, Levinas argues, characterised not only by the non-reciprocal and asymmetric responsibility of the self for the other, but also by the fact that the other is by definition un-thematisable. The otherness of the other rests in the fact that the other disrupts the ontological horizon of the self, as Levinas (1969) argues in a critique of Heidegger's (1962) ontology of being. Hence, the other resists a thematisation which would represent him or her as a particular type of phenomenon within a universal order of being. Since the otherness of the other represents precisely that which does not fit into a universal order of being, he or she may not be thematised through the traditional categories of phenomenology. The other transcends the limits of (self-) consciousness and its ontological horizon. Levinas thus argues that

> The face [of the other] is present in its refusal to be contained. In this sense it cannot be comprehended, that is, encompassed. It is neither seen nor touched – for in visual or tactile sensation the identity of the I envelops the alterity of the object, which becomes precisely a content.
>
> (Levinas 1969: 194)

Since the other may not be thematised, it does not represent a phenomenon, but rather what Levinas (1987) terms an enigma which may not be defined in purely phenomenological terms. This draws attention to the radical otherness in terms of which Levinas conceptualises the relationship between self and other. Since the otherness of the other may not be thematised, a thematic relationship becomes impossible. To thematise the otherness of the other would represent an attempt to deny it.

The problem is thus, Levinas argues, that while it may be possible for the self to establish contact with the other through interaction, that which represents the otherness of the other disappears as soon as language thematises the utterance of a speech act. Since a relationship between self and other by necessity implies thematisation (that is, an act of violence in which the otherness of the other is reduced to a moment of the Same), it is necessary for the self perpetually to unsay that which is said. The self may unsay that which is said, a piece of ontology produced by the saying, by recognising that the unsaying, in its turn, will change into a said which must be said again. As Levinas argues, 'There is therefore a need to unsay all that comes after the nakedness of signs, to set aside all that is said in the pure saying proper to proximity' (1981: 198). In other words, only by facilitating a perpetual thematisation/de-thematisation of the otherness of the other (that is, by saying and unsaying that which is said) may the self avoid reducing the otherness of the other into a moment of the Same.

Levinas' argument that an ethical relationship between self and other may only be established if the self facilitates a perpetual thematisation/de-thematisation of the otherness of the other provides an important counter-argument to the one levelled by Benhabib. From an organisation-theory perspective, Levinas' argument draws attention to the fact that it is not adequate for the corporation to thematise rather than bracket the values which underlie the knowledge-claims of its stakeholders. Rather, his argument implies, in order not to render the otherness of the other invisible (that is, to reduce the other to a moment of the Same), it is necessary to facilitate a perpetual de-thematisation of the values which underlie their knowledge-claims. In concrete terms, this implies that the corporation ought to engage in a perpetual questioning of its own understanding of the knowledge-claims of its stakeholders, and of the values upon which they appear to be based.

Yet Levinas' approach to ethics implies that more radical steps should be taken on the part of the corporation than to facilitate a perpetual thematisation/de-thematisation of the values which underlie the knowledge-claims of its stakeholders. In particular, it requires that the corporation (as a self) also becomes the object of a perpetual de-thematisation (or self-deconstruction) in the face of its stakeholders (as others). On this particular point, which is significant to our attempt to develop the conceptual foundation for an ethic of knowledge construction in corporations, Levinas' approach to ethics differs fundamentally from the approaches of Habermas and Benhabib.

Self-deconstruction/construction in the face of the other

Levinas argues not only that the otherness of the other is by definition unthematisable (since the other disrupts the ontological horizon of the self) but also that the other appears as other before the self (only insofar as his or her appearance destroys the ontological horizon of the self without ever permitting the self to restore its previous order). The subjectification of the self thus does not represent an original closure which produces a self-contained entity, but rather represents an openness which destroys the ontological horizon of the self, and at the same time subjectifies it. The self does not proceed from itself, but rather returns to itself in a retrograde movement which Levinas (1981) terms recurrence. The confrontation with the other is the condition upon which the subjectivity of the self becomes uncovered to itself; it depends upon confrontation with the other for its articulation as self. This retrograde movement from self-deconstruction in the face of the other to an ethically charged self-construction thus represents a movement away from naïve (self-)consciousness to responsible consciousness on the part of the self.

Levinas' argument that an ethical relationship between self and other may only be established as the result of self-deconstruction in the face of the other followed by an ethically charged self-construction differs fundamentally from the arguments of Habermas and Benhabib. On the most general level, both Habermas and Benhabib are primarily concerned with one aspect of self–other relations, that of the other. In both of their accounts, the concept of the self is virtually left unproblematised. They both assume that the subjectivity of the self is produced prior to their interactions with others, and not vice-versa. Benhabib's account differs the most in this respect since she argues that the self ought to assume the standpoint of the concrete other in relation to others, which assumes that both self and others exist as fixed subjectivities prior to their interactions. Yet Habermas' discourse ethics also operates upon the basis of a conception of self-deconstruction in the face of the other. Habermas argues that differences in the values which underlie the interests and knowledge-claims of the participants ought to be bracketed rather than thematised during interaction through the assumption of the standpoint of the generalised other. In contrast to Levinas, however, Habermas' conception of self-deconstruction is problematic for organisation theory, since it is likely to lead to a situation in which individuating characteristics of self and other disappear entirely. Levinas' conception of self-deconstruction, on the contrary, implies that the individuating characteristics of self and other are maintained.

Without taking sides on this complex issue, Levinas' conception of self-deconstruction arguably draws attention to important aspects of the relationship between self and other which are not well captured by Habermas and Benhabib. In particular, it draws attention to the fact that an ethically sound basis for knowledge construction in the corporation may arguably not be achieved either by conceptualising and relating to others in a radically reciprocal and symmetric manner (Habermas/Benhabib) or by thematising rather than bracketing the values which underlie the knowledge-claims of the corporation's stakeholders (Benhabib). Rather, it implies that the corporation (as a self) ought to transcend its fixed subjectivity by recovering latent, yet legitimate, conflicts between its multiplicity of potential selves. If the corporation does not attempt to recover its own internal conflicts, it is unlikely that it will be able to help recover and recognise those of its stakeholders. In a Levinasian perspective, the purpose of such a self-deconstruction on the part of the corporation is not to recover a more unitary self, but rather to self-construct into a more responsive self.

The importance of providing the corporation's stakeholders with representation rights within its internal knowledge-generating processes thus rests upon the opportunity not for successful self-expression, but rather for self-deconstruction in the face of the other. The interactions between the corporation and its stakeholders ought to be potentially productive rather than reproductive (see Deetz 1995a, esp. ch. 6, for development), aimed at producing what neither of the participants had access to prior to their interactions rather than successfully reproducing either or both of their respective values and knowledge-claims.

It should be considered, however, that to self-deconstruct in the face of the other is likely to be an unsettling experience for the corporation. To do so successfully, the company must overcome a profound sense of ontological insecurity (Giddens 1992) or Cartesian anxiety (Bernstein 1984) – that is, a natural anxiety associated with a sense of loss of subjectivity. Yet it is precisely such a self-inflicted loss of subjectivity which is required of the corporation if it is to establish ethically sound relationships with its stakeholders.

Conclusion: towards an ethic of knowledge construction in corporations

The prior discussion indicates that to develop the conceptual foundation for an ethic of knowledge construction in corporations is a complex endeavour. The question of how the corporation ought to construct knowledge should be considered not only an epistemological issue, but also (and perhaps more fundamentally) an ethical issue. This requires a radical reconception of the relationship between the corporation and its stakeholders. In particular, it implies that the corporation should consider not only upon what methodological bases and through which means it constructs knowledge of its stakeholders, but also (and perhaps more fundamentally) whether these reflect an ethically sound stance towards them. These two concerns are closely interrelated, however, and only recognition of the complex relationship between them may provide the conceptual basis for such an ethic of knowledge construction in corporations.

First, and perhaps most importantly, an ethic of knowledge construction in corporations should be considered intrinsically linked to the question of self–other relations. The prior discussion indicates that the relationship between the corporation and its stakeholders may be conceptualised as a concrete manifestation of a more abstract relationship between self and others. It is important to maintain the distinction between the corporation (as a self) and its stakeholders (as others), not only for conceptual purposes, but also due to the unique historical context in which the modern corporation operates. One of the most significant characteristics of a modern heterogeneous society, such as the United States, is that it is associated with considerable, and increasing, value dissensus among different societal (and stakeholder) groups. Under such circumstances, the corporation may not assume that its multiplicity of stakeholders adhere to the same underlying values as itself. If the corporation is to conceptualise and relate to its stakeholders in an ethically sound manner, it has no choice but to conceptualise and relate to them as others – that is, as groups of people with different, and potentially conflicting, yet legitimate, knowledge-claims in need of representation within its internal knowledge-generating processes.

The important question is, then, how the corporation may establish an ethically sound basis for knowledge construction. Habermas' discourse ethics provides important ethical ideals which may serve as an initial response to this question. Only when the force of the better argument rather than various types of systematic distortion in the form of discursive closures governs the interactions between the corporation and its stakeholders does the corporation facilitate genuine stakeholder representation within its internal knowledge-generating processes. The problem with Habermas' discourse ethics is, however, that it is based upon a narrow conception of the moral point of view, associated with a distinction between moral-practical discourses (about normative questions of justice and rights), which are amenable to rational-critical discourse under conditions stipulated by the ideal speech situation, and ethical-existential discourses (about evaluative questions of the good life), which are only amenable to rational-critical discourse within the unproblematic horizon of a concrete historical form of life.

While the distinction between moral-practical discourses, to which Habermas' discourse ethics thus applies, and ethical-existential-discourses, to which it does not, is appropriate for traditional homogeneous societies characterised by considerable value consensus among different societal (and stakeholder) groups, it is problematic in modern heterogeneous societies, such as the United States, characterised by considerable, and increasing, value dissensus among different societal (and stakeholder) groups. In particular, the distinction between moral-practical and ethical-existential discourses implies that both the corporation and its stakeholders ought to assume the standpoint of the generalised other. This requires them to bracket rather than thematise differences in the values which underlie their respective knowledge-claims. But if both the corporation and its stakeholders are to bracket rather than thematise the values which underlie their respective knowledge-claims, the distinction between the corporation (as a self) and its stakeholders (as others) is likely to collapse entirely, a distinction which, as previously discussed, it is so important to maintain, since the modern corporation operates in a historical context characterised by considerable, and increasing, value dissensus among different societal (and stakeholder) groups. To require the corporation and its stakeholders to bracket rather than thematise the values which underlie their respective knowledge-claims is thus not only ethically problematic (since it provides the corporation with much opportunity systematically to distort its interactions with its stakeholders), but also likely to be associated with negative epistemological consequences. If the nature of the knowledge-claims deemed amenable to rational-critical discourse is determined in advance of communicative interaction, important types of knowledge-claims are likely never to enter the corporation's internal knowledge-generating processes.

Some of the problems with Habermas' discourse ethics, and especially the problematic conception of self–other relations, may be addressed by attending to

Benhabib's reconsideration thereof. Most importantly, her delineation of the principles which underlie the moral conversation represents a broadening of self–other relations in which others ought not only to be conceptualised and related to as generalised others (*à la* Habermas), in the sense of equal moral agents, but also as concrete others, in the sense of individuals with irreducible differences. This implies not only that the problematic distinction between moral-practical and ethical-existential discourses ought to be transcended, but also (and perhaps more importantly) that the values which underlie the knowledge-claims of, respectively, the corporation and its stakeholders ought to become thematised rather than bracketed during interaction. This thematisation of the underlying values of the corporation's stakeholders is significant since it serves to maintain the important conceptual distinction drawn between the corporation (as a self) and the stakeholders (as others). This way of conceptualising the ethical basis upon which knowledge ought to be constructed in the corporation thus not only represents an ethically more sound stance on behalf of the coporation towards its stakeholders than the one advanced by Habermas, but is also likely to be associated with positive epistemological consequences, since it is not associated with epistemological limitations as to the types of knowledge-claims deemed amenable to rational-critical discourse.

The discourse-ethical approaches of Habermas and Benhabib may, however, only provide partial responses to how the construction of knowledge in the corporation may be achieved in an ethically sound manner. Most importantly, they are both primarily concerned with problematising one aspect of self–other relations: that of the other. The concept of the self is virtually left unproblematised in both of their accounts, which is problematic for organisation theory.

It is in this important respect that it becomes important to consider Levinas' approach to ethics. For Levinas, the relationship between self and other is characterised by the non-reciprocal and asymmetric responsibility of the self for the other. This implies that the responsibility of the corporation (as a self) towards its stakeholders (as others) is antecedent to its (self-)conscious (or freely determined) choice to engage in an ethical relationship with them, but also (and perhaps more fundamentally) that the question of how to conceptualise and relate to them as others in an ethically sound manner is not adequately resolved by arguing that their interactions ought to be based upon the ethical ideals of reciprocity and symmetry which underlie, respectively, the ideal speech situation (Habermas) and the moral conversation (Benhabib). Furthermore, since the otherness of the other rests in the fact that he or she is by definition unthematisable, not only should the corporation engage in a thematisation rather than bracketing of the values which underlie the knowledge-claims of its stakeholders (Benhabib), but rather it should facilitate their perpetual thematisation/de-thematisation. In concrete terms, this implies that the corporation ought to engage in a perpetual questioning of its own understanding of the knowledge-claims of its stakeholders, and the values upon which they appear to be based.

Yet for the corporation to facilitate a perpetual thematisation/de-thematisation of the values which underlie the knowledge-claims of its stakeholders is not adequate in a Levinasian perspective. An ethically sound ethical relationship between the corporation (as a self) and its stakeholders (as others) may only be established if the corporation self-deconstructs in the face of its stakeholders, and follows this with an ethically charged self-construction. This implies that the corporation ought to transcend its fixed subjectivity by recovering latent, yet legitimate, conflicts between its multiplicity of potential selves. If the corporation does not attempt to recover its own internal conflicts, it is unlikely that it will be able to help recover and recognise those it of its stakeholders. In a Levinasian perspective, the purpose of such a self-deconstruction on the part of the corporation ought not to be to recover a more unitary self, but rather to self-construct into a more responsive self. The importance of providing the corporation's stakeholders with representation rights within its internal knowledge-generating processes thus rests upon the opportunity not for successful self-expression, but rather for self-deconstruction in the face of the other. The interactions between the corporation and its stakeholders ought to be potentially productive rather than reproductive, aimed at producing what neither of the participants had access to prior to their interactions, rather than successfully reproducing either or both of their respective values and knowledge.

References

Benhabib, S. (1985) 'The utopian dimension in communicative ethics', *New German Critique* 35: 83–96.

Benhabib, S. (1986) *Critique, Norm and Utopia: A Study of the Foundations of Critical Theory*, New York: Columbia University Press.

Benhabib, S. (1987) 'The generalized and the concrete other', in S. Benhabib and D. Cornell (eds) *Feminism as Critique: On the Politics of Gender*, Minneapolis: University of Minnesota Press.

Benhabib, S. (1990) 'Afterword: Communicative ethics and current controversies in practical philosophy', in S. Benhabib and F. Dallmayr (eds) *The Communicative Ethics Controversy*, Cambridge, MA: MIT Press.

Benhabib, S. (1992) *Situating the Self: Gender, Community and Postmodernism in Contemporary Ethics*, New York: Routledge.

Bernstein, R. (1984) *Beyond Objectivism and Relativism: Science, Hermeneutics and Praxis*, Philadelphia: University of Pennsylvania Press.

Carroll, A. (1989) *Business and Society: Ethics and Stakeholder Management*, Cincinnati, OH: South-Western.

Deetz, S. (1992) *Democracy in an Age of Corporate Colonization: Developments in Communication and the Politics of Everyday Life*, Albany, NY: State University of New York Press.

Deetz, S. (1995a) *Transforming Communication, Transforming Business: Building Responsive and Responsible Workplaces*, Cresskill: Hampton Press.

Deetz, S. (1995b) 'Transforming communication, transforming business: Stimulating value negotiation for more responsive and responsible workplaces', *International Journal of Value-Based Management* 8: 255–78.

Freeman, R.E. (1984) *Strategic Management: A Stakeholder Approach*, Boston: Pitman Publishing.

Freeman, R.E. and Gilbert, D. (1988) *Corporate Strategy and the Search for Ethics*, Englewood Cliffs, NJ: Prentice-Hall.

Freeman, R.E. and Gilbert, D. (1992) 'Business, ethics and society: A critical agenda', *Business and Society* 31: 9–17.

Giddens, A. (1992) *Modernity and Self-Identity: Self and Society in the Late Modern Age*, Stanford: Stanford University Press.

Haas, T. and Deetz, S. (2000) 'Between the generalised and the concrete other: Approaching organizational ethics from feminist perspectives', in P. Buzzanell (ed.) *Rethinking Organizational and Managerial Communication From Feminist Perspectives*, Thousand Oaks., CA: Sage

Habermas, J. (1970) 'On systematically distorted communication', *Inquiry* 13: 205–18.

Habermas, J. (1973) 'Wahrheitsteorien', in H. Fahrtenbach (ed.) *Wirklichkeit and Reflection: Walter Schultz zum 60*, Pfullingen: Neske.

Habermas, J. (1979) *Communication and the Evolution of Society*, trans. T. McCarthy, Boston: Beacon Press.

Habermas, J. (1984) *The Theory of Communicative Action*, vol. 1: *Reason and the Rationalization of Society*, trans. T. McCarthy, Boston: Beacon Press.

Habermas, J. (1987) *The Theory of Communicative Action*, vol. 2: *Lifeworld and System*, trans. T. McCarthy, Boston: Beacon Press.

Habermas, J. (1990) *Moral Consciousness and Communicative Action*, trans. C. Lenhardt and S.W. Nicholsen, Cambridge, MA: MIT Press.

Habermas, J. (1993) *Justification and Application: Remarks on Discourse Ethics*, trans C.P. Cronin, Cambridge, MA: MIT Press.

Heidegger, M. (1962) *Being and Time*, trans J. MacQuarrie and E. Robinson, New York: Harper & Row.

Levinas, E. (1969) *Totality and Infinity*, trans A. Lingis, The Hague: Martin Nijhoff.

Levinas, E. (1981) *Otherwise than Being, or Beyond Essence*, trans. A. Lingis, The Hague: Martin Nijhoff.

Levinas, E. (1986) 'Dialogue with Emmanuel Levinas', in R.A. Cohen (eds) *Face to Face with Levinas*, Albany, NY: State University of New York Press.

Levinas, E. (1987) 'Language and proximity', in *Collected Philosophical Papers*, trans A. Lingis, The Hague: Martin Nijhoff.

Levinas, E. (1994) *Beyond the Verse*, trans G.D. Mole, Bloomington, IN: Indiana University Press.

Levinas, E. (1996) 'Transcendence and height', in A.T. Peperzak, S. Critchley and R. Bernasconi (eds) *Emmanuel Levinas: Basic Philosophical Writings*, trans T. Chanter, S. Critchley and N. Walker, Bloomington, IN: Indiana University Press.

Mead, G.H. (1934) *Mind, Self and Society: From the Standpoint of a Social Behaviorist*, Chicago: University of Chicago Press.

Townley, B. (1993) 'Foucault, power/knowledge, and its relevance for human resource management,' *Academy of Management Review* 18: 518–45.

12 Gender citizenship in organisations

Silvia Gherardi

Introduction

The extension in recent decades of the sphere of rights connected, directly or indirectly, with the condition of women in society is undoubtedly of great social and cultural importance. Furthermore, the changes which, at least in Europe, have been made to labour law have had a major impact on the organisation and on the organisational culture of so-called everyday rights. But it is not at the level of the law and the de facto change induced by it that I wish to proceed; I shall concentrate instead on cultural and symbolic change in the social construction of gender within organisations that has progressed in parallel. To do so, I shall explore a metaphor – gender citizenship – in order to show how gender can assume different connotations internally to an organisational culture and generate a multiplicity of courses of action. My aim is to have 'gender' recognised as a social relation, instead of being denied by supposed gender-neutrality.

I have chosen the concept of citizenship principally because of its strong symbolic value as a complex of meanings handed down to us by previous generations. These meanings have undergone a process of transformation, and this transformation has been institutionalised. The analogy with gender should be clear.

My second reason for choosing citizenship is that it provides common terrain for broader debate encompassing the condition of postmodernity and the demands for affirmation by various diversities. This sets up the interesting paradox where the concept of citizenship suggests a common identity even though many citizens are excluded from it or wish to differentiate themselves from it. Citizenship is the sign of membership, of 'sameness' rather than of diversity, and it generates further paradoxes and ambiguities when we interrogate ourselves on the presence/absence of women as title-holders of citizenship.

Feminist political scientists (Sapiro 1981; Diamond and Hartsock 1981; Zincone 1984, 1992; Jones 1990) have conducted a rich debate on the ambiguity of the concept, and certain contributions to this debate will be drawn upon here, although my principal concern is to explore the metaphorical force of the concept when it is transported to a more restricted setting, from the state to the organisation. As a further case of institutional reflexivity, current debate on citizenship can also be transferred into organisations. In both cases the leitmotif is the same: difference and how to accommodate the models of universality and particularity in thought and action. 'Equal and different' has been a feminist slogan which one can use to indicate many other diversities but the same problem. The practices of citizenship have helped to change the concept of citizenship into tolerance for diversity and ambiguity; and the jurisdiction is both accepting these deferrals of meaning and actively diffusing them through its normative action. Thus, today, one may justifiably talk of gender citizenship as women's right to be equal and different, and as a universal right (of women and men as well) to be released from the prison of gender.

'Equal and different'

In order to link the argument of gender equality to the organisation, I shall illustrate how the term 'difference' has changed in only very recent times. I shall map three semantic paths and refer to the field of labour law, since this is automatically reflected in managerial philosophies of human resource management.

There is an extremely interesting debate in progress within labour law which, although it takes different forms in different countries, links all the European countries together and has inspired common female labour policies throughout the European Economic Community (EEC). The principal issue of debate is the passage from neutral law to gendered law, or from the rights of women to rights for women (Andrini 1991; De Leonardis 1991). The metaphor of gendered law (Holtmaat 1989; Pitch 1991) raises a theoretical challenge against a policy of justice. Admitting a situated and partial subject, with differences recognised as legitimate and safeguarded in their constitutive elements, signifies that differences are no longer differences from the norm (the abstract individual); they are differences among subjects, they are interdependencies (Minow 1990). The problem for law is the creation of a system of rights which are neutralistic but not neutral, impartial but articulated on differences (De Leonardis 1991; Forbes 1991). This debate has touched upon the role itself of law to reveal an alternative use for it, where the law is not solely normative but also serves to encourage behaviour worthy of social recognition and to enhance the humanity and dignity of subjects. The acceptance of these norms and of the principles that inspire them, together with the demands of women in the workplace, has served to alter the cultural meaning of gender difference.

Admittedly it is possible to talk in general of an organisational culture as a set of meanings shared by a group of individuals in a certain timespan; we can, however, identify a number of stages in the semantic change undergone by the concept of difference since the Second World War. Difference used to be almost exclusively sexual, biologically given, stemming from a social destiny which differed between the sexes and was naturally unequal. Within certain limits, there was no labour law for women (apart from the tutelage of their reproductive function). Their unequal status stemmed from childbearing and other impediments that their social function raised against their productive function. A first phase of women's struggle pursued the goal of the social valorisation of their participation in the labour market and of their contribution – economic as well – to society's resources through domestic and family work. Stressing that housework was work in every respect, and not just love, highlighted the interdependencies between market and non-market, between direct remuneration, transfer systems and the production of non-market wealth, between production and reproduction. It became no longer natural to be discriminated against, and some women demanded equal treatment.

The era of equal rights and egalitarian goals was thus born. Difference had a substantially negative meaning; it was the attribution of otherness. The woman represented diversity and all the social attributes of the diverse: inferiority, inadequacy, the 'second sex'. The equality demanded had the significance of formal equality, because it was supposed to fill a void, to compensate for a loss or a distancing from the norm. It was agreed that all people – male workers and female workers – should be considered equal. The principle of equality was not descriptive of a situation but prescriptive of a desirable state. This ushered in the period of what, with hindsight, has been called 'emancipationism' and which witnessed the mass entry of women into new occupations and the attenuation of occupational segregation.

Equal rights, however, soon revealed the contradictions that arose from the failure to take initial diversities into account: full achievement of workplace parity between the sexes required the affirmation of the specific rights of women and measures which compensated for initial disparities. Thus the subjects who had always been the embodiment of the norm, the paramount object of the law, found themselves discriminated against, found themselves to be the bearers of further differences, expressed as anxieties and fears of discrimination.

Alongside formal equality stood substantial equality, and a sharper distinction was drawn between personal diversity (of race, sex, religion, political opinion, etc.), which was to be recognised, respected and safeguarded, and inequalities, which were to be eliminated or compensated for in order to create equality. Formal or political equality was ensured by 'rights of' (freedom), and diversity, in this sense, was a positive value to be guaranteed. Substantial or social equality was ensured by 'rights to' (work, dignity), and in this case difference was a negative value to be eliminated. In the 1970s the distinction between difference and inequality marked the transition from a doctrine of equality to one of diversity. The same process of thought that had opposed the definition of difference as otherness first discovered that a definition 'in positive' was necessary, and then transformed difference into superiority. This was made possible by the discovery of difference as a resource, and of the female body as a specific resource for knowledge and an epistemic relation with the world.

The theoretical path pursued by Luce Irigaray (1977) is emblematic of what happened in the many European feminisms, but the repercussions of this debate were less explosive within organisations than at the level of the theoretical and political practice of feminism. Nevertheless, and ironically, in organisational practices the female as a resource encountered a certain managerial ideology which was receptive to it, and which sought to destabilise certain excessively single-dimensional features of masculinity that were impeding the flexibilisation of production processes. There thus appeared a rash of management courses which acknowledged and developed nurturing skills and attitudes, and there likewise arose the metaphor of the 'listening organisation' (Crozier 1989), one able to assimilate, to be passive, to receive rather than to dominate. The organisational exploitation of the female resource was only at the beginning, however; it was not envisaged as an equal exchange, as a relationship between adults, or as a guarantee of citizenship, but rather as a predatory act, with the replacement of one type of workforce with another that the passage of time and the exigencies of production had made more attractive because its diversities had acquired market value. Language of this kind is part of the so-called 'new wave management' (Willmott 1993), a sort of hegemonic project which attempts to build consent while favouring an already privileged group and one form of masculinity, the hegemonic one (Connell 1995).

With their spread and self-recognition in a condition of postmodernity, all the phenomena varyingly involved in the dialectic between diversity and inequality, between rights to difference and rights to compensation – in short, all the requests for citizenship – demanded a different position and posited the issue as being not of the subject's autonomy but of the subject's interdependence, in a complex social network, with other subjects.

Organisational citizenship

In the literature of organisational studies since Barnard (1938), an examination has been conducted of the participation of the members of an organisation in producing that common good known variously as organisational life, the culture of the workplace, the organisational climate, well-being (or the lack of it) and the material conditions of its production, the civilisation of the workplace. Common to all these reflections is the notion that there is something more than economic exchange involved in the regulation of the individual/organisation relation, and that it is constituted by a 'willingness to co-operate', by a pro-social form of behaviour, by an organisational commitment.

The concept of organisational citizenship behaviour (OCB) has been proposed by Bateman and Organ:

> to denote those organisationally beneficial behaviours and gestures that can neither be enforced on the basis of formal role obligations nor elicited by contractual guarantee of recompense. OCB consists of informal contributions that participants can choose to proffer or withhold without regard to considerations of sanction or formal incentives.
>
> (Bateman and Organ 1983: 589)

The literature has continued in its endeavour to measure this behaviour and to understand its motivational basis (Organ 1990; Podsakoff *et al.* 2000).

There has recently been a revival of the concept of organisational citizenship which has engendered heated debate on the meaning of this concept in the rhetoric of managerial discourses (Parker 1997; Hancock 1997). Parker argues that the new managerial style which uses the rhetoric of the corporate 'mission' and 'responsible autonomy', which propounds the idea of self-fulfilment through work and career, and which envisages a workforce which 'sings the company song and wears its tie', is forced to recognise the bond of reciprocity that ties the management and the workforce together. If the intention is to rely on affiliation and identification – i.e. on motivation rather than control – and metaphorically to transform the job description into a bill of rights, one ends up by using the vocabulary of rights and obligations. Parker thus maintains that organisational citizenship is the discursive terrain on which the colonisation of the employees' hearts and minds can be transmuted into an extension of participatory democracy. It thus has a boomerang effect on management, which is compelled to review the terms of the social contract between the parties.

Parker's views have been criticised by Hancock, who argues that the so-called 'new management style' prefigures a return to the Middle Ages (to the New Middle Ages also discussed by Minc (1993)) because it constructs a corporate culture which emphasises individual adherence to an ethereal and transcendent world in which the organisation is symbolically personified as a benevolent but demanding feudal lord, to whom all the ritual forms of obeisance must be paid.

The sense is therefore reversed: in a post-solidaristic age in which the traditional bonds of occupational, class and primary-group solidarity have dissolved, employees are not citizens but vassals. Even the trade unions have been unable to counteract the rhetoric of 'new-style management' and have lost credibility. In the recent revival of the concept of organisational citizenship – as Loveridge (1997) points out – the concern is more with the responsibilities of employees towards the employer than with the social responsibility of the firm towards the community. Interestingly, therefore, the notion of citizenship can be expressed in rhetorics of both participation and control. Here I wish to suggest that behaviour that expresses gender citizenship within an organisation should be included among the behaviours that constitute organisational citizenship, bearing in mind Parker's admonition that any attempt to introduce civil and political citizenship into the workplace cannot rely on organisations alone.

Assessment of this proposal requires us to ask if and how gender citizenship can become part of a conception of 'civic virtue' and in what sense fairness in the gender relationships may be considered as 'organisationally beneficial behaviour'. One can straightforwardly answer the first question by saying that for civil society today the justification of social inequalities as 'natural' is repugnant, and that, since civil society condemns discrimination, the behaviour which endeavours to achieve substantive equality is therefore a civic virtue. Graham (1986) has argued that OCB logically comprises those behaviours which define civic virtue, and that the concept of citizenship entails an obligation to participate appropriately in the government of the common good (if I may anticipate the second point).

If the organisation is the beneficiary of OCB, then it is necessary to specify what the organisation is and what it is that organisational citizens co-operate over when they express a civil commitment. Obviously, if the term 'organisationally beneficial' is synonymous with 'managerial', the suspicion of manipulation and of an attempt to extort more effort for unilateral gain is legitimate. There is no doubt that organisations – as corporate bodies – have understood the benefits that derive from non-discriminatory behaviour and from commitment to equal opportunities (Fletcher 1998). Indeed, the development of affirmative action programmes has pivoted on the image of the firm and on indirect benefits. What one fails to understand is why simple members of the organisation, workmates, should commit themselves to behaviour designed to achieve gender citizenship when they do not stand to gain any benefit from it for themselves.

My proposal is to consider the expression 'organisationally beneficial' in terms of the social dimension of organisational life, of the organisation as the social construction of a delimited sphere of civil society. Life-quality in this sphere of our social existence is a common good produced by all those involved in the process, and it is enjoyed or consumed by these same producers. The willingness to co-operate therefore takes as its goal the social construction of an environment which respects human dignity, favours the development of human characteristics and enhances human well-being. The equity of exchange in asymmetric power relationships thus becomes of crucial importance; and so too does individual moral responsibility for the production of that common good which we call organisational life. Consequently, participating – as producer and beneficiary – in organisational cultures more or less respectful of differences (not only of gender differences, but of all of them) and more or less concerned to redress inequalities makes a difference both for the individual and for a society which contains more or less fair organisations. Accordingly, the way in which one 'thinks' gender and 'does' gender within an organisation is part of a civic discourse and is integral to the process of civilisation. That which is socially fair in the social arrangements between the genders is historically produced by the social institutions, and one such social institution is the organisation (Gherardi 1996).

The concept of 'fairness' is crucial for understanding OCB. One of the principal conclusions of this line of thought is that willingness to engage in OCB depends on a perception of fair treatment by the organisation. This entails an exchange which is both economic and social, and based on different ideas of fairness. Organ (1990) maintains that whereas fairness in economic exchange requires a specific 'quid' for a particular 'quo', fairness in social exchange requires diffuse obligations which are vaguely defined in their nature, value, and temporal definition of benefits given and received. Social exchange 'requires only a sense that the relationship is based on "good faith" recognition of each other's contributions' (Organ 1990: 63). Social exchange presupposes trust, reciprocity relations, interdependencies between the parties to it, connection. Fairness in the social exchange with the organisation also entails appraisal of how gender relations have been constructed at the symbolic level in the imagination of the male and the female, and at the level of social practice in men/women relationships. It is, therefore, an appraisal of the symbolic order of gender (Gherardi 1995).

Gender citizenship as civic discourse

Gender and citizenship have much more in common than appears at first sight. Both – as Scott (1986) and Saraceno (1989) suggest – are symbolic constructs which contain ambivalences, tensions and contradictions which express themselves in contradictory practices: the equality at the basis of equal opportunity practices conflicts with the inequality and difference between men and women, but also among men and among women; individualism contrasts with needs for solidarity; the value of independence and autonomy contrasts with needs for nurturing and therefore for dependence and interdependence.

Gender and citizenship are symbolically interwoven with the dichotomy between public and private: a public woman is she who grants public access to the supremely private dimension – sexuality; a public man is he who influences the collectivity, the man of power. The woman symbolises the private domain, of nurture, of individuality, of difference and of specificity; the man symbolises the public, the political, the rights and the citizenship that homogenise. Symbolically, therefore, women are non-citizens, second-class citizens, excluded by law, the embodiment of inequality and discrimination; at the same time, however, by practising the dual presence, women in the Western democracies, in the welfare state, are the principal actors in the interdependencies between private and social life (consider redistributive social policies), between institutions and individuals (consider nurturing and solidarity work), and between the suppliers of a service and its users.

The figure emblematic of all these interdependencies is the 'working mother' (a term for which there has been no corresponding 'working father'). The 'working mother', at the level of rights and of social meanings, is the social representation of the individual who has both social, work and public responsibilities and responsibilities for family care. If the 'working mother' tries to shift the work involved in caring for children, the elderly and the family onto the collectivity, or if she questions the social division of labour in her family, then she is 'playing dirty', she is surreptitiously attempting to change the rules that govern the production of common goods. However, the ambiguity of the construct 'working mother' goes further: for, according to whether it is framed by an egalitarian or traditional ideology of gender, a different paradox arises. 'Working mothers' take part in organisational cultures in which they find their identity negated in the responsibility of nurture when an egalitarian gender regime cancels its difference, or negated in social responsibility when a traditional ideology of gender assigns the 'working mother' a priority role in the family. When an organisational culture 'thinks' in terms of egalitarian gender citizenship it assumes that men and women have the same work behaviours. When it 'thinks' in terms of traditional gender citizenship it presumes that there is a pattern of male working life and a female one, the job remaining equal.

Consequently, there are two philosophies and two practices of human resource and career management.

To provide a concrete example of how organisational cultures differ in terms of gender citizenship, I shall compare the rhetorics employed in two organisations (one in the large-scale distribution sector, the other in the information-technology sector) when talking about maternity. One presumes in fact that personnel policies ensue from them, and that (at a deeper-lying level of awareness) these rhetorics are introjected and appear 'natural', so much so that they are used to justify and explain individual and organisational patterns of behaviour. These examples are taken from a study (Gherardi and Poggio 2003) on narratives – recounted by both women and their male colleagues – about entry by women into male-dominated environments.

The first example concerns a women who had been appointed the manager of a shop. Her choice of career – her breaking through the invisible ceiling between female work and managerial male work – was not supported by her husband, who worked in the same shop, or by her colleagues. The reasons given by the latter to explain why women should not embark on managerial careers centred on possible pregnancy and the irreconcilability between work and family due to working hours:

> It's pointless. Sooner or later a woman is going to have a child, and then she can't do the hours that we work because ours is a ten-hour-a-day schedule, or at any rate an eight-hour one. So it's a special working day which a woman on her own can do. But some day a woman has a child and that changes everything, and then what will we do? We'll find ourselves without a manager, but with someone with the grade of manager. I told this to the inspectors at the time, not that [she] shouldn't become manager; but I think it's absurd, because, I mean, it's not a job for a woman.
>
> (interview no. 6; the respondent is a man)

The second example is taken from a computer company with two women in top management. Both men and women in positions of authority stressed the importance of collaboration, of a participatory leadership style and of involvement. One result of this working climate was that the gender issue was addressed directly, and not defensively, even by the men. How the problem of maternity and discrimination was treated in this culture was symptomatic of greater gender equality. Absence on maternity leave was obviously a problem, but it was not an individual problem:

> There are a lot of women here – this is a young company – they often get married and then a few months later – fortunately – they're on maternity leave. So, when planning, this creates problems of substituting people going on leave, for usually unpredictable periods, because you don't know if the person is going to return, when she'll return, for how long…and so we say when this aspect comes up, because every month we assess the situation, how

many people are there, how many should we take on, how many new pregnancies? There's always this joke with a question mark. These are things that are handled straightforwardly and positively.

(interview no. 3; the respondent is a woman)

In one culture, maternity was viewed as a biological fact, as a natural event which concerned only women and did not call the division of labour in the family into question. In the second culture, maternity was described as an organisational problem handled by means of substitutions – that is, as a problem of uncertainty for which a solution had to be found. Note also that only in the former case were the long hours worked in both organisations considered to be – from an organisational point of view – a barrier against female employment in managerial positions. Organisations, therefore, produce a culture of citizenship and do not only reflect the conception of citizenship institutionalised in society. This, of course, is implicitly to accept the metaphor of organisation as a democratic political system, and to acknowledge that every metaphor illuminates certain aspects of organisation while leaving others obscure (Morgan 1986). We should bear in mind, however, that the extension of the conception of citizenship from an exclusively political sphere to one of everyday rights is a historical process which has also affected the economic and productive sphere. Civil society demands democracy and citizenship in other areas apart from politics: the economy, the social, the private and gender relationships.

I consider citizenship to be principally a practice; that is, a way of life pursued by people – inside and outside organisations – who share a historical context in which they contest the meaning of social or legal norms and struggle to define collective and individual identity. Yet the very concept of citizenship is extremely contested in the literature (Turner 1990, 1991).

I shall develop this argument by examining how different conceptions of citizenship give rise to diverse organisational cultures, and how these cultures contain a plurality of conceptions of what is 'fair' in the relationships between the sexes.

Western thought has developed two principal conceptions of citizenship (Oldfield 1990, 1991), and these have given rise to different definitions of the nature of individuals and of the social ties that exist among them qua citizens. On the one hand, there is the liberal or liberal-individualist conception of citizenship as status; on the other, the classical or civil-republican conception of citizenship as practice. The difference between the two can be summarised thus:

- The constitutive elements of citizenship as status are needs and rights. Individuals are sovereign and morally autonomous beings whose duty is to respect the analogous rights of other citizens, to pay their taxes and to defend the state when it is threatened. They have no other obligations to society except those freely accepted by contract. Social ties are therefore contractual ties.

- Citizenship as practice is based on duties which individuals must fulfil if they are to be granted the status of citizens. Individuals are members of a community, and they are citizens because they not only respect the autonomy of others, but commit themselves to a socially defined practice. The social ties among individuals derive from the fact that they share and establish a life-system.

In the former case individuals born in democratic countries need do nothing to become citizens because they are such by right, while in the latter case individuals prove themselves to be citizens by what they do. Action sustained by a mental attitude constitutes, in this latter case, citizenship, and it maintains a community whose members assume joint responsibility for its continuity and identity.

Translated into an organisational setting, this analogy prompts a crucial question: are the members of an organisation such by virtue of a status created by a contract which sanctions rights and duties, or are they such by virtue of a practice of responsibility towards the community? Depending on the answer to this question, the problem of membership, of its role and of organisational boundaries assumes different connotations. At the same time, the individual/organisation relationship, too, takes on a different meaning: hence, Oldfield (1991), like Rousseau before him, admits that the practice of citizenship is an unnatural practice, that it is the price to pay for entry into social life.

Since citizenship is a complex and ambiguous topic, before examining its general implications I shall first explore a more specific issue: namely, how the ability to construct a social practice of gender citizenship varies according to the way an organisational culture constructs the idea of fairness in gender relationships, and consequently the way in which it reacts to the set of juridical norms that guarantees/imposes equal opportunities and translates them into personnel policies, on the one hand, and into culture on the other.

Put otherwise, organisational cultures differentiate themselves according to the concept of gender citizenship that they express and make possible (see the second column of Table 12.1). For ease of exposition I shall use the six models of citizenship (as universality; as neutrality; as communality; as the amelioration of class conflicts; as self-sufficiency; as a hermeneutic endeavour) set out in Alejandro (1993), since I share his assumption that citizenship is a problem of interpretation and of the discourse-based construction of meanings within a community of practices. The analogies with gender citizenship are my own responsibility.

Gender citizenship as legal ratification

In the conception of citizenship as universality and as a legal construction – as, for example, in Dahrendorf (1974) – citizenship is viewed primarily as an idea expressed in law. It produces a social order based on ties which are not natural

Table 12.1 Conceptions of citizenship and gender citizenship

Citizenship	Gender citizenship
Citizenship as universality and as a legal construct	Gender citizenship as legal ratification
Citizenship as neutrality	Gender citizenship as permanent membership and cultural integration
Citizenship as communality and participation	Gender as the affirmation of specific gender resources
Citizenship as amelioration of class conflict	Gender as tension towards substantial equality
Citizenship as self-sufficiency	Gender as moral obligation to work
Citizenship as hermeneutic endeavour	Gender as civic discourse

but which are instead created ad hoc by the law (see, for example, Dahrendorf 1974). It protects citizens against each other and against outsiders. This, therefore, is the liberal notion which conceives first the individual and then the citizen as a right-bearer and which expresses an abstract dimension of equality: citizenship is a generalised right. The citizen has neither gender nor sex!

The abstract universality of rights is a notion of especial significance in both what it says and what it leaves unsaid: the historical-social formation of these rights, their origin in conflicts and struggles between the strong and the weak. Citizens have rights qua individuals – that is, as abstract persons; but they conduct their daily lives as members of specific groups and within a social order fragmented by class, race, gender. The discourse of universality and of rights silences the narration of particular identities, of the origins and evolution of equality/inequality. But simultaneously it marks out and guarantees a political arena in which the abstract principle can be challenged.

When we shift this concept to an organisational setting, we have an organisational citizenship based on the legal definition of membership. The labour contract and trade union agreements define a sphere of consensual obligations which turn the organisation's members into participants in a system of rules for economic and social exchange.

A definition of organisational citizenship based on the abstract universality of rights creates a discourse space where the logic of the labour law may prevail and trigger social struggles based on the principle of equal wages and equal working conditions. Thus expressed is the idea of social justice as the safeguarding of the contractual positions of the weaker components of the labour force: immigrants, women, young people. What this discourse obscures in organisational life is effective participation and the exercise of rights: those who are disadvantaged in a class system are also largely unable to join a citizenship system and to render citizenship substantial rather than formal.

As regards gender citizenship, the discourse of rights is the discourse that eclipses difference and every difference: citizens have rights qua individuals, and the legal definition of the individual transcends every particularity. Women are no longer women; they are individuals, and the relationships between men and women are subject to the same rules of social communality that regulate the relationships between men and men or between women and women. The problem of justice in gender relationships does not arise, since gender plays a secondary role in the constitution of individuality. Women may constitute a disadvantaged social group, but a woman is a bearer of rights on a par with a man. That she is then unable to exercise them is another matter. Thus, women who participate in the organisation are individuals with the same rights and duties as their male colleagues, and they will be assessed and rewarded according to their effective performance. They will participate in the social and political life of the organisation according to their position in the internal hierarchy of power and prestige. Social differentiation will operate internally to groups, and among women and among men, according to a class structure. The specific action of gender in creating occupational segregation, in the marginalisation of discretionary power, in effective political participation, has no place in this discourse, which founds citizenship on individuality.

Gender difference is denied or ignored in norms establishing the formal equality of rights, and the ban on discrimination is the symbol of cultural commitment and sensitivity to the problematics of gender. An organisational culture based on this conception of gender difference usually refrains from taking specific measures to promote equality, and it uses the ban on discrimination more as an excuse for failing to act than as a goal to achieve. Non-discrimination is only formal, while invisible barriers, for example, are not a topic of organisational discussion. Occupational segregation is the 'natural' outcome of the unequal social distribution of human capital. Economic theories of human capital, from Mincer (1958) to the present, have explained the inequality between men and women in the workplace in terms of unequal investments in education and training. Under this conception of gender citizenship, the organisation bears no moral or social responsibility for inequalities.

Gender citizenship as cultural integration

In Rawls' (1971) view of citizenship as neutrality, the moral and political diversity of citizens is based on the distinction between the public and private spheres. Citizenship is both permanent membership of a well-ordered society and an effort, in the context of a democratic society, to found justice on a political conception of justice.

In Rawls' model of citizenship the state is neutral with respect to what constitutes a good civic life. On the other hand, it is the interests of justice which guide the actions of citizens, as well as the separation between their most profound private convictions and the principles of the public search for consensus.

The private is the sphere of the moral personality, of pluralism and of diversity. The public, by contrast, is the sphere of stability, of order, of agreement and of an 'overlapping consensus' on justice. For Rawls (1971), modern societies are characterised by non-commensurate conceptions of what a good life is. For this reason the state is neutral vis-à-vis the definitions that citizens give to it. In the public sphere, citizens are free individuals who have the right not to be identi-fied, or not to identify themselves, with a specific system of ends; in the private sphere, both personal and associative, citizens may possess strong attachments and commitments which they refrain from displaying in public.

The construction of political consensus through the exercise of public neutrality presupposes a social order in which everyone co-operates by accepting this polit-ical assumption and by freely choosing to mutilate the public self and to confine the more authentic self to restricted, private or internal, ambits. On the one hand, this entails reasoning in terms of multiple selves, the end of comprehen-sive doctrines, the interweaving between the differences and pluralities of the worlds of sense in which they are simultaneously immersed. On the other hand, they call to mind the well-known model of the double moral standard whereby, for example, adultery committed by a man or a woman is judged differently. Or they recall societies of weak democracy where a person's most profound convic-tions are revealed in private not in public.

By analogy, organisational citizenship as neutrality commits the organisation to neutrality vis-à-vis the ways in which its members elaborate the contents of a democratic culture and put the principles of a good life into practice. In turn, its members are committed to guaranteeing civil consensus on the idea of justice. The good organisational life should thus be founded on the beliefs of its members, and, as a system of government, the organisation should respect these beliefs.

If we look specifically at the citizenship of gender, the above assumption entails that both men and women enjoy permanent membership. However, what is considered 'fair' in gender relationships is elaborated by the local culture and within social relationships among people of different sex. The organisation is not affected by the private values of its members. Since public life is based on the effort to reach consensus, and since the power relationships between the genders is a private matter, it is highly likely that consensus will be reached on male values and on the cultural hegemony of male over female. Cultural integration, homosociability, becomes the ticket of entry to civil society and civil organisa-tions.

Gender difference is indeed recognised but minimised in its effects on social relations: male workers and female workers must be considered equal despite the fact that they are different. If there is historical inequality in the initial opportunities available to each sex, this can be corrected by measures designed to achieve egalitarian goals. Emblematic of this conception and of the limits of formal equality is, for example, the prohibition of dismissal for pregnancy. Although originally designed to render women equal with men in the work-place,this provision in fact penalised women because employers were reluctant to hire them in case they became pregnant and incurred costs for the organisation.

Like the culture oriented to legal ratification, an organisational culture which embraces this assumption on what is fair in gender relationships denies the consequences of gender difference although it acknowledges such difference.

This is the culture of formal equality which considers as equal only those who achieve the same performance or who embrace the same values, and these have been historically inscribed in the body of the male worker. In this culture, the organisation's social responsibility is expressed in its respect for formal equality and in its even-handed treatment of workers who achieve commensurate performances. But the organisation bears no responsibility for the fact that formal equality may have a backlash effect on those rendered unequal by gender, race or class. Here, too, one notes with interest how economic theories on the labour market have sought to explain gender inequalities, and how certain cultural constructs such as gender citizenship are conveyed by similar discourse practices in different disciplines. How, though, does one account for that part of discrimination (by sex or race) which differentials in productivity fail to explain? Becker (1971) introduces the concept of 'taste of discrimination' to define the situation where employers, but also occupational communities, will sustain extra real costs rather than assume the psychological cost of working with people for whom they feel an aversion. This amounts to saying that, performance and behaviour remaining equal, there is a further 'irrational', non economic-cultural, factor which induces discrimination.

Gender citizenship as a specific resource

The conception of citizenship as communality and participation gives priority to the construction of communal life by means of active political participation. Citizenship is a mode of social being, and the citizen is the product of a process of participation within a community. Walzer's (1983) conception of citizenship, for example, assumes a community of shared values in which citizens share a culture, and are determined to continue to do so in the future, since the community is in itself the most important good to be distributed. The community and the sense of a communal life cement together the traditions, conventions and expectations which underpin the shared experiences and values that almost everybody subscribes to.

What is obscured here is the fact that not everybody attributes the same value to the same traditions, that a universal category like 'people' is composed of a diversity of components which live the same communal experience differently, and that traditions can be questioned and criticised, as well as provoking conflict. The presumption is, therefore, that the community in question is solely a legitimate community, one in which all its members are equally committed to preserving its dominant values.

Organisational citizenship in analogy to a conception of communality and participation is almost synonymous with a conception of organisational culture where the members of an organisation are such because they participate in a historical community of meanings shared by the pooling of sensitivities and intuitions.

Gender citizenship within this conception of organisational democracy is recognition of the diversity of human types, but only within the legitimate community. Contribution to the community and participation in the common good is also acknowledged by organisational citizens of the female sex, but only within the confines of their traditional social position as the affirmation of the specific resources of the female. Occupational segregation results from different modes of participation in the formation of the organisation as a common good by men and women.

In this conception, gender difference no longer arises as the attribution of otherness, difference-from, the biologically determined social destiny of the previous conceptions. Instead, the female body becomes a resource, the means to enter domains barred to the male. Femaleness becomes a resource for the organisation, which develops special policies for the management of female human resources.

The definition 'in positive' of femaleness and the assertion, in theory and practice, of its superiority swiftly turned into an urge to dominate. This transformed the traditional male/female dichotomy but did not change its philosophy of asymmetric power - giving rise to mostly circumscribed organisational cultures, like the committees for affirmative action in large organisations, or women's organisations within trade unions, or the cultures of specific feminist organisations. Most organisations contain a cultural nucleus, of varying size, which conceives the female as a specific resource and attributes special skills to women qua women. The implicit risk here is of a unilateral, as well as normative, definition of femaleness.

Research programmes display the same conception whenever, in different ways and for different purposes, they compare working groups of different sex seeking to quantify the variance engendered by the variable 'sex' and endeavour to define the femaleness that women have and men do not. This formulation, the poverty of its results and its evident character as a self-fulfilling prophecy have been widely criticised (see Calás 1988, as regards management).

Nevertheless, the glamour of female leadership, by way of example, remains intact because it is part of the same discourse strategy which in the past femaleness employed to justify discrimination and occupational segregation and which today is employed to obtain a competitive advantage. Organisation rhetoric has always exalted the specifically 'female' virtues: in the past to celebrate the secretary, today to extol the woman manager. The contents of gender change, but the trap of gender and of fixed identities for men and women is still firmly in place, and the winner is always the hunter. Paradoxically, the moral responsibility coherent with this conception is the responsibility to exploit – to a greater or lesser extent – this resource.

Gender citizenship as tension towards substantial equality

Marshall (1950) divides citizenship into three successive phases between the 18th and 20th centuries: civil, political and social. Marshall discerns a constant historical improvement in class conflict, because the extension of citizenship rights has weakened the system of privileges even if social inequality has not been eliminated.

Citizenship rights have assaulted the entire structure of social inequalities, and whatever inequality still remains no longer constitutes a class distinction in the sense given to the term in the past. A major factor in the progress of citizenship towards greater economic and social equality has been the expansion of social services backed by more egalitarian legislation.

The welfare state, especially before its crisis, was of crucial symbolic importance because it represented the idea of a more equable system of income distribution and of social reproduction. The task of the social services was to mark out new boundaries between production work and reproduction work, and one of their principal intended effects was the releasing of new productive forces – especially female – for the market.

By analogy, the organisation has undergone a similar evolution towards the elimination of the system of class inequalities, although in this case it would be more accurate to say that it was class conflict and workers' struggle which brought an extension of citizenship rights. Organisational citizenship rights, in this sense, signify opposing and assessing the justice of the unequal system within the workplace, in particular the inequalities of gender in access to the status of organisational citizen. For example, the persistent obligation for women to work what Hochschild (1989) has called 'the second shift' in order to denote the accumulation of family, domestic and nurturing work impedes women from acquiring full citizenship in organisational life. Since women have a second job outside the workplace, their investments of time and emotional resources are smaller; or, if they wish to maintain these investments at the same level as men, they incur psychological and real costs which men do not. Consequently, those able to exercise citizenship rights, able to discuss them and to enjoy them, are those organisational citizens who are freed from the second shift either by gender privilege or by economic privilege.

Gender difference is formulated in terms of the elimination of inequality: male and female workers are socially and economically unequal; accordingly, they must be made equal. Compensation for inequality is the symbolic action which affirms the value of difference and of the search for equity. The organisational culture which conceives gender citizenship as the elimination of the causes of inequality is that which, in consequence, commits itself to democratic participation in the construction of organisational life. Policies of substantial equality pursue two goals: re-equilibrating women's chances of effective participation, and ensuring just and equable participation for both women and men. As an example, recall the debate on the ban on night work for women and whether or not it should be abolished. Simultaneously with the abolition of this protective measure, the demand was advanced for regulation of the practice in the interests of men and women and in order to safeguard workers outside the workplace.

As regards my personal experience in this area, I find that the philosophy of equal opportunities committees in organisations has changed in recent years. From measures aimed exclusively at women, the emphasis has now shifted to ones addressed to all workers in order to redress the balance between working life and family and extra-work life in general.

Gender citizenship as the equal moral obligation to work

Under this conception, the principal component of citizenship is the duty to work and citizens are defined as self-supporting members of the community. This conception often crops up in debates on poverty, unemployment and so-called 'welfare mothers' – that is, women who choose to live on welfare rather than work in low-paid jobs (Mead 1986).

This debate is being conducted in the United States of America, and therefore in a socio-economic context which differs in many respects from Europe's and from its approach to labour policies, but the basic concept remains the same. The legal character of citizenship is not sufficient: a citizen cannot only be the bearer of rights; s/he must work, for this is the entry ticket to society. Having a job means being empowered to enjoy a series of other rights by virtue of one's status as a worker, an assertion whose validity is proved *a contraris* by the status of unemployed worker. But there is in this conception a worrying ambivalence between the 'duty to work' and the 'right to work'.

Work, as a means of sustenance, is part of a final vocabulary and assumes the force of a moral obligation, like paying taxes and ensuring that they are paid. The presumption is that work, any work, is gratifying, that full employment is possible, and that to work is to perform a political as well as normative act. This assertion suppresses or overlooks the fact that non-work is also a political act, but more importantly it induces us to interrogate ourselves about the 'goodness' of work, about the intrinsic equity of its allocation and about the justice of its social distribution. In the debate between welfare dependency and subsidiarity, the two opposing views are in fact complementary, and they coincide in accepting the justice of an economic structure which produces both work and unemployment.

What is the analogy with organisational citizenship here, if being a worker in an organisation means already being self-sufficient? In this case the moral obligation to work is paralleled by the obligation to be committed to the organisation. Being an organisational citizen means responding to the organisation's appeal to identify with it, to share the organisational culture, to join a collective 'us', to be motivated workers.

The commitment thus required is based principally on an emotional and ethical investment, while economic or 'contractual' exchange is secondary. The organisation not only pays money in exchange for work, but also disburses more important and intangible things: identity resources, social position, prestige, priority access to welfare benefits, and therefore opportunities to become first-class citizens.

The fairness of the exchange cannot be subjected to open scrutiny and it is therefore regulated in private: it is only in their own hearts that workers judge the 'goodness' of their contracts with the organisation and decide how motivated they are willing to be.

Regarding the justice of gender relationships in society and in the organisation, much has already been implicitly said: female citizens, precisely because they are women, have less chance of being self-sufficient; they are often self-sufficient, not as themselves, but because they are tied to a man; and they frequently slide into poverty because they have fewer resources to offer in exchange for citizenship. That one talks of 'welfare mothers' is indicative of the fact that the theoretical model does not take account of the gender structuring of social relationships and therefore of the unequal distribution of chances of being first- or second-class citizens. The same applies to the structuring between male and female workers of participation in the organisation.

In this case, gender difference is seen neither as difference nor as inequality. Indeed, the assumption is that women exploit loopholes in the system to avoid badly paid and unrewarding work. Doubt is cast on their loyalty to the organisation, the insinuation being that their primary dedication to their families may induce them to treat work as of secondary importance, as merely providing a second wage, and that family responsibilities may subtract effort and time from work. This conception is akin to that of gender citizenship as cultural integration. Both aspire to formal equality despite the fact that female participation in the labour market has not changed patterns of the sexual division of labour in society or in the household, and women are therefore forced into double jobholding. The two conceptions differ to the extent that those who look with suspicion on women's contribution to the organisation may nevertheless turn a blind eye, for it is a private matter and does not concern the organisation; or they may regard it as a factor which reduces competition between men and women over the distribution of income, restricting women's aspirations to female work. The organisational culture based on this conception may be called 'traditionalist' in its view of gender relationships because it believes that women are predominantly oriented to the home.

This is a cultural model too well known to require further elaboration. However, it is worth noting that, while on the one hand a person acquires citizenship if s/he works, on the other women may or may not become citizens via the family. When workers are considered not as individual suppliers of labour but as constituting households rationally deploying their resources and choosing to allocate time between domestic and extra-domestic work, value-assumptions on the social role of the division of labour come to light. For example, the new home economics (Becker 1965; Mincer 1972; Gronau 1973) argues that since male activities receive greater remuneration in the market the maximisation of the family's utility will induce the man to invest his time outside the home, while the woman will seek extra-domestic work only when the wage on offer is higher than the loss of productivity in domestic work.

This justifies the lesser value of extra-domestic work by women based on the rigid sexual division of labour in society, but it does not call into question the conditions of employment connoted by a rigid temporal model. In other words, women do not resort to domestic work because their extra-domestic work has lower value; it is work that has lesser value because women are in any case committed to domestic work. An organisational culture that takes the priority commitment of women to domestic work for granted is an organisational culture which considers men to be free from such encumbrances and therefore entirely available – as regards their time, mental energy and priority interest – to the organisation. Paradoxically, this is an organisation which systematically under-utilises female human resources and systematically abuses male ones; although it considers both men and women to have an equal moral obligation to work, it believes that their jobs are not of equal weight in their lives.

Gender citizenship as civic discourse

Alejandro's (1993) critique of citizenship models and his proposed reading of citizenship in hermeneutic terms lays primary emphasis on citizens' interpretation of what constitutes citizenship and how this interpretation is a historical and social construct. The legal model, the productivist and participative models, Marshall's conception of the extension of social rights, and Rawls' notion of the exclusion from politics of comprehensive doctrines all fail to recognise the importance of the interpretation of legal principles and social practices or the diversity of interests in contemporary society.

Alejandro's proposal is to conceive citizenship as a terrain – a hermeneutic horizon or a space of memories and struggles – on which individuals interpret the past, re-examine their traditions, accept or reject social practices. To claim that citizenship is a social practice is to imply that 'citizenship as a practice has to do with the discourses and symbols that establish the collective identity of a community' (Alejandro 1993: 37). Citizenship can thus be conceived as a text which opens itself to a plurality of readers, a text which can be used in different settings and for different purposes. As a text, citizenship represents the possibility that its subjects – the citizens – are also the authors of the text – that is, that they reflect and act upon the meaning of constructing a communal life because they are concrete persons who belong to specific social groups, who have conflicting political agendas, specific interests and contrasting systems of meanings for the same concepts. Citizenship within a hermeneutic model 'appears as a social construction; namely, as a dimension of connectedness and distance as well as a metaphor of fluid borders' (Alejandro 1993: 39).

The analogy with my conception of gender as a discourse practice (interpretable in the light of two metaphors of separation and inseparability) and as positionality in the interaction between the symbolic universes of gender should at this point be self-evident. Organisational citizenship thus becomes the terrain on which the interpretations and interests of the various members of the organisation meet and clash over the definition of membership, everyday rights, justice – namely citizenship.

Gender citizenship is therefore a text which expresses what is deemed 'fair' in the social relationships between the sexes in a certain context and in a certain historical-social setting. In any given organisational culture, gender citizenship constitutes that discourse terrain on which different interpretations confront each other, and where different collective identities struggle to define not only their contents but also the material contexts – circumstances, groups and ideas – that produce them. Hence it follows that every organisation produces its text on citizenship in that organisation, on the fairness of the relations between men and women, and on how the symbolic universe of male and female is socially constructed. An organisation's culture is also characterised by its particular narrative structure of gender citizenship and by the voices and silences which confront each other over gender inequalities.

The social processes whereby individuals are differentiated are now slowly changing according to distinctions more complex and subtle than sex. The social construction of gender relationships is a dialectical process which makes it possible to overcome the dichotomy between two and only two genders, or types of individual. The reciprocity of the relationship acquires concrete form through discourse practices which position gender as one of the many principles of differentiation. The ethics of difference thus become a key criterion in assessing the fairness of gender relationships, and a key instrument in increasing freedom for gender identity. 'Equal and different', as a basic concept of equality, begins to change its meaning when it abandons the unquestioned foundation of diversity, looks to the dual presence and moves increasingly far into the field of ambiguity, of the fluid boundaries between the genders, of the liminality condition between one gender and another; that is, as it moves towards an unstable process of difference and in-differentiation. It is the possibility of in-differentiation – contingently inherent to specific social practices – which may give innovative contents to differentiation, and which map out game-spaces of reciprocal gender positioning which are less stereotypical and less tyrannical.

I have not yet encountered an organisational culture truly aware of and committed to a discourse on gender citizenship as a civic duty and as a civil practice. However, I have seen nuclei of awareness emerging, and I have met people ready to assume the risk of uncertain, changing and fluid gender boundaries.

Conclusions

Initiating a discourse on the positioning of gender within organisational ethics entails the organisation's commitment to developing discourse practices which are not paternalistic or discriminatory in their effects. Such an undertaking involves the assumption of a moral and political stance in which one accepts or declines to take part in discourse practices which, with their tenets, images or metaphors, are contrary to the beliefs of those who participate in the conversation or to one's own beliefs.

Since I am not a political scientist, I prefaced my remarks on theories of citizenship by pointing out that they would be somewhat superficial and that my interest in the concept of citizenship lay in its potency as a symbol of societal participation. Gender citizenship in organisations is the metaphor that I propose in order to position gender discourse differently in organisations, and which I used in my foregoing discussion to show the various ways to gender an organisational culture:

- An organisational culture which claims to be neutral and which denies every relation between organisation and the gender of the people who work in it establishes a gender regime based on universality as the negation of gender differences.
- An organisational culture which expresses the belief that women are as good as men, and which promises equality of treatment for equality of performance, establishes a gender regime based on cultural integration.
- An organisational culture which regards the female to be a specific resource for the organisation establishes a gender regime based on the dichotomisation and stereotyping of what is specifically female and male.
- An organisational culture which declares itself committed to substantial equality is one which implements an equal opportunity policy and recognises that men and women are not equal but should be made so. The value inspiring this culture is emancipation, although one rarely finds a gender regime systematically predicated on substantial equality.
- An organisational culture which expresses a traditional conception of gender roles establishes a gender regime where, despite its commitment to both genders, the work of men is primary and that of women is auxiliary.
- A postmodern organisational culture is aware of the gender trap and seeks to establish a gender regime which respects the constant deferral of the meaning of gender and of the practices that sustain it.

The endeavour to pose gender citizenship as an interpretative task of civic discourse helps to break the tyranny of gender as a discourse based on dichotomy and hierarchisation, and it may become a discourse of liberation from biological destiny for both men and women.

In this sense it moves towards in-differentiation – not to negate it, however, but to incorporate it into a network of manifold differentiation – where gender is only one of the criteria for the formation of identity and difference.

Today, citizenship is becoming the theme of a new historical cycle – no longer as an institution guaranteeing social integration under the banner of universalism, but as a factor in the development of new solidarities under the banner of respect for differences and substantial equality. The critique of modernity has evidenced how certain features of the segmentation of the social are changing: the social movements that brought collective actors (from the proletariat to feminists) to the fore are in constant decline, and are unable to ensure a stable cultural identity. Certain strong distinctions such as public/private, state/market are blurring into much more indistinct social and economic organisations, like proximity services. Or again, as Eisenstadt (1992) argues, there has been a decline in demand for a centre (ideal and symbolic) which seeks to govern functional differentiation, and a burgeoning of autonomous spheres which are ideologically and concretely independent from the centre. According to

Eisenstadt, what is changing is the relationship between '*volonté générale*' and '*volonté de tous*', in the sense that there is a tendency for new and different arenas to appear in which the *volonté de tous* can be exercised without the ideological totalitarianism of the *volonté générale*.

This historical-cultural climate has engendered numerous movements for civil liberties, for the reconstruction of rights, one of which may be the right to sexual difference and to gender citizenship.

Like all differences, gender difference is a symbolic terrain for the image-making of an otherness and of a plurality of othernesses which are neither subordinate nor totalising. A semantic path of postmodern gender difference is an interpretation of difference as liminality, as irresolvable ambiguity which defers – in time and in interpretation – the meaning of gender as the symbol of differ-ence/*différance* – that is, of becoming. Symbolically standing at the threshold is the image of suspension, of repeatedly traversing the symbolic universes of male and female, of living the ambiguity of gender and denying the dichotomous and hierarchical relation between them. What divides and differentiates also unites.

References

Alejandro, R. (1993) *Hermeneutics, Citizenship, and the Public Sphere*, Albany, NY: State University of New York Press.

Andrini, S. (1991) 'Differenza e in-differenza', *Democrazia e Diritto* 5–6: 237–63.

Barnard, C.J. (1938) *The Function of the Executive*, Cambridge, MA:Harward University Press.

Bateman, T.S. and Organ, D. (1983) 'Job satisfaction and the good soldier: the relationship between affect and employee "citizenship"', *Academy of Management Journal* 26: 587–95.

Becker, G.S. (1965) 'A theory of the allocation of time', *Economic Journal* 5(2): 65–83.

—— (1971) *The Economics of Discrimination*, Chicago: University of Chicago Press.

Calás, M. (1988) ' "Gendering" leadership: the differ(e/a)nce that matters', paper presented at the Academy of Management Meetings, August.

Connell, R.W. (1995) *Masculinities*, Cambridge: Polity Press.

Crozier, M. (1989) *L'Entreprise à l'écoute*, Paris: InterEditions.

Dahrendorf, R. (1974) 'Citizenship and beyond: the social dynamics of an idea', *Social Research* 41(4): 673–701.

de Leonardis, O. (1991) 'Diritti, differenze e capacità: sulla giustizia come processo sociale', *Democrazia e Diritto* 5–6: 197–218.

Diamond, I. and Hartsock, N. (1981) 'Beyond interests in politics: a comment on Virginia Sapiro's "When are Interests Interesting? The Problem of Political Representation of Women" ', *American Political Sciences Review* 75: 712–21.

Eisenstadt, S. (1992) 'La perdita di carisma dei centri politici', *Democrazia Diretta* 7(1): 53–60.

Fletcher, J. (1998) 'Relational practice: a feminist reconstruction of work', *Journal of Management Inquiry* 7(2): 163–86.

Forbes, I. (1991) 'Equal opportunity: radical, liberal and conservative critiques', in E. Meehan and S. Sevenhuijsen (eds) *Equality, Politics and Gender*, London: Sage.

Gherardi, S. (1995) *Gender, Symbolism and Organizational Cultures*, Sage: London.

—— (1996) 'Gendered organizational cultures: narratives of women travellers in a male world', *Gender, Work and Organizations* 4: 187–201.

Gherardi, S. and Poggio, B. (2003) *Donna per fortuna, uomo per destino*, Milan: Etas.

Graham, J. (1986) 'Organizational citizenship informed by political theory', paper presented at the Academy of Management Meetings, Chicago.

Gronau, J. (1973) 'The intra-family allocation of time: the value of the housewife time', *American Economic Review*, September: 354–71.

Hancock, P. (1997) 'Citizenship or vassalage? Organizational membership in the Age of Unreason', *Organization* 4(1): 93–111.

Hochschild, A.R. (1989) *The Second Shift*, London: Viking.

Holtmaat, R. (1989) 'The power of legal concepts: the development of a feminist theory of law', *International Journal of the Sociology of Law* 17: 67–85.

Irigaray, L. (1977) *Ce Sex qui n'est pas un*, Paris: Les Edition de Minuit.

Jones, K. (1990) 'Citizenship in a woman-friendly polity', *Signs* 15(4):781–812.

Loveridge, R. (1997) 'Social science as social reconstruction: a celebration of discontinuity or a test of the resilience of belief?', *Human Relations* 50(8): 879–84.

Marshall, T.H. (1950) *Citizenship and Social Class*, Cambridge: Cambridge University Press.

Mead, L. (1986) *Beyond Entitlement: The Social Obligations of Citizenship*, New York: Free Press.

Minc, A. (1993) *Le Nouveau Moyen Age*, Paris: Folio Actuel.

Mincer, J. (1958) 'Investment in human capital and personal income distribution', *Journal of Political Economy* 66: 89–103.

—— (1972) 'Labour force participation of the married women', *Aspects of Labour Economics*, Princeton, NJ: Princeton University Press.

Minow, M. (1990) *Making all the Difference*, Ithaca, NY: Cornell University Press.

Morgan, G. (1986) *Images of Organizations*, Beverly Hills, CA: Sage.

Oldfield, A. (1990) 'Citizenship: an unnatural practice?', *The Political Quarterly* 2: 48–62.

—— (1991) *Citizenship and Community*, London: Routledge.

Organ, D. (1990) 'The motivational basis of organizational citizenship behaviour', *Research in Organizational Behaviour* 12: 43–72.

Parker, M. (1997) 'Organizations and citizenship', *Organization* 4(1): 75–92

Pitch, T. (1991) 'Differenza in comune', *Democrazia Diritto e* 5–6: 219–35.

Podsakoff, P. MacKenzie, M., Scott, B. and Bachrach, D. G. (2000) 'Organizational citizenship behaviors: a critical review of the theoretical and empirical literature and suggestions for future research', *Journal of Management* 26(3): 513–24.

Rawls, J. (1971) *A Theory of Justice*, Cambridge, MA: Harvard University Press.

Sapiro, V. (1981) 'When are interests interesting? The problem of political representation of women', *American Political Sciences Review* 75: 701–11.

Saraceno, C. (1989) 'La struttura di genere della cittadinanza', *Democrazia e Diritto* 5: 273–95.

Scott, J. (1986) 'Gender: a useful category of historical analysis', *American Historical Review* 91: 367–75.

Turner, B. (1990) 'Outline of a theory of citizenship', *Sociology* 24: 189–217.

—— (1991) 'Further specifications of the citizenship concept', *Sociology* 25: 215–18.

Walzer, M. (1983) *Spheres of Justice*, New York: Basic Books.

Willmott, H. (1993) 'Strength is ignorance; slavery is freedom: managing culture in modern organizations', *Journal of Management Studies* 30: 515–52.

Zincone, G. (1984) *Gruppi sociali e sistemi politici: Il caso donne*, Milan: Angeli.

—— (1992) *Da sudditi a cittadini*, Bologna: Il Mulino.

13 Laying new foundations

Manufacturing management knowledge in a post-industrial knowledge economy

Roy Stager Jacques

Science has been compared to pursuit of the horizon; each step forward reveals more to be taken.

(Editorial, Administrative Science Quarterly, 1956, 1(1): 1)

Introduction: hidden in plain sight

The thesis of this collected volume is that the foundations of management knowledge are in transition. In this chapter I will argue that responding to the challenges this poses cannot be done by focusing solely on new objects of study (e.g. 'knowledge work') or on new methods for studying them (e.g. 'qualitative methods'). The most critical problems facing explorers venturing into post-industrial realities will not be related to the elusiveness of the phenomena sought; the phenomena are 'hiding in plain sight'. Our critical problems of understanding will be related to the heavy but unfelt blinkers[1] we wear as we grope into emergent worlds, unaware that the virtual (un)reality we so vividly perceive is merely an old picture of an industrial landscape painted on the inside of these blinkers. The first challenge we face as explorers is to become more conscious of the active role played by these habits of perception in limiting what we can see and how we understand it.

Speaking in very broad demographic terms, there are two groups of workers ascendant in the emerging post-industrial order of world capitalism.[2] One is the 'nouveau proletarian', the burger flipper, personal service and/or contingent worker. The other is the so-called 'knowledge worker', the quasi-professional worker who does not contract to deliver a discrete product (as does the self-employed contractor) but whose discretionary action cannot be controlled by now-traditional methods of managing human 'resources'. This chapter will focus on the latter group, but has implications for the study of the former. My argument is that, through a process of social forgetting, the industrial roots of today's assumptions about the rights and responsibilities of the worker, the meaning and role of the organisation in society, and even the meanings of human 'nature' have been lost. This has been exacerbated by the dominance of a physical science model for organisational inquiry which eschews the production of narrative knowledge about organisations, aspiring instead to a paradigmatic science of measurable, testable knowledge. In this drive, historically and culturally bound assumptions and problems have come to be reified as fundamental variables of human interaction. Before we can proceed to create useful knowledge of the post-industrial, I will argue, we must proceed in what I have only half-facetiously termed a necrological manner, to become aware of and to dislodge the 'dominant but dead' (Calás and Smircich 1987; Habermas 1983) corpse of positivist-industrial knowledge that is lying upon us.

A topic I will use to illustrate my points is the production and distribution of organisational knowledge by the American-style business school, ubiquitous in the US[3] and highly influential in many other countries. Having outlined some of the basic issues, I will use the example of understanding 'knowledge work' to illustrate some ways the legacy of industrial reality actively hinders apprehension of the emergent aspects of this phenomenon within the discursive boundaries of the business school. In the final section, I will attempt to frame some of the key issues and challenges facing those who would be involved with the production of organisational knowledge in this time of shifting foundations.

Masters of the (knowledge) universe

Remember Michael Milken, the undisputed master of Wall Street's 'masters of the universe', the junk bond power-broker whose name was synonymous with the merger frenzy and crash of the 1980s? Well, like the Terminator, he's back. Unlike Arnold's Hollywood Terminator, however, he isn't confined to the petty cash of a $100 million budget. According to *Fortune* magazine, Milken is already overseeing a company with 'more than $1 billion [US] in revenues, thanks to an acquisition rampage' (Martin 1998: 113).[4] OK, the master of acquisitions is doing what he does best; so what? This is what: Milken's new company, Knowledge Universe (KU), is the first company credibly poised to become the General Motors of education, an integrated provider of 'cradle to grave learning tools' (*Los Angeles Times*, 25 September 1998: D4).

> At Knowledge Universe, we believe that minds are the world's most valuable resource. On the brink of the twenty-first century, people, corporations and traditional education face unprecedented change. These are opportune times for us to become both learners and educators. Knowledge Universe is dedicated to providing services, products and environments to meet the learning needs of individuals, schools and corporations. We affirm the principle of lifelong learning and invite you to join us in this adventure.
>
> (mission statement from KU website www.knowledgeu.com)

As we begin the millennium with KU, should we consider Milken a prophet of the Messiah or should we look for three sixes on his brow? I'm afraid much of the discourse about KU and other similar institutions will take this polarised form. A major purpose of this chapter is to help place the situation in a more useful context. It remains to be seen how thoroughly KU will fulfil its nominal goal of becoming an integrated provider of cradle-to-grave education crowned by the still-hypothetical Knowledge University. To what extent will the KU vision serve merely to ennoble the construction of a corporate conglomerate that adds only a layer of value-extraction to a collection of already viable companies? Whether the standard-bearer of a radically reorganised educational universe turns out to be KU or another organisation not yet on our radar, my research on the industrial period, its emergence and its passing (Jacques 1996) has convinced me that there is currently (to paraphrase Santayana) 'a hole in the shape of KU' within the institutional relationships through which knowledge is now supplied to the work organisations of society. The foundations have already been marked out for the construction of post-industrial institutional knowledge relationships. These relationships will dramatically transform our present industrially dominated configuration. The question is not whether construction will occur on this new foundation, but when – and the answer I believe is 'soon'.

What role will we, as academics, students and citizens, play in the creation of these new relationships? My hope is that as the relationships emerge a critical dialogue will emerge along with them that will provide broad input from the constituencies these pervasive relationships of power will influence. My fear is that, instead of an engaged dialogue, some will sanctify the new uncritically, others will demonise it, and the terms of debate on both sides will continue to be bounded by an oppositional, binary, industrial common sense. This futile passing of hot air will be the default condition unless a great deal of work is done to create an institutional context within which a more productive debate can occur. If an engaged debate is not constructed, very narrow constituencies such as the KU strategic team will go about their work of engineering the new order while other constituencies re-rehearse tired industrial scripts elsewhere. Even if we accept that such agents act in the best of faith, it is probably bad policy to turn a key social resource over to the unchallenged vision of a very few. Before we can engage on the immediate issues, however, we must take a step back to ask ourselves how our present 'common sense' and our present institutions – more than the emergent phenomena themselves – actively obstruct constructive engagement.

The post-industrial knowledge economy and our industrial blinkers

I will not retrace the numerous arguments for and against the possibility that these are times of a 'paradigm shift'.[5] With reference to the present arguments, my main assumptions regarding these changes are as follows:

- It is meaningful to treat present problems of work in complex, bureaucratised organisations as entering a new chapter, perhaps as radical in its effect on work relationships as industrialisation itself.
- It is not yet meaningful to state in positive terms what the next chapter will look like (as some writing as postmodernists have attempted to do) because such knowledge will require historical distance.

- Whatever changes are afoot are inherently neither emancipatory nor oppressive. It will be necessary to understand these changes in terms of emancipatory or oppressive potential in relationship to specific contexts.
- It is fruitless to attempt to understand the problems of emerging post-industrial work relationships without a historical perspective placing these changes in the context of the emergence of industrial work relationships.
- The future of the management disciplines as privileged academic specialities cannot be taken for granted. These are times for honest dialogue about whether our fields have a future and what can be done to change that future in ways we would desire.
- There is the danger that academia will not respond effectively to these changes and will atrophy, like the fields of phrenology, eugenics and physiognometrics, due to having failed to reconfigure our knowledge in a way that does not reflect the realities of a past, industrial order.

In *Manufacturing the Employee* (Jacques 1996), my central goal was to provide a context for understanding the present shifts in the relationships of power that structure work by studying the shifts introduced by industrialism as it emerged. In the process, I was struck by the degree to which the emergence of industry produced an 'industrial revolution' in education. In the US, which is the specific case I know best, the 19th century produced:

- A shift from a system modelled on England to one modelled on the technical-industrial form of production emerging in Germany.
- New technically oriented forms within tertiary education, such as graduate education linked to the research laboratory and a bureaucratic (as opposed to medieval) hierarchy of expertise.
- New technically oriented Germanic credentials – such as the Ph.D. – to certify achievement.
- New institutions created *de novo* for the new order, e.g. the shift in power from the (US) East Coast colleges to the new 'Big Ten' universities of the Midwest.[6]
- New 'knowledge worker' organisations, such as the American Association of University Professors, which have strongly influenced much of the present-day conception of the meaning of tenure and academic freedom – i.e. the freedom of the professorate to 'manufacture' knowledge useful to the military/corporate/industrial powers who were the midwives of the industrial university's birth.[7]

Today (*pace* Hegel) this 'shape of life' is growing old. The owl of Minerva has indeed flown, and our academic norms and practices often constitute little more than veneration of its droppings beneath the empty perch. In my interaction with colleagues I have often encountered the perception that the university is a form with a continuous history stretching back to the venerable medieval institutions at Paris and Bologna, Oxford and Heidelberg. This inappropriately links the university to the monastery, the monastery to the classical age, and the classical age to all that is good, right and true. Such a metanarrative apotheosises the university as the holy custodian of the timeless search for Truth and marginalises the social relations of power that have sustained and changed the academic institution over time. That this spirit of enquiry is often found in professors and sometimes found in students is a phenomenon I applaud. That the university's performance of this role (to the extent that it does this at all) assures it an institutional role in society, I question. More to the point are the words of Margaret Schaffner (yet another forgotten woman of organisation studies), whose doctoral dissertation reminds us that 'no industrial relation can long survive the reasons for its being' (1907: 132).

Industrial knowledge, owl-scat, knowledge work: the proctology of knowledge?

In this section I will present an example from practice in order to illustrate how the content of knowledge manufactured within the industrial knowledge factory of the business school not only fails to illuminate, but also actively obscures, important dimensions of phenomena. Subsequently, I will discuss why it is insufficient merely to look at the content of the knowledge produced and will argue that the very structure of the industrial university must change if knowledge appropriate to the problems of today is to be produced.

It is hardly controversial at this late date to state that the attention of organisational theorising is increasingly being drawn to work situations where the coalescence of several long-term changes in markets, production technologies and labour markets has resulted in the growing prominence of work situations where the work is relatively complex and thus discretionary, difficult to specify and thus to control, and, for both of these reasons, reliant upon the voluntary decision of the worker to give her/his best effort. By now there seems to be some consensus to term this 'knowledge work' and to consider the site in which knowledge work is done the 'knowledge-intensive form' (KIF) or the 'learning organisation'. Now, what does the body of management knowledge contribute to our understanding of knowledge work?

Predictably, some early responses to this question were merely repackaged of the problem to fit existing solutions. Argyris (1992) presumes to speak to this emerging issue by republishing several articles stretching back decades. Senge (1990) adds little to Weick (1969), and Weick, though creative and insightful, was building on ideas popularised in the 1950s. Practitioners can benefit from Senge and theorists from Weick or Argyris, but, to the extent that the phenomenon of knowledge work is emergent, old theories will, by definition, fail to reflect it. For instance, one of the greatest popular effects of *The Fifth Discipline* (Senge 1990) seems to have been catalysing the insight that organisations are organic systems. How novel is this when Drever stated – in 1929! – that the 'mechanical phase' of considering society to be composed of 'standard economic individuals' had already been followed by 'the *organic* phase', viewing society as 'a complex organism', and that this phase was already being seen to be inadequate, since work relationships 'depend essentially on the interests, impulses, sentiments, and passions of human beings' (Drever 1931: 26; emphasis in original).

This illustrates the procrustean manner in which new phenomena are regularly imported into organisational discourse. The aspects of, in this case, knowledge work that are consistent with existing theories and old perspectives are represented as the phenomena themselves. Not only does this bury whatever is genuinely emergent in the phenomena; it also makes it more difficult to create dialogue about the emergent aspects because certified experts (with a vested stake in the existing order) have already bounded the debate so that the boundaries exclude the novel.

So, are knowledge workers 'new professionals'?

Theorists such as Kelley (1985), Raelin (1984) and Von Glinow (1988) have attempted to understand knowledge workers as a form of professional:

> In some sense, the entire work force is changing to reflect increased specialization, differentiation and knowledge. Few would dispute that knowledge is power; thus, the new breed of professional worker might be called a 'knowledge worker'.
>
> (Von Glinow 1988: 11–12)

This elision of knowledge work and professionalism says less about the emergent quality of such work than it does about the poverty of subject positions one can use within the discourse of management theorising to represent work. Little has changed since Etzioni (1969), in his study of 'semi-professionals', asked why such workers sought full professional recognition when the structure of their occupation failed to support that claim. His answer was that

> The only alternative status is that of the non professional employee.... Unable to find a niche between these white collar statuses and the professions, and not wishing to be identified with the lower status group, [semi-professionals] cling to the higher aspiration of being a full professional.
>
> (Etzioni 1969: vi–vii)

Elsewhere, I have referred to this as the 'tripartite box' of industrial-era organisational theorising:

> Imagine a box with three partial partitions [manager, employee, professional]. It is possible to move from one area to another and even to stand at the juncture of two or all three partitions. One cannot, however, leave the

box. In order to become a working subject in the industrial order...one has
to take a place in such a box.

(Jacques 1996: 93)

If one is to appear in organisational theorising, one must appear as a
manager, an employee[8] and/or a professional. This is not accidental. One of the
founding principles of organisational science was the belief that occupation-
specific knowledge[9] could be replaced by a general theory of the person at work
(e.g. Blackford and Newcomb 1914; Person 1926; Jenks 1960). As examination of
any OB textbook indicates, the primary distinction between workers has been
made between those who manage and those who are managed. This has, of
course, also constituted the basis for asymmetric authority and voice between the
two groups. The organisational disciplines participate in this relationship of
power, having been constituted so that one is institutionally (discursively) constrained
to speak to managers about workers. The sole exception of note is the professional worker – and s/he has been constituted not so much as a unique
subjectivity but as a combination of managerial and employee characteristics – a
residual of whatever does not fit into the binary representation manager/employee.

This creates a discursive black hole.[10] Managerial membership is more or less
objectively definable by employment status. All else is the domain of 'the
employee', i.e. the generic worker unless the work can successfully claim professional status. 'Professional', then, functionally signifies nothing more than all that
which has (partially) escaped managerial control within the binary manager/employee
representation of workers. Since all that is not managerial or proletarian labour
can only be signified as 'professional', or as nothing at all, knowledge work is
tautologically professional, and as professional work it is already understood with
reference to existing (industrial) occupational relationships. In 1902 Andrew
Carnegie was already telling workers, '[t]his is the age of the specialist' (1913:
36). Goode (1960: 902) generalised that '[a]n industrializing society is a professionalizing society' – note 'industrialising', not post-industrialising. This reminds
me of an old Rocky and Bullwinkle cartoon show in which Boris Badenov, a
caricature of a cold-war Russian communist, is explaining to Bullwinkle why the
tax on Bullwinkle's 5,000 Pottsy inheritance is 10,000 Pottsies:

In Pottsylvania, if you got 5,000 Pottsies, that make you capitalist. And
everybody knows capitalist got lots more than 5,000 Pottsies.

We laugh at Boris and Bullwinkle; we read the literature on employed professionals with a straight face. Our ingrained 'common sense' makes professional a
category that appears to have specific content, while it functions as a garbage
can for all knowledge-intense or semi-autonomous occupational structuring and
phagocytoses all that does not fit the relationships produced by industrial reality:
manager and employee. Imposing a unified signifier upon diverse relationships
buries the emergent aspects of those relationships; hence the signifier 'professional' preserves the apparent adequacy of the entrenched discourse, but at the

expense of making the discourse unable to represent subjects other than those of interest to industrial-era employers.

Continuing the example: nurses as knowledge workers

Picture a knowledge worker. Male? Sitting in front of a computer? Engineering background? Working in 'high tech'? No doubt many of the people who fit this description can help us better understand some knowledge work, but how does this stereotypical representation limit us? How many knowledge workers are doing complex work in other conditions which, if we could recognise them, would help us to remove the sexist and industrial blinkers ('blinders')?

In my prior research, as part of an attempt to shift the object of enquiry from knowledge work itself to the ways knowledge work is represented, I used a method of structured observation to record the work of a group of bedside medical/surgical nurses working in an American teaching hospital (Jacques 1992). If one sums up the amount of time these workers spent in knowledge-intensive work with forms and direct communication, these nurses actually spent slightly more time working with knowledge than with bodies. This figure is conservative, since it does not consider the knowledge intensity blended into other activities, including direct patient care. So, is this 'professional' work?

In Jacques (1996: 90), based on a review of the literature on professions,[11] I made two suggestions for understanding 'profession' in its specificity. The first is explicitly to distinguish between an 'attitude of professionalism' and any partic-ular occupational structure. This refers to what is casually meant when we point to any rocket scientist, truck driver or chimney cleaner and say something like: 'his/her professionalism in doing the job really shows'. Second, I suggest that 'profession' be understood as a set of discursive relationships, not something an occupation has, but part of the context within which occupations form and contest with each other for power in the world of work. Professional relation-ships of power, then, could be understood as part of the discursive medium of work. Representing an occupation successfully as a profession can be understood with reference to these relationships and can be understood to have certain consequences for the occupation (occupational autonomy, limited entry, rela-tively high compensation, proprietary knowledge, etc.). Specifically, these relationships would be between the occupation as an entity and:

- science: proprietary body of knowledge, explicitly rule based, built on testable hypotheses;
- the university: legitimates the scientific status of the knowledge and controls access to practice through credentialising;
- the law: professions are granted monopoly privilege within their domain and are legally answerable for any abuse of that privilege;
- the community: accountable through ethical codes and peer review; good faith shown through 'pro bono' work;

•   the client: to exist at all, a profession must be seen as critically important by a constituency that has the power to support the profession.

The *bête noire* of functionalist sociology of the professions has been that there is no 'pure' profession, even medicine. However, as a script of sorts, these relationships form a well-known set of relationships that 'professionalising' occupations quite deliberately emulate (e.g. Kalisch and Kalisch 1986; Etzioni 1969; Wilensky 1964). So, to what extent does this describe the nurses I observed? In a word, poorly.

What is of interest to the present argument is not describing the work as professional, unprofessional or anywhere in between, but it is especially enlightening relative to understanding the content of the work. The construct (professional) itself is partly distorting, partly irrelevant. There were aspects of the work that involved complex knowledge and occupational management of that knowledge – but within a structure differing qualitatively from that described above. In Jacques (1993) I noted four dimensions of the nursing knowledge I observed being applied and the structure of professional discursive relationships:

1   academic vs. experiential knowledge
2   acontextual/durable vs. contextual/transient
3   bounded vs. permeable
4   ethic of exclusivity vs. ethic of sharing.

In brief, a central feature of a profession is the ability of an occupation to stand between a proprietary body of knowledge legitimated as science[12] and a client, who receives instructions based on the knowledge (not access to the knowledge itself). For the nurses, this was not possible because, while the knowledge they employed was complex and the context in which they applied it was important – literally a matter of life and death – the knowledge content was eclectic in quality, combining oral, experiential and situational elements with abstract principles to such an extent that the abstract portion could not be claimed to be central. The knowledge overlapped with many knowledge domains exclusive to medicine, therapies and technical areas. The knowledge content often looked unimportant unless one could see the implicit context of reasoning within which a mundane piece of data like 'Mrs Petrini had a glass of water this morning' might or might not take on significance. Finally, where the *sine qua non* of professional status is maintaining proprietary access to the body of knowledge, the nurses worked with a body of knowledge permeable to other occupations and they exacerbated this permeability through an ethos of sharing the knowledge with other caregivers and with patients – for instance through educating patients about their condition prior to discharge.

Nursing, professionalism and the limits of discourse

This nursing practice[13] is bounded by a relatively explicit set of discursive relationships, but the relationships governing practice differ from those specified above as professional. In order to become subjects of management theory, however, these workers have to illustrate something about the subject positions manager, employee or professional, since that 'tripartite box' (Jacques 1996) exhausts the positions one can refer to within the industrially produced discourse of organising as it has sedimented in the business school. It is not enough that we observe new subjectivities. We can look at new work practices until the sun cools ,and as long as the only representation available for them is non-managerial and non-professional they will not lead us to see new patterns. Rather, we will impose old patterns on them. Before these subjectivities can be represented, it is necessary (1) to recognise that the language of organising is a discursive formation and, as such, that it actively constrains and conditions what can be said and how it can be interpreted, and (2) to challenge the boundaries of this discourse in order to make space for new subjectivities.

For the nurses described above (and, consequently, for healthcare) this has practical implications. Professionalisation has been an explicit strategy used by nursing to gain authority and recognition over recent decades. To the extent that this has permitted the complexity of nursing work to be valued, I support the strategy, but unless the limits of discourse are simultaneously challenged, this becomes a double bind for nurses:

> Nursing has claimed legitimacy and recognition through appealing to the occupation's technical expertise…. At best, technical proficiency leads to representation of the nurse as 'almost a doctor'…. The core activity of nursing may be the relationship with the patient. However, without a framework for valuing the structural importance of this relationship, it is easily trivialized into the nurse-as-cheerleader…where the 'real' work is done by doctors.
>
> (Jacques 1993: 6)

What is experienced in this case by one occupational group can be extended to the large majority of those in knowledge-intensive work situations who are not members of established professions. How many other patterns of relationships remain unrepresented or misrepresented? Where do these practices exist? What are their consequences? What violence is done to knowledge, effectiveness and social equity by the procrustean process of forcing these practices on to industrial templates and amputating everything that fails to conform to prior experience?

…and the role of social identity

Because nursing is constituted largely by women performing a stereotypically feminine organisational role, it offers an excellent example of the way industrial blinkers also marginalise the importance of social identity. The fantasy of industrial organisational knowledge has been the dream of the generic employee. Again, OB textbooks offer an excellent example of the attempt to construct a single grid of knowledge practices into which any body (*sic*) can be dropped. The idea of discrete knowledges (pl.) particular to a multiplicity of worker communities and their social relationships runs counter to another foundational principle of the industrial practices that produced management knowledge and the business school. It is not enough to add marginalised identities of race, gender and other cultural signifiers of asymmetrical power into the already constituted discourse that has been formed by a relatively homogenous (and dominant-identity) group looking at a similar group of subjects. It is necessary to abandon altogether the idea of norm and deviance before we can represent the complexity of the interacting web of social identities constituting society (Jacques 1997a). Consider one example from the nurse knowledge- workers I studied.

Why does the non-nurse more readily see the nurse as a mother surrogate doing bodily and emotional care work that can be done by any woman with a good heart,[14] rather than as a knowledge worker? Several months after leaving the field, I realised there was a systematic pattern to some categories I had constructed to account for the general ways the nurses had used their time. Of 11 categories I had subjectively derived, 6 were relatively visible while 5 were mostly invisible. Specifically:

1   Visible work:

- feeding patient
- patients' physical comfort
- medications/specimens, etc.
- giving treatments
- patients' personal hygiene
- routine administrative items

2   Invisible work:

- getting clinical information
- giving information, educating, instructing
- communicating between patient and others
- 'rapport talk' (Tannen 1990), communication to establish relationship
- 'above and beyond', work neither required nor expected

Because the nurses spent much of their time doing two or more of these activities simultaneously, the total time spent in all activities added up to 137 per cent. This is significant because what is visible is systematically the more mundane work. What is more complex and discretionary is almost completely hidden. Furthermore, if the visible activities were all I expected to see, I would find the nurse's time fully occupied since these accounted for 96 per cent of her time. What would be unsuspected is that embedded within this visible structure 41 per cent, almost half, of the nurse's time is also spent in knowledge-intensive discretionary activity requiring numerous specific skills and a highly trained orientation to the work.

This is not an issue of doing good or bad research. It is about the lens through which the work we are exposed to becomes data (as Popper,[15] among others, has admonished us, there is no data that is not already an interpretation). In reviewing the organisational research which used nurses as subjects (Jacques 1992), I found no hint of awareness among these hypothesis-testing studies that the phenomena I discuss here exist – and at the level of design and data collection, that is good science. 'Extraneous' factors were 'controlled'. This is bad science only from the perspective that there is no narrative context to create a generative context for discussion of what might best merit testing and measurement and for considering what might be important that exists outside the subdivision of experience that is quantitatively testable.

This work is perpetually on display and is performed by the largest occupational group in the US, yet it remains hidden. 'Seeing' the work, in the sense of meaning what it means to those who perform it and those affected by it, means viewing the work from a paradigmatic perspective derived from the 'indigenous language' (realities, values, concerns) of the practitioners. In my case, what I 'objectively' observed was conditioned by reading in the nursing literature and in feminist theorising. Without this questioning of the dominant discursive boundaries, the organisation of nursing care could be understood only with reference to healthcare (dominated by medicine), professional (dominated by medicine) or management (dominated by large corporate organisations) knowledge. In every case, these bodies of knowledge reflect the gendered discursive boundaries sedimented as men interact with men.[16] Over time, these norms have ceased to be seen as masculine and are considered merely 'organisational'. Nursing, however, is constructed on values congruent with feminine socialisation, values more or less antithetical to those of medicine, management or professionalism. As a result, 'objective' study, in which enquiry is made only into the work data and not into the constraining/shaping role of the framework within which the data takes on meaning, inherently matches the work against a deficit model in which peripheral aspects of the work become visible – and seem to be 'the work itself' – while other, more central aspects, remain hidden.

Fletcher (1994) identifies similar patterns in workers other than nurses and elaborates the specific categories of work that are marginalised, not because they are unimportant, but because of their association with the feminine and, through that association, with being inappropriate to the workplace. For instance, an engineer who sends thank-you notes to those her project team needs co-operation from (but cannot control hierarchically) is seen as doing this, not to advance the project, but because she is a 'nice person'. Fletcher argues that this process is not random; such practices actively 'get disappeared' through structural dynamics in which feminine practices are discursively inappropriate and for which no 'language of competency' exists to represent the importance of the work.

Throughout this section, it has been a theme that one cannot learn about new phenomena merely through study of the phenomena. This can be understood with reference to Thomas Kuhn's (1970) distinction between normal science and paradigm shift. While it is not novel to invoke Kuhn, it would be novel if the management disciplines were seriously to heed the implications of his work. As we see in Kuhn's examples, a paradigmatic framework does not constitute a universal language within which everything that exists can be represented. Quite the contrary; its very usefulness derives from its exclusion of most of the phenomena of experience. One main reason why paradigms are replaced by other paradigms is that for influential members of the knowledge community the utility of the paradigm is eventually outweighed by a desire to represent phenomena beyond the paradigmatic boundaries of representation. In such times (and for the industrial university this is such a time) 'research' means concentration not on solving 'normal science' puzzles, but on debating the rules and values of the context that determines which puzzles are important, what will constitute a solution and what the solution will mean.

The emerging knowledge economy, the business school, the possible

> When you have buried us told your story
> ours does not end we stream
> into the unfinished the unbegun
> the possible.

> (Adrienne Rich, 'Phantasia for Elvira Shateyev')

It would be unfortunate if the preceding is read only as a defence of bringing poststructuralist, feminist critical enquiry into specific research projects. Whether in the interest of organisational effectiveness or social equity, unless we see in this situation a need to critically examine and reconfigure the discursive norms, institutional practices and social power relationships constituting academia our ability to represent emergent phenomena will change little. It is of some comfort that since the early 1980s little ghettos of post-positivist enquiry have appeared in the management disciplines, but in a discursive formation where doing 'qualitative research'[17] is still often considered an act of courage we should not feel too smug.

If the present order were effectively serving the interests of effectiveness but marginalising some constituents one might attempt to work within the discourse to expand it. If there were any credible evidence that knowledge was developing towards a paradigmatic science, it might be advisable to have patience. But the discourse of organising signified by 'management' has a body of knowledge that compares in scientificity with phrenology, alchemy and physiognometrics. Where enough studies have been done to create a major body of knowledge (i.e. motivation, leadership), the promised paradigmatic coalescence – if it ever does arrive – will give us answers to questions posed at the advent of industrialisation. Yes, we are better than we have ever been at getting Henry Ford's River Rouge plant running like clockwork, but another clock has been ticking while we have pursued the muse of motivational Truth. Even the post-Fordist factory has but limited use for management practices and theoretical formations directed at getting the worker to sit down, shut up and do as s/he is told.

Historical perspective shows the 20th century to be the second century in a row in which experts speaking of business relationships herald the new century in terms of transformational changes in technologies, internationalisation of markets, a shift to a service economy, and a growing awareness that the key to strategic advantage lies in the knowledge and attitude of the worker. In an industrialising 19th century, these claims were new observations, representing newly emerging social values and marking sites of dramatic shifts in work relationships. In an increasingly post-industrial 21st century, recycling the same claims reinscribes old meanings on changing experience. Worse, because the recycled claims are presented as 'leading edge' it is not even possible to question the sameness of the supposed change (Jacques 1992: 287).

In studying the proletarianisation of labour that accompanied industrialisation, my sympathies are generally pro-labour and anti-deterministic regarding the supposed 'evolution' of the industrial order. As a tactical point, however, I think that labour's bet to back traditional technologies against the mass technologies being developed was a bad choice because labour did not possess the social power to prevent the implementation of the systems they resisted. As a result, labour positioned itself as an outsider to what eventually became the established order. Had labour been able to see the future, it might have been more successful at seeking a place at the table within the emerging system it was going to have to enter one way or another. There is a lesson in this for the present.

In discussions to date in which I have heard my colleagues debate new technologies and their possible influence on teaching, most opinions fall fairly neatly into two categories. There are the technophiles, for whom CD-ROMs, distance teaching and so forth are simply interesting technical problems to solve. At the opposite pole are those who sanctify the classroom 'chalk and talk' format as self-evidently important. What I have heard much less of is considered debate about where technology can usefully substitute for a live instructor and where the personal connection offers something distinct. For instance, much of the study of statistics can take place more effectively with programmed learning packages than in a lecture hall, but the intervention of a skilled instructor to help with difficulties – emotional and technical – is also important. Neither adding computers while retaining the traditional class nor eliminating teachers in favour of unsupported programmed learning realises the potential of redesigning the course structure, the teaching load, degree requirements and so forth to create a different set of learning relationships. In my own teaching I am painfully aware that my best lectures are abysmal 'product' when compared with even the average television documentary. Nonetheless, I will continue to participate in a system I know to be ineffective until there is an institutional commitment to replace lectures with well-designed media products and a commitment to provide the time and funds for the initial investment, to redesign workloads, to reshape the process of getting a degree. At the present time it is understandable that there should be little clarity of vision regarding where all of this is headed. What is more of a problem is the lack of a framework for creating informed debate about the issues.

It requires no prognostication to predict an impending revolution in academia. The dynamite is in place around the old foundations. The coalescence of a host of digital and telecommunications technologies has, in just a few years, radically changed the limits of possibility for both the production and the distribution of knowledge. To date, this potential has been utilised only in a very limited manner. We are flooded with digital data, but this is not knowledge. Changes in work technologies, worker skills and values, world markets, and the relationship of society with the corporation have changed the core problems of organising. Yet the main body of organisational knowledge and the academic business disciplines are still largely focused on the prior set of problems, which emerged with industrialisation and were central for a century, but which are becoming increasingly marginal today. To date, responses to these changes have been almost non-existent.

> Researchers of stature regularly lament the field's stasis or crisis...the status of the MBA appears to be eroding...lack of interest in theoretical production by 'the practitioner' is regularly lamented.... But, if anything, the discursive boundaries of the field are narrower than they were a few years ago. New voices are more timid...the mainstream of organizational studies in North America is engaging in necrophilia with the [dominant but] dead modern/industrial worldview. It is toward this necrophilia and its eradication that a necrology of knowledge must be directed...[and] through which we can metabolize the dead shell of an accreted industrial knowledge cementing us to the hull of a sinking industrial reality.
>
> (Jacques 1997b: 133–5,139)

Producing a necrology of organisation science

A fundamental flaw in the design of the foundation upon which management knowledge now rests is the axiom that 'the methods of thought developed by the physical sciences, which have given to mankind such unprecedented control over material things, could and should be applied to man [*sic*] himself' (Urwick 1956: ix). Had this argument been limited to 'the application of scientific methods to the subject of administration' (Thompson 1956: 103) – i.e. use of statistics to identify measurable regularities within a narrative discipline – the scientific project would have been merely a tool, useful or not as its results over time determined. What made this axiom dangerous was the hubristic inversion of the appropriate relationship between method and philosophy of knowledge – by stuffing the narrative of management into the methodolatrist's

Frankensteinian dream of 'the possibility of a science of administration' (*ibid.*: 103).

A discourse of truth

> Computing body counts, masturbating
> In the factory
> Of facts.

> (Adrienne Rich, 'The phenomenology of anger')

Limited to the language of tests and measures, organisational scholarship has functioned as a discourse of truth. Admittedly, this particular ideal of science has been a caricature of the physical sciences (as is evident if one, even briefly, considers the arguments of Kuhn 1970). But caricature or no, the signifier 'science' functions powerfully to marginalise questions of value, social construction, interpretation, feeling and aesthetics.

This has dovetailed with a romanticised view of the status of the university in society in which the university represents a (relative) haven from power and politics whose essential function is to free scholars for the pursuit and communication of their truths. But a review of the history of the university since industrialisation tells another story (e.g. Bledstein 1976; Jacques 1996) and makes the idea of any essential role difficult to accept. Disciplines are supported by producing knowledge for constituencies which value the knowledge produced enough to continue their support. This need not be the nominal content of the body of knowledge. The university may act as a gatekeeper for an occupation; it may legitimate the occupation's status or certify the 'objectivity' of the knowledge applied in an area. It may socialise entrants into a field or pre-stratify them so that they may be selected on 'merit' and still be from certain social classes. It may offer students a chance to make the social connections that will serve them later in their careers. All of these are powerful, knowledge-intensive activities more or less unrelated to the content of a discipline.

Nonetheless, when all bets are on the table, the sum of nominal and other functions provided must secure the support of constituencies or the discipline withers. I think it debatable whether English literature or polymer science offers more to society. Both are of value. But the relatively privileged status of polymer science relative to English literature in the university has more to do with the relatively specific needs of relatively identifiable constituencies than it does with the overall contribution of either to the general welfare. Somehow, this Machiavellian context seems to have been lost in debates about the status of the management disciplines. I know of no equivalent discussion to that engaged by Rosenhead (1986) in British operations management, in which he attempts to raise this question of knowledge, value and constituencies. Even Pfeffer (1993), when explicitly looking at disciplinary status as a power issue, frames the problem of disciplinary status as one of political negotiation rather than one of identifying and meeting core needs of constituencies. This issue embodies two related problems. First, in management, 'constituency' has been too narrowly interpreted to mean 'managers', and 'management' to mean a custodian of investor interests. Second, the field as it has coalesced is of questionable value in serving even this portion of the potential web of constituents.

Webster and Starbuck (1988) recommended that academic research programmes be subjected to a Stalinist regime of control so that progress could be made in what a central committee defined as the most important areas of the field. At the time I rejected this idea out of hand. In retrospect, I believe this proposal deserves reconsideration, at least as a starting point for discussion. To those who would howl 'academic freedom' I would reply that such academic freedom as does exist is an artefact of relationships of power with the university in which core constituencies have been served by the outputs this freedom produced. The funded basic research laboratory is one example. What some would celebrate as paradigm diversity in organisational studies, coupled with a discipline that long ago became decoupled from any meaningful relationship to practitioner communities (any practitioner communities: managers, labour groups, consultants, governments, etc.), seems to be producing no critical mass of energy around topics that could support a constituency. Where energy has developed – such as in the organisational ecology literature – it is easier to see congruence with abstracted norms of empirical science than with any concrete issues of practice.

Perhaps it is time to begin to ask how to generate critical mass between communities of research practice and practitioner communities. This would indeed mean infringing any idealised notion of academic freedom. I would prefer to think of such freedom as part of a relationship rather than as a mere privilege: the freedom to take the initiative in contributing to identifying and producing useful knowledge for client communities. Diversity of values, approaches and topics must be defended; it would not be acceptable to produce a paradigm of '*Blut und Eisen*', but efforts are needed to see that individual efforts accumulate into something larger. After all, no individual study is that important. Influence belongs to the research stream, not the single product of an individual. Of immediate consequence is the question of how this project might be started. In the absence of a discourse where there is space for discussion of such a topic, how can such space be produced?

A discourse of amnesia

'The struggle of humanity against power', says a character in a Milan Kundera novel, 'is the struggle of memory against forgetting' (Kundera 1981: 3).[18] One might transpose this aphorism into the struggle of memory against science. While it is broadly accepted, especially since Kuhn (1970), that science has a history, this does not change the basically oppositional discursive roles of science and history. If one accepts that the primary criteria for knowledge are statistical significance, reliability and validity, what is relevant is the stock of validated findings, not the process through which they were produced. In training new producers, the primary skills to emphasise are techniques, not philosophies of knowledge – Kuhnian 'problem-solving', not paradigmatic critique.

Over time, this emphasis on the techniques of testing produces an amnesiac culture that is not merely unwilling, but thoroughly unable to self-critique its own legitimating narrative. One reason that the ridiculous debate over the 'validity of qualitative research' continues to run after two decades (e.g. Hunt 1994) is that most participants in the debate have been trained to judge all knowledge-claims on their reliability and validity, unaware that judging claims on reliability and validity is itself a value-laden, power-laden choice. Since debate cannot happen at this level, the level required for intelligent engagement, it goes in circles, with many genuinely well-intentioned organisational 'scientists' unaware that their efforts to include 'qualitative research' in organisational science are marginalising a plethora of post-analytic, critical and identity-centred schools of thought by imposing on them the inapplicable criteria of hypothesis-testing.

This is not a problem caused by malicious or closed-minded individuals. Its main elements are institutional/discursive. As Bion (1959) long ago noted, the group's first task over time is to assure its own reproduction. Journals devoted to hypothesis-testing come to be seen as the 'best' journals of the field '*tout court*'. Reviewers trained only in tests and measures can be relied upon more systematically to see the value of test-and-measure submissions. Tenure – continued survival as a producer of knowledge – comes to be influenced by 'A'-journal publications, and a circular process is created. At every level, from consideration of doctoral student applications, through appointment to tenure, distribution of honours and allocation of gatekeeping authority, what is the 'best' scholarship is determined objectively – in the sense that all contenders are judged within the boundaries of a discourse bounded by the dreams and norms of positivist[19] science. This comes to be reproduced by the folklore of how to succeed in the field. People are strongly governed by rumours about what one supposedly can and cannot do. These urban myths are one of the most powerful control mechanisms on academics and on the production of academic knowledge, yet they have no centre to their authority, no falsifiability, no concrete subjective form.

In addition, we who have been critical of scientism have often contributed to reifying the old discursive boundaries by accepting the dichotomy 'positivist/anti-positivist' (Burrell and Morgan 1979) as a meaningful distinction. A question we have too seldom considered is the more nuanced issue of what role varieties of empirical enquiry can play in a post-positivist world. Is the statistical hypothesis per se an enemy? I know of no uneducated people so simple-minded as to declare their allegiance to numbers or words; they use whichever best meets the needs of the moment. Yet I know many fairly intelligent people with expert training who seem to find it reasonable that one be required to swear a loyalty oath exclusively to either the hypothesis or the narrative proposition.

A discourse of yesterday's news

If we compare the needs of knowledge development in the research world of particle physics and the social world of Silicon Valley, we find very different constraints on what counts as useful knowledge. The objects of physics are, for all intents and purposes, fairly stable, fairly universalisable. Neither are they self-aware. Perhaps measuring the electron changes the electron's trajectory, as we have learned from Heisenberg, but the electron's intentions are something we have, since Newton, profitably ignored. It took centuries to develop a paradigmatic science of, for instance, mechanics, but in that time the problems, and the value of being able to explain them, changed only marginally.

For the Silicon Valley manager, the world is a social construction that is perpetually in the process of reconstruction. Interactions between self-aware subjects and a kaleidoscopic environment mean that, even if reliable and valid information about emerging problems was created, by the time the solution was available the problem would have mutated beyond recognition (for instance the literature on the relationship between task-worker satisfaction and industrial productivity; cf. Jacques (1996: 175–6)). To the extent that statistics and hypotheses can contribute to the production of useful knowledge in this environment, the key question is not the place of organisational studies within the sciences, but the place of scientific method within organisational studies.

Questioning the discursive boundaries

What is lacking in organisation studies is an awareness of history that is integrated into the process of knowledge generation in a manner that results in constant scrutiny of the social relevance of the problems addressed by the field and the processes through which this is done. This failure stands in the way of developing organisational knowledge for post-industrial organising because the field is harnessed to cumulatively adding to problems that were of concern to early industrialists, using methods more appropriate to those problems than to those emerging today. If we are to facilitate the ability of management knowledge to represent emergent phenomena, I suggest that in addition to investigating the phenomena themselves and unintentionally moulding them into familiar, but inappropriate, industrial shapes we consider questions like the following:

- What constituencies do or could support the field? What is the best way to serve their needs? What conflict between constituency groups must be recognised? How can we help to negotiate these conflicts equitably?
- What practices lead to 'voice' in determining how organising will be done? What voices do the theorist community hear? What voices does it contribute to suppressing? What is the appropriate role of academics in relation to both knowledge and social equity?

- What are the core problems of organising in our time? Do these differ from the core problems of organising as defined by our cumulative knowledge? (Yes.) What response to this situation is appropriate?
- How is our knowledge historically and culturally specific? How can we retain the useful generalisations produced to date while more appropriately contextualising these observations in time and place?
- How are our knowledge practices, research methods and 'media' (e.g. a journal system based on pre-electronic, physical science communication needs) appropriate or inappropriate for present and emerging knowledge-production needs?
- How do basic terms and concepts such as 'employee', 'the organisation', 'management', 'leadership' reflect needs of previous decades and/or other cultures? What are the implications in terms of a need to remap the variables, constructs and concepts of organisation studies? What is the emerging language ('langue', not 'parole', in a Saussurian sense) of post-industrial organising in the workplace and what academic language will most usefully communicate with it?
- And finally, what new institutional forms are emerging to provide knowledge? What roles will exist for knowledge producers within these forms (e.g. consultants, researchers, trainers)? What does this mean regarding credentialising, careers, strategies for knowledge development? What social needs will be met and what social problems will be created by these new forms? What is to be done other than to fantasise that business as usual in academia will not result in eventual catastrophe?

By analogy, the management disciplines today are in the position of a rider in a limousine, enjoying the company of friends, listening to a good stereo and opening a bottle of champagne. The position is comfortable and one may want it to continue. Whether the position is comfortable or not is secondary, however, if the car is about to run over the edge of a cliff (Jacques 1992: 288).

Into the land of Milken honey

Fernand Braudel (1982) illustrates the tremendous institutional flexibility shown by capitalism over the last several centuries. He reminds us that the institutions of capitalism take no necessary form, but are adaptable to time and place: 'The chief privilege of capitalism, today as in the past, remains the ability to *choose*' (*ibid.*: 622; emphasis in original). The relationship of the university to business as a 'supplier' has been a product of late industrialisation. Neither capital-market economies, manufacturing nor international trade inherently require a relationship of businesses with tertiary-education providers. Is there any reason to imagine that the relationship between the university and business should be immune from the institutional contingency that has been a condition of all other relationships with business?

I have been making arguments such as those in this chapter for some time (e.g. Jacques 1988), with the implicit goal of contributing to change within what has initially been constituted as the industrial business school. Along the line, however, my focus has been shifting. In writing *Manufacturing the Employee* (Jacques 1996), I came to appreciate the knowledge-production revolution that accompanied industrialisation. What this taught me was that the relationships of power structuring industrial society did not result merely from the transformation of old institutions and interests. The manager, for instance, was neither the old foreman nor the old owner-operator capitalist, but the occupant of a new social space borrowing from, but not congruent with, these older social actors. The employee was not a continuation of the pre-industrial worker, but was 'manufactured' within the industrial system. Strange alliances were forged, such as that between socialist reformers such as Jane Addams and industrialists like General Electric's Jacob Steinmetz (Struck 1930).

And this has been true institutionally of the provision of knowledge for the corporation. Crafts and the apprentice system carried much pre-industrial knowledge. As these were destroyed, corporation schools, night classes, revised public-school education, the production of 'vocational' schools for the trades and other expediencies were attempted as responses to changing times. Only late in the game did universities enter, and these were radically transformed through an industrialisation of the educational process. This experience also shows that the old power-brokers did not disappear; nor did they generally make the jump to the new order. There is still a theology department at Harvard and Yale, but these formerly dominant players in tertiary education now exist in the shadow of the business schools. Into what shadow might the business schools fade tomorrow? And, if they survive, will they be transformed beyond present recognition, as the pre-industrial university was a century ago, when, like the factories growing up around it, it became a mass producer of standardised knowledge?

Bringing this insight forward to the present, what new relationships, what new providers of knowledge are imminent? To what extent will the university remain a privileged provider for businesses and to what extent will it be supplanted by new providers and new forms? What are the changing needs and emerging crises that will determine what is most needed by constituents? It is in this sense that Michael Milken's Knowledge Universe looms ominously. The stage is set for actors like Knowledge Universe. Whether those who will actually be influential are in this organisation or another is unimportant. What is important for us, as producers and consumers of knowledge, is that neither scientific validity nor academic freedom will be worth a damn if the relationships that – just coincidentally – uphold them shift. Like the workers of early industrialisation, we are witnessing the emergence of a new system for producing and distributing knowledge. This system will bring with it new relations of power, new constituencies, new winners and losers. It is uncertain who the big winners and losers in the emerging order will be. But whether our central concern is organisational effectiveness, social equity or both, we can be assured that we will not be winners if we are not in the game.

Notes

1 'Blinkers' to the Anglo world; 'blinders' to Americans.

2 Neither has the old industrial order disappeared, as the maquila worker, the Haitian sewing T-shirts for Disney for 28 cents an hour, the Burmese worker who undercuts the Haitian worker's labour rate and others can testify. This chapter is not about such work, but in the rush to be fashionably post-industrial let us not forget the now long-standing issues of deskilling and exploiting labour in Fordist and sweated-labour situations.

3 See Jacques (1996: xii, xvi) for several reasons why I consider my study of the US case to be more directed at decentring American hegemony than at perpetuating American ethnocentrism.

4 Knowledge Universe was initially capitalised privately with US$500 million put up by Michael, his brother Lowell and Lawrence Ellison, CEO/founder of Oracle. Because it has no public reporting requirements and no investor community to massage, relatively little information exists about this rapidly growing giant already valued (speculatively of course) at US$4–6 billion.

5 For lengthier treatment of my views on these themes, I refer the reader to Jacques (1996) or White and Jacques (1995).

6 For more detail, see Bledstein (1976), especially the later chapters.

7 There is not space in this chapter to discuss the interesting contrast between this technical legitimation of professorial freedom and a more seigneurial history such as that of Oxford and Cambridge, especially as the power of both as signifiers of academic authority is intertwined.

8 In Jacques (1996) I stress the significance of the fact that managers are also employees. At the same time, in our terminology 'employee' has come to mean the one who is managed, except where explicitly noted otherwise.

9 This previous configuration of knowledge is illustrated, for instance, in turn-of-the-20th-century trade journals where 'railroad men' read about their trade in railway journals while their compatriots in, say, steel, were reading the steel trade journals. At this point, the idea of a generic knowledge of management (e.g. the Taylor, Gilbreth, Gant, Person, Fayol element) was quite radical.

10 Writing under different astrological influences, I have also referred to this phenomenon as 'semantic eclipse' (Jacques 1996: 159).

11 The review itself is more extensive in Jacques (1992).

12 In law and theology, the legitimation is more hermeneutic, but in today's world the scientific technical profession is the more relevant template for understanding the actions of occupational groups seeking to distinguish themselves from the proletarian world of the generic 'employee'.

13 I say 'this' nursing practice because even within this one occupation the patterns of relationships between skill, credential, worker and work are so diverse that very little can be said about nursing '*tout court*' – another reminder that one epistemological challenge of entering the networked world of post-industrial power relationships will be to jettison the constraining, generic concept of 'the employee' and to replace it with a more multidimensional understanding of the qualitative differences between groups of workers.

14 This has been discussed in the nursing literature; see Jacques (1992).

15 '[P]ure observational knowledge, unadulterated by theory, would, if at all possible, be utterly barren and futile' (Popper 1985: 48–9).

16 See Mills and Tancred (1992), especially the chapters by Calás and Smircich, Acker, and the editors' introductions.

17 The term itself indicates the poverty of dialogue. I can understand the meaning of qualitative methods, but what is qualitative research? Must one choose ideologically between the digit and the phoneme? Is 'qualitative' a philosophy of knowledge?

(Indeed, is 'quantitative'?) What possible meaning can the term have except in a hypothesis-testing order where a particular species of quantitative research is represented as research itself, and an absence of informed dialogue is a prerequisite for maintaining this epistemologically untenable position?

18 What was translated as 'man' I have reinterpreted as 'humanity'.

19 I am aware that this term rankles with those to whom I am applying it. I would be happy to apply a term of their choosing if they would choose something more specific than 'science', since not all science is constrained by the same norms, and multiple possibilities exist for the creation of more and less positivistic organisational sciences. However, the absence of a term by which to refer to the present values illustrates the points I am trying to make – others have values, ideologies, beliefs and power-interests, while the mainstream has none of these but only 'science'.

References

Argyris, C. (1992) *On Organizational Learning*, Oxford: Blackwell.

Bion, W. (1959) *Experiences in Groups*, New York: Basic Books.

Blackford, K.M.H. and Newcomb, A. (1914) *The Job, the Man, the Boss*, Garden City, NY: Doubleday, Page & Co.

Bledstein, B. (1976) *The Culture of Professionalism*, New York: W.W. Norton.

Braudel, Fernand (1982) *Civilization & Capitalism 15th–18th Century*, vol. 2: *The Wheels of Commerce*, New York: Harper & Row.

Burrell, G. and Morgan, G. (1979) *Sociological Paradigms*, Portsmouth, NH: Heinemann.

Calás, M.B. and Smircich, L. (1987) 'Post-culture: is the organizational culture literature dominant but dead?', paper presented at the Third International Conference on Organizational Symbolism and Corporate Culture, Milan, Italy, June.

Carnegie, A. (1913) *The Empire of Business*, New York: Doubleday.

Drever, J. (1929) 'The human factor in industrial relations', in C.S. Myers (ed.) *Industrial Psychology*, London: Thornton Butterworth Ltd.

—— (1931) 'The human factor in industrial relations' in B.V. Moore and G.W. Hartmann *Readings in Industrial Psychology*, New York: D. Appleton–Century Company.

Etzioni, A. (ed.) (1969) *The Semi-Professions and Their Organization*, New York: Free Press.

Fletcher, J.K. (1994) 'Toward a theory of relational practice in organizations: a feminist reconstruction of "real" work', unpublished doctoral dissertation, Boston University, Boston, MA.

Goode, W.J. (1960) 'Encroachment, charlatanism, and the emerging profession: psychology, sociology, and medicine', *American Sociological Review* 25(3): 902–14.

Habermas, J. (1983) 'Modernity – an incomplete project', in H. Foster (ed.) *The Anti-Aesthetic: Essays on Postmodern Culture*, Port Townshend, WA: Bay Press.

Hunt, S.D. (1994) 'On the rhetoric of qualitative methods: toward historically informed argumentation in management inquiry', *Journal of Management Inquiry* 3(3): 221–34.

Jacques, R. (1988) 'Post-industrialism, postmodernity and O.R.: toward a "custom and practice" of responsibility and possibility', in M.C. Jackson, R. Keys and S.A. Cropper (eds) *Operational Research in the Social Sciences*, London: Plenum.

—— (1992) 'Re-presenting the knowledge worker: a poststructuralist analysis of the new employed professional', unpublished doctoral dissertation, University of Massachusetts, Amherst, MA.

—— (1993) 'Untheorized dimensions of caring work: caring as a structural practice and caring as a way of seeing, *Nursing Administration Quarterly* 17(2): 1–10.

—— (1996) *Manufacturing the Employee: Management Knowledge From the 19th to 21st Centuries*, London: Sage.

—— (1997a) 'The unbearable whiteness of being: reflections of a stale, pale, male', in M.P. Prasad, A.J. Mills, M. Elmes and A. Prasad (eds) *Managing the Organizational Melting Pot*, Thousand Oaks, CA: Sage.

—— (1997b) 'Classic review "The Empire Strikes Out": Lyotard's postmodern condition and the need for a "necrology of knowledge" ', *Organization* 4(1): 130–42.

Jenks, L.H. (1960) 'Early phases of the management movement', *Administrative Science Quarterly* (3)1: 421–47.

Kalisch, P.A. and Kalisch, B.J. (1986) *The Advance of American Nursing*, 2nd edition, Boston, MA: Little, Brown & Co.

Kelley,. R.E. (1985) *The Gold-Collar Worker: Harnessing the Brainpower of the New Work Force*, Reading, MA: Addison-Wesley.

Kuhn, T.S. (1970) *The Structure of Scientific Revolutions*, 2nd edition, Chicago: University of Chicago Press (first published in 1962).

Kundera, Milan (1981) *The Book of Laughter and Forgetting*, New York: Penguin.

Martin, J. (1998) 'Lifelong learning spells earnings', *Fortune*, 6 July: 113–15.

Mills, A.J. and Tancred, P. (eds) (1992) *Gendering Organizational Analysis*, Newbury Park, CA: Sage.

Person, H.S. (1926) 'The management movement', in H.C. Metcalf (ed.) *Scientific Foundations of Business Administration*, Baltimore, MD: Williams & Wilkins.

Pfeffer, J. (1993) 'Barriers to the advance of organizational science: paradigm development as a dependent variable', *Academy of Management Review* 18(4): 599–620.

Popper, K.R. (1985) 'Knowledge without authority', in D. Miller (ed.) *Popper Selections*, Princeton, NJ: Princeton University Press (first published in 1960).

Raelin, J.A. (1984) *The Salaried Professional*, New York: Praeger.

Rosenhead, J. (1986) 'Custom and practice', inaugural address as President of the Operational Research Society, Society for Long-Range Planning, *Journal of the Operational Research Society* 37(4): 335–43.

Schaffner, Margaret Anna (1907) 'The labor contract from individual to collective bargaining', *Bulletin of the University of Wisconsin* 2(1): 1–182.

Senge, P.M. (1990) *The Fifth Discipline*, New York: Doubleday.

Struck, F.T. (1930) *Foundations of Industrial Education*, New York: John Wiley & Sons.

Tannen, D. (1990) *You Just Don't Understand: Women and Men in Conversation*, New York: William Morrow & Co.

Thompson, J.D. (1956) 'On building an administrative science', *Administrative Science Quarterly* 1(1): 102–11.

Urwick, L. (1956) *The Golden Book of Management: A Historical Record of the Life and Work of Seventy Pioneers*, London: Newman Neame Ltd.

von Glinow, M.A. (1988) *The New Professionals: Managing Today's High-Tech Employees*, Cambridge, MA: Ballinger.

Webster, J. and Starbuck, W.H. (1988) 'Theory building in industrial and organizational psychology', in C.L. Cooper and I. Robertson (eds) *International Review of Industrial and Organizational Psychology*, New York: Wiley.

Weick, K.E. (1969) *The Social Psychology of Organizing*, Reading, MA: Addison-Wesley.

White, R. and Jacques, R. (1995) 'Operationalizing the postmodernity construct for efficient organizational change management', *Journal of Organizational Change Management* 8(2): 45–71.

Wilensky, H. (1964) 'The professionalization of everyone?', *American Journal of Sociology* 70(2): 137–58.

Index

Printed in the United States
by Baker & Taylor Publisher Services